THE BLACK DEATH
TRANSFORMED

THE BLACK DEATH TRANSFORMED:

DISEASE AND CULTURE IN EARLY RENAISSANCE EUROPE

Samuel K. Cohn, Jr

A member of the Hodder Headline Group
LONDON
Co-published in the United States of America by
Oxford University Press Inc., New York

First published in Great Britain in 2002
Paperback edition published in 2003, by
Arnold, a member of the Hodder Headline Group,
338 Euston Road, London NW1 3BH

http://www.arnoldpublishers.com

Distributed in the United States of America by
Oxford University Press Inc.,
198 Madison Avenue, New York, NY10016

British Library Cataloguing in Publication Data
A catalogue record for this book is available from the British Library

Library of Congress Cataloging-in-Publication Data
A catalog record for this book is available from the Library of Congress

ISBN 0 340 70646 5 (hb)
ISBN 0 340 70647 3 (pb)

1 2 3 4 5 6 7 8 9 10

Typeset in 10 on 12 pt Sabon by Cambrian Typesetters, Frimley, Surrey
Printed and bound in Malta

What do you think about this book? Or any other Arnold title?
Please send your comments to feedback.arnold@hodder.co.uk

Table of Contents

CONCLUSION

Table of Figures

Acknowledgements

This book began with the preparation of a special subject course at the University of Glasgow in 1995. I wish to thank three classes of students for their interaction with the ideas that became the first raw materials of this work.

From 1997 to 1998 I benefited from a Royal Society of Edinburgh fellowship, which allowed me to visit libraries and archives in London, Douai, St Étienne, and Rouen. I wish to thank the directors Vincent Doom at the Archives Municipales de Douai and Pascal Allais of the Archives Départementales de la Loire. Many others came to my assistance with bibliographical details, book loans, and more: Davit Braun with advice on Irish and Scottish chroniclers, Thomas Clancy with Welsh poetry, John Thomson with French and English chronicles, Truus van Bueren with Dutch, Christiane Klapisch-Zuber with her own library and note cards in Paris, Father Armando Verde and Salvatore Camporeale with theirs at Santa Maria Novella, and Helen Marlsborough with general bibliographic assistance.

With further funding from a Wellcome Project Grant in 1998, I was able to return to these archives on several occasions and extend my research at others in Paris, Rodez, Siena, and Florence. In addition to travel and microfilm costs the grant allowed me to profit from the skills of Peter McKinney and Peter Illing, who coded most of the non-Italian testaments used in this study.

An Arts and Humanities Research Board study leave grant combined with study leave from the University of Glasgow (October, 2000 to April, 2001) enabled me to be a visiting scholar at the American Academy at Rome. Here, I wrote two drafts of this book and expanded my research at the Academy's library, the Biblioteca Apostolica Vaticana, the Biblioteca Nazionale Centrale di Roma, the École française di Rome, the Herziana, the Istituto Superiore di Sanità, the Archivio di Stato, Roma, the Archivio Capitolino, the Archivio di Stato di Bologna, and the Biblioteca Nazionale Centrale di Firenze. I wish to thank the archivists and librarians for their assistance. In particular I am grateful for the intellectual exchange with a remarkable group to scholars at the Academy and for the hospitality of Professor Lester Little and Lella Gandini.

For airing earlier views on this project I was able to give lectures at the Medical School of the University of Alabama (Birmingham), the Wax Chandlers Guild (London), twice at the Wellcome Unit for the History of Medicine (Glasgow), for the history society at the University of Edinburgh, at the Santa Fe Institute (New Mexico), the École des Hautes Études en Sciences Sociales (Paris), the American Academy in Rome, the Villa Spelman (Florence), and at conferences in Ghent, Oslo, and Utrecht. In these venues and others I have benefited from the questions and criticisms of doctors, scientists, historians, and the general public.

This book demanded new departures for me as a historian. I ventured into countries where I had done no previous research and into a subject, the history of medicine and epidemiology, in which I had little prior training. I must thank my colleague Graeme Small for his help with chronicles and other bibliographic sources for France and the Low Countries and Lawrence Weaver, Professor of Child Health at the University of Glasgow, for help with concepts and definitions in microbiology, medicine, immunology, and evolution. For the chapters on India I am grateful to Bruce Fretter and Saul David, who read my first two chapters.

Finally Lawrence Weaver, John Henderson, Rosemary Horrox, William Bowsky, Rudolph Binion, and Christopher Wheeler read through earlier versions of the manuscript. They may not be happy with my final product, but it is a better one thanks to their patience and criticisms. This book is dedicated to my father.

Glasgow, July 2001

For
Samuel Cohn, MD

Introduction

The Black Death in Europe, 1347–52, and its successive waves to the eighteenth century was any disease other than the rat-based bubonic plague
(now known as *Yersinia pestis*), whose bacillus was discovered in 1894.[1]
No contemporary evidence links the Black Death or its successive strikes in
Western Europe to rats. While the Black Death circumnavigated most of the
then known world in five years, modern plague, tied to the homey rat, travels slowly. Thus the so-called Third Pandemic of plague began in the
Yunnan peninsula in the mid 1850s, if not before, but took 40 years to
travel to Hong Kong, a distance swept by the medieval Black Death in a
matter of months without assistance from railways or the steamship. Along
with this speedy transmission, medieval commentators were astounded by
their plague's lightning contagion. By contrast, health workers in India at
the end of the nineteenth century were surprised by the opposite with
theirs—the seeming absence of interpersonal contagion: one plague report
after another concluded that the safest place to be in times of plague was

---

[1] To distinguish between the plagues of the later Middle Ages and the so-called 'Third
Pandemic' of bubonic plague at the end of the nineteenth century, I will call the latter 'modern
bubonic plague', even though descriptive evidence from as early as the Old Testament, Samuel
I, suggests that this disease may have been an ancient malady. In addition to the plague of the
Philistines described in I Samuel IV and I Kings V and VI, historical evidence from India as
early as the seventeenth century suggests that what I am calling 'modern bubonic plague'
(*Yersinia pestis*) was probably an ancient disease. Unlike the later-medieval plague, the sources
reveal that rodents played a prominent role in modern plague and boils formed predominantly
in the region of the genitals. For these earlier plagues, see L. Fabian Hirst, *The Conquest of
Plague: A Study of the Evolution of Epidemiology* (Oxford, 1953), p. 7; *Manson's Tropical
Diseases: A Manual of the Diseases of Warm Climate*, ed. by Philip H. Manson-Bahr, 7th ed.
(London, 1921), p. 257; Carlo Tiraboschi, 'Les rats, les souris et leurs parasites cutanés dans
leurs rapports avec la propagation de la peste bubonique', *Archives de Parasitologie*, VIII, no.
2 (1904), p. 163; and Wu Lien-Teh, 'Historical aspects', pp. 1–12, in Wu Lien-Teh, J.W.H.
Chun, R. Pollitzer, C.Y. Wu, *Plague: A Manual for Medical and Public Health Workers*
(Shanghai Station, 1936), pp. 1–2.

the hospital plague ward. Third, while the Black Death killed upwards of three-quarters of urban and village populations, modern plague in its worse plague-year since the bacillus's discovery has yet to kill over 3 per cent of an urban population. Finally, while modern plague is unusual in that humans possess no natural immunity to it and cannot acquire it, the European populations of the late Middle Ages adapted to their plague over its first hundred years with remarkable speed.

The discovery of the modern plague's bacterium may have marked a leap forward in the conquest of the late nineteenth- and twentieth-century disease; it has, however, retarded our understanding of the late-medieval plague. Without argument, historians and scientists have taken the epidemiology of the modern plague and imposed it on the past, ignoring, denying, even changing contemporary testimony, both narrative and quantitative, when it conflicts with notions of how modern bubonic plague should behave. When the accounts of contemporary chroniclers appear to accord with a so-called theory of modern plague, historians have praised them for empirical precision; when they do not, they are accused of rhetorical exaggeration or of seeing only what their miasmic, scholastic, or humanistic theories supposedly require.

This book begins with the late nineteenth and early twentieth centuries, charting the experience of the plague researchers in India. I begin here not only to understand and distinguish the modern from the late-medieval plague, but also to show the heavy hand of the Middle Ages on medicine in the halcyon years of microbiological investigation, the age of Louis Pasteur and Robert Koch. While knowledge of the medieval past and fear of a return to the Black Death's unprecedented mortalities spurred new levels of international research into a single disease, it also led to new levels of conflict between modern and traditional medicine in India, to major social rioting, and to an initial refusal by scientists to accept the epidemiological realities of their current plague. Given their knowledge of the Black Death's swift sweep through the then known world, these scientists were reluctant to accept the complex, slow, and relatively non-contagious mechanisms of their present bubonic plague—a rat-disease transmitted to humans by fleas regurgitating the bacillus. Even today, despite the vast differences in transmission and contagion between the two plagues and the lack of any evidence of rats or fleas for the earlier one, the medical community continues to view them as the same. Symptomological evidence is crossed from one to the other, and the modern plague continues to be called the 'Third Pandemic', supposedly the same disease that crossed Europe in the time of Justinian (the sixth century) and again in the mid-fourteenth century.

Rejecting the preconception that the Black Death and the plague whose agent was discovered in 1894 had to have been the same disease, this book turns to the sources afresh, first the narrative ones—over 400 chronicles,

250 plague tracts, 50 saints' lives, merchant letters and more. From County Kilkenny to Uzbekistan, Sicily to Scotland, these sources describe the signs and symptoms of the late-medieval plague, provide clues about its epidemiology, and chart changes in mentality over the Black Death's first hundred years. I then turn to archival sources—over 40,000 death documents. From last wills and testaments, mendicant and confraternal obituaries, and the earliest surviving burial records, I plot the late-medieval plagues' temporal cycles, seasonality, and patterns of mortality by class, sex, age, occupation, and neighbourhood, north and south of the Alps.

These sources show that the signs and symptoms of the late-medieval and modern plagues do not match one another nearly so closely as present-day doctors and historians continue to proclaim. Further, the epidemiological evidence of the late-medieval plague—its cycles, seasonality, contagion, speed of transmission, the age and sex of its victims, and occupational and topographical incidence of mortality—frees from suspicion two supposed protagonists of Western civilization—the rat and the flea. In addition, modern plague has a characteristic that, more than plague boils, distinguishes it from most other infectious diseases—the absence of any natural immunity on the part of humans.[2] Thus, each new strike of modern plague is as though the disease is invading a population for the first time—a 'virgin-soil population'; no change in the age structure of its victims ensues with successive strikes, and annual mortalities first rise, not fall, and then vary from year to year almost randomly without downward or cyclical patterns seen for other diseases where human immunity plays a role.[3]

By contrast, the steep and steady fall in mortality with successive strikes of the late-medieval plague over its first hundred years shows Europeans adapting to their new microbial plague enemy with striking speed and success, and this without the benefit of the late nineteenth century's medical discoveries. The last chapter explores the cultural and psychological consequences of this biological success story, the connection between plague and the rise of the Renaissance, not only in Florence or for a handful of humanist intellectuals, but in places as far removed from the supposed centres of Renaissance culture as Danzig and for unknown authors of plague tracts, mendicant chroniclers, and even peasant testators. From the utter despondency felt with the plague's first strike, contemporaries expressed a new

---

[2] Another bacterium for which humans possess no natural immunity is *Helicobacter pylori*, the commonest clinical bacterial infection of mankind, but it does not kill us and may even be beneficial in its interaction with other parasites living off the body.

[3] No immunisation against *Yersinia pestis* is effective for humans for more than six months. At the beginning of 2000, *The Guardian* reported that British intelligence, MI5, had developed such a serum against Saddam Hussein's threat of biological warfare using *Yersinia pestis*. On the failures to find a long-term vaccination, see Norman F. White, 'Twenty years of plague in India with special reference to the outbreak of 1917–18', *Indian Journal of Medical Research*, VI, 2 (1918), 190–236, esp. 215.

sense of confidence in their powers of healing and ability to tame nature. From God and the stars, they turned to cures and socially grounded explanations. The change, I argue, centred on the particular character of the disease—the swiftness with which Europeans adapted to their new bacillus (whatever it might have been).

PART

I

THE MIDDLE AGES
CONFRONTS THE
TWENTIETH CENTURY

|1|

Scientists square the circle

Almost every year a new book or article extols the enigmatic Alexandre Yersin, his courage in discovering the plague bacillus, which in 1954 was named *Yersinia pestis*.[1] It is a tale of David and Goliath, the young Yersin standing alone against the German–Japanese scientific alliance headed by perhaps the most prominent biologist of his day, Robert Koch.[2] On hearing of the outbreak of plague in Hong Kong, the Swiss-born Yersin, student of Louis Pasteur and assistant to Dr Émile Roux, rushed off to Hong Kong in 1894, only to find the Japanese student of Koch, Shibasaburo Kitasato, and his army of assistants entrenched at the Kennedy Town Hospital, the principal plague hospital in Hong Kong. In the competition to discover new and dangerous bacteria between the two leading schools of microbiology, those of Koch and of Pasteur, Yersin's arrival was hardly greeted with enthusiasm.

Yersin was not allowed to enter the Kennedy Town Hospital or given access to plague corpses. Instead, to conduct his research, he had to build a straw hut outside the hospital and to bribe orderlies to smuggle out plague victims for his examination. Within a few days matters worsened with Yersin's sole assistant running off with his money and equipment. Yet against the odds, Yersin succeeded in first identifying correctly the plague bacillus as Gram-negative and immobile, as opposed to Kitasato's culture

---

[1] Until 1900 it was called '*Bacterium pestis*', then '*Bacillus pestis*' until 1923, when it became '*Pasturella pestis*', a term still found in some texts today. On this nomenclature, see Thomas Butler, *Plague and Other Yersinia Infections* (New York, 1983), p. 25.

[2] See Noël Bernard *et al.*, *Yersin et la peste* ... (Lausanne, 1944); H.H. Mollaret and J. Brossollet, *Alexandre Yersin ou le vainqueur de la peste* (Paris, 1985); O. Barrett, 'Alexandre Yersin and recollections of Vietnam', *Hospital Practice*, 24 (1989); N. Howard-Jones, 'Kitasato, Yersin and the plague bacillus', *Clio Medica* 10 (1975): 23–7; H. Kupferschmidt, 'Development of research on plague following the discovery of the bacillus by Alexander Yersin', *Revue Médicale de la Suisse Romande*, 114 (1994): 415–23.

(Gram-positive and immobile) made at almost exactly the same time but which doctors since the 1950s have recognised as mistaken.[3]

On his discovery, Yersin dramatically proclaimed in letters to his mother, in his diary, and in a classic paper published in the *Annales de l'Institut Pasteur* that he had found the bacillus that had caused not only the present plague in China but the sixth-century plague of Justinian and the Black Death of 1348, whose successive waves continued to haunt Europe until it supposedly disappeared after the plague of Marseilles in 1720–22.[4] This view of plague history continues to be standard both for historians and doctors[5]—its three pandemics and its Francocentric view of its European end in 1722, forgetting Messina's plague in 1743 with 48,000 victims and Moscow's in 1771–72, with over 100,000.[6]

Afterwards, Yersin directed a Pasteur Institute in Nhatrang, Vietnam, dedicated to research in animal diseases, and mapped uncharted regions of

---

[3] Mollaret and Brossollet, *Alexandre Yersin*, p. 141. Kitasato's results were published in the *Lancet* on 25 August 1894. Some historians and biologists continue to give Kitasato equal weight in the discovery of the plague bacillus; see for instance Graham Twigg, *The Black Death: A Biological Reappraisal* (London, 1984), p. 171. With Pollitzer's *Plague* (Geneva, 1954), the bacillus was placed 'in the family of bacteria Enterobacteriaceae and included *Y. enterocolitica* and *Y. pseudotuberculosis*, as well as the plague bacillus. Thus plague joined the same bacterial family as *Escherichia coli* and became easier to think of it as a Gram-negative rod bacterial infection. There evolved concurrently a growing awareness of *Y. enterocolitica* as a pathogen capable of causing febrile gastroenteritis, as well as acute appendicitis-like syndrome'; Butler, *Plague and Other Yersinia Infections*, p. 3. Also see Robert B. Craven, 'Chapter 159: Plague', in *Infectious Disease: A Treatise of Infectious Processes*, ed. by P. Hoeprich, M. Jordan and A. Ronald, 5th ed. (Philadelphia, 1994), pp. 1302–11.On the DNA structure of *Yersinia pestis* and its relation to *Y. pseudotuberculosis*, see B. Joseph Hinnebusch, 'Bubonic plague: a molecular genetic case history of the emergence of an infectious disease', *Journal of Molecular Medicine* 75 (1997): 645–52.
[4] Butler, *Plague and Other Yersinia Infections*, p. 17. Yersin, 'La peste bubonique à Hong-Kong', *Annales de l'Institut Pasteur* [hereafter *AIP*] 8 (1894), 662–7: 'the current plague presents all the symptoms and clinical characteristics of the ancient *peste à bubons*, which many times over the centuries has decimated the people of Western Europe and the Levant until it disappeared at Marseilles in 1720, when the disease became restricted to Persia, Arabia, and the Chinese province of Yunnan' (pp. 662–3). Kitasato made a similar historical proclamation in his discovery of the bacillus, except Asia instead of France was emphasised; see Andrew Cunningham, 'Transforming plague: the laboratory and the identity of infectious disease', in *The Laboratory Revolution in Medicine*, ed. by Cunningham and Perry Williams (Cambridge, 1992), p. 241.
[5] See *Manson's Tropical Disease*, ed. by P.E.C. Manson-Bahr and D.R. Bell, 19th ed. (London, 1987), p. 586.
[6] Hirst, *The Conquest of Plague*, p. 16; John Alexander, *Bubonic Plague in Early Modern Russia: Public Health and Urban Disaster* (Baltimore, 1980), pp. 257–9. Further, Lorenzo del Panta and Massimo Livi-Bacci, 'Chronology, intensity and diffusion of mortality in Italy, 1600–1850', *The great mortalities: methodological studies of demographic crisis in the past*, ed. by Hubert Charbonneau and André Larose (Liège, 1979), p. 77, describe a plague in the small village of Noia (Apulia) in 1815; Balint Ila, 'Contribution à l'histoire de la peste en Hongrie au XVIIIe siécle', in ibid., pp. 133–8, plague in Hungary in 1739/40; and August Hirsch, *Handbook of Geographical and Historical Pathology*, tr. by Charles Creighton (London, 1886), III, pp. 660–8, a disease of boils and carbuncles that spread through various parts of Europe and the world from 1834 to 1853.

Vietnam.[7] But his significance for plague research faded, taking a path that has yet to bring lasting success. In the spirit of the late nineteenth-century conquest of new diseases (especially within the Pasteur tradition), after identifying the bacillus, Yersin immediately turned to laboratory experimentation with serums for combating plague. Later researchers would realise that modern bubonic plague possessed a trait that made such a turn problematic—human inability to acquire long-term immunity to it. As for uncovering the complex mechanisms of the plague's transmission, recurrence, and decline, the immediate consequences of Yersin's discovery were limited and his further laboratory endeavours brought scientists no closer to understanding elementary aspects of the plague's epidemiology.

In addition to discovering the plague bacillus, some have claimed that Yersin was the first to identify rats as essential to the transmission of the disease.[8] These claims are misleading. First, from some point in the distant past as seen in folklore and common practice in Africa, India, and China, native peoples had long before noticed the connection between the onset of human plague and a previous or concurrent appearance of dead rats, their fall from rafters, their drunken stagger, and exodus from their nests and holes.[9] Chroniclers, local gazetteers, doctors, and government officials had observed the same in India and China as early as the seventeenth century. Emperor Ichangir Schangir recounted in his memoirs the dying of rats in great numbers during the plague at Agra (India) in 1618.[10] In Yunnan, a local gazetteer during a plague at Shiping (China) in 1810 reported: 'In each family that got sick, the rats first jumped out without any reason, faltered, and fell dead in front of people. Those who saw them became sick in a very short while. Once sick, they could not be saved.'[11]

More to the point, such a picture that centres on Yersin's laboratory finding or even that adds to it Paul-Louis Simond's rat-flea hypothesis of four years later foreshortens the protracted discovery of the plague's mechanisms and epidemiology. Instead, it is a story that carried on into the second

---

[7] See Brossollet and Mollaret, *Alexandre Yersin*, and idem, *Pourquoi la peste? le rat, la puce et le bubon* (Paris, 1994), pp. 86–91.

[8] According to Brossollet and Mollaret, *Alexandre Yersin*, p. 144, it was 'totally unknown in 1894'; also see Michael W. Dols, *The Black Death in the Middle East* (Princeton, 1977), p. 69.

[9] See Charles Creighton, *History of Epidemics in Britain*, 2nd ed., ed. by D.E.C. Eversely, E.A. Underwood and L. Ovenall, I: *A.D. 664–1666* (Cambridge, 1894; London, 1965), pp. 168 and 169 for Yunnan and the Gulf of Tonkin in the 1870s; Patrick Manson, *Tropical Diseases: A Manual of the Diseases of Warm Climates* (London, 1898), pp. 153–4: based on British reports in China and the Himalayas in 1864: 'people, taught by experience, on seeing the exodus [of rats] recognised it as a warning'.

[10] Tiraboschi, 'Les rats', p. 163.

[11] Cited in Carol Benedict, *Bubonic Plague in Nineteenth Century China* (Stanford, 1996), pp. 22–3.

decade of the twentieth century. Yersin, along with W.J. Simpson,[12] Patrick Manson, and other colonial doctors and authorities on tropical diseases, continued to believe that the rat (or rodents more generally) were not the sole or even principal carriers of plague. For Yersin, pigs and buffaloes carried the disease, and flies could transmit it.[13] He had no idea that fleas played any part, and unlike medical observers in Yunnan and the Himalayans earlier in the nineteenth century, Yersin only speculated that rats were 'probably the principal vehicle of plague'.[14] He saw 'human plague preceded by heavy mortalities of mice, rabbits, and guinea pigs' in addition to rats.[15] Further, along with most of the scientific community, he continued to believe that bubonic plague was highly contagious, that as with other infectious diseases a vaccine would confer long-term immunity, and that the bacillus lived in the soil and was communicated from exposure to dirt, through clothing, and by open sores.

In China the role of the flea in the transmission of plague was doubted longer than in India. The principal British plague researchers there, Simpson and Hunter, added calves, hens, turkeys, geese, and pigeons to Yersin's list of animals that generally contracted the disease, and they thought that pigs, poultry, and buffaloes, in addition to Yersin's flies, spread it to humans.[16] Moreover, Simond's flea hypothesis was roundly rejected on its appearance, and even after the Indian Plague Commission's demonstrations aided by massive data collection and repeated experimentation, the scientific community was not totally convinced of the rat–flea–human transmission until Glen Liston's tests published in 1910.[17] The mechanism by which blocked rat fleas regurgitated the plague bacillus into the blood stream came later still, at the time of the outbreak of the First World War.[18] And even after that, some Indian health and sanitary authorities continued to treat plague as a highly contagious disease, failed to understand the rat–flea–human nexus, and disinfected homes and neighbourhoods in the hope of killing the bacillus instead of employing

---

[12] Simpson, *A Treatise on Plague dealing with the Historical, Epidemiological, Clinical, Therapeutic and Preventive Aspects of the Disease* (Cambridge, 1905).

[13] Others in China, such as Rocher, 'observed' that oxen, sheep, deer, pigs, and even dogs (now recognised to be among the most immune to plague) died because of plague: Manson, *Tropical Diseases* (London, 1898), p. 154. Yersin, 'La peste bubonique à Hong-Kong', *AIP*, VIII (1894), p. 667.

[14] Yersin, 'La peste bubonique à Hong-Kong', p. 667.

[15] Yersin, Calmette and Borrel, 'La peste bubonique', *AIP*, IX (1895), p. 589. While these animals can carry plague, they have never precipitated a human plague of epidemic proportions, even in the United States, where rodents other than rats form the plague focus. On various animals as possible carriers, see Craven, 'Plague', p. 1305.

[16] Hirst, *The Conquest of Plague*, p. 150.

[17] David Arnold, *Colonizing the Body: State Medicine and Epidemic Disease in Nineteenth-Century India* (Berkeley, 1993), p. 210.

[18] A.W. Bacot and C.J. Martin, 'Observations on the mechanism of the transmission of plague by fleas', *Journal of Hygiene* [hereafter *JH*] (1914), pp. 432–4.

effective rat controls.[19] While the plague bacterium remains one of the mostly deadly microbes known to man, it is one of the least infectious of epidemic diseases as far as human hosts go.[20]

Successive editions of Sir Patrick Manson's monumental textbook, *Tropical Diseases: A Manual of the Diseases of Warm Climates* first published in 1898, chart the scientific consensus about plague at various moments through the twentieth century. Its massive near-2000-page twentieth edition, published in 1996, remains the authoritative text for tropical medicine with scientists and health workers around the world.[21] In the first edition, Manson defined bubonic plague as 'a communicable epidemic disease common to man and many of the lower animals'; that it was 'innoculable' and 'communicable either through the atmosphere or by contact'; that its transmission depended on a lack of personal cleanliness, that it entered through wounds in hands and feet, from clothing, food, dishes, and water; that it could be communicated to the lower animals by feeding them on the tissues of plague patients and on cultures of the specific bacillus, and that it might be conveyed to man in food and drink. Lice, fleas, bugs, and perhaps flies might act as carriers from person to person. Supposedly 'a considerable mass of evidence' showed that clothes, skins, textile fabrics, and other similar materials, 'preserved the virus in an active state for several months'. Manson called for the isolation of plague-stricken patients, and, following Kitasato, advised that convalescents be isolated for a month before being allowed to mingle with an uninfected community.[22] Over the next decade and a half the researchers of the Indian Plague Commission with detailed and repeated observations and experimentation would demonstrate that all these contentions were either false or of trifling importance.

---

[19]   Ira Klein, 'Plague, policy and popular unrest in British India', *Modern Asian Studies*, 22, 4 (1986), pp. 752–3.

[20]   Even after the complex chain of events, less than 15 per cent of the bites of infected fleas are successful in transmitting the bacillus into the human blood stream; see Hirst, *The Conquest of Plague*, pp. 29, 186, and 459–63. On the other hand, still reflecting the heavy hand of the medieval historical past on modern medical research, Hirst in the same sentence concluded that 'Pneumonic plague is probably the most infectious . . . of all epidemics'. But more than 30 years earlier, while Hirst was investigating bubonic and septicaemic plague in Ceylon, Wu Lien-Teh was mapping the slow and ineffective contagion of pneumonic plague in Manchuria during the worst recorded incidents of this type of plague. He published his results in the same journal as Hirst, the Cambridge-based *Journal of Hygiene*. More recently, the molecular scientist Hinnebusch, 'Bubonic plague', p. 648, after describing the difficulties of fleas regurgitating the bacillus, has made the same claims for pneumonic plague's transmission (without any new research or references to older work). In fact, since the Second World War, pneumonic plague has been extremely rare.

[21]   On Manson and his school of tropical diseases, see Michael Worboys, 'Germs, malaria and the invention of Mansonian tropical medicine: from "diseases in the tropics" to "tropical diseases"', pp. 181–207, in *Warm Climates and Western Medicine: The Emergence of Tropical Medicine, 1500–1900*, ed. by David Arnold (Amsterdam, 1996).

[22]   Manson, *Tropical Diseases* (London, 1898), pp. 144–63.

The next edition of Manson, published in 1903, mostly repeated these assertions. Besides adding new information drawn from the international plague commissions in India, such as the narrow temperature bands in which epidemics exploded and the fact that the death of rats usually preceded an outbreak of human plague,[23] it extended (incorrectly) the number of plague carriers to lice and other bugs. In keeping with current scientific consensus, Manson rejected Simond's radical speculations of 1898[24] that fleas were the key for understanding the plague's transmission.[25]

Even as late as the seventh edition of *Manson's Tropical Diseases*, published in 1921 by his son-in-law, Philip H. Manson-Bahr, certain misconceptions lingered on such as the notion that oxen, sheep, deer, pigs, and dogs were the carriers of the disease.[26] Moreover, the sections dedicated to ancient and medieval plagues had become more prominent in framing the understanding of the current plague's epidemiology.[27] To Manson's credit, even before the first India plague commissions, he reported hospital workers' observations that plague was 'not so infectious as scarlet fever, measles, smallpox, or even typhus' and that the disease rarely infected medics or nurses.[28] Yet, like others, he could not wean himself from the conviction based on the evidence gained from the late Middle Ages that the plague of their own time was also highly contagious. Manson speculated that the absence of the present plague's infection must be explained by the cleanliness and ventilation of hospitals and that modern health workers must not have had open wounds or remained long in close proximity with their patients.[29]

The weight of the past, particularly that of the late Middle Ages, had a triple effect on the discovery of modern bubonic plague. First, under international pressure, the British reacted against the outbreak of plague in India in 1896 with levels of medical and sanitary intervention not seen with other diseases in India. This forceful intervention came even before the disease had become rampant in India.[30] The callousness and severity of British medical and sanitary measures provoked in turn an unparalleled reaction

[23] Manson, *Tropical Diseases*, 3rd ed. (London, 1903), 'Plague', 231–63, esp. p. 242.
[24] Paul-Louis Simond, 'La propagation de la peste', *AIP*, XII (1898): 625–87.
[25] Manson, *Tropical Diseases* p. 243. Likewise in China, the principal plague researchers, Simpson and Hunter, doubted the flea's essential role in 1904 and probably later; see W.J. Simpson, *Report on the Causes and Continuance of Plague in Hongkong* (1903); Hirst, *The Conquest of Plague*, p. 159; W.B. Bannerman and R.J. Kápadiâ, Chapter XXVIII, *JH*, 8 (1908), pp. 209–20.
[26] *Manson's Tropical Diseases*, 7th ed., p. 258.
[27] Ibid., pp. 256–58.
[28] Manson, *Tropical Diseases* (1898), p. 152.
[29] Ibid., p. 152.
[30] See Arnold, *Colonizing the Body*, pp. 200–39, notes 313–18. Arnold fails to explain why plague should have created so much European attention and hysteria in contrast to earlier outbreaks of other diseases.

by Indians that led to widespread riots against the British medical establishment in Bombay, Pune, Calcutta, and elsewhere.[31]

On the other hand, fear of a return to Europe's monumental mortalities of 1348 prompted an unprecedented international scientific response to the outbreak of a new disease. Through the first two decades of the twentieth century the plague became more intensively studied microbiologically and epidemiologically than any other tropical disease, even though its mortalities never surpassed those of malaria, influenza, tuberculosis, or six other diseases in early-twentieth-century India—the subcontinent hit by far the hardest by plague, accounting for 95 per cent of the twentieth century's plague mortalities.[32] In four months alone, the influenza epidemic of 1918–19 in India eradicated almost twice those taken there by plague, and the Number One killer, malaria, killed as many as ten times more than the plague.[33] Yet these other diseases, which were also more threatening to colonial European populations,[34] failed to bring into India numerous European and Asian commissions to collect and classify millions of rodents and insects, to conduct thousands of experiments throughout the Indian subcontinent, and to examine differential mortalities according to geography, climate, housing materials, social class, religion, and habits of the people.

Even as late as 1914, after the Manchurian plague of 1911 but also after the first ports-of-call of the 'Third Pandemic' had killed only in the tens, not the millions, as had been expected in places such as San Francisco and Glasgow,[35] calls were made for Europeans to stand guard against an invasion of plague that could repeat the Black Death's mass destruction. Such was the message of an article in the *Fortnightly Review* of 1914:

> According to many eminent authorities, we have here in Europe still cause to fear the sudden appearance of the unwelcome guest [the plague]. We must not

---

[31] On these riots, see chapter 2.

[32] Klein, 'Urban development and death: Bombay City, 1870–1914', *Modern Asian Studies* 20 (1986), p. 744.

[33] Rajnarayan Chandavarkar. 'Plague panic and epidemic politics in India, 1896–1914, *Epidemics and ideas*, ed. by T. Ranger and P. Slack (Cambridge, 1992), p. 204.

[34] Early on, Simond, 'La propagation de la peste', pp. 644 and 649, observed that cases among Europeans in India were 'entirely exceptional' and maintained that the difference between European and native susceptibility rested not on any difference in immunity but on habits of storing food and the separation of the domestic lodgings from the kitchen.

[35] Sydney and San Francisco were among the most severely stricken of non-Asian ports in 1900; Sydney had 303 cases and 103 deaths in 1900 (J. Ashburton Thompson, 'A contribution to the aetiology of plague', *JH*, I, [1901], p. 153); San Francisco, 159 cases and 77 deaths between 1900 and 1907 (Rupert Blue, 'Anti-plague measures in San Francisco, California, USA', *JH*, IX [1909]: 1–8). In Glasgow, despite its slums and although plague created a major political embarrassment for the city in 1900, only 36 cases appeared with 16 deaths; see A.K. Chalmers, *Corporation of Glasgow, Report on Certain Cases of Plague Occurring in Glasgow in 1900 by the Medical Officer of Health* (Glasgow, 1900), p. 1; and Twigg, *The Black Death*, p. 147.

deceive ourselves, or permit ourselves to be lulled into a false sense of security; for if we do, when we least expect it, the dreadful scourge will be in our midst. It will then be too late to take precautions, and it will, if it once obtains a foothold, be a far greater danger than when the terror-stricken Romans cried: 'Hannibal ante portas!'[36]

Third, despite obvious differences between the medieval Black Death and modern plague as to mortality, speed of transmission, and levels of contagion, scientists continued (and continue) to assume that the microbiology of the two is the same. This assumption delayed progress in the discovery of the modern plague's epidemiology: how could a disease tied to rats and transmitted by fleas spread with the speed and contagion of the Black Death? As early as 1896 the Japanese microbiologist Ogata and, in the following year, the German Bombay Plague Commission found plague bacillus in fleas but refused to assign them a major role in the transmission of the plague to humans. In harmony with Yersin and the renown entomologist G.F.H. Nuttall, Ogata also saw flies as carriers and added mosquitoes. Further, he saw mice, pigs, rabbits, and cats as carriers.[37]

In 1898 a French microbiologist from the Pasteur Institute, Paul-Louis Simond, speculated that the flea was the vital link in the transmission of plague to humans.[38] His argument rested almost entirely on epidemiology: that the plague spread irregularly from one street to the next, that people unconnected with one another caught it while those residing with victims or visiting them in hospitals remained largely unaffected, that the plague season occurred outside the hottest months of the Indian calendar, and that successive outbreaks were usually separated by 12-month periods.

These speculations would become the principal arteries by which plague research would develop over the next 20 years. However, there was no simple progression between these hypotheses of 1898 and the painstaking and massive research carried on almost exclusively by British doctors, epidemiologists, geographers, and statisticians from the turn of the century to the First World War.[39] Nuttall, founding editor of the Cambridge-based *Journal of Hygiene*, who would publish the path-breaking plague reports of the Indian Plague Commission, attacked

---

[36] William B. Steveni, 'The ravages of the Black Death in the fourteenth century and its reappearance in the twentieth century', *Fortnightly Review*, 95 (1914), p. 164.
[37] M. Ogata, 'Ueber die Pestepidemie in Formosa', *Centralblatt für Bakteriologie, Parasitenkunde und Infektionskrankheiten*, XXI (1897): 769–77; E.H. Hankin, ' On the epidemiology of plague', *JH*, 5 (1905), pp. 81–2; Harriette Chick and C.J. Martin, 'The fleas common on rats in different parts of the world and the readiness with which they bite man,' *JH*, 11, no. 1 (1911): 122–36; and Hirst, *The Conquest of Plague*, p. 108.
[38] Simond, 'La propagation de la peste'. On Simond, see Brossollet and Mollaret, *Pourquoi la peste?*, pp. 91–6.
[39] Brossollet and Mollaret, *Pourquoi la peste?*, gives a progressive francocentric history of the plague's conquest without any mention of the post-1900 British contribution.

Simond's flea hypothesis most vigorously. Until 1905, his conclusions had sway over Simond's.[40]

Such a slow and irregular tangle of transmission did not square with scientists' knowledge of the medieval and early modern plagues in Europe, which they referred to often in their scientific essays published in the *Annales de l'Institut Pasteur*, the *Journal of Hygiene*, the *Archives de Parasitologie*, *Centralblatt für Bakteriologie, Parasitenkunde und Infektionskrankheiten* as well as in books by plague specialists such as W.J. Simpson.[41] In one of the earliest of the Indian plague reports, those from the Presidency of Bombay, one hospital after another reported the plague's surprising inability to infect hospital doctors, nurses, and attendants or to spread among the relatives who clustered around plague patients on whom they showered affection by receiving the sputa of the sick in their hands and who used their hands and clothing to wipe away discharges from the patients' mouths.[42] The report from the head of one of the largest of these plague hospitals concluded: 'I do not think infection is spread by human intercourse. . . Of about 400 people. . .who either visited their sick friends or remained constantly by their bedsides. . .in not a single instance did any of these persons contract the plague'.[43] Yet, despite these observations, which Brigadier-General W.F. Gatacre recorded with care in his general report of 1897, his conclusions were just the opposite: 'The disease appears to be both infectious and contagious'.[44] As we have seen, the early editions of Manson's *Tropical Diseases* were riddled with similar inconsistencies: while Manson reported having learnt from the field that 'one of the safest places during an epidemic is the ward of a sanitary plague hospital',[45] he insisted that the plague was a communicable disease, that plague patients had to be isolated from the community, and that convalescents should not mix with relatives for as long as a month.

Even in the latest editions of this venerable text, notions from the Middle

---

[40] On the supposed importance of flies, see Nuttall, 'Zur Aufklärung der Rolle, welche die Insekten bei der Verbreitung der Pest spielen', *Centralblatt für Bakteriologie*, XXII (1897): 87–97; on Nuttall's as the authoritative opinion, see Thompson, 'A contribution to the aetiology of plague', p. 163; Hankin, 'On the epidemiology of plague', p. 77. On the Nuttall–Simond controversy, see Tiraboschi, 'État actuel de la question du véhicule de la peste', *Archives de Parasitologie* XI (1907), p. 546. Also, the prominent plague specialist, Galli-Valerio of Lausanne in 1900 rejected Simond's hypothesis; see W.B. Bannerman, 'The spread of plague in India', *JH*, 6 (1906), p. 206.
[41] *A Treatise on Plague*.
[42] J.K. Condon, *The Bombay Plague . . . September 1896 to June 1899* (Bombay, 1900), p. 72.
[43] W.F. Gatacre, *Report on the Bubonic Plague, 1896–97* (Bombay, 1897), p. 94.
[44] Ibid., p. 231.
[45] Ibid., p. 51. This dictum was to be repeated often in plague reports and articles in the *Journal of Hygiene* and elsewhere through the early years of the twentieth century; see for instance, Simond, 'La propagation de la peste', p. 649; Hankin, 'On the epidemiology of plague', pp. 180–1; 'Plague in Parel village', *JH*, 7 (1907), p. 876; and Hirst, *The Conquest of Plague*, p. 118.

Ages and the early modern period have influenced its clinical descriptions. It continues to report that 'occasionally' bubonic plague produces 'carbuncles, pustules, and abscesses'. But neither it nor any other modern text that I have seen cites an example of such skin disorders that comes after Yersin's discovery of the bacillus. In the case of *Manson's Tropical Diseases* the latest evidence for such a spread of pustules was the London plague of 1665.[46] On the other hand, the largest database of signs and symptoms for any modern plague, that gathered by Gatacre for the Bombay plague of 1896–7, with over 3000 clinical observations, does not report a single case of boils or pustules spreading all over the body.[47]

The cultural sophistication, knowledge of foreign languages and awareness of the historical past, both European and Asian, of doctors such as E.A. Hankin, W.J. Simpson, Charles Creighton, and Georg Sticker is impressive.[48] In addition to knowing Latin and Greek and a number of European languages, they saw history as a vital link for understanding current infectious diseases. Several of them even engaged in historical research using primary sources. In the early days of plague research such historical interest in the plague of Athens, the Justinian plague, the Black Death, and the seventeenth-century plagues, especially in Britain, was not just an afterthought or a later sideline of retirement after active lives in the laboratory;[49] the historical past entered into their scientific arguments and accompanied results from the laboratory.

One of the most prominent examples of such concern with the historical past to probe the epidemiology of the modern plague appears in the arguments of the early twentieth-century plague researcher Hankin. In a seminal article, he surveyed the medieval and early-modern sources on plague, both European and Indian, concluding (against what would later be proven by the Indian Plague Commission) that 'rats were not a necessary cause or agent in the spread of plague' in his present-day India, because the historical record for late-medieval Europe (as he rightly observed) showed that they did not suddenly surface in those earlier plagues.[50] The presumed identity between these two epochs of bubonic plague also led him to impose conclusions derived from the present epidemiology of plague on the European past. With the new epidemiological discovery that modern plague mortalities were inversely correlated with the population size of an infected locality, Hankin

---

[46] *Manson's Tropical Diseases*, 19th ed., pp. 591 and 593. The same goes for Pollitzer's classic work, *Plague*, p. 426.

[47] See chapter 4.

[48] Hankin, 'On the epidemiology of plague'; Simpson, *A Treatise on Plague*; Creighton, *History of Epidemics in Britain*; Sticker, *Abhandlungen aus der Seuchengeschichte und Seuchenlehre*, I (Gissen, 1908).

[49] For such examples of later historical work, see Hirst, *The Conquest of Plague*, and J.F.D. Shrewsbury, *A History of Bubonic Plague in the British Isles* (Cambridge, 1970).

[50] Hankin, 'On the epidemiology of plague', p. 66.

stated boldly that the same was found for the Black Death, asserting that
mortalities had been high in English villages but that 'no evidence of such
depopulation exists for London or other towns'[51]—this despite Creighton's
analysis of wills from the Court of Hustings published several years earlier
that showed a fifteen-fold increase in London's mortality in 1348–49.[52]

Following on from the new discoveries made by the Indian Plague
Commission that the most destitute of India's population seemed to escape
the plague, Hankin concluded the same for the late Middle Ages, seeing it
confirmed by Simon de Couvin's, Black Death poem, which alleged that
tanners escaped the plague.[53] True or false, tanners, almost invariably a
guild occupation, hardly comprised Europe's most destitute circa 1348 as
Hankin assumed to make the past fit his present. Using another new and
unexpected recent finding—plague in India did not follow trade routes as is
normally the case with diseases that spread person-to-person—Hankin
assumed the same for late-medieval plague but for this he did not bother to
cite any contemporary evidence.[54] Finally, Hankin rightly noted from
chroniclers characteristics of fourteenth-century plagues that had no paral-
lels with the Indian plague experience, such as children as the principal
victims of the second outbreak of plague in Europe in the 1360s.[55] Yet,
despite discordances between the two plague periods, he concluded with
confidence: 'all the known plagues of Western India resemble the Black
Death and the epidemics to which it gave rise'.[56]

Hankin and others also turned to India's past plagues to mould a uniform
image of epidemic disease as between past and present, even though earlier
chroniclers described the death of rats preceding human plagues in some
cases and no such rat epizootics with others.[57] Indeed, those with prior rat
epizootics appear to fit within the frame of modern bubonic plague as with
a plague in Pali within the Presidency of Bombay in 1836. The first human
cases were preceded by 'the death of all the rats of the village of Taiwali . . .
They lay dead in all places and directions, in the streets, houses, and hiding-
places of the walls . . . this death of the animal attended or preceded the
disease in every town that was attacked in Marwar, so that the inhabitants
of any house instantly quitted it on seeing a dead rat'. Furthermore, the
death of rats and men occurred in the latter half of April, which corresponds
with the cooler plague season for Bombay.[58]

[51] Ibid., p. 58.
[52] Ibid., p. 60. Creighton, *History of Epidemics in Britain*, p. 118.
[53] Hankin, ' On the epidemiology of plague', p. 57.
[54] Ibid., p. 56.
[55] Ibid., p. 64.
[56] Ibid., p. 58.
[57] Ibid., pp. 708–27; more recently, see Klein, 'Plague, policy and popular unrest', pp. 735–7.
[58] Hankin, 'On the epidemiology of the plague', p. 55, cited from the report of Mr White,
published in *Bombay Medical and Physical Society's Transactions*, II (1839), p. 1.

On the other hand, no chronicler pointed to epizootics of rats for the plague of 1687–90, whose early signs were swellings in three principal zones of the body—behind the ears, in the armpits, or in the groin. Instead, the descriptions suggest a disease that might have been the same as those bubonic plagues of late-medieval and early-modern Europe. Such were the laments of the contemporary Khāfi Khān, whose images of this plague echo the descriptions of late-medieval European commentators of the Black Death but do not conform with the mortalities or mechanisms of the modern plague's transmission:

> it spread so fast and suddenly . . . A hundred thousand people are said to have fallen victim. The disease began with a slight swelling, attended with inflamed lungs and severe fever; the attack generally proved fatal in a few hours. So numerous were the victims that the usual burial rites could not be performed, and the dead were thrown into carts and hurried into the open spaces beyond the town. In one day 700 carts full of dead bodies are said to have passed through the Shāhāpur gate. Whole families were carried off in a night and their bodies were left to decay where they lay. None attended to the wants of others.[59]

Further, the chronicler Muntakhabu-l Lubāb of Muhammad Hāshim cites the conditions that brought on this plague—'famine, drought, and the scarcity of grain'.[60] As we will see, these conditions were just the opposite of those that fan bubonic plague in the modern period. It depends on high levels of humidity, is fuelled by bumper crops of grain, and travels via the grain trade. Moreover, unlike diseases of the poor such as typhus and typhoid, it attacks relatively healthy bodies with requisite levels of iron in the blood for the bacillus to multiply effectively.

Another account also stressed the swiftness of the disease's spread in the 1680s without the telltale warnings of dead rats first appearing: 'So sudden and fierce was this plague that seventy men of the Emperor's suit are said to have been struck down by it and to have died on the road, as Aurangzeb

---

[59] Exactly where Hankin found this quotation is not clear. He cites the translation of in Sir H.M. Elliot and John Dowson, *The History of India as Told by its own Historians: The Muhammadan Period* (London, 1867–77), VII, p. 337, which however, is different: 'The plague (*tā'ān*) and pestilence (*wabā*), which for several years had been in the Dakhin as far as the port of Surat and the city of Ahmadābād, now broke out with violence in Bijāpār, and in the royal camp. It was so virulent that when an individual was attacked with it, he gave up all hope, and thought only about his nursing and mourning. The black-pated guest-slayer of the sky sought to pick out the seed of the human race from the field of the world, and the cold blast of destruction tried to cut down the tree of life of every being. . . . The visible marks of the plague were swellings as big as a grape or banana under the arms, behind the ears, and in the groin, and a redness was perceptible round the pupils of the eyes, as in a fever or pestilence (*wabā*). It was the business of heirs to provide for the interment of the dead, but thousands of obscure and friendless persons of no property died in the towns and markets, and very few of them had the means of burial. It began in the 27th year of the reign, and lasted for seven or eight years.'

[60] Elliot and Dowson, *The History of India*, VII, p. 328.

was being borne from his palace to the Jāma mosque, a distance probably of about three quarters of a mile.'[61] Further, the mortaliáties of the plague appear on a different level of magnitude from those of the worst hit villages and towns of India during the early twentieth century. Nor must we rely on supposed hyperboles of chroniclers for the plague of the 1680s. Several years before it struck, the Emperor Aurangzeb ordered a census in the two principal cities of Bijāpur and Shāhāpur, which numbered nearly 2,000,000.[62] Immediately after the plague he ordered another. Only 984,000 survived, a loss of 1,016,000 people! Such devastation corresponds with figures for Florence, Avignon, and Paris in 1348[63] or for Genoa and Naples in the plague of 1656 but hardly with figures for modern plague; the worst yet to be recorded for any plague since Yersin's discovery has been Bombay City, 1903, when it lost 2.68 per cent of its population.[64] Unfortunately, Indians of the early-modern period did distinguished between these two very different diseases; nor do their terms *tā'ān* for plague and *wabā* for pestilence in general[65] correspond with these two differing forms of epidemic, one with vast mortalities and no signs of rats, often spread by armies and brought on by famine and drought; the other a rat disease in which contemporaries described a prior rodent epizootic and which subsided with the heat of late spring and summer.

Even with a plague researcher of the second generation of the Indian Plague Commissions, L. Fabian Hirst, insistence that modern and medieval bubonic plague were the same led him into self-contradictions and other complications. Faithfully, he reported previous Plague Commission results, recounting an early twentieth-century study in Java, which examined the clothing and hand baggage of over 56,000 natives passing from a plague-ridden area. Their belongings showed plenty of lice, bugs, and human fleas, but only three rat fleas. First, he followed the commission's conclusion—'as a rule very few rat fleas can be recovered from clothing or

---

[61] James Campbell, *Gazetteer of the Bombay Presidency* (Bombay, 1884), XXIII, p. 524.

[62] There is no evidence that the census exists or survived at the time of Campbell's *Gazetteer*.

[63] Campbell, *Gazetteer*, XXIII, pp. 437 and 592. Whether or not this plague was similar to those of the mid–fourteenth or seventeenth century in Europe will require further research. Unfortunately, none of the sources in the Dawson or Campbell collections records the season when the plague occurred and one description maintains that the survivors were maimed for life (perhaps as from smallpox). I have found no such remarks about the survivors of the late-medieval plagues, only hints from a few miracle cures appearing in saints' lives. Also, unlike the fourteenth-century plagues (but not dissimilar from those of the fifteenth century), the Ahmadābād plague lingered on for eight years running. This plague may have been the same that struck Bombay City and its island in 1686. The chroniclers provide less information but stress its extreme violence and high mortalities and further do not mention the death of rats; ibid., XXVI (Bombay, 1893), p. 101.

[64] Klein, 'Urban development and death', p. 744.

[65] On these terms, see Lawrence I. Conrad, 'Tā'ān and wabā': Conceptions of plague and pestilence in early Islam', *Journal of the Economic and Social History of the Orient*, XXV (1982): 268–307, and Dols, *The Black Death in the Middle East*, pp. 315–16.

baggage of travellers' and thus was not an important mode of plague transmission.[66] But when he turned to the Middle Ages, he reported Venetian legislation banning the transport of merchandise and their lists of suspected articles and woven fabrics as being justified in plague time. He did not, however, question that the earlier plague might have been different from the one of his own time.[67]

Similarly, Hirst's lifetime thesis, repeated from his first field research in Ceylon in the 1910s[68] to his magisterial survey of the plague across the ages in the 1950s,[69] was brushed aside to explain how the fast-spreading, contagious fourteenth-century and the slow-moving modern plagues could be the same. For the twentieth-century plagues, Hirst's thesis turned on a single factor—the prevalence of one rat flea, *Xenopsylla cheopis*. According to Hirst, its dominance as the rat-flea determined whether plague would spread from rats to humans with epidemic consequences.[70] Like other plague researchers such as Wu Lien-Teh, he vigorously refuted the claims of some French plague researchers working in Morocco in the 1930s and 1940s who saw the human flea, *Pulex irritans*, as effectively transmitting plague person-to-person without the rat intermediary. Hirst argued first that plague never reached epidemic proportions in Morocco; furthermore, there was no evidence to suppose that X. *cheopis* had not been the chief vector of plague to humans there; and, most importantly, 'all the available evidence' points to *Pulex irritans* as 'a feeble transmitter of plague' anywhere. The reverse transmission of plague from humans to rats, other mammals, or other humans was highly unlikely: the *bacillaemia*, or concentration of bacilli in the blood of human plague victims, is far lower than in rats, too low, in fact, to induce blockage of the flea's proventriculus, thus forcing it to transmit the plague bacillus to any animal. As Graham Twigg would later put it, 'man is a biological dead end' as far as plague goes.[71]

Yet when it came to explaining the much more rapid and efficient spread of plague in the late Middle Ages that far exceeded anything seen in Morocco or even the worst plague years anywhere in the twentieth century,

---

[66] Hirst, *The Conquest of Plague*, p. 308. According to Twigg, *The Black Death*, p. 129, only two X. *cheopsis* were found among the clothes and baggage of 56,790 passengers, and he adds: 'Even the clothes of a group of 1829 persons, among whom there were 393 plague patients, yielded only 7 X. *cheopis*'. On the unlikelihood of plague spreading in clothing and luggage, see also Robert Pollitzer and Karl F. Meyer, 'The ecology of plague,' in *Studies in Disease Ecology*, ed. by Jacques M. May (New York, 1961), p, 435.

[67] Hirst, *The Conquest of Plague*, pp. 307 and 311.

[68] W.M. Philip and L.F. Hirst, 'A report of the outbreak of the plague in Colombo, 1914–16', *JH*, 15 (1915–17): 527–64, esp. 558; Hirst, 'Plague fleas with special reference to the Milroy Lecture', *JH*, 24 (1925): 1–16.

[69] Hirst, *The Conquest of Plague*, esp. pp. 209, 222, 240, and 302: 'No epidemic of human plague nor rat epizootic of any magnitude has ever occurred anywhere during the course of the recent pandemic in the absence of an adequate density of X. *cheopis*.'

[70] Hirst, *The Conquest of Plague*, p. 362.

[71] Twigg, *The Black Death*, p. 170.

Hirst turned to the improbable *Pulex irritans* to account for the differences, now seeing this flea as an 'important auxiliary in transmitting the infection' in the late Middle Ages. Such a flea as the late-medieval plague's vector made it possible to explain away another discordant feature between the two plague pandemics: earlier, characteristic of highly contagious diseases that spread person-to-person, plague deaths clustered in households, while twentieth-century plague shows no such tendency.[72] Thus to maintain the identity between the two waves of disease, Hirst was willing to forego the cornerstone of his life's work, the central importance of one rat-flea, *X. cheopis*, for explaining when plague reached epidemic proportions among humans.[73]

Turning back to that other supposed protagonist of Western civilization—the rat—some, such as Hankin and Tiraboschi,[74] admitted its absence as the disseminator of plague in the later Middle Ages but still did not question the identity of the two plagues. Others, such as the plague-doctor Charles Creighton, rightly argued that an epizootic of rodents must precede human bubonic plague and then dug through the historical past until he thought he had found it.[75] His evidence, however, was slim indeed, a single reference from an Edinburgh plague tract of 1604: 'And when as

---

[72] Hirst, *The Conquest of Plague*, p. 246.

[73] Ibid., pp. 240 and 244. Earlier, other field workers in northern Africa (Tunisia and Algeria) looked to *Pulex irritans* for an explanation but found no evidence of it as a carrier; see A. Billet, 'La Peste dans le département de Constantine en 1907: recherches particulières sur les rats, leurs ectoparasites et leurs rapports avec l'épidémie', *AIP*, 22 (1908), 658–81, esp. p. 671. Yet historians continue to pin their assertions of the two plagues' identity on the much less efficient conveyor of plague, *Pulex irritans*, to explain the much more efficient and rapid spread of the disease from person to person in the Middle Ages. See S.R. Ell, 'Interhuman transmission of medieval plague,' *Bulletin of the History of Medicine*, 54 (1980): 497–510. His speculations also depend on plague spreading in cold climates when people were more likely to wear loose clothing. As we shall see, the most rapid and ferocious spread of plague, particularly in the Mediterranean zones of Europe, came consistently in the hottest months of year. Nonetheless, Ell recognised that the 'transmission of plague by the human flea is still far from universally accepted as a major mode of [the plague's] spread' (p. 503). Similarly, M.W. Flynn, 'Plague in Europe and the Mediterranean countries', *Journal of European Economic History*, 8 (1979): 131–47, favoured the possibility of the human flea to explain plague transmission past and present but raised doubts. Other historians have not been as cautious; see J.-N. Biraben, *Les hommes et la peste en France et dans les pays européens et méditerranéens* (Paris, 1976), I, 13; Emmanuel Le Roy Ladurie, 'A concept: the unification of the globe by disease (fourteenth to seventeenth centuries)' in *The Mind and Method of the Historian*, tr. Siân and Ben Reynolds (Brighton, 1981; 1973), 28–83, esp. 36 (first published in *Revue Suisse d'Histoire* (1973): 627–96); Leslie Bradley, 'Some medical aspects of plague,' in *The Plague Reconsidered: A New Look at its Origins and Effects in 16th- and 17th- Century England*, Local Population Studies supplement, 1977, pp. 13–15; Paul Slack, *The Impact of Plague in Tudor and Stuart England* (London, 1985), pp. 7–10; and Geoffrey Hawthorn, *Plausible Worlds: Possibility and Understanding in History and the Social Sciences* (Cambridge, 1991), p. 43. On the other hand, biologists and other specialists of modern plague have now rejected the possibility of the human flea as a significant vector of plague, past or present; see Butler, *Plague and Other Yersinia Infections*, p. 51.

[74] Tiraboschi, 'Les rats', p. 163.

[75] Creighton, *History of Epidemics in Britain*, p. 170.

rats, moles, and other creatures (accustomed to live underground) forsake their holes and habitation, it is a token of corruption in the same . . .'[76] From this passage alone Creighton concluded: 'The very same observation of the rats leaving their holes, which is so abundantly confirmed from the recent plague-spots of Southern China, of Yun-nun, of Kumaon, and of Gujerat, was familiar in the plague-books of London and of Edinburgh in the Elizabethan period'.[77] Yet, instead of an observation, this literary topos taken from Avicenna (980–1037) or even an earlier source was a theoretical proposition about the corruption of the atmosphere that supposedly caused an inversion of the animal kingdom. Had he dug deeper into doctors' tracts, he would have found many more of these statements going back to the Middle Ages, but he would have also found that they said many other 'reptiles' came out of their holes, including moles, frogs, snakes, and snails. In addition, by the same theory of atmospheric corruption, birds accustomed to living on high came down to the plains to presage the coming of plagues.[78] Even if these formulae of inversion were true observations, which they were not, none of them describes an epizootic (unlike the medical and folkloric evidence from Africa, India and China). In these tropes the animals lived on, even if in new and unaccustomed habitats. Also, Avicenna's mice came out of their holes as if intoxicated,[79] a detail curiously not added by any of the later European tracts. To date, no one has found a description of a rat epizootic preceding or accompanying a plague in late-medieval or early modern Western Europe.

* * *

The Chinese doctor Wu Lien-Teh was the one plague scientist, even if only momentarily, to doubt the connection between the modern and late-medieval plagues. Wu (called Tuck for his British readers) was the chief medical researcher for the Manchurian plagues of 1911 and 1922—the only two incidents to date when pneumonic plague reached epidemic proportions. He pointed to the exceptional circumstances that gave rise to these two extraordinary events. The sudden rise in the price of tarabagan skins brought a rush of inexperienced trappers into northern Manchuria. They resided in cramped, unventilated underground huts, with forty living in spaces 15 by 12 feet.[80] His conclusions were the opposite of those that historians Christopher Morris,

---

[76] Ibid., p. 172.

[77] Ibid., pp. 172–3.

[78] On these 'remote signs' of plague, see chapter 6.

[79] Charles-Edward Amory Winslow, *The Conquest of Epidemic Disease* (Princeton, 1943), p. 95.

[80] Wu Lien-Teh, 'First Report of the North Manchurian Plague Prevention Service', *JH*, 13 (1913–14), 237–90, expressed doubts about modern and medieval plague as the same early on but later was convinced that the two were the same; see also, *A Treatise on Pneumonic Plague* (Geneva, 1926); idem, 'Historical aspects', 1–55, in Wu Lien-Teh, J.W.H. Chun, R. Pollitzer, C.Y. Wu, *Plague: A Manual for Medical and Public Health Workers* (Shanghai Station, 1936); and *Plague Fighter: The Autobiography of a Modern Chinese Physician* (Cambridge, 1959).

Emmanuel Le Roy Ladurie, Gunnar Karlsson, and others have attributed to him to argue an identity between medieval and modern plague and to explain the high mortalities, rapid transmission, person-to-person contagion, and absence of rats for the former. In a report on the worst of the pneumonic plagues, that of 1911, Wu was clear: pneumonic plague, like bubonic, is dependent on a prior epizootic of rodents, in the case of Northern Manchuria, the tarabagan. Even in the exceptional conditions of the 1911 plague, its transmission from the rodent population to humans is 'negligible'.[81] In the first of these outbreaks, which infected far more people than any other modern pneumonic plague, killing as many as 50,000, the death toll amounted to only 0.3 per cent of the population exposed to the disease; thus it was less dangerous than bubonic plague in India and hardly comparable to the mass mortalities of the Black Death or its successive waves of destruction.

With his investigation of the second Manchurian plague in 1922, Wu went further: 'Pneumonic plague epidemics arise as a secondary manifestation of Bubonic plague';[82] 'despite regular steamship travel between endemic southern ports of Canton, Hong Kong, etc. and northern ports like Shanghai, Dairen ... plague seldom visits these parts'; 'the rooms where patients have died of pneumonic plague are not particularly dangerous'; 'in all four instances recorded, sick patients travelling in railway carriages have not infected their fellow passengers'.[83] In other words, pneumonic plague was not the lightning-rapid contagion that historians and even recent scientists have attributed to it and in turn have used to explain away the uneasy fit between Black Death's massive spread and destruction and the much more limited ravages of modern plague.[84]

In an overview of the Manchurian experience written with two younger collaborators, Wu was still convinced that the seventeenth-century plague of London was bubonic plague but had doubts about the late-medieval plague: 'The Black Death which ravaged the whole of Europe and a large part of Asia might have been plague or a virulent type of influenza such as that encountered in 1918.' But neither Wu nor his collaborators—one of whom, Robert Pollitzer, 31 years later would publish what still stands as the major survey of the plague across time and space—gave the idea any further thought. By 1954 for Pollitzer there was no longer any question: the Black Death was modern bubonic plague.[85]

---

[81] Ibid., p. 275.
[82] On this point also see Pollitzer, *Plague*, p. 504.
[83] Wu Lien-Teh, 'Plague in the orient with special reference to the Manchurian outbreaks', *JH*, 21 (1922–23): 62–76, esp. pp. 63, 75 and 76.
[84] See for instance, Michael Dols, 'The Second Plague Pandemic and its recurrence in the Middle East: 1347–1894', *Journal of the Economic and Social History of the Orient*, XXII (1979), p. 169: 'The appearance of pneumonic plague, either alone or, as is usual, in conjunction with bubonic plague, is important because its is probably the most infectious epidemic disease ...'
[85] Pollitzer, *Plague*, p. 13.

Yet Wu and his collaborators provided reasons for doubting the connection between the two diseases: (1) pneumonic plague usually arises as result of earlier bubonic infections, which produce pulmonary symptoms, and not the other way around as Guy de Chauliac described the successive modes of plague in the late autumn of 1347 to the spring of 1348;[86] (2) patients died usually within 16 hours of the onset of coughing and not the three to five days or even longer recorded by chroniclers and doctors during the later Middle Ages;[87] (3) bubonic plague builds up at a slow rate before the pneumonic type fully develops;[88] there is no sudden explosion and spread of disease such as chroniclers recorded in 1348. Finally, the descriptions of intense pain gruesomely retold by Gabriele de' Mussis[89] and other chroniclers of the Black Death—the sharp pangs of San Sebastian's piercing arrows, that made him the Renaissance's pre-eminent plague saint[90]—do not correspond with clinical observations of the twentieth-century's pneumonic plague: 'Owing to CO_2 intoxication' the patients instead experience little pain; death is swift and delirium, rare.[91] Before comparing the signs and symptoms of the two periods of plague, let us turn to the unsung heroes of the plague's discovery, the British, and to their findings, many of which have been forgotten, ignored, or never learnt by successive generations of scholars of plague, both scientists and historians.

[86] Guy de Chauliac, *Chiurgia*, Tract. II, cap. 5, text found in Heinrich Haeser, *Geschichte der epidemischen Krankheiten* in *Lehrbuch der Geschichte der Medizin und der epidemischen Krankheiten*, II (Jena, 1865) [hereafter, Haeser], p. 175.

[87] Again, see Guy de Chauliac. Monna Filippa, a patient of the Lucchese doctor Ser Iacopo di Coluccino in the plague of 1373, survived coughing and spewing of blood for at least four days after she had come into Ser Iacopo's care (*Il Memoriale di Iacopo di Coluccino Bonavia Medico Lucchese (1373–1416)*, ed. by Pia Pittino Calamari in *Studi di Filologia Italiana*, XXIV [Florence, 1966], p. 397).

[88] Wu, Chun, and Pollitzer, 'Clinical observations', pp. 292–3.

[89] Haeser, pp. 157–61.

[90] Jérôme Baschet, 'Image et événement: l'art sans la peste (c. 1348–c. 1400)?', in *La Peste Nera*, pp. 25–48; and Avraham Ronen, 'Gozzoli's St Sebastian altarpiece in San Gimignano', *Mitteilungen des Kunsthistorischen Institutes in Florenz*, XXXII (1988), p. 77.

[91] Wu, Chun and Pollitzer, 'Clinical observations', p. 298.

|2|

The conquest of plague

Recent accounts of the discovery of the plague's aetiology, transmission, and conquest have stressed the French contribution, starting with Yersin's discovery in 1894, jumping to Simond's flea hypothesis in 1898, and ending with Yersin's and Roux's development of a plague serum and vaccination.[1] Yet Yersin's discovery did not change certain engrained assumptions about the plague seen in medical and sanitary reports from Yunnan and the Gulf of Tonkin since the 1860s, if not before, and Simond's hypothesis was roundly rejected until proven by British scientists around 1905. Finally, the Pasteur Institute's laboratory search for a long-lasting vaccine for plague was a wild goose chase. Still, there is no certainty that one has been developed. Instead, the crucial phase in the discovery of the modern plague, that which took place after 1900, has yet to receive the historical attention it deserves,[2] and the attention it has received, almost exclusively from historians of colonial India, has placed it in a negative light. The present consensus is that the Indian Plague Commission's results were contradictory and at best limited, and that its Western scientific hubris provoked riots, resentment, and a lack of cooperation from the native populations of India.

With the more threatening spread of plague in India by the early years of the twentieth century, medical research into the plague changed tack, reversing the direction of earlier discoveries in microbiology from the laboratories of Koch in Germany and of Pasteur, Roux, and Yersin in France. From the 1820s to the 1840s, medical writers collected statistics on diseases, 'priding themselves on their new statistical sense'. Parallel to this development was the growth of medical geography and topographical

---

[1] See Brossollet and Mollaret, *Pourquoi la peste?*
[2] For the political developments, see I.J. Catanach, 'Plague and the tensions of empire: India 1896–1918', in *Imperial Medicine and Indigenous Societies*, ed. by D. Arnold (Manchester, 1988), pp. 149–71.

surveys.[3] By contrast, toward the end of the century 'the new tropical medicine' tended to eschew analysis of climate and topography in favour of microbiological analysis of bacilli and protozoa.[4]

The discovery of plague, however, was an exception to this straightforward linear progression in modern medicine. While certainly the doctors and statisticians of the twentieth century made use of Yersin's discovery of the bacillus for conducting their experiments, their breakthroughs rested on the collecting of unprecedented quantities of statistical data on rats, fleas, and on the human populations exposed to plague. Their endeavours turned first largely to field work, not the laboratory, [5] with careful mapping of the spread of this enigmatic disease, the counting and identification of over two million rats and many more fleas, the plague's seasonality in numerous ecozones based on temperature and humidity, its relationship to topography, building materials, habits of the people, and more. Their early reports even eschewed the microscope, concluding that their native attendants were better equipped to identify plague-infected rats with the naked eye than laboratory experts with microscopes.[6]

The first plague report compiled by the British in India came from the army, edited by Brigadier-General W.F. Gatacre.[7] Its data and analysis pertained to the first strike of plague in the Presidency of Bombay in 1896–97 and was limited to the clinical hospital records of daily temperatures, pulse readings, signs and symptoms, dates of entry, discharge, or death of plague patients. Although later Reports of the Indian Plague Commission were on a much grander scale, geographically and analytically, for the symptomatology of the plague, I know of no other source for any outbreak that can rival Gatacre's report in the quantity of cases or clinical detail.

Subsequent attention to plague in India by the British (and in particular its special reports issued by the Advisory Committee appointed by the Secretary of State for India, the Royal Society, and the Lister Institute) turned from the patient to the environment. Experimentation with rats and

---

[3] D. Arnold, 'Introduction' in Tropical Medicine before Manson', in *Warm Climates and Western Medicine: The Emergence of Tropical Medicine, 1500–1900*, ed. Arnold (Amsterdam, 1996), p. 9.
[4] Ibid., p. 10.
[5] On the endeavours of W.M. Haffkline to create a serum, see Catanach, 'Plague and the tensions of empire', pp. 154–9, and articles in *JH*.
[6] 'Characteristic appearances in plague-infected rats recognisable by naked-eye examination', *JH*, 7 (1907): 324–58: 'The results of tests carried out for the purpose of comparison make it manifest that the naked eye is markedly superior to the microscopical method as an aid in diagnosis' (p. 368). Later analysis caused these researchers to distrust further the microscope: 'Additional observations on the septicaemia in human plague', *JH*, 8 (1908): 'Microscopical examination of the blood cannot be regarded as a trustworthy index of the degree of septicaemia' (p. 234).
[7] On the politics of Gatacre's appointment to head the Bombay plague committee, see Arnold, *Colonizing the Body*, p. 208.

guinea pigs or data on the transmission of the disease and the conditions that brought it to fruition were mixed with comparative sociological, climatic, and topological surveys. Across much of the infected subcontinent, the commissioners collected data on nutrition, class, religion, and occupations of plague victims as well as on their housing—types of flooring, masonry on walls, tiling of roofs, ventilation, neighbourhood, and more. From the Bombay Presidency the British team's analysis spanned the varied climatic belts of India with detailed reports in sample places, not only in subtropical climes but also in temperate regions in the hills and mountains, places such as Belgaum City at 2500 feet in altitude and the Coimbatore district at 8000 feet, where plague had been severe in the first decade of the twentieth century. The reports are models of interdisciplinary and comparative research. Unfortunately, one question they failed to ask was why plague was so much more severe in India than elsewhere in the world, even within the subtropics.

By its first inquiry conducted in 1904 and published in 1906, the plague researchers came to a number of surprising conclusions, given earlier assumptions about the disease. Several confirmed what Simond had hypothesised at the end of the nineteenth century. First, they reiterated Robert Koch's dictum put succinctly in 1901: plague was 'a disease of rats in which men participate'.[8] Second, as had been observed in the hospital reports of the first outbreak of plague in 1896–97, plague was rarely communicated person to person; third, by the meticulous counting of various species of rat fleas, by charting the rise and fall in rat and human cases of plague in numerous places, and through experimentation, they proved that the plague's transmission required rat fleas to bite infected rats and then transmit the disease to humans only after a rat epizootic had reached or passed its peak.

Other conclusions were new, even if anticipated earlier, such as the fact that plague was a disease of place. Here, the charts of the plague's irregularities, its seemingly haphazard jumps from one house to the next or one street to the next that made no sense in terms of human sociability, confirmed long-known practices of indigenous villagers who on the appearance of increasing numbers of dead rats saw the comings of plague, evacuated their villages en masse, and camped together as little as 200 yards from their homes until the plague season had run its course.[9] However, the most striking conclusion of these early plague reports regarded the marked seasonal consistency of plague outbreaks in any given locality; once endemic to a

---

[8] 'Digest of recent observations on the epidemiology of plague', *JH*, 7 (1907), p. 696.

[9] In addition to the stories of such movements collected by Hutchison from the 1870s and 1880s in Twigg, *The Black Death*, pp. 25–7, see those recorded by the Indian Plague Commission, 'General considerations regarding the spread of infection, infectivity of houses, etc. in Bombay City and island', *JH*, 7 (1907), p. 882.

locality, it reappears, rises, declines, and disappears at about the same time, year after year.[10] From this, the researchers pinned the plague's appearance on the fertility cycle of rat fleas and maximum rat flea 'indices'. The ideal temperatures for plague ranged between daily means of 68°F and 78°F with human plague often peaking well below this maximum.[11]

In later plague reports, the researchers would add to their temperature charts relative humidity and the more complex index of saturation points to argue that humidity might be even more important than daily average temperatures for predicting yearly recurrences of rat epizootics and human plague. The maximum temperature of plague epidemics would be considerably lower in dry conditions or may not occur at all.[12] Still other findings surprised the plague researchers who insisted on confirming their results with an avalanche of local comparative studies and repeated experimentation. Yet, despite the Plague Commission's care and repeated testing, later historians as well as bacteriologists often have lost sight of these conclusions and continue to report the opposite as secure facts about modern bubonic plague. Here are some examples.

Against repeated assertions in history texts that in addition to the fleabite, plague is spread to humans by scratching rat faeces into the bloodstream, the commissioners found that even when the infected faeces or blood contained abundant bacteria, they were not highly infective and played little part in the spreading of an epizootic or plague.[13]

Against earlier speculations,[14] the commissioners found that plague was not transmitted through clothing or baggage of travellers, or other effects of infected persons. Instead, adult fleas outside their normal host, the rat, rarely live more than five days and do not travel in passengers' baggage, in wool packs, or cotton bales as recent historians such as Le Roy Ladurie, John Aberth, and Norman Cantor for medieval Europe,[15] Paul Slack for

---

[10] 'On the existence of chronic plague in rats in localities where plague is endemic', *JH*, 6 (1906), p. 530.

[11] Hugh A. Fawcett, 'Preliminary rat-flea survey and some notes on its relation to local plagues, Hongkong', *JH*, 30 (1930), p. 485, where the human plague peaks fell in May when average daily temperatures heated up to 72.4°F.

[12] R. St J. Brooks, 'The influence of saturation deficiency and of temperature on the course of epidemic plague', *JH, Plague Supplement V* (1917), p. 898.

[13] 'On the infectivity of floors grossly contaminated with cultures of *B. pestis*', *JH* (1906), p. 523, and 'General considerations regarding the spread of infection, infectivity of houses, etc. in Bombay City and Island', *JH*, 7 (1907), pp. 875–6.

[14] Ibid., p. 541: 'We have no ground for suspecting that the infection of plague can be spread by clothing, bedding, or other articles of household use'. Also, see Pollitzer and Meyer, 'The ecology of plague', p. 435.

[15] Le Roy Ladurie, 'A concept', p. 32; Norman F. Cantor, *In the Wake of the Plague: The Black Death and the World it Made* (New York, 2000), p. 46; J. Aberth, *From the Brink of the Apocalypse: Confronting Famine, War, Plague, and Death in the Later Middle Ages* (New York, 2000), p. 113: 'Rats, for instance, are not essential for the disease. In addition to airborne contagion, plague bacilli can travel long distances in fleas that burrow in merchandise such as wool packs.'

Tudor and Stuart England,[16] Ole Jørgen Benedictow for late-medieval Scandinavia,[17] and Klein for twentieth-century India, [18] continue to report as solid epidemiological facts of modern plague. Grain with infested plague-ridden rats was the conduit by which plague moved over long distances, and as plague researchers of the late nineteenth century observed in Bombay, Karachi, and elsewhere, 'plague first broke out among the grain dealers and their employees'.[19] Unlike the plagues of the late Middle Ages and early modern periods, where the bacillus seems to have travelled readily in clothing and cloth merchandise of all varieties, later plague researchers showed that rat-infested fleas did not travel with textiles, and especially not in bales of cotton because cottonseeds are poisonous to rats.[20]

Building construction and the state of an accommodation bore no relation to whether a dwelling became plague-infested. Indeed, often the better and more newly built stone chawls with cement floors counted more infested rats and human plague cases than wooden or thatched buildings with ground floors within the same village or town. In 1907 the plague researchers found for Bombay City the opposite of what they expected: 'of 9527 plague cases, 57.7 per cent resided in houses with stone or cement floors, 41.5 per cent in houses with cow dung or earthen floors, and 0.7 per cent in houses with uncovered wooden floors'.[21] The new chawls of Morland Road constructed in 1906, 'solidly built of brick and supported on a high masonry plinth, with floors of concrete . . . the lighting and ventilation of the whole building leaving nothing to be desired' were so plague-infested that the residents 'had to abandon the chawls and live in huts made of bamboo and matting'.[22] Instead of housing and its materials, the Plague Commission concluded that the principal determinant of whether a house

---

[16] P. Slack, *Plague in Tudor and Stuart England*, p. 12; idem, 'The Black Death past and present, 2: Some historical problems', *Transactions of the Royal Society of Tropical Medicine and Hygiene* (1989) 83, p. 461.

[17] Ole Jørgen Benedictow, *Plague in the Late Medieval Nordic Countries: Epidemiological Studies* (Oslo, 1992), p. 272.

[18]   Klein, 'Plague, policy and popular unrest', p. 737: 'Indian travellers played a crucial role in disseminating plague . . . as carriers in their clothing or baggage of *X. cheopis* across the country'; also see Carol Benedict, *Bubonic Plague*, p. 5.

[19]   Hirst, *The Conquest of Plague*, p. 131. See also Hankin, 'On the epidemiology of plague', p. 72; and 'Observations made in four villages in the neighbourhood of Bombay', *JH*, 7 (1907), p. 852; 'Observations on plague in Eastern Bengal and Assam', *JH*, 12 (1912), p. 188; 'Epidemiological observations in the United Provinces of Agra and Oudh, 1911–1912', *JH: Plague Supplement V* (1917), p. 826; W.M. Philip and L.F. Hirst, 'A report of the outbreak of the plague in Colombo', p. 522.

[20]   J. Isgaer Roberts, 'The relation of the cotton crop to plague and its role as a vehicle for rats and fleas in East Africa', *JH*, 34 (1934): 388–403; and G.H.C. Hopkins, 'Cotton and plague in Uganda', *JH*, 38 (1938): 233–47.

[21]   'The epidemiological observations made by the commission in Bombay City', *JH*, 7 (1907), p. 773.

[22]   Ibid., p. 783.

was struck by plague were 'habits'—the desire on the part of some Indians to protect rats and to store grain and food in living areas.[23]

Here the assumptions of historians and scientists of the Black Death is doubly perplexing in attributing low or no plague incidence to the well-built stone buildings of the rich, which supposedly prevented the penetration of rats.[24] Not only does the assumption that rats could not enter stone-built castles and monasteries fail to conform to what the plague researchers found with modern bubonic plague; it does not correspond with the mortality losses of the later Middle Ages. In 1348, some of the highest death statistics came from the well-fed living in well-built stone structures—the Dominicans at Santa Maria Novella (Florence), Siena, Pisa, Lucca, Montpellier, and Maguelonne (where only seven of 160 survived), and the Franciscans at Marseilles and Carcassonne, where all the friars are said to have perished in 1348.[25] At Westminster the mortalities may not have been quite as dramatic, but at least half the community died in 1348–9 despite a standard of living that Barbara Harvey has meticulously shown was on a par with the substantial gentry and whose buildings and plumbing was 'of a splendour and proportions fit for the nobility'.[26]

Against the present assumptions about modern plague held by medievalists, early modernists, and even students of modern plague, the plague researchers found no relation between the severity of plague and overcrowding in the neighbourhoods of Bombay City.[27] Moreover, other cities, such as Madras, Lucknow, and Calcutta, with living conditions as appalling or more so than those of Bombay were relatively unscathed by plague.[28]

---

[23] Ibid., p. 782.

[24] See Le Roy Ladurie, 'A concept', pp. 32–3; Ell, 'Immunity as a factor in the epidemiology of medieval plague', *Reviews of Infectious Diseases*, 6 (1984), p. 869; M. Hulton, 'Introduction' to *The Black Death in Coventry*, ed. by Hulton (Coventry, 1998), p. 9; Benedictow, *Plague in the Late Medieval Nordic*, pp. 136–7; Aberth, *From the Brink of the Apocalypse*, pp. 112–13; Shrewsbury, *A History of Bubonic Plague*, p. 35: 'There is nothing surprising about the almost complete exemption of the English nobility and landed class from 'The Great Pestilence'; it just happened that the house-rat could not make itself at home in their castles. . .'

[25] Yves Renouard, 'Conséquences et intérêts démographiques de la Peste Noire de 1348', *Population*, 3 (1948), pp. 462–3; and P. Angelus Walz, OP, *Compendium Historiae ordinis praedicatorum* (Rome, 1948), p. 55.

[26] B. Harvey, *Living and Dying in England, 1100–1540: The Monastic Experience* (Oxford, 1993), p. 78. Also, historians of modern plague have assumed the same; see Klein, 'Urban development and death', p. 733: 'Their [the Bombay elite] "pucca" houses resisted the incursions of rodents . . .'

[27] It is common for historians to set the stage of the plague by invoking pictures of the terrible hygienic conditions that must have existed circa 1348; see for instance, Renouard, 'Conséquences,' p. 461: 'les villes où l'hygiène était déplorable . . . tous les quartiers avec les puces . . .' Curiously, Renoud then follows by telling us that the worst afflicted in 1348 were the privileged Dominicans and Franciscans.

[28] See Klein, 'Plague, policy and popular unrest', p. 738, for his description of the severe overcrowding and deprivation of Madras, where plague hardly existed. Yet Klein, p. 754, still concluded that the reasons for the exceptional mortality from bubonic plague in the early twentieth-century India resulted largely from overcrowding and poor housing.

Although Jews, Europeans, and often the wealthy escaped plague more than others in India, it related to their habits of keeping food and not to their nutrition. A privileged caste such as the Brahmins of Saara experienced high mortalities from plague, and wealthy grain dealers were often the first to contract plague and experienced the worst mortalities because of their proximity to grain depots, and thus infected rats and fleas.[29] By contrast, the impoverished caste of the byragees, who lived in the open air, had few casualties. The difference did not hinge on religious beliefs or the open air as was first thought, but on keeping rats out of their households.[30] The researchers also found that the very poorest, those who could not afford to leave scraps of food, were free of plague infestation.[31] In South Bihar plague even had an upper caste bias because of the high incidence of death among tradesmen in sweats and other foodstuffs and the fact that the upper classes evacuated their homes for other houses susceptible to rat-infestation, while the poor left their houses to sleep on mats in the open air.[32]

In addition, modern plague is more likely to follow good harvests rather than droughts or famine, because increased grain boosts rat population and higher humidity their fleas. Consistently, grain deposits were the epicentres from which plague was ignited and spread.[33] No historian, however, has shown such a positive correlation between outbreaks of late-medieval plagues and good grain harvests. Indeed, usually, the argument goes the other way: it was overpopulation, poverty, and unhygienic conditions that brought on the Black Death and can explain its super mortalities that far exceeded any of modern plague.[34]

With the Black Death of 1348, the testimony from the chroniclers is mixed. Two chroniclers of northern France, Jean de Venette and Richard the Scot, remarked with astonishment that famine had not sparked the mortality of 1348; indeed, here it was preceded by abundance.[35] But these conditions

---

[29] Simond, 'La propagation de la peste', p. 644; Hankin, 'La propagation de la peste', *AIP*, 12 (1898), p. 709.

[30] Hankin, 'La propagation de la peste', p. 739.

[31] 'Plague in Parel village', *JH*, 7 (1907), p. 853; in addition, later researchers have shown *Yersinia pestis*'s need of sources of iron for growth and replication, giving those with iron-deficient diets a certain immunity to modern plague; see Ell, 'Immunity as a factor', p. 873.

[32] Alok Sheel, 'Bubonic plague in south Bihar: Gaya and Shahabad districts, 1900–1924', *Indian Economic and Social History Review*, 35 (1998), p. 433.

[33] Hirst, *The Conquest of Plague*, p. 281: 'Good rain also means good crops, and a good harvest only too often means more rats and still more fleas'.

[34] See most recently, Adriano Prosperi, *Dalla Peste Nera alla guerra dei trent'anni* (Turin, 2000), p. 43; Cantor, *In the Wake of the Plague*, p. 75; Aberth, *From the Brink of the Apocalypse*, p. 112: 'Undoubtedly medieval hygiene was a major factor in the spread of the disease. One can speculate about how rarely the average person of the Middle Ages took a bath.'

[35] *Chronique latine de Guillaume de Nangis (Continuatio)*, II, p. 213; and *Chronique de Richard Lescot*, p. 82.

72601

cannot be generalised elsewhere. For an anonymous chronicler of Pistoia whose account ends abruptly in 1348, famine and plague accompanied one another in 1347-8.[36] The principal chronicle of Perugia records extreme dearth in 1347, the year before the plague reached Umbria.[37] The punctilious record-keeper Giovanni di Pagnolo Morelli was more precise for Florence, saying that the city was overflowing with people, 'a larger number never before being known', which he estimated at 120,000. Further, throughout that year, 1348, the city suffered from a 'great famine'.[38] And the diarist Marino Sanudo recorded a dearth of grain for Venice brought on by wars in southern Italy that blocked trade and caused grain prices to soar.[39]

According to Biraben, no clear correlation between the outbreak of plague and a preceding period of dearth emerges for the Black Death and its ensuing strikes over the late-medieval and early modern periods.[40] After 1348, however, more often than not, from the Low Countries to Puglia, plague, like many other crowd diseases (but unlike modern plague), followed periods of dearth—in 1366–7, 1373, 1374, 1390, 1400, 1405, 1411, 1418, 1437, 1438 and 1439.[41] Furthermore, Elizabeth Carpentier has argued that the decade preceding the Black Death was generally for Europe a period of hardship, and afterwards, 'plague was the child of famine'. According to Henri Dubois, from 1437 to the end of the century, plague was consistently accompanied by bad harvests.[42] More than one

---

[36] *Annales Pistorienses*, col. 524.
[37] *Cronica della città di Perugia*, p. 143.
[38] Morelli, *Ricordi*, p. 209.
[39] Sanuto, *Vitæ Ducum Venetorum*, col. 614.
[40] Biraben, *Les hommes et la peste*, I, p. 148. For the significance of Biraben's work, see Flynn, 'Plague in Europe and the Mediterranean countries'.
[41] For the plague of 1366–67 in Mainz, see *Chronicon Moguntinum*, pp. 173–4; for the plagues of 1373–75 in the territory of Florence, see Cohn, *Creating the Florentine State: Peasants and Rebellion, 1348–1434* (Cambridge, 1999), pp. 228–9; Stefani, *Cronica fiorentina*, p. 289; and *Cronichette antiche di varj scrittori*, p. 202; for Pistoia, *Specimen Historiæ Sozomeni*, col. 1094; for Piacenza, *Chronicon Placentinum*, col. 520; for Milan, *Annales Mediolanenses*, cols 756–7; for Rome, the Marche, and Tuscany, see *Cronache Malatestiane*, p. 35; for Avignon, *Chronicon Moguntinum*, p. 192. For the 1390 plague in Perugia, Alfonso Corradi, *Annali delle epidemie occorse in Italia dalle prime memorie fino al 1850*, I, (Bologna, 1865), p. 237; for 1400 in Florence, *Cronica volgare di Anonimo Fiorentino*, p. 274; and for Parma, *Storia della città di Parma*, p. 274; for plague in Padua in 1405, Gatari, *Cronaca carrarese*, pp. 559–60; for plague in Siena in 1411, Corradi, *Annali delle epidemie*, V, p. 225; for plague in Paris and Rouen in 1418, *Chroniques de Perceval de Cagny*, p. 113, and *Chronique de Jean le Févre*, I, p. 352; for northern France and the Low Countries and Germany in 1437 and 1438, Jacob Meyer, *Commentarii sive Annales rerum Flandricarum* (Antwerp, 1561), p. 293; *Chroniques de Perceval de Cagny*, p. 252; Gruel, *Chronique d'Arthur de Richemont*, p. 140; *La chronique d'Enguerran de Monstrelet*, V, pp. 319–20; for plague in Erfut in 1439, *Chronicon Elwacense*, p. 45.
[42] Elizabeth Carpentier, 'Famines et épidémies dans l'histoire du XIVe siècle', *Annales: E.S.C.* 17 (1962), pp. 1076 and 1081; and Dubois, 'La dépression: XVIe et XVe siècles', in *Histoire de la population française*, ed. by Jacques Dupâquier (Paris, 1988), I, p. 327. W.P. Blockmans, 'The social and economic effects of plague in the Low Countries 1349–1500', *Revue belge de philologie et d'histoire*, 58 (1980), p. 863, has found the same for the entire fifteenth century.

chronicle pointed to war and its social and economic deprivations to explain why pestilence ignited as with the plague of 1405 in Padua, whose social conditions—war followed by overcrowding, filth, and dearth—the Gatari chroniclers described in brutal detail. These conditions give rise to infectious diseases such as dysentery, cholera, and typhus but not to modern bubonic plague with its dependence on rats, slim temperature ranges of the flea's reproductive cycle, the availability, even abundance, of grain and high humidity. Yet on occasion, chroniclers, such as the Gatari in 1405, reported the signs we generally associate with medieval bubonic plague, the 'nociellete' or little nuts that form on the neck, under the armpits, or in the groin and which killed within two to three days, but they always followed dearth and drought.[43]

* * *

The breakthroughs of the Indian Plague Commissions of the second decade of the twentieth century were not as surprising or exciting as those made in 1906 and 1907. The researchers tried to explain the decline of plague, which began in some places as early as 1910 and for the subcontinent as a whole by 1917. The key now turned from the flea to the rat, which unlike humans can develop immunity.[44] Further, comparative work for other places corroborated most of the Commissioners' earlier findings only with more sophisticated testing and with more emphasis on the variable of humidity and saturation points. The Ninth Plague Report in 1915 extended research to the Presidency of Madras on the east coast of India, where plague had failed to penetrate in epidemic proportions.[45] Here, differences in climate offered no easy explanations; nor, according to the researchers, did the facts of fleas and rats, living conditions, or the habits of the people resolve Madras's absence of plague. By a process of elimination the scientists reasoned 'that the city had escaped because the infection had been unable to reach it, in spite of the fact that considerable traffic exists between Madras and the badly plague-infected town of Bangalore'.[46] Fleas, they speculated, could not endure the passage over the hot and dry lowland plains that separated the plague-infested west from the east coast.[47] For other places such as Lucknow, the fourth largest city in India, other explanations were offered. Although periods of the year were climatically

---

[43] For this citation, see chapter 9. Furthermore, Klein, 'Plague, policy and popular unrest', pp. 735–6, has argued that drought and famine sparked 'plagues' in India before 1896, but from his evidence it is not clear that any of these were modern plague connected with rats.

[44] See for instance A.S. Burgess, 'Virulence, immunity and bacteriological variation in relation to plague', *JH*, 30 (1930): 165–79. On humans' lack of natural immunity, see *Manson's Tropical Diseases*, 19th ed., p. 591.

[45] Captain J.C. Kunhardt and Captain J. Taylor, 'Epidemiological observations in Madras Presidency', *JH: Plague Supplement IV* (1915), pp. 683–751.

[46] Ibid., 683–4.

[47] Ibid., p. 744.

suitable for plague and Lucknow's dilapidated housing and abject poverty
were second to none in India, the Commission pointed to the absence of
large grain depositories to explain the plague's low incidence.[48]

Later, Hirst vigorously contested that it was the hot and dry plains that
blocked the plague's transmission from west to east. In its place he
proposed a single cause: 'Wherever *X. [Xenopsylla] cheopis* prevails in a
suitable climate the rats are liable to acute epizootics and human beings
to epidemic bubonic plague'. Moreover, since *X. cheopis* is the principal
flea of the *Mus* (or *Rattus*) *rattus*, the black rat,[49] and *Ceratophyllus
fasciatus* that of the brown rat, Hirst's thesis may have been the zoological basis for Shrewsbury and others thereafter assuming mistakenly that
only the black rat was responsible for plague.[50] Some (Hirst included)[51]
have fabricated the story of an underground war between *Rattus rattus*
and the brown rat to explain the plague's sudden disappearance from
Europe in the eighteenth century. Supposedly the larger and stronger
brown rat eradicated his black brother, ending conditions favourable to
human plague.[52]

Specialists on rats and their archaeological remains find that that struggle never took place. *Rattus rattus* was always rare in Europe and confined
largely to coastal cities.[53] But the story never needed fabrication in the first
place. The black rat has never been the sole or even the principal carrier of
plague, either amongst rats or in its transmission to humans. The Plague
Commissioners in their meticulous counts of thousands of rats in Bombay
City in the early twentieth century found brown and black rats of equal

---

[48] 'Epidemiological observations in the United Provinces of Agra and Oudh, 1911–1912', *JH:
Plague Supplement* V (1917), p. 817.
[49] Hirst, *The Conquest of the Plague*, pp. 143, 345, and 359.
[50] The researchers of the Indian Plague Commission ('Observations on the bionomics of
fleas', *JH*, 8 (1908), p. 245), utilizing the research of Rothschild and others (Tiraboschi, 'Les
rats', p. 266), concluded that *C. fasciatus* is the common flea found on *Mus decumanus* (the
brown rat) and *X. cheopis* on *Mus rattus* (the black rat) in Western Europe. But in India and
other subtropical places, *X. cheopis* was equally common on the black rat; a variety of fleas
can feed on more than a single species of rats. Further, Chick and Martin ('The fleas common
on rats', p. 128) found in experiments conducted in 1911 that *C. fasciatus* fed on man as readily as on rats, even if experiments from other entomologists found that *X. cheopis* bit humans
more readily than did *C. fasciatus*.
[51] Hirst, *The Conquest of the Plague*, p. 141.
[52] See for instance Le Roy Ladurie, 'A concept', p. 33, and Shrewsbury, *Bubonic Plague in the
British Isles*, p. 9: 'It is indisputable that the field-rat could not have been responsible for the
epidemics ... The distinctions belongs exclusively to *R. rattus*'. The notion still prevails in
general works on the history of disease; most recently, Robert Desowitz (*Tropical Diseases
from 50,000 BC to 2500 AD* (London, 1998), pp. 64–5) mixes up his brown and black rats,
claiming that the brown instead of the black arrived with the crusaders. And with a complete
ignorance of the Indian Plague Commission reports, historians of modern India also assume
that the spread of plague in medieval as well as modern times depends on the black rat; see
Klein, 'Plague, policy and popular unrest', pp. 735–6.
[53] David E. Davis, 'The scarcity of rats and the Black Death: an ecological history', *Journal
of Interdisciplinary History*, XVI (1986): 455–70.

importance in the spread of plague.[54] In other subtropical areas the black rat was less important even though it existed in substantial numbers side by side other rat species. For the 1907 plague in Tunisia and Algeria, the brown rat (*Mus decumanus*) led the count of infected rats collected in the houses of plague victims in the towns and *Mus alexandrinus* in the countryside; *Rattus rattus*, although it coexisted with the other rat populations, was rare in both city and countryside as the bacillus's host.[55] Later, Robert Pollitzer and Karl Meyer concluded that '*R. novegicus* [yet another name for the brown rat] was twice as liable to natural plague infection as R. rattus.'[56]

Further, Hirst's own evidence weakens his thesis. In the Mediterranean ports of Marseilles, Genoa, and Salonika, *X. cheopis* is the predominant flea in the plague months of August and September, but against what Hirst claimed: these cities have not been 'precisely those [within temperate zones] which have been most subject to plague in modern times'.[57] Rather, when plague spread from its subtropical base in China and India in 1899–1900 as many or more plague cases sprung up in Atlantic Opporto, San Francisco, Hamburg, and Glasgow—among the few places in the world where *X. cheopis* does not predominate as the rat flea.

Moreover, modern plague has never prevailed in Mediterranean Europe or for that matter in most places where *X. cheopis* is the principal rat flea. In 1953 Hirst painted a foreboding picture for the future of bubonic plague in Europe and other temperate areas, claiming that with increased contact and commerce with India, *X. cheopis* was a flea on the rise and thus plague would once again threaten Europe.[58] Already by 1911 the plague commission entomologists, Harriette Chick and C.J. Martin, had found *X. cheopis* as the principal rat flea in the temperate zones of Japan, Sydney, and Marseilles at the end of summers.[59] But no such scenario has ensued. In fact, *X. cheopsis* was on the rise in the Indian heartland of plague, Bombay, from 1920 to 1956, at the very moment when plague was on the decline[60]. Other areas of the subtropics such as Shanghai with the right temperatures and supposedly the right flea, *X. cheopis*, have

---

[54] *JH*, 7 (1907): No. 3 Extra 'Plague Number', pp. 703 and 743, based on the plague of 1905; however, afterwards, for plagues from 1907 to 1911, they found that human plague correlated more closely with plague in the brown rat. See John Brownlee, 'Certain Aspects of the Theory of Epidemiology in Special Relation to Plague', *Proceedings of The Royal Society of Medicine*, XI (1918), p. 110.

[55] A. Billet, 'La Peste dans le département de Constantine', p. 667.

[56] Pollitzer and Meyer, 'The ecology of plague,' p. 452. Also, see *Manson's Tropical Diseases*, 19th ed., p. 597. Brownlee, 'Certain aspects', p. 94, calculated that the brown rat 'is at least two and a half times more frequently affected with plague than the black rat'.

[57] Hirst, *Conquest of Plague*, pp. 343–4.

[58] Ibid., p. 302.

[59] Chick and Martin, 'The fleas common on rats', p. 125.

[60] I.J. Catanach, 'The "globalization" of disease? India and the plague', *Journal of World History*, 12 (2001), p. 143.

remained plague free even during the height of the supposed 'third pandemic', from 1900 to 1908, despite regular contact and trade with plague-stricken areas.[61]

Furthermore, Hirst's reliance on Cragg's Indian rat-flea survey overstated its results. As Cragg admitted, it was a 'preliminary' study of 46 stations in India, all from towns and not a one from a village, even though 'plague is much more severe in country villages than in large towns'.[62] It was hardly a systematic survey even of all of India, much less the world as Hirst implies. Nor were plague cases and the per centages of *X. cheopis* as the principal rat flea so highly correlated as Hirst claimed the study proved. Except for the tropical south, this flea was the dominant one at almost every station—in plague-free Madras as well as in the Punjab, where plague cases and mortalities towered over the rest of India and the world. In fact, the foremost flea expert of his day, the Honourable N. C. Rothschild, found that *X. cheopis* is the principal rat-flea in most places around the world, northwest Europe being the exception.[63] While it has had only a slim majority in the plague-ridden Punjab,[64] it constitutes near 100 per cent in the upper Nile,[65] where modern plague has never risen to levels comparable with many areas in India (especially in the Punjab), and 80 to 90 per cent in Brisbane and Sydney,[66] where cases can be counted only in the hundreds.

Neither Hirst nor those who followed, making his conclusions now the only view of plague and fleas in entomology text books, contested, or even cited earlier studies, such as the Shanghai case, that contradicted his generalisations or have entertained alternative hypotheses such as the one proposed by the plague commissioner Norman White in his analysis of India's first 20 years of plague.[67] The line he drew separating plague-India from non-plague India corresponded closely with wheat growing as opposed to rice-growing India. In 1917 when plague-free Vizagapatam on the Madras coast began to import grain because of a sudden problem in the supply of railway rolling stock, plague in epidemic proportions was, for the

---

[61] E.P. Hicks, 'The relation of rat-fleas to plague in Shanghai', *JH*, 26 (1927): 163–9.

[62] W.B. Bannerman, 'The spread of plague in India', *JH* 6 (1906), p. 195. Also, see the later confirmation in the Sixth Plague Report, 'Statistical investigations', pp. 88–91.

[63] Rothschild, 'Note on the species of fleas found upon rats, *Mus rattus* and *Mus decumanus*, in different parts of the world', *JH*, 6 (1906), p. 485.

[64] Major F.W. Cragg, 'The geographical distribution of the Indian rat-fleas as a factor in the epidemiology of plague: preliminary observations', *Indian Journal of Medical Research*, 9 (1921), p. 379, Table I.

[65] A. Bacot, George Petrie and Captain Ronald E. Todd, 'The fleas found on rats and other rodents, living in association with man, and trapped in the towns, villages and Nile boats of upper Egypt', *JH*, 14 (1914), p. 502.

[66] Rothschild, 'Note on the species of fleas', p. 485.

[67] See for instance Karl Jordan, 'Suctoria,' in *Insects of Medical Importance*, ed. by John Smart, K. Jordan and R.J. Whittick, 3rd ed. (London, 1956), pp. 211–46, and G.B. White, 'Fleas', in *Manson's Tropical Diseases*, 19th ed., pp. 1482–6.

first time, imported as well.[68] There is no evidence that the rat-flea population suddenly changed.

*   *   *

In the 1920s and 1930s plague research, still principally published by the *Journal of Hygiene*, extended its reach beyond India to Java,[69] parts of Africa[70] and China,[71] but concentrated less on the macroscopic and more on problems that might be solved in the laboratory, such as producing a plague serum.[72] After 1937 articles on plague in the *Journal of Hygiene* disappear; the recrudescence of plague in India in the 1940s failed to rekindle interest in this journal or from other international commissions. The next significant site of human plague research was Vietnam in the 1960s, where the number of known cases reached 4503 in 1965.[73] While the study of plague was now more sophisticated in some respects, in terms of macroscopic analysis—the relation of plague to climate, topography, class, and social customs—it was much more limited than the Indian Plague Commission Reports had been two generations earlier.

The American researchers had learnt little from earlier studies in India; few, if any, turned to the pages of the *Journal of Hygiene* and its lengthy plague supplements. An essay by five researchers in 1967 concludes without references to the Indian past and makes 'discoveries' which would have been obvious to any plague researcher in India even as early as 1900; such as that 'the transportation of grain appears to have played a major role in the spread of plague to the cities'.[74] Further, the American researchers cautioned: 'Any program of rodent eradication, whether initiated as a plague control or as a crop saving measure, must take into account the presence of large numbers of potentially infected fleas which could trigger an even greater plague epidemic among the human population'.[75] The Indian Plague commissioners had already crossed that bridge several times, finding

---

[68] White, 'Twenty years of plague', p. 212.

[69] See for instance L. Otten, 'The problem of the seasonal prevalence of plague', *JH*, 32, 3 (1932): 396–405.

[70] J. Isgaer Roberts, 'The relation of the cotton crop to plague'; idem, 'Plague conditions in an urban area of Kenya', *JH*, 36 (1936): 467–84; idem, 'Plague conditions in a rural area of Kenya', ibid.: 485–503; idem, 'The carriage of plague', ibid.: 504–6; G.H.C. Hopkins, 'Cotton and plague in Uganda', *JH*, 38 (1938): 233–47.

[71] Hicks, 'The relation of rat-fleas to plague in Shanghai'.

[72] See for instance the many articles by S. Rowland on plague vaccination and the relation between pseudo-tuberculosis and plague.

[73] J.D. Marshall, Jr, R.J. Joy. N.V. Ai, D.V. Quy, J.L. Stockard, and F.L. Gibson, 'Plague in Vietnam, 1965–1966', *American Journal of Epidemiology*, 86,(1967): 603–16; and Thomas Butler, 'A clinical study of bubonic plague: observation of the 1970 Vietnam epidemic with emphasis on coagulation studies, skin histology and electrocardiograms,' *American Journal of Medicine* 53 (1972): 268–76.

[74] Marshall *et al.*, 'Plague in Vietnam', p. 615.

[75] Ibid., p. 616.

across a diverse range of ecologies that fleas separated from their rat hosts did not pose a threat and that rat control in critical places such as in and around grain depositories was the very first measure that sanitary commissions must enact.

While new articles celebrate Yersin's heroism and discovery of the plague bacillus almost yearly, historians have nearly forgotten the British achievement in India, where the mechanisms of plague and the conditions of its rise and decline were discovered over the next two to three decades. When the British experience in India is recalled at all, it is cast negatively. The picture is one of colonial hubris, riots against isolation of plague victims, resistance against neighbourhood disinfection, rejection of vaccination,[76] and 'the unavoidable clash of two different, often antagonistic value-systems, the one Indian, the other European'.[77]

David Arnold has commented that 'bubonic plague provoked an unparalleled crisis in the history of state medicine in India'.[78] Yet the evidence for this negative judgment comes exclusively from the first four years of the plague, before its sharp rise in mortalities and before the Indian Plague Commission allied with the Lister Institute and the Advisory Committee for the Investigation of Plague in India had begun its work.[79] The riots in Calcutta, the Rand murder, and those of Grant Road, Bombay, Cawnpore, Karnataka, and Mysore all preceded 1901.[80] By 1898, the Indian Medical Service came to an about-face and began hiring traditional Indian doctors (hakims and vaids) to supervise public and private hospitals and camps.[81] To collect its massive evidence from villages and towns across most of northern and central India, the commissioners relied on native Indians. The picture given by the British plague commissioners is one of respect for the native populations and cooperation in turn. Far from the hubris of modern medicine, they trusted their Indian assistants' trained eyes over the microscope and marvelled at village traditions in avoiding plague by systematic

---

[76] Arnold, *Science, Technology and Medicine in Colonial India*, The New Cambridge History of India, III, 5 (Cambridge, 2000), p. 74. For a detailed account of these riots and the circulation of rumours of vicious treatment by British doctors, see Arnold, *Colonizing the Body*, pp. 214–26 and 230–1.

[77] Chandavarkar, 'Plague panic', p. 207.

[78] Arnold, *Colonizing the Body*, p. 202.

[79] As early as 1897, Brigadier-General W.F. Gatacre, *Report on the Bubonic Plague in Bombay*, commented: 'from this date the plague operations worked smoothly and well. In fact, instead of the people obstructing me, they gave me every assistance' (p. 194). On the politics of the formation of the Advisory Committee, see Catanach, 'Plague and the tensions of empire'.

[80] On these riots, see Catanach, 'Plague and the tensions of empire', p. 157; Klein, 'Plague, policy and popular unrest', pp. 739–52; B. Leela, 'Plague in Karnataka: 1896–1900', *Indica*, 35 (1998): 133–46; and idem, 'Plague in Karnataka. Part 2: Mysore (1896–1900)', *Indica*, 36 (1999): 39–49.

[81] Catanach, 'Plague and the tensions of empire', p. 157. Also, see Arnold, *Colonizing the Body*, pp. 227–39.

migration to nearby woods once the first rats began to die. Often articles in the *Journal of Hygiene* would break from their academic reportage of data to recognise the cooperation received from individual villagers and urban populations.

In part, this negative picture of the British accomplishment in India derives from the racism of plague researchers outside of India, such as J. Ashburton Thompson, who directed plague research in Sydney at the turn of the century. In 1901 and again in 1906 he claimed that all previous epidemiological investigation into plague had been limited, especially in India, because:

> Plague has almost always appeared in countries inhabited by races foreign to the observer in their language and modes of thought, who were of little instruction, of an education limited to ancient and immutable conventions, and who lived for the most part under conditions which unavoidably obscured the phenomena.[82]

By contrast, when plague invaded Sydney, Thompson welcomed the new opportunity: 'The invaded population was not merely wholly white, of English extraction and speech, and fully civilised, but intelligent, instructed, and orderly, accustomed to direction and amenable to it'.[83]

In retrospect, the chronology and geography of Thompson's interpretation of the plague's conquest must be seen as incorrect: India, not Australia was the principal focus of research, where the plague's unusual transmission and the means for combating it were discovered. Thompson's own hypotheses on the mechanisms of plague transmission, published in 1901 and 1906, followed exactly the lines first published by Simond and Hankin and added little if anything to what they had discovered in India before the plague had even arrived in Australia. Moreover, the British plague researchers demonstrated that these hypotheses were correct and elaborated further on them, again, almost exclusively from field research in India. Nonetheless, 50 years later, a researcher in the last stages of the Indian Plague Commission, L.F. Hirst, lost sight of this early twentieth-century history. Instead, he followed Thompson's racist version of events, concluding that the Australians 'enjoyed a considerable advantage over workers in Bombay' because 'investigation in Sydney had been conducted in the midst of a civilised and homogenous community speaking the language of the investigator.'[84] Even today, historians clearly of an anti-colonialist bent use different words to say much the same, claiming that 'the conflict of cultures' or the 'lack of education of the indigenous peoples' and 'fatalistic Muslims' hampered investigation into plague in India and implementation of sanitary policies:

---

[82] Thompson, 'On the epidemiology of plague', p. 537. Also, see 'A contribution to the aetiology of plague', p. 162.
[83] Ibid., p. 538.
[84] *The Conquest of Plague*, p. 145.

'Villagers generally trusted the charms and incantations of their spiritual advisers in preference to the councils of government.'[85] Certainly, the early articles on plague research in India published in the *Journal of Hygiene* give another version of these events.

Further, recent historians such as Klein have judged the British efforts to contain the plague to have been 'almost a complete failure'.[86] I.J. Catanach has gone further, asserting that it was not until the use of DDT and strep-tomycin in the 1940s and 1950s that scientific and medical intervention made any difference in the struggle against plague in India, and by that time the plague had already gone into steep decline.[87] Indeed, plague cases and mortality climbed sharply in India as a whole for the first 12 years since its appearance in 1896. What this curve of cases and mortality had to do with human intervention, either because of new scientific understanding of the plague's transmission or with plague controls such as rat-proofing grain deposits and ports, is difficult to know. Certainly, the Plague Commissioners were modest about their accomplishments. Although they discovered and initiated policies of rat control and advised villagers and townspeople to change their habits of allowing, even harbouring, rats in their living areas, they saw rising levels of rat immunity as the key to the plague's decline.

On the other hand, should the Indian Plague Commission be blamed for the rising curve of cases and deaths during the first decade or so after plague had first appeared in a locality? The subsequent histories of plague in India in the 1940s, in Thailand in the 1940s and 1950s, in Brazil and Vietnam in the 1960s and 1970s, and in almost every other place in the subtropical world show similar curves of rising cases through the first five to ten years after the plague had infected human populations, even after the implemen-tation of DDT, medical advances, and the widespread availability of inex-pensive antibiotics, principally tetracycline.[88]

Regardless of how we judge the Plague Commission's impact on the plague in India, the several thousand pages of reports, maps, and scientific analysis is without doubt the most important scholarly repository for anyone studying the history of plague. Many of its findings confirmed by meticulous research, engaging teams of doctors, entomologists, epidemiol-ogists, and zoologists have now been forgotten, not only by historians but also by the scientific community. One objective of this book is to convince scholars that these pages are worth revisiting.

---

[85] Klein, 'Plague, policy and popular unrest', p. 750.
[86] Ibid., p. 753.
[87] Catanach, 'Plague and the tensions of empire', p. 166. Following Catanach, Arnold, *Colonizing the Body*, pp. 236 and 318, came to the same conclusion.
[88] See Pollitzer, *Plague*, pp. 16–27.

|3|

Historians square the circle

Fear of a return to Black Death mortalities led early plague researchers at the end of the nineteenth century to study their plague with more resources than for any other disease until at least the Second World War. At the same time, their idée fixe that the late-medieval and modern plagues were the same hampered understanding of their own plague, delaying acceptance of key phenomena such as modern plague's inability to spread rapidly or effectively person to person even in its pneumonic form. The traffic in ideas along this historical street passed in both directions, causing plague researchers to draw 'facts' from the past and pin them as aspects of modern plague. Thus in the latest editions of medical texts pustules are said occasionally to spread over plague victims' bodies, though no case is cited later than the London plague of 1665.[1] To their credit, by 1906 the researchers of the Indian Plague Commission were willing to put aside the past and state their findings no matter how opposed to common knowledge of the late-medieval plague. By the 1920s the historical introductions to plague found less space in *Manson's Tropical Diseases* and by its nineteenth edition comprised a single sentence. Nonetheless its editors had no doubts that the modern plague was the 'Third Pandemic' of the same disease.[2]

Following in the footsteps of these medical, zoological, bacterial authorities, historians have also been chary to question the Black Death as anything other than that bubonic plague first cultured in Hong Kong in June 1894, even if historians, such as David Herlihy and Christopher Morris have pointed to the extraordinary character of the Black Death and the ways it has failed to mesh so well with epidemiological facts of the present *Yersinia pestis*. They have described the Black Death's swift

---

[1] See chapter 4.
[2] 'Plague and Melioidosis' in *Manson's Tropical Diseases*, 19th ed.

dissemination through Europe, its contagion and high mortalities, but have sought more to mend the paradigm rather than question the disease. The escape valve usually is the claim that the Black Death and its subsequent strikes were predominantly pneumonic plague.

Reliance on the pneumonic as the Black Death's principal form has raised other problems. In this form plague has reached epidemic proportions in modern times only in cold winters with populations closely huddled together as were the tarabagan trappers of Northern Manchuria in 1911 and 1922. By contrast, the Black Death raged in Barcelona, Florence, and other Mediterranean centres, scoring its record mortalities during the hottest summer months. As Herlihy recognised: 'That a pulmonary infection should have spread "like fire" in summer and disappeared in winter is difficult to explain.'[3] To square this circle, he turned to the dates of grape harvests at Pistoia set by the government from 1330 to 1355—although no date was given for 1348—and argued that with half the dates in October the summers must have been unusually cool, cloudy, and humid.[4] Yet, as Herlihy would later show in criticizing Le Roy Ladurie's use of similar data for judgments about climatic change, taste may have been more critical than weather in governing grape harvests.

Furthermore, the chronicles are filled with comments about unusually hot summers particularly in the second half of the fourteenth and early fifteenth centuries, so much so that peasants died in the fields from the Mediterranean sun[5] and suffered even in places north of the Alps.[6] In addition, H.H. Lamb has argued that in southern Europe 'no extraordinary predominance of blocking anticyclones' produced the weather extremes with colder winters as in the north. In the Mediterranean, summers may have continued to be as much as +1°C warmer than they are today (that is, circa 1970), despite global warming since the Industrial Revolution.[7] Moreover, as we will see, 1348 was not an exceptional year as far as the seasonality of plague goes. Throughout the Mediterranean basin and particularly in Italy the late-medieval plagues recurred with remarkable consistency during the hottest and driest months of the Mediterranean calendar, June and July.

Other historians, more confident than Herlihy about the identity of the late fourteenth-century disease, have dealt differently with the conflicting evidence between the medieval past and a 'theory' of modern bubonic

---

[3] D. Herlihy, *Medieval and Renaissance Pistoia: The Social History of an Italian Town, 1200–1430* (New Haven, 1967), p. 108.
[4] Ibid., p. 109. Without any evidence, others such as Shrewsbury, *Bubonic Plague in the British Isles*, pp. 38–9 and 104, had earlier claimed the same.
[5] *Practica Antonii Guainerii papiensis doctoris clarissimi et omnia opera* (Florence, 1517), p. 140v. For more on climate and plague in the fourteenth and fifteenth centuries, see ch. 7.
[6] *Chronique et annales de Gilles le Muisit*, p. 269; *Journal d'un bourgeois de Paris*, p. 111.
[7] H.H. Lamb, *Climate, History and the Modern World*, 2nd ed. (London, 1995), p. 207.

plague. Thus Robert Gottfried rightly questioned Gabrielle de' Mussis's account of the plague's origins and transmission to the West as an accurate description of the behaviour of modern plague—the Knights of the Golden Hoard's early use of biological warfare by catapulting plague corpses into Genoa's compound at Caffa on the Black Sea.[8] As Gottried remarked, plague corpses do not usually spread modern plague; rather it depends on a much slower, complex, and less efficient means of transmission: first, rats need to become infected, then have time to give rise to a rat epizootic, and only some time later might the rat disease pass via blocked fleas to humans, assuming the proper climatic conditions, adequate densities of rats, the right fleas, and more. But instead of questioning the disease, Gottfried dismissed the source.[9] Further, he found it 'surprising that virtually all of the medical observers failed to make the connection between plague and the plethora of dead rodents that preceded an epidemic'.[10] Why insert 'virtually'? Neither he nor anyone else has cited a plague tract, chronicler, or any other scrap of evidence that points to a epizootic of rodents preceding plague in the late-medieval West.[11]

*   *   *

With the bacteriologist and historian of plagues in Britain, J.F.D. Shrewsbury, the choice of epidemiological theory over the historical record was more extreme. First, he expressed a confidence in matters for which no sources exist. As for the 'responsibility' of the Black Death 'it is indisputable . . . The distinction belongs exclusively to *R. rattus*'.[12] He was not bothered that, unlike the Chinese, African, and Indian observers before the bacillus's discovery,[13] not a single medieval source from Britain or elsewhere in Western Europe mentioned a prior epizootic of any rodents—much less *Rattus rattus*—the distinctive drunken prance of the plague-infected rat, their unusual appearance in daytime, or their fall from rafters as the sign

---

[8] See Vincent Derbes, 'De Mussis and the great plague of 1348: A forgotten episode of bacteriological warfare,' *Journal of the American Medical Association*, 196 (1966): 59–62.

[9] Robert S. Gottfried, *The Black Death: Natural and Human Disaster in Medieval Europe* (London, 1983), pp. 36–7.

[10] Ibid., p. 110.

[11] The most oft-cited source for arguing that the Black Death was rat-based comes from Nicephorus Gregoras's mention of rats when plague invaded the Aegean Islands in 1348. Those, however, such as Le Roy Ladurie, who cite it fail to mention, that the rats in Gregoras's version of events are listed after people, dogs, horses, and various kinds of birds. These other animals possess a high natural immunity to *Yersinia pestis*, and more to the point it does not testify to a prior epizootic of the rats (for Nicephorus's text, see the German translation in Haeser, pp. 167–8).

[12] Shrewsbury, *Bubonic Plague in the British Isles*, p. 9.

[13] See Otto Neustatter, 'Mice in plague pictures', *Journal of the Walters Art Gallery*, IV (1941), p. 112 on prior rat epizootics in African folklore: '"If you see mice behaving like this", they say in Africa, "be on your guard, plague is near!"' On China, see Creighton, *History of Epidemics in Britain*, I, pp. 167–70. On India, see Hankins, 'La propagation de la peste', pp. 706–12, and *Manson's Tropical Diseases*, 19th ed., p. 598.

that human disease was on its way. Others, such as Philip Ziegler following Shrewsbury's example, have explained away the absence of dead rats preceding the Black Death by claiming that such ubiquity was hardly worthy of attention.[14] Why then did Indian villagers before Yersin's discovery notice them, comment on their sudden strange appearance, and understand them as the alarm bells to abandon their huts for a two-month vacation in neighbouring woods?

Despite Shrewsbury's training as a bacteriologist, he made pronouncements on the character of modern bubonic plague that fail to accord with what the researchers of the Indian Plague Commission discovered or has been sanctioned since by plague research. One was that 'the human disease must have been proportionate in its extent to the density of the human population' as with other crowd diseases.[15] The plague researchers found nearly the opposite; plague cases varied inversely with the population of a city or village.[16] Another was that 'Bubonic plague was essentially an urban disease'.[17] The most cursory glance at the late nineteenth- and twentieth-century evidence for China, India, Vietnam, and elsewhere disproves this assertion. A third was that 'the pain of the erupting bubo is often so agonizing that many patients . . . attack their attendants . . . jump out of windows . . . No other bacterial disease of man shows with such constancy an equivalent degree of frenzy'.[18] Shrewsbury fails to cite his source; rather, Indian plague doctors found that often no pain precedes or accompanies the formation of the bubo and instead of wild delirium, 'depression and stupor' were the more likely physiognomy. As Gatacre reported from his clinical survey in 1897: 'The patient has a furtive look . . . gazes about him vacantly and does not seem to care to talk or to notice persons or things about him.'[19] Fourth, Shrewsbury asserted that 'Modern studies of bubonic plague show that woollen and cotton material, grain, fodder, forage, hides, and furs are the most favourable goods for flea-dissemination',[20] and

---

[14] Philip Ziegler, *The Black Death* (Harmondsworth, 1970), p. 27. Shrewsbury, *Bubonic Plague in the British Isles*, p. 14: 'This is hardly telling evidence either way, since silence may reflect lack of interest as well as of occurrence'. For a similar view, see Cantor, *In the Wake of the Plague*, p. 172. Dols, *The Black Death in the Middle East*, p. 158, points to the 'curious failure in the Middle Eastern sources, as there is in the European accounts, to mention the extermination of plague-carrying rodents'.

[15] *Bubonic Plague in the British Isles*, p. 21.

[16] Early on, Hankin, 'La propagation de la peste', p. 734, noted that high density of population had no effect on the number of plague cases. Major Greenwood, statistician to the Lister Institute,'Statistical investigation of Plague in Punjab. Third report', *JH: Plague Supplement I* (1912), from an analysis of the mortalities recorded in Punjab villages went further: 'the rate of plague mortality tends to increase as the absolute population of the infected community diminishes' (p. 98). He also thought the same applied to the plague experience in late medieval and early modern Europe.

[17] Shrewsbury, *Bubonic Plague in the British Isles*, p. 141; also, pp. 98 and 109.

[18] Ibid., p. 5.

[19] Gatacre, *Report on the Bubonic Plague in Bombay*, pp. 55–6.

[20] See previous chapter.

'blocked fleas could be spread by clothing'.[21] Again, he cites no sources; again, except for grain, the plague reports found through numerous observations and experimentation that human plague was not transmitted through fleas travelling in furs, woollens, cotton, or clothing. Fifth, Shrewsbury held that 'there is nothing surprising about the almost complete exemption of the English nobility and landed class from 'The Great Pestilence'; it just happened that the house-rat could not make itself at home in their castles'. Again, the plague researchers showed the opposite: building materials had no effect whatsoever on the penetration of either rats or plague in India. Sixth, Shrewsbury asserted that according to 'modern observations, in ill-developed countries urban communities commonly lose about one-third of their members from a severe epidemic of bubonic plague'.[22] Again, Shrewsbury's 'modern observers' are not cited, and, to the contrary, no bubonic or pneumonic plague since the discovery of the bacillus has registered a population loss anywhere near this level. For a large urban centre, Bombay City's plague in 1903 was the highest with less than 3 per cent dying.[23]

More problematic, Shrewsbury sought to rewrite British demographic history with a disregard for the contemporary sources:

> It is absolutely certain therefore that the great national outburst of bubonic plague in 1348–50 afflicted only a part, and in all probability much the smaller part of the population of England . . . in the rest of England and Wales it is extremely doubtful if as much as one-twentieth of the population was destroyed by it. These are not random assertions; they are inherent in the aetiology of bubonic plague.[24]

He rejected out of hand narrative sources such as the chronicle of Geoffrey le Baker, calling it 'total nonsense', because the chronicler said 'many country villages were totally destitute of human beings'. Such a claim did not abide with Shrewsbury's notions of rat density in rural Britain at the time of the Black Death.[25] To shore up the necessities demanded by modern bubonic plague, he rejected mortality rates of the plague based on vacant benefices of clergymen caused by death and the deaths of tenants appearing in manorial rolls: the levels of mortality were simply far too high for modern bubonic plague (even by his inflated estimates), especially for sparsely populated rural areas. They defied 'the laws governing the genesis, spread, and epidemicity of bubonic plague'.[26] Further, he labelled as 'extremely improbable' Rees's discovery

---

[21] Ibid., p. 156.
[22] Ibid., p. 40.
[23] See previous chapter.
[24] Shrewsbury, *Bubonic Plague in the British Isles*, p. 36.
[25] Ibid., p. 40.
[26] Ibid., pp. 55, 77 and 104.

in Wales that the mountainous regions suffered more than the plains and that the Great Pestilence overran Snowdonia. For Shrewsbury such a conclusion was inconceivable because such a sparsely populated region with such inclement weather 'could not have been colonised by the house rat [*Rattus rattus*]'.[27]

He rejected the comments of chroniclers who said that the plague was spread between England and Scotland by invading armies, because armies do not transmit bubonic plague.[28] He rejected a chronicler of Scotland's observations that the plague spared no age or sex, because 'the assertion . . . is at variance with modern knowledge of the epidemic'.[29] He castigated a historian of Nottinghamshire who documented that 'superiors with their more commodious rooms and better food . . . suffered as heavily as any class', saying it 'reveals regrettable ignorance of the nature of bubonic plague'.[30] In other places, Shrewsbury was more circumspect. To explain Lunn's finding that the Forest of Dean was devastated by the Black Death, Shrewsbury imagined a more complex and indirect scenario: 'In all probability what actually happened in the Forest of Dean was that *P. pestis* sneaked into one or two of the hamlets on the fringe . . . fugitives and rumour then depopulated the De Briane estate'.[31]

Shrewsbury's book received immediate acclaim[32] as well as sharp criticism. But his critics did not fault him for his cavalier dismissal of the historical sources; instead his supposed fault was turning 'a blind eye to pneumonic plague'.[33] His principal critic, Christopher Morris, also made up theory as he went along in order to retain modern plague as the Black Death's disease, asserting without any medical reference that 'when plague is invading virgin territory, it is particularly likely to assume pneumonic form'.[34] Further, to justify the plague's large-scale mortalities in the British Isles and the swiftness of its contagion, he turned to the Manchurian plagues of 1911 and 1922 to argue his case, citing Wu Lien-Teh but without reading (or at least) heeding Wu's conclusions: like its bubonic form, pneumonic plague was not spread person-to-person very effectively and because of the lightning lethality of the latter was even less a killer of populations. To date, the most serious pneumonic plague—that of 1911—killed less than 0.4 per cent of the population it invaded. Moreover, against what Morris assumed, pneumonic plague also must stem from a prior epizootic

---

27 Ibid., p. 119.
28 Ibid., p. 142.
29 Ibid., p. 43.
30 Ibid., p. 107.
31 Ibid., p. 69.
32 See Le Roy Ladurie, 'A concept', p. 33ff.
33 Christopher Morris, 'The plague in Britain,' *Historical Journal*, 14 (1971): 205–15, p. 207.
34 See Twigg's criticisms of Morris, in *The Black Death*, p. 163, and those of Lawrence R. Poos, 'Population and resources in two fourteenth-century Essex communities: Great Waltham and High Easter, 1327–1389' Ph.D Fitzwilliam College, 1983, p. 327.

of rodents; it too is essentially a rat or rodent disease in which humans sometimes participate.

*   *   *

To square the circle, Ann Carmichael, who combines an expertise in medicine and medieval history, was subtler than Shrewsbury and understood better the characteristics of modern plague. But, despite discordances between modern bubonic plague and descriptions and epidemiological patterns of the late-medieval plagues, which she aptly reveals, she claimed confidently: 'Boccaccio leaves no doubt that bubonic *Y. pestis* ravaged Florence in 1348', and generalised further: 'If the bubo predominated as a sign, we could still be reasonably comfortable after five centuries that there was not much error in the ascription of a death to plague.'[35] She knew, for instance, that unlike most other contagious diseases, modern plague shows no predilection for children with successive strikes of the disease. Yet, from data taken from Herlihy and Klapisch-Zuber that showed as much as 70 per cent of the mortalities in the plague year 1400 had been children,[36] she did not question *Yersinia pestis* as the disease and insisted that the children must have died of other causes: 'it was a fact readily explained by assuming that the delivery of food and normal sanitary care was [sic] disrupted [by the plague] and that the individuals needing these services most (children) succumbed to secondary infections'.[37] First, as she admits, this is an assumption unsupported by any sources. No evidence points to any breakdown in basic services in Florence in 1400 or for lesser plagues, which before and after 1400 took strikingly disproportionate numbers of children.[38] Moreover, as Biraben has shown, the late-medieval plagues did not always trigger bad harvests and periods of dearth. Further, even the worst period of medieval famine, 1315–22, did not produce levels of mortality on a scale with the Black Death or other major plagues through the fourteenth century.[39] Finally, for the most disruptive plague of them all, that of 1348, when social services such as burials, church services, and even the basic fabric of family life collapsed according to the chroniclers, children

---

[35] A. Carmichael, *Plague and the Poor in Renaissance Florence* (Cambridge, 1986). Nor had Carmichael's confidence slackened a decade later: 'Because of these sudden and abnormal swellings on different places of victim's bodies, we can now confidently identify the epidemic's cause as *Yersinia pestis*' (p. 60); 'Bubonic plague: The Black Death', in *Plague, Pox and Pestilence*, ed. by Kenneth F. Kiple (London, 1997).

[36] D. Herlihy and Christiane Klapisch-Zuber, *Les Toscans et leurs familles: Une étude du Catasto de 1427* (Paris, 1978), p. 463.

[37] Carmichael, *Plague and the Poor*, pp. 93–4.

[38] See chapter 8.

[39] Carpentier, 'Famines et épidémies', pp. 1076–7; William C. Jordan, *The Great Famine: Northern Europe in the Early Fourteenth Century* (Princeton, 1996), pp. 184–6; Bruce Campbell, 'Population-pressure, inheritance and the land market in a fourteenth-century peasant community', in *Land, Kinship and Life-Cycle*, ed. by Richard M. Smith (Cambridge, 1984), p. 120, goes further: the crisis 1314–17 (at least in Norfolk) passed 'without any departure from the demographic status quo'.

did not then die in disproportionate numbers. Unlike subsequent strikes, that one, according to the chroniclers (and, as we shall see, quantitative evidence) showed no age discrimination.

Subtler still (and more perplexing) is her argument about contagion. She contends that promulgation of plague legislation in most places had to wait until the mid-fifteenth century, when 'because of mixture of diseases by mid century legislators could be convinced that the feared plague was contagious'.[40] Before mid century she asserts doctors refused to believe that the plague was contagious, and (except for 1348) they were able to persuade republics and princes alike not to pass laws to control the spread of disease. Yet she cites no evidence whatsoever for either proposition. Any glance at the chroniclers or the doctors, who in increasing numbers wrote plague tracts from 1348 onwards, shows that none doubted the plague's contagion. Rather, they claimed that it blazed when crowds formed, spreading person-to-person by smell, breathe, touch, and sweat, and with such rapidity that some saw it as contracted also by sight. By the fifteenth century chroniclers and doctors even distinguished 'true' plague from other epidemic diseases not by the plague boil but by its rapid infectivity.[41]

Nor, is it evident from her own survey of plague legislation in Milan, Mantua, and Venice that plague controls had to await the mid-fifteenth century before becoming serious. As she shows, the Milanese Visconti introduced draconian measures in 1348 and 1374 to guard against the plague's contagion, as did rulers in Mantua in 1374.[42] The imposition of the first quarantine, though only a trentine, was in Ragusa as early as 1377, and Marseilles extended it to forty days in 1383. In 1385, Venice had already created a competent administration, the Magistro della Sanità, to enforce plague legislation and invented the first lazzaretto in 1423,[43] though already anticipated by Giangaleazzo Visconti's 'mansiones' conceived in the plague of 1399.[44] Plague legislation that restricted both travel and trade can

---

[40] Carmichael, *Plague and the Poor*, p. 123. Also, see 'Contagion theory and contagion practice in fifteenth-century Milan', *Renaissance Quarterly*, XLIV (1991): 213–56.

[41] For this evidence, see chapter 6. Also see the criticisms by Henderson, 'The Black Death in Florence: medical and communal responses', *Death in Towns: Urban Response to the Dying and the Dead, 100–1600*, ed. by Steven Basset (Leicester, 1992), pp. 136 and 145; idem, 'Epidemics in Renaissance Florence: medical theory and government response', in *Maladies et Société (XIIe XVIIIe siècles) Actes du colloque de Bielefeld*, ed. by Neithard Bulst and Robert Delort (Paris, 1989), pp. 136 and 145, and Jon Arrizabalaga, 'Facing the Black Death: perceptions and reactions of university medical practitioners,' *Practical Medicine from Salerno to the Black Death*, ed. by Luis García-Ballester, Roger French, Jon Arrizabalaga and Andrew Cunningham (Cambridge, 1994), pp. 259 and 287.

[42] Carmichael, *Plague and the Poor*, pp. 110–16.

[43] George Sarton, *Introduction to the History of Science* (Baltimore, 1948), III, p. 1659.

[44] Aldo Bottero, 'La Peste in Milano nel 1399–1400 e l'opera di Gian Galeazzo Visconti', *Atti e Memorie dell'Accademia di Storia dell'Arte Sanitaria. La Rassegna di Clinica, Terapia e Scienze Affini*, XLI, fasc. VI (1942), p. 18; and Antonia Pasi Testa, 'Alle origini dell'Ufficio di Sanità nel Ducato di Milano e Principato di Pavia', *Archivio Storico Lombardo*, CII (1977): 376–86.

be easily spotted in a number of northern Italian towns by the 1420s—
Perugia, Forlì, Udine, Venice, Mantua.[45] In 1395 Valencia passed new laws
regulating public hygiene to curtail the plague's spread.[46]

In a thoroughgoing examination of plague legislation in Milan and
Pavia, Antonia Pasi Testa has shown that the 'notable step forward' in
plague legislation came not with the mid-fifteenth century (as Carmichael
asserts) but with the plague of 1399–1400. In addition to developing earlier
controls on the movement of peoples from plague-infected areas,
Giangaleazzo Visconti created new specialised plague hospitals with
remarkably humane care for the infirm. Further, by the plague of 1424 his
son Filippo Maria had established a permanent health board in Milan to
consider policy in plague time. Thirty years later, the reforms of the Sforza
in the duchy showed no further innovations.[47] The reasons merchant
republics such as Florence lagged behind principalities had nothing to do
with ideas of contagion or doctors' supposed power to block communal
legislation;[48] instead, it rested on merchants' will and ability to block legislation that would seriously hamper trade. Such tension between disease
control and mercantile profits would continue well into the nineteenth
century, if not later.[49]

To her credit and unlike Shrewsbury, Gottfried, and others, Carmichael
did not so readily reject the sources when they refused to cooperate with
notions of the twentieth-century bubonic plague. Instead, she strove to have
it both ways, accepting the sources while affirming that the plague of 1348
and many (most?) thereafter were the same disease as discovered in Hong
Kong in 1894.[50] She accomplished this by a retrospective diagnosis, separating those medieval descriptions that matched modern bubonic plague
from those that did not, maintaining that the fourteenth-century plague was
one of several diseases that interacted with one another.[51] By this means,
she explains the striking mortalities, perplexing contagion, speed of transmission, and signs such as pustules and freckles, which resemble smallpox

---

[45] Ibid., pp. 116–17.

[46] Agustin Rubio, *Peste Negra: Crisis y comportaminetos sociales en la España del siglo XIV:
La cuidad de Valencia (1348–1401)* (Granada, 1979), p. 76.

[47] 'Alle origini dell'Ufficio di Sanità nel Ducato di Milano'.

[48] Nonetheless, the views on plague and contagion show no conflict between merchant
communes and doctors. Often, Italian communes such as Perugia, Genoa, and Udine commissioned tracts from prominent university physicians such as Gentile da Foligno and Giovanni
da Santa Sophia. Further, many others dedicated their tracts to their fellow citizens.

[49] For governments' reluctance to admit the presence of plague out of fear of injuring trade
in the seventeenth century, see Cipolla, *Faith, Reason and the Plague*. For yellow fever and the
threat to commerce in New Orleans in the mid-nineteenth century, see Desowitz, *Tropical
Diseases*, pp. 105–8. For Florence's reluctance to pass laws to assist plague-stricken communities in its hinterland, see Cohn, *Creating the Florentine State*, pp. 225–8.

[50] This idea was first floated by Shrewsbury, *Bubonic Plague in the British Isles*, pp. 60, 107,
119, and 125.

[51] Carmichael, *Plague and the Poor*, p. 26.

or typhus more than modern bubonic plague. But it is not clear from her analysis whether the plague somehow raised the 'penumbra' of these existing diseases to new heights of infectivity and levels of mortality or whether for some unexplained reason they just happened to appear in Europe for the first time just as the plague crossed from the Black Sea to Sicily.

Both conjectures are improbable. First, unlike the New World in the period of Columbus or the antipodes in the eighteenth century, mid-four-teenth-century Europe was not suddenly exposed to new peoples, animals, and parasites by the opening of new trade routes.[52] In fact, just the opposite was happening: trade with the Orient was in decline and contact with the East much less frequent than it had been a century earlier. If Europe had been on the downward slope of a disease gradient extending from East to West, the demographic catastrophe should have struck it a century earlier, if not before, but no such sanitary crisis accompanied the crusades or merchant explorations to Mongolia and China.

Second, modern plague does not show significant synergy with other diseases, as happens when malnutrition weakens resistance to infection with many other crowd diseases. Influenza accompanied a minor outbreak of plague in Calcutta in 1900,[53] and typhoid accompanied plague in Vietnam in 1965.[54] But the major plagues in India and elsewhere during the late nineteenth and early twentieth centuries did not suddenly spur on the proliferation of other diseases, even in neighbourhoods of abject poverty and wretched sanitation. The researchers of the Plague Commission instead found the opposite: the plagues in India 'consist almost entirely of bubonic plague'.[55] Moreover, since humans have no natural immunity to modern plague, nutrition by itself is not a factor in raising the risk of catching the disease or of dying from it. It depends simply on the chance that a blocked infected rat flea successfully regurgitates the plague bacillus into the blood stream of the hapless individual. As we have seen, plague is more likely to spread in times of grain abundance than scarcity; grain, not poverty, was the sinew of this disease. The disease of the later Middle Ages was different; as Carmichael has shown, it became increasingly a disease of the poor, sprouting in the poorest neighbourhoods with the worst overcrowding, even though the general welfare of artisans and workers in places such as Florence was

---

[52] See Alfred Crosby, *Ecological Imperialism: The Biological Expansion of Europe, 900–1900* (Cambridge, 1986).
[53] C. Hossack, District Medical Officer, Calcutta, 'Influenza and plague,' *British Journal of Medicine* 1900, II, Oct. 27: 1244–7.
[54] Marshall *et al.*, 'Plague in Vietnam, 1965–66', p. 612. Recent research from the Sanger Centre Cambridge Genone Project shows a link between typhoid and bubonic plague in DNA sequencing; see Steve Farrar, 'Bug that bears the mask of death', *THES* (14 April 2000), pp. 20–21 and the centre's web site—www//Sanger.ac.uk/Project/S_typhi/.
[55] 'Interim report by the Advisory Committee', *JH*, 10 (1910), p. 566.

improving during the latter years of the fourteenth to the end of the fifteenth century.[56]

* * *

More recently, Ole Jørgen Benedictow's study of plague in Nordic Countries (primarily Norway and Iceland) shows an impressive but highly selected reading of the epidemiological materials on modern plague. He argued that Y. *pestis* was the bacillus and bubonic the form of the plague that spread to the most unlikely places for a rat-based, rat-flea transmitted disease.[57] Because of the inhospitable temperatures of these Nordic countries and the narrow temperature bands in which bubonic plague can operate—circa 50° to 78°F—historians have argued that the plague there must have been primary pneumonic plague.[58] Curiously, the late-medieval plagues tended to erupt later in the year in the North of Europe than in the Mediterranean south and could last until January, when temperatures in Bergen, Oslo, and places further to the West and North dipped to freezing temperatures, well below the rat-flea's margins of survival.[59] Further, while the little optimum of warm temperatures persisted in the Mediterranean basin into the fifteenth century, for northern Germany, Scandinavia, and Scotland, climate by 1300 had become more inclement with lower winter temperature extremes than today.[60]

Of course, once plague becomes an air-borne disease it can detach itself from rats and fleas and can survive even in Arctic conditions. But Benedictow vigorously attacked this possibility, insisting that the disease had to be bubonic with secondary pneumonic complications as occurred in twentieth-century India. First, he rightly argued that the most devastating of the known epidemics of primary pneumonic plague, that in Manchuria in 1910–11, killed less than 0.4 per cent of the population.[61] Unlike most historians, Benedictow also recognised that this form of plague was too lethal for its own good as an effective destroyer of human populations. But instead of questioning the nature of the disease, he insisted that it was modern bubonic plague and by it the problems surrounding the late-medieval plague's seasonality, spread, lethality, morbidity, and high mortalities could be resolved. Yet to give the epidemiology of the late-medieval

---

[56] See S.K. Cohn, *The Laboring Classes in Renaissance Florence* (New York, 1980).

[57] Benedictow, *Plague in Late Medieval Nordic Countries*.

[58] Most recently, see Gunnar Karlsson, 'Plague without rats: the case of fifteenth-century Iceland,' *Journal of Medieval History*, 22/23 (1996): 263–84.

[59] Even with the protection of the Gulf Stream on the west coast of Norway, average low temperatures in Bergen rise above 50°F only in July and August (for both months, it is 51°F), *Washington Post* Historical Weather Data website.

[60] H.H. Lamb, *Climate, Present, Past and Future*, II (London, 1977), pp. 405–7.

[61] Benedictow, *Plague in Late Medieval Nordic Countries*, p. 27.

plague this new twist, he had to rely on much slimmer data than are available for other areas of Europe. In contrast to the burial records, obituaries, hundreds of chronicles, thousands of last wills and testaments, plague tracts and more, the historian of the Black Death in Nordic Countries must rely on one brief chronicle description, ten mentions of death in one necrology for 1350, and eight last wills and testaments for mid-fourteenth-century Scandinavia.

To argue that the contagion was bubonic plague followed by secondary pneumonic and not primary pneumonic or any other disease, Benedictow relies on a two-line description from the one narrative source for the Black Death in Norway (1350), the Icelandic chronicle *Lawman's Annal*:

> people did not live more than a day or two with sharp pangs of pain/ After that they began to vomit blood.[62]

This chronicle does not even mention the telltale buboes in the groin, the arm-pits, or elsewhere; instead, pain and blood spitting sufficed for Benedictow to diagnose the disease not only as *Yersinia pestis*, but even as the bubonic followed by the secondary pneumonic as opposed to primary pneumonic plague. Apart from many other diseases causing pain and blood spitting, clinical reports of plague, as we have seen, show that often no pain precedes or accompanies the bubo; instead, most often patients are lulled into a dull, mindless state of indifference and depression. Further, in cases of bubonic plague, the patient did not usually die so fast as within a day or two as the Icelandic chronicler reports.[63]

Similarly, Benedictow squeezes from a mere ten death records found in an obituary of monks at Lunn a reading that is far beyond the statistical probabilities of these records:

> Intense epidemic activity is also suggested by an unusual incidence of deaths of upper-class persons from the last week of July until the beginning of September. The epidemiological pattern indicated is one in which the plague arrives in late autumn or in the spring, as always commencing its course in the quarters of the miserable.[64]

Not only do these records say nothing about the cause of death (Benedictow has assumed that all must have died from plague); they tell us little about social class. What evidence is there for the supposed first deaths of Norway's 'miserables'? Benedictow goes on to claim that these ten deaths show the typical bi-modal curve of modern bubonic plague 'with two peaks and a winter trough', yet he does not even produce their

---

[62] Ibid., p. 44.

[63] See the more than three thousand clinical reports in Gatacre, *Report on the Bubonic Plague in Bombay*.

[64] Benedictow, *Plague in Late Medieval Nordic Countries*, p. 51.

monthly distribution.[65] In addition, a Norwegian spring or autumn hardly corresponds with those seasons in Bombay City. If modern bubonic plague were to break out any time in Norway, summer could have been the only possibility and an usually hot one at that.

Even more than those who ascribe the disease in Nordic countries to pneumonic plague, Benedictow has the problem of explaining a bubonic plague based on adequate densities of rats in countries as cold and sparsely populated as Norway and Iceland. Here the problem is more vexed than in Britain, where at least archaeological evidence has uncovered rats that lived in the Middle Ages. For these Nordic countries no skeletal remains of rats has been found. In the spirit of Shrewsbury, Benedictow simply pushes the evidence aside, attributing this absence to the primitive state of zooarchaeology in Scandinavia. Instead, evidence of the plague itself (which he is trying to prove was the rat-based bubonic plague of the modern subtropics), is itself proof for *Rattus rattus*'s presence in medieval Iceland and Norway.[66]

Finally, historians' vitriolic rejections of Graham Twigg's findings perhaps best illustrate their emotional attachment to the Black Death as modern bubonic plague. Instead of addressing his arguments showing the failure of the late-medieval plague in Britain to fit the seasonality, incubation periods, and transmission of modern bubonic plague, they have seized on his closing suggestion that the Black Death might have been anthrax.[67] For Robert Gottfried: 'Twigg falls short at every juncture . . . He is ahistorical . . . we will not have to ponder or consider this work'.[68] Others such as Brossollet and Mollaret[69] and Benedictow cite Twigg in their bibliographies but in their texts give his arguments no hearing at all.[70] Still others have misconstrued Twigg's arguments to assert that, 'like Shrewsbury', he claimed that plague 'affected a much smaller fraction of the population'[71]— something he never suggests.

In closing, I turn to Carlo Cipolla, whose numerous small books on early modern plague in Italy have captivated audiences of general readers and specialists alike over the past three decades. I will let Cipolla speak for himself:

---

[65] Benedictow has misread what the researchers of the Plague Commission meant by a 'bimodal pattern': although plague usually occurred in India in one of two seasons separated by the hot dry months, it rarely occurred in both, or twice a year, in any one locality.
[66] Ibid., pp. 159–60. On the absence of any evidence of rats in late-medieval Iceland, see Karlsson, 'Plague without rats', pp. 263–4.
[67] See my introduction to Herlihy, *The Black Death and the Transformation of the West*, ed. by S.K. Cohn (Cambridge, Ma., 1997), pp. 6–7.
[68] Review in *Speculum* 61 (1986): 217–9.
[69] *Pourquoi la peste?*, p. 152.
[70] The one historian to give Twigg a reasonable hearing has been David Herlihy, *The Black Death*, pp. 29–30 and most recently, Cantor, *In the Wake of the Plague*.
[71] Benedict, *Bubonic Plague*, p. 77.

Doctors were quick to notice that those who dealt with furs, carpets and bales of wool and cloth were more likely to contract plague than those who dealt with marble, iron or wood . . . [that the former] might harbor infected fleas did not even cross the doctors' minds; the theoretical paradigm did not leave any room for microbes and their vectors. The doctors saw in the correctly observed facts proof that the atoms of poisonous miasmas, being 'sticky', obvious stuck or adhered more easily to hairy surfaces than to smooth ones.[72]

How and why a totally erroneous paradigm maintained for centuries its uncontested domination of the field of medical science has been and remains one of the most fascinating problems in European cultural history. For example, doctors soon observed correctly that plague epidemics broke out during the hot summer months. It never entered their heads that this might be in some way connected with the proliferation of insects such as fleas.[73]

As we have seen, the researchers of the Indian Plague Commission found no plague-infected fleas or the bacillus in a free or potentially contagious state clinging to furs, carpets, wool, or any other merchandise with the clear exception of rat-infested grain. Also, as we shall see, it makes good sense that men and women of late-medieval and early-modern Italy never connected the consistent summer seasonality of their plagues with the appearance of fleas, as Cipolla insists they should have. June and July, instead of being at the apex of the flea cycle in the Mediterranean, was at or near its nadir.[74]

Historians' unbending attachment to the Black Death as the same as modern plague illustrates with uncanny precision Cipolla's observation: 'Paradoxical as it may sound, the lesson of history is that all too often people find it easier to manipulate the facts to fit their theories than to adapt their theories to the facts observed.'[75]

---

[72] *Environment in the Pre-Industrial Age*, tr. by Elizabeth Porter (New Haven, 1992), p. 5; for similar propositions, see his *I pidocchi e il Granduca: Crisi economica e problemi sanitari nella Firenze del '600* (Bologna, 1979), p. 73.
[73] C. Cipolla, *Miasmas and Disease: Public Health and the Environment in the Pre-Industrial Age*, tr. by Elizabeth Porter (New Haven, 1992), p. 5; for much the same see idem, *I Pidocchi e il Granduca*, p. 73.
[74] See chapter 7.
[75] C. Cipolla, *Fighting the Plague in Seventeenth-Century Italy* (Madison, 1981), p. 14.

PART

II

THE BLACK DEATH:
SIGNS AND SYMPTOMS

|4|

Signs: chronicles, plague tracts, and saints' lives

It is difficult to know why historians and medical scientists have held on so passionately to the notion that the Black Death and its successive waves of pestilence must have been the same disease whose bacillus was discovered in 1894. Despite conflicting data between the two in mortality rates, presence of rats, seasonality, speed of transmission and more, few of these scholars have felt forced to argue their corner. For Robert Gottfried and Michael Dols (fourteenth and fifteenth centuries), Paul Slack (early-modern Britain), Brossollet and Mollaret (the plagues from the sixth century A.D. to Marseilles, 1720), and many others, the plague's bacteriology is simply indisputable; no argument need be made: 'The nature and dissemination of the Black Death are no longer the gruesome mystery they were in the Middle Ages. Modern scientific research has disclosed the complex pathology of plague'.[1] They then proceed to impose their notions of the aetiology and mechanisms of transmission of the twentieth-century bubonic plague on those of late-medieval and early modern Europe. Worlds of rats and fleas, rat epizootics, and regurgitated bacilli are invented for 1348 and beyond with picturesque vignettes without any grounding in the historical sources[2] or regard for the ecological differences between temperate Europe and subtropical India.

Other historians have stated their reasons, even if only briefly. As we

---

[1] Dols, *The Black Death in the Middle East*, p. 9. Gottfried, *The Black Death*; Slack, *The Impact of Plague*; and Brossollet and Mollaret, *Pourquoi la peste?*; the latest with this 'knowledge' that I have seen is Prosperi, *Dalla Peste Nera alla guerra dei Trent'anni*, p. 43; and Cantor, *In the Wake of the Plague*, p. 11.

[2] For the latest of such inventions, see Cantor's descriptions of scurrying 'plague-carrying rats' and infected fleas in bales of cotton on the docks of Bordeaux as Princess Joan and her entourage made their way in 1348 for her marriage to Prince Pedro of Castille (*In the Wake of the Plague*, p. 46). The only evidence for his elaborate scenario was that the Princess happened to die in 1348.

have seen, Boccaccio's description of the *gavòccioli* left Ann Carmichael with no doubts about the late-medieval plague's identity. Similarly, for Elizabeth Carpentier, Marchionne di Coppo Stefani's description of swellings in the armpits, groin, the rush of fever, the spitting of blood—was sufficient to conclude: 'the bubonic plague is here briefly but exactly described'.[3] Even more surprising are the comments of the great immunologist and Nobel Prize winner Sir Macfarlane Burnet. First, he cautions his readers that to understand diseases in past times, the historian must go beyond the signs and symptoms of a disease and study its epidemiology.[4] But when Sir Macfarlane reached the Black Death, he apparently forgot his lesson. Boccaccio's description of the symptoms are 'enough to make it easy to recognise the disease . . . we can be sure that the two greatest European pestilences, the plague of Justinian's reign (A.D. 542) and the Black Death of 1348, were both the result of the spread of the plague bacillus'.[5]

The assumption has often been that swellings in the lymphatic glands with haemorrhagic points, found in the groin, armpits, or other places is unique to bubonic plague. But as doctors and other health workers in the subtropics are taught, such swellings are insufficient for treating a disease as bubonic plague. Early on, *Manson's Tropical Diseases* insisted that health workers go beyond the bubo and take cultures of the infected area before treatment, even though bubonic plague (*Y. pestis*) is a quick killer. As later editions enumerated, such swellings could equally well signify other diseases such as relapsing fever, severe cases of malaria, typhoid, typhus, glandular fever, tularaemia, lymphogranuloma inguinale, and various forms of filariasis.[6] With scrub typhus, for instance, the abscesses form in the armpits and the scrotum, and with filarial orchitis the lymph gland enlargements may be as large as a fist (5–7.5 cm in diameter).[7]

In addition, Boccaccio's description may not be such a perfect description of modern plague as historians and scientists have assumed. It does not end with the plague swellings in one of two glands; rather the disease's course continued:

> From the two areas already mentioned [the groin and the armpit], the afore-mentioned deadly *gavòcciolo* would begin to spread, and within a short time would appear at random on every part of the body. Afterwards, the illness would change with the appearance of black or blue spots (*macchie nere o*

---

[3] *Une ville devant la peste: Orvieto et la peste noire de 1348* (Paris, 1962), p. 113; also 'Famines et épidémies', p. 1071.

[4] Burnet, *Natural History of Infectious Disease*, 3rd ed. (Cambridge, 1962), p. 296

[5] Ibid., p. 323. The fourth edition of 1972, updated by David O. White, left this remark intact, p. 225.

[6] *Manson's Tropical Diseases*, 7th ed., p. 270; *Manson's Tropical Diseases*, 19th ed., pp. 594–5; Michael Smith and Nguyen Duy Thanh, 'Plague', in *Manson's Tropical Diseases*, 20th ed., ed. by Gordon Cook (London, 1996), p. 920. Also, Ell, 'Immunity as a factor', p. 871.

[7] *Manson's Tropical Diseases*, 19th ed., p. 359.

livide) forming on their arms, thighs, and other parts of the body, sometimes large and few in number, at other times tiny and closely spaced.[8]

As we shall see, neither the plague boils nor such spots were to spread over the body in more than 3000 clinical cases reported in Bombay in 1896–97 or in 36 cases in Glasgow in 1900. In 95 per cent of cases only one plague boil formed and with no modern plague have black pustules spreading randomly all over the body been reported. At most, a few points might form around the fleabite, but such marks are rare and usually occur with pneumonic or septicaemic plague, when buboes do not have time to form at all.[9]

Boccaccio's description cannot be simply dismissed as poetic license to heighten the plague's horror. Other chroniclers and doctors from 1347 on described the same spread of spots, carbuncles, pustules, and anthraces in plague time. The earliest Black Death description, that of Emperor John IV Cantacuzenos for 1347, told of 'black blisters' and 'black spots' that spread all over the body: 'in some they were few and very manifest; in others they were obscure and dense.'[10] The Dominican chronicler of the convent of Santa Maria Novella, Florence, did not even mention the typical single bubo for the plague victims of his order in 1348; instead, 'pustules, spots, or other similar formations (*carbunculi, seu antracis aut alicuius similis*) formed in the groin and under the arms.'[11] Giovanni of Parma, chronicler and canon at Trent in 1348, noted 'swellings' (*glandularum*) in the groins and the armpits, followed by the spread of spots (*carbunculorum*).[12] A fragment of a necrology of Cividale del Friuli in 1348 reported that plague took three forms: glandular swellings, spots, and the spitting of blood.[13] A chronicler from Rimini described the sign in 1348 as either a spot (*carbunculo*) in the singular or as ulcers or blisters (*fistulis*) in the plural. He also described those who mixed with the plague stricken as becoming visibly and lethally spotted ('visibiliter maculabant', 'letaliter maculabat').[14] For the chronicler of Spalato (Split) in Dalmatia, the plague's sign was glandular swellings or spots (*glandis vel carbunculi*) that formed in several parts of the body.[15] The chronicler of the monastery in southern Austria called the 'signs of pestilence' red ulcers dotted around the genitals and in the armpits.[16] Geoffrey le Baker described the English as being gripped by ulcers in various parts of the body: some were so hard and dry that hardly

---

[8] Boccaccio, *Decameron*, ed. by Vittore Branca (Milan, 1976), pp. 10–11.

[9] Smith and Thanh, 'Plague', p. 920. Also see Butler, *Plague and Other Yersinia Infections*, p. 17; *Manson's Tropical Diseases*, 10th ed. (London, 1935), p. 254 and 19th ed., p. 591.

[10] Translated by Christos S. Bartsocas, 'Two fourteenth-century Greek descriptions of the "Black Death"', *Journal of the History of Medicine and Applied Sciences*, 21 (1966), p. 396.

[11] 'Necrologio' di S. Maria Novella, I, p. 65.

[12] *Cronica inedita di Giovanni da Parma*, p. 50.

[13] 'Fragmenta Historica', p. 43.

[14] *Marcha di Marco Battagli da Rimini*, p. 54.

[15] *Ecclesia Spalatensis*, p. 324.

[16] *Codex Novimontibus in Continuatio Novimontensis*, p. 675.

any liquid seeped out; others had small black spots (*pustulos*) that formed on the skin covering the entire body. The latter signs were the more deadly; from them 'hardly any survived'. The same combination of boils and pustules also afflicted the Scots in 1349/50.[17] Finally, the first sign of plague at Messina in 1347 was a spot (*quedam pustula*) that took the form of a lentil (*ad modum lenticule*); the larger glandular swelling that formed near the thigh (*circa femur*) and under the arms here came later.[18] When plague spread to Catania 'not only did these spots (*pustule ille*) called *antrachi*, but also glandular swelling (*glandule*) spread over various parts of the body, first on the breasts, some on the thighs (*in tibiis*), others on the arms, others on the throat'. The chronicler Michele da Piazza then went into greater detail: 'it grew in the shape of a nut, then into the shape of a hen's or a goose's egg, and from it came unusual pain and filled with a putrid liquid which expelled blood from the body'.[19] The cutaneous progression in Sicily was the reverse of what it would assume in Boccaccio's Florence.

For successive waves of plague, some chroniclers continued to distinguish the disease by its combination of glandular swellings and spots. For the second plague of 1361, the Piacentine Giovanni de' Mussis (not his more famous brother) spoke of 'a coagulated liquid that formed under the skin in the armpits or in the groin and, with some, pustules or ulcers (*pustulae sive apostemata*) ringed the back of the head behind the ears'.[20] A poem once thought to be that of the Welsh poet Jeuan Gethin but recently attributed to the mid-fourteenth-century Llywelyn Fychan laments the death of his four children during the plague; another had died nine year earlier in what was probably the first plague of 1348–49.[21] After describing the 'swelling under the armpit, grievous sore lump', he described a 'shower of black peas'.[22] As in Boccaccio's Florence (but not as in Michele da Piazza's Sicily), the pustules followed the larger lumps:

> a swelling under the armpit, grievous sore lump,
> white knob, poisonous misfortune,
> pommel of a sword of sift strife,
> . . .shape of an apple full of pain,
> bitter head of an odious onion,
> a little boil which spares no one. . .
> Evil provision of grief quite openly,
> a reaping of black pangs,
> ugly pox, dreadful is its haste,

---

[17] *Chronicon Galfridi le Baker*, p. 100.
[18] Michele da Piazza, *Cronica*, p. 82.
[19] Ibid., p. 86.
[20] *Chronicon Placentinum*, cols 506–7.
[21] *Galar Y Beirdd: Marwnadau Plant/ Poets' Grief: Medieval Welsh Elegies for Children*, ed. and tr. by Dafydd Johnston (Cardiff, 1993), pp. 56–8.
[22] Ibid., pp. 53–5.

is it not similar to seeds of black peas?
Inflamed burning of brittle coal fragments,
tempestuous host like studs;
crowds from the brink of death,
a heavy sickness produces them, horrible to us.
A shower of peas giving rise to affliction,
messenger of swift black death;
parings from the petals of the corn-poppy,
murderous rabble, evil omen;
black plague, they don't come with any good intent,
halfpennies, seaweed scales;
a grim throng, humble speech,
berries, it is painful that they should be on fair skin.

Giovanni of Parma called the plague of 1371 an 'illness of spots and glandular swellings (*infirmitas carbunculi et glandulae*)'. With his 'own eyes', he drew a curious unexplained difference between those that formed on the right as opposed to the left side of the body, claiming that none survived with them on the right, whereas some, even if only a few, recovered with them on the left.[23] Further, he commented that the plague of 1373–74 took three forms: (1) swelling in the groin or under the arms; (2) spots; and (3) 'of sleeping', in which none survived after the fifth day.[24] Descriptions of both cutaneous signs continue to be reported in the fifteenth century. The chronicler of Saint-Denis (Paris) recorded that 'after severe headaches a collection of swollen pustules almost exploded on and just under the skin killing its victims in two or three days'.[25]

In addition, plague tracts of the later fourteenth and early fifteenth centuries, written mostly by university-trained doctors, referred to black spots they called ants, carbuncles, or spots (*formicae vel carbunculi vel antracis*). These accompanied or followed (*trahens*) the appearance of the plague ulcers or apostemes.[26] Some, such as Colle of Belluno and Alphonse de Cordova, said that both the spots and the larger ulcers spread over the body.[27] By the fifteenth century, doctors even classified the plague swellings according to size, type, and colour—'Carbunculus, Carbo, et Glandula';[28] 'green and black, sometimes red and yellowish

---

[23] *Cronica inedita di Giovanni da Parma*, p. 52.
[24] Ibid., p. 52.
[25] *Chronique du religieux de Saint-Denys*, VI, p. 270.
[26] Karl Sudhoff, 'Pestschriften aus den ersten 150 Jahren nach der Epidemie das "schwarzen Todes" 1348', *Archiv für Geschichte der Medizin*, vols IV–XVII (1910–25). See for instance, [24], p. 52; [39], p. 373; [38], p. 361; [116], p. 125; [98], p. 120. For these and the following Sudhoff references see Appendix III. The numbers within brackets correspond to Sudhoff's own numbers.
[27] 'Ex libro vetusto Dionysii Secundi Colle', in Haeser, p. 169; Coville, 'Écrits contemporains sur la peste', p. 367.
[28] [215], p. 131.

(*citrinas*)'.[29] Like the chroniclers, they often found that the smaller pustules covering various parts of the body were more deadly and painful than the larger lymphatic buboes.[30] The distinction was also important for the treatments prescribed. The famous doctor Giovanni da Santa Sofia, professor of medicine at the University of Padua, advised that a plaster of pig fat be applied to the larger plague boils but a plaster made from pigeon dung (*de stercore columbino*) be put on the smaller anthrax and carbuncles because of their more 'vehement heat'.[31]

Perhaps we should conclude along with Shrewsbury and Carmichael, that contemporaries were describing a synergy of diseases, bubonic plague followed possibly by smallpox, measles, or typhus. Several plague tracts might support such an interpretation by the various words they used to describe the pustules. A late-fourteenth-century doctor in Bologna reported 'that smallpox (*variolae*), measles (*morbilli*), and many other poisonous diseases with anthrax, carbuncles, and herpes (*et aegritudines multae venosae ut antrax, carbunculus, herpes*)' followed from the larger plague boils.[32] Others, such as a doctor from Lübeck in 1411, saw smallpox, measles, worms and snails preceding the formation of plague boils and afterwards the outbreak of anthrax and carbuncles.[33] However, the bulk of these descriptions do not afford such a reading. First, as recent historians of medicine have cautioned us, it is hazardous to translate terms such as measles, smallpox, anthrax, or others as necessarily being the equivalents of the modern diseases whose bacteria or viruses were discovered in laboratories during the late nineteenth and twentieth centuries.[34] These words were more often intended as descriptions of skin disorders rather as a nomenclature for distinct diseases.[35] When chroniclers and doctors wished to distinguish among diseases, as indeed they could and sometimes did, they rightly turned to epidemiological criteria, such as how fast the illness spread, how long it took to kill, and whether many died from it.[36] Second, the chroniclers and doctors consistently described the pustules as an integral part of the plague, sometimes forming before, sometimes after, but usually alongside the plague boils. Finally, Boccaccio, Geoffrey le Baker, the Tridentine canon, Giovanni Morelli, and

---

[29] See for instance, [232], p. 160; [140], p. 95; and *Practica Antonii Guainerii*, p. 107r; and Marsilio Ficino, *Consiglio contro la pestilenza*, ed. by Enrico Musacchio (Bologna, 1983), p. 92.
[30] [89], p. 269; [140], 95; *Practica Antonii Guainerii*, p. 107r.
[31] [50], p. 348.
[32] [46], p. 330; also see [9bis], p. 87; and [95], p. 57.
[33] [119], p. 151: 'In pueris interdum precedunt variole, morbilli, vermes seu lumbrici . . .'
[34] See for instance, Jon Arrizabalaga, John Henderson, and Roger French, *The Great Pox: The French Disease in Renaissance Europe* (New Haven, 1997), pp. 1–3; and Cunningham, 'Transforming plague'.
[35] See the examples above and *Practica Antonii Guainerii*: 'De signis febris pestilentialis . . . est variolas vel morbillos, antrace, carbunculum vel bubonem demonstrare . . .' (106r–v).
[36] See chapter 6.

many plague doctors saw the tiny 'black peas', carbuncles, and anthraces as more virulent and lethal than the dry or suppurating boils as big as apples. Yet, smallpox, measles, and *pondi* (possibly dysentery) had been around and when chroniclers such as the Brut, the Parisian bourgeois, and Minerbetti referred to them as distinct diseases, they described them as principally childhood diseases which killed slowly and with much lower levels of mortality. They were not the new 'big death', which the chroniclers and doctors distinguished by its new, 'unheard of' mortalities and speed of contagion.[37]

Perhaps like measles, tuberculosis, and most other infectious diseases, the first time the plague struck its skin disorders were different from when it became more endemic.[38] Indeed, Michele da Piazza's distinction of the plague's first appearance in Messina from its further spread into the heartland of Sicily suggests such a transition. Yet the pustules and buboes continued to accompany one another with plagues into the seventeenth century.[39]

*   *   *

The descriptions of the Florentine chronicler Marchionne di Coppo Stefani, John da Bazano of Mantua, an anonymous chronicler from Flanders, a chronicler of Ferrara, the Gatari of Padua, and the chroniclers of Saint-Denis might suggest that the cutaneous signs of the late-medieval plagues resembled more closely modern bubonic plague in that they used the singular to name the skin disorder and described it as a boil (*gavòcciolo, grossetto, grosso, apostemata pessima, turber, angum, glandula*) and not a rash or rings of spots spreading over the body.[40] But as often, chroniclers referred to these swellings in the plural—*glandulae incurabiles, glandule, aposteme, apostemate, gaudusse a l'inguinaie, inguinarie* in Italian chronicles;[41] *boches* in a chronicle from Rouen,[42] *boce* in two early fifteenth-century plagues in Paris,[43] *bossas* and *apostematibus* in the north of France,[44] *glauces* in a chronicle of Frankfurt commenting on a plague of 1356.[45]

---

[37] See chapter 6.

[38] See Arno Karlen, *Plague's Progress: A Social History of Man and Disease* (London, 1995), 'When zymotics first raged through ancient cities, they often took forms we would not recognise . . . a vicious changeling' (p. 56).

[39] See the numerous plague tracts edited by Sudhoff, and Manson's citation to the plague of London in 1665.

[40] *Cronichetta d'incerto*, p. 183; Stefani, *Cronica fiorentina*, pp. 230–2 and 426; Iohannis de Bazano, *Chronicon Mutinense*, p. 177; Sanctus, p. 466; Dominici de Gravina, *Chronicon de rebus in Apulia gestis*, p. 49; *Chronique du religieux de Saint-Denys*. I, p. 475; II, p. 693, IV, p. 690.

[41] Gatari, *Cronaca Carrarese*, p. 559; *Cronica volgare di Anonimo Fiorentino*, p. 110; *Chronicon Placentinum*, pp. 506–7; '*Aliprandina*', p. 133; '*Necrologio*' *di S. Maria Novella*, I, p. 65.

[42] *Chronique Normande*, p. 72.

[43] *Journal d'un Bourgeois de Paris*, pp. 111 and 295.

[44] *Chronique latine de Guillaume de Nangis (Continuatio)*, II, p. 211; *Richardi Scoti Chronicon*, p. 82.

[45] *Annales Francofurtani*, pp. 394–5.

Of course, from a phrase such as that of Minerbetti in 1390—'And again in this time [1390] some began to have certain plague boils dying in a few days'—it difficult to know whether he meant that several boils formed on an individual plague victim or whether the plural referred to single boils on numerous victims.[46] Doctors also almost invariably used the plural to refer to the plague scars—'apostemata'.[47] However, on occasion they were more explicit. The 1382 plague tract of the Florentine Niccolò de Borgo reported that when the disease spread to the emunctory glands either a 'raised tumour' would appear or 'in other parts one or more spots (*antrax unus vel plures*)'.[48] Similarly, another Italian plague doctor at the end of the fourteenth century, referred to the anthraces as appearing either as one sore or as many that formed in various parts of the body.[49] But despite references to specific plagues, the tracts rarely described individual case histories. One exception in Sudhoff's collection of plague tracts is in fact not a plague tract at all but an obituary for Prince John, Duke of Bavaria, who died of plague in 1463. His doctor described the prince as having two plague boils—one in the groin, the other up the nostrils.[50]

With modern bubonic plague between 55 and 75 per cent of the plague boils form in the groin, followed by 10 to 20 per cent in the armpits with the remaining 10 per cent or so forming in other glands, mainly in the cervical region. Most form in the groin: although the flea can jump a hundred times its own height, usually it can bite no higher than just above the ankles; thus the first glandular node where blood and bacillus concentrate is in the groin. On first impression, the historian might well conclude that the literary sources suggest a similar pattern. Particularly in Florence after 1348, a word for plague derives from the boil's position in the groin—'inguinarie', 'pietolenzia dell'anguinaia', 'la mortalità dell'anguinaia'.[51] It was also used elsewhere in Italy and north of the Alps, though rarely. An anonymous early-fifteenth-century chronicler of Mantua called the 'illness' of 1348 the 'Inguinariam',[52] and a chronicler of Mainz used a similar term for plague in 1365 and the scribe of the Monastery of Melk (southern Austria) for plague in 1365 and in 1495 ('lues igwinaria cruetissima').[53] Despite this occasional linguistic connection, however, I know of only three chroniclers who mentioned the groin alone as the place where plague boils

---

[46] *Cronica volgare di Anonimo Fiorentino*, p. 110: 'E ancora in questo tempo cominciano alcuni ad avere certe aposteme pestilenziose, e questi morivano in pochi dì.'
[47] See for instance [98], p. 119; [50], p. 348.
[48] [38], p. 361.
[49] [43], p. 314.
[50] [150], pp. 138–9.
[51] Matteo Villani, *Cronica*, I, pp. 273, 300, 514, 585–6, 660–1, and 663.
[52] *Annales Veteres Mutinensium*, 'Additamenta varia', p. 82.
[53] VI. *Chronicon Moguntinum*, p. 169; and *Continuatio Mellicensis*, p. 526.

formed,[54] and no chronicler, not even the statistically minded Florentines, ever suggested that the vast majority of plague boils appeared there.

The most often noted combination of places was the double location of boils in the groin and the armpit as described by the Sienese Agnolo di Tura, the Parisian Jean de Venette, the Florentines Marchionne di Coppo Stefani, Matteo Villani, Boccaccio, and several others in southern Austria, Frankfurt, and Flanders.[55] Yet almost as many chroniclers gave prominence to three bodily areas. As we have seen the Piacentine Giovanni de' Mussis described them around the head behind the ears in addition to the groin and armpits.[56] For the plague of 1405 in Padua, the Gatari said the 'little nut' appeared 'with some on the throat, some on the arm and some in the groin'.[57] The early fifteenth-century Florentine Giovanni Morelli, claiming 'Giovanni Bocacci' as his source, went beyond him, no doubt reading back into 1348 his own lifetime of plague experiences. In addition to giving a more reasonable figure for the 1348 fatalities,[58] his description differed from Boccaccio's in finding the plague boils 'in the groin, under the arms, or on the throat at the bottom of the ears (*o nella gola, da piè dell'orecchie*)'.[59] More vaguely, the Cortusii brothers of Padua reported that in 1348 the plague boils 'were born' near the groin, under the arms, and in other places.[60] An Egyptian chronicler described the boils 'first forming behind the ears, where rapidly they suppurated and then under the arms with death following quickly'. The groin was not mentioned.[61]

But more chroniclers, even those who mentioned plague boils or other skin disorders, did not locate them as forming predominately in any gland. Even a chronicler as meticulous as the anonymous Minerbetti, who described the plague swellings, reported precise mortality figures based on government figures, and distinguished plague from other diseases, did not specify that the boils formed in the groin and armpits.[62] In fact, the vast majority of chroniclers did not even mention boils at all. On the other hand,

[54] 'Aliprandina', p. 133; and Dominici de Gravina, *Chronicon de rebus in Apulia*, p. 49; and *Kalendarium Zwetlense*, p. 692.

[55] *Cronaca Senese attribuita ad Agnolo di Tura del Grasso*, p. 555; *Chronique latine de Guillaume de Nangis (Continuatio)*, II, p. 211; Stefani, *Cronica fiorentina*, pp. 230, 289, and 426; Matteo Villani, *Cronica* , I, pp. 9 and 300; 'Necrologio' di S. Maria Novella, I, p. 65; *Codex Novimontibus*, p. 675; *Annales Francofurtani 1306–1358*, pp. 394–5; Sanctus, p. 466; and *Chronique Normande*, p. 72

[56] *Chronicon Placentinum*, p. 506.

[57] Gatari, *Cronaca Carrarese*, p. 560.

[58] Morelli, *Ricordi*, p. 209, estimated that the population of the city of Florence had climbed to 120,000 just before the plague and that three-quarters or 80,000 died from it in 1348 (and not 100,000 as Boccaccio claimed); for the most recent population estimates, see Herlihy and Klapisch, *Les Toscans*, pp. 173–7.

[59] Morelli, *Ricordi*, p. 207.

[60] Cortusii, *Historia de Novitatibus Paduae*, col. 927.

[61] *Maqrīzī, Sulūk*, p. 370.

[62] *Cronica volgare di Anonimo Fiorentino*, pp. 110 and 250.

another source, the plague tract, specified the place of these cutaneous signs far more consistently. While the plague tract was not entirely a new genre of medical writing in 1348, I know of only three to have survived between Avicenna's *Canon of Medicine* of the eleventh century and the appearance of the Black Death.[63] With the Black Death and even more so afterwards during the later fourteenth and fifteenth centuries, these tracts explode in number.[64] Between 1348 and 1500, perhaps a thousand or more circulated in Europe, of which 288 have been mentioned or edited in part by Karl Sudhoff in various numbers of his journal, *Archiv für Geschichte der Medizin*, from 1910 to 1925.[65]

Collectively, they are a difficult source to use. Scholars often take Sudhoff's selection from numerous libraries in the early twentieth century as the corpus of these works before 1500 or a representative sample of them. It is neither, as was pointed out in the 1930s.[66] Because of his access to German, Austrian, and Czech libraries, tracts from these areas have been listed or edited out of proportion to their survival vis-à-vis other national libraries. His most important quarries were the libraries of Munich, followed by those in Leipzig.[67] As a consequence, the number of tracts from German-speaking areas exceeds the rest, almost doubling the Italian sources, but Sudhoff missed many important tracts.[68] Most remarkable of these omissions are perhaps the second most famous plague tract of the fifteenth century—that of the Paduan doctor Giovanni Michele Savonarola—and the most celebrated of the early authors of Montpellier, Bernard Alberti.[69] On the other hand, Sudhoff also listed at least one plague tract—that of Ugolino da Montecatini—for which no surviving manuscripts could be uncovered.[70]

---

[63] [22], pp. 39–41; [81], pp. 214–5; and Lynn Thorndike, 'A pest tractate before the Black Death', *Archiv für Geschichte der Medizin*, XXIII (1930): 346–56.

[64] To find these signs of plague, Herlihy turned to saints' lives as a source but produced only two examples of such descriptions from the lives of two saints of the Middle Ages; see idem, *The Black Death*, p. 79.

[65] Under the title 'Pestschriften aus den ersten 150 Jahren nach der Epidemie des "schwarzen Todes" 1348', these are scattered in a somewhat haphazard fashion through most of the volumes, IV to XVII.

[66] Alfred Coville, 'Écrits contemporains sur la peste de 1348 à 1350', in *Histoire littéraire de la France*, XXXVII (Paris, 1938), p. 372.

[67] Sudhoff, 'Nachträge und Verbesserungen', Sudhoff, XVII (1925), pp. 286–91.

[68] Arturo Castiglioni, 'I libri italiani della pestilenza', in *Il Volto di Ippocrate: Istorie di medici e medicine d'altri tempi*, ed. by Castiglioni (Milan, 1925), p. 153.

[69] Savonarola is only mentioned in Sudhoff, XVI, p. 180, but does not receive a number as a plague tract. His long tract was finally brought out in a modern edition in 1953: *I trattati in volgare della peste e dell'acqua ardente*, ed. by Luigi Beloni (Milan, 1953). On the Montpellier doctors, see Melissa P. Chase, 'Fevers, poisons, and apostemes: authority and experience in Montpellier plague treatises', in *Science and Technology in Medieval Society*, ed. by Pamela O. Long (New York, 1985), p. 154.

[70] Ugolino's most famous tract, on sanitation ('Consiglio medico di maestr' ad Averardo de' Medici', ed. by F. Baldasseroni and G. Degli Azzi, *ASI*, 5th ser. 38 [1906]: 140–52), does not mention plague; see [42], pp. 395–6; and [42 bis], p. 140.

While Sudhoff did venture to Florence and consulted several libraries there, he certainly did not exhaust their resources.[71] On the other hand, he spent even less time in libraries and archives in France and most of the French tracts he edited he found housed in German and Austrian libraries. Moreover, in a great number of the cases Sudhoff did not provide the entire texts; sometimes he cited only the incipit or nothing at all from the text. In other instances, it is difficult to know whether he has included the entire text or only a selection. Yet, despite these difficulties, we are indebted to Sudhoff for his prodigious efforts in making these sources available. Although a number of new plague texts have come to light since he finished his collection in 1925,[72] no one has seriously attempted to fill the gaps left by his ambitious plan of the early twentieth century.[73]

While many of these tracts framed their arguments in good scholastic fashion by citing classical authorities—Hippocrates, Galen, Avicenna, Averroes, Rhazes, Maimonides—and occasionally their own contemporaries—Gentile da Foligno,[74] Tommaso Del Garbo,[75] and Marsilio da Santa Sophia[76]—it is remarkable how many did not mention a single authority, classical or modern, to substantiate their claims for their recipes and treatments for plague. Instead, they launched straight into

---

[71] See the criticisms of Castiglioni in 'I libri italiani della pestilenza', p. 153, who considers a number of Italian plague tracts not mentioned or edited by Sudhoff.

[72] Almost immediately scholars such as Thorndike signalled new plague tracts but only a handful of them have been published since 1925. See Thorndike, 'Some Vatican manuscripts of pest tractates' 'A pest tractate before the black death' *Archiv für Geschichte der Medizin*, XXII (1929): 199–200 and XXIII (1930): 346–56; Castiglioni 'I libri italiani della pestilenza'. Most recently, see the Dutch plague tracts published in *Koninklijke Academie voor Geneeskunde van België*, LXI/2 (1999).

[73] For works on these tracts, see Dorothea Waley Singer, 'Some plague tractes (fourteenth and fifteenth centuries),' *Proceedings of the Royal Society of Medicine* IX: 2 (1916), 159–214; Castiglioni, 'I libri italiani della pestilenza', IX/2; Ann Campbell, *The Black Death and Men of Learning* (New York, 1931); Winslow, *The Conquest of Epidemic Disease*, pp. 95–116; Séraphine Guerchberg, 'The controversy over the alleged sowers of the Black Death in the contemporary treatises on plague', in *Change in Medieval Society: Europe North of the Alps 1050–1500*, ed. by Sylvia Thrupp (1965), pp. 208–24; L.I. Conrad, 'Arabic plague chronologies and treatises: social and historical factors in the formation of a literary genre,' *Studia Islamica*, LIV (1981): 51–93; Chase, 'Fevers, poisons, and apostemes'; Ron Barkai, 'Jewish treatises on the Black Death (1350–1500): a preliminary study,' in *Medicine from the Black Death to the French Disease*, ed. by French, Arrizabalaga, Cunningham and García-Ballester (Aldershot, 1998), pp. 6–25; Sabine Krüger, 'Krise der Zeit als Ursache der Pest? Der Traktat De mortalitate in Alamannia des Konrad von Megenberg', in *Festschrift für Hermann Heimpel zum 70. Geburtstag am 19. September 1971* (Göttigen, 1972), II, pp. 839–83; Arrizabalaga, 'Facing the Black Death'; and Nancy Siraisi, *Medieval and Early Renaissance Medicine: An Introduction to Knowledge and Practice* (Chicago, 1990), pp. 128–52. For a list of early printed plague tracts in France, see A.C. Klebs and E. Droz, *Remèdes contre la peste: facsimilés* (Paris, 1925).

[74] [35], p. 341; [97], pp. 70 and 73; [220], p. 136; [223], p. 141 and 144; [239], p. 173; [173], p. 10.

[75] [220], p. 136; [194], p. 95.

[76] Savonarola, *I Trattati in volgare della peste*, p. 28.

practical advice and procedures. Far from being theoretical texts, slavishly following antique authorities, removed from the realities of current
plagues, these fourteenth- and early fifteenth-century plague tracts
turned on practical experience of treating plague patients.[77] As the
doctors themselves intended and chroniclers such as Giovanni Morelli
attest, by the end of the fourteenth century these tracts had penetrated
beyond the university, entering the homes of merchants and literate artisans. With increasing numbers written in the vernacular and some, such
as the tract of Tommaso Del Garbo, surviving in a large numbers of
manuscripts scattered across Europe, Arturo Castiglioni has claimed that
the genre had become a form of popular literature by the fifteenth
century.[78] If not then, certainly later: the only book mentioned in the
post-mortem inventory of the seventeenth-century artisan Miquel Paret
of Barcelona was a plague tract.[79]

*   *   *

To date, our sense of where the plague boils formed in 1348 and later
comes from impressions given by chroniclers who mostly did not
describe them at all. Doctors, by contrast, because of their attempts to
cure the plague by addressing its surface manifestations, focused consistently on these cutaneous signs. The positions of the buboes pinpointed
in these texts are at variance with those given by the chroniclers. Only
one plague tract, and that one not by a doctor but by a German school-
teacher, located the plague boils in a single bodily spot. Furthermore, it
was in the armpit as opposed to the most usual place with modern
plague, the groin.[80] Even more curious, the pairing of boils in the groin
and under the armpits, which the chronicles to some extent and modern
historians more often have seen as the late-medieval plague's unmistakable signs, is almost wholly missing from the tracts. The only exception
I have spotted comes from a Neapolitan doctor in 1348, who placed the
'external boils in the underarms and groin (*titilicorum et inguinum*)', but
even he spoke of other 'internal apostemes' that formed in the lungs and
the breasts and later in his tract said they formed externally in three
places.[81]

Instead, almost all the doctors identified the plague boils as forming in

---

[77] For this impression, see Andreina Zitelli and Richard J. Palmer, 'Le teorie mediche sulla
peste e il contesto veneziano', *Venezia e la peste 1348–1797* (Venice, 1979), pp. 21–8, esp.
p. 24. For these doctors' emphasis on practical experience, see chapter 9.

[78] Castiglioni, 'Ugo Benzi da Siena ed il "Trattato utilissimo circa la conservazione della sanitate"', *Rivista di storia critica delle scienze mediche e naturali*, XII (1921), p. 75.

[79] James S. Amelang, *The Flight of Icarus: Artisan Autobiography in Early Modern Europe*
(Stanford, 1998), p. 110.

[80] Konrad von Megenberg, 'Tractatus de mortalitate in Alamannina', in Sabina Krüger, 'Krise
der Zeit als Ursache der Pest?', p. 865.

[81] [35], p. 348.

three principal areas of the body linked to Galen's three 'emunctoria'.[82] Heinricus Rybbinis put it succinctly in his tract addressed to the citizens of Bratislava in 1371: 'if any of you are invaded by plague boils, they usually form in three places, according to the triplex of *emunctoria*, that is the *emuctorium* of the brain, the heart, and the liver (*epatis*) where water is passed'.[83] From these three *emunctoria* or springs of life, poison passes to the nearest glands. From the liver, boils form on the thighs or in the groin; from the heart, in the underarms as well as on the arms, the chest, or under the breast. The brain was the most complex of these and produced a range of possibilities—behind the ears, on the back of neck, and occasionally on the face.

Except for the two tracts mentioned above, every other one that pointed to plague boils (at least 55 tracts) said they formed in these three zones.[84] According to the position of the boils, the doctors would then advise where to place their plasters and of what materials they should be composed, and more often, which veins were to be tapped for bloodletting (*fleubotomy*). In these discussions, the groin never took pride of place; instead doctors began their instructions with those boils that formed on the throat, neck, and behind the ears. If no boils appeared here, they proceeded to discuss treatment of those under the arms, and finally, if not in these two zones, those in the groin as if these were the least likely place of the three.

An easy reading of these texts would be to infer that ancient theory fixed doctors' mindset so that they saw the boils forming according to the dictates of Galen's *emunctoria*. But even if we should conclude that these men were so enslaved to the 'auctores'—a hypothesis that the most cursory glance at a few tracts would dispel—not all the antique sources agreed and the doctors had a choice of which to follow. Here, the plague tracts show a fundamental break in an intellectual tradition. From the end of the thirteenth century to 1348 the most influential medical authority was Aristotle.

---

[82] Two authors listed six zones, but these were the right and left sides of the body that derived from the same three *emunctoria*; see [45], p. 325; and Ficino, *Consiglio contro la pestilenza*, p. 92. It is interesting to note that of the 1348 tracts studied by Arrizabalaga, 'Facing the Black Death', p. 284, only Gentile da Foligno referred to the *emunctoria*. By the second plague, this Galenic notion was universal with all the tracts that mentioned bloodletting.

[83] [9], p. 209.

[84] These include [2], p. 197; [5], p. 393; [9], p. 209; [9bis], p. 87; [19], p. 58; [24], p. 48; [24bis], p. 33; [26], p. 28; [27 and 28], pp. 64–5; [38], p. 361; [39], pp. 383–4; [43], p. 314; [44], p. 317; [45], p. 325; [49], pp. 342–4; [56], p. 371; [58], pp. 374–5; [61], pp. 68–72; [63], pp. 73–4; [64], p. 93; [75], p. 181; [89], p. 269; [97], p. 77; [98], p. 119; [99], p.138; [103], p. 161; [111], p. 69; [113], p. 73; [114], pp. 83–4; [116], pp. 124, 129; [117], p. 138; [119], p. 161; [161], p. 159; [182], p.38; [184], p. 55; [192], p. 68; [193], pp. 92–3; [215], p. 128; [256], p. 28; [260], pp. 48–9; [279], p. 123; [285], pp. 136–8; *Practica Antonii Guainerii*, p. 106v; Ficino, *Consiglio contro la pestilenza*, p. 92; Raymundus Chalmelli de Vivario, in Robert Hoeniger, *Der Schwarze Tod in Deutschland: Ein Beitrag zur Geschichte des vierzehnten Jahrhunderts* (Berlin, 1882) [hereafter Hoeniger], p. 171. It is not as if the other plague tracts did not designate the positions of the apostemes: particularly towards the end, Sudhoff often included only incipits, fragments of texts, or often no texts at all.

With the earliest plague texts of 1348 (most prominently that of the Paris Medical Faculty), he held his own over Galen and all the Arabic doctors, but afterwards, by the second plague, he curiously fades from these medical texts until around 1450, when he enjoys a slight revival but only within the astrological sections of several plague tracts.[85]

According to Nancy Siraisi, the most important Italian doctor before the plague, Gentile da Foligno (who dies of plague in Perugia in 1348), 'showed himself a convinced Aristotelian, stressing the primacy of the heart . . . he made no mention of Galen's views on the role of the brain.'[86] Other early tracts of 1348 such as that of Magister Petrus de Amousis from Remis, composed two months after Gentile's first tract and two months before the Report of the Faculty of Medicine, as well as the poem by the Parisian doctor Simon de Couvin, show the same allegiance to Aristotle and his primacy of the heart.[87]

According to Siraisi, the debate over whether to follow Aristotle or Galen in the late Middle Ages turned on different notions of where disease originated in the body. In the Hippocratic–Galenic tradition, the body possessed three sources of life, whereas for Aristotle, there was only one— the heart.[88] Here, the plague experience appears vital to Aristotle's decline in the fourteenth and fifteenth centuries at least as far as medicine is concerned. The choice of theory lay with what the doctors were observing, and the system revealed by the plague experience was one of threes as opposed to a single source of life and death. After the first tracts of 1348,

---

[85] For this revival of Aristotle in the tracts, see *Il Libro della Pestilenza di Giovanni de Albertis da Capodistria (A.D. MCCCCL)*, ed. by Ugo Castiglioni in *Archeografo Triestino*, ser. III, 39 (1924), pp. 196–7; [78], p. 198; [109], p. 58; [193], p. 79; [238], p. 170; [282], p. 127; Ficino, *Consiglio contro la pestilenza*, p. 57; Alessandro Simili, 'Saladino Ferro da Ascoli', in *Atti e Memorie dell'Accademia di Storia dell'Arte Sanitaria*, 29 (1963), p. 37.

[86] Siraisi, *Taddeo Alderotti and his Pupils: Two Generations of Italian Medical Learning* (Princeton, N.J., 1981), p. 206; also see Coville, 'Écrits contemporains', p. 347. Roger French, 'Gentile da Foligno and the *via medicorum*', in *The Light of Nature*, ed. by J.D. North and J.J. Roche (Dordecht, 1985), pp. 21–34, has shown the influence of Galenic and Hippocratic medicine from Taddeo in the early fourteenth century to Gentile before the plague, but Gentile's plague tracts substantiate Siraisi's point: unlike authors of later tracts, he continued to rely heavily on Aristotle.

[87] Coville, 'Écrits contemporains,' pp. 328–33. Despite Gentile's call for practical cures and investigation (according to Ann Campbell), his text like that of the Paris Faculty and the doctor from Remis is heavily grounded in Aristotelian as opposed to Galenic ideas and is immersed in astrological theory. Coville (pp. 378–82) has shown the affinities between Gentile's tracts and the philosophical *Compendium of the Medical Faculty of Paris*, especially in contrast to Guy de Chauliac and later developments (pp. 347 and 357). Also see 'Opuscule relatif à la peste de 1348 composé par un contemporain', ed. by E. Littre, *Bibliothèque d'École des chartes*, II (1841), pp. 201–43. Another 1348 tract missed by Sudhoff, that of André Benedict, vicar of Narbonne, also stressed the alignment of the planets taken from Aristotle; see David Nirenberg, *Communities of Violence: Persecution of Minorities in the Middle Ages* (Princeton, 1996), p. 233.

[88] Siraisi, *Taddeo Alderotti*, pp. 187–9: 'In the thirteenth century Aristotle's teachings were often easier to come by than those of Galen and a growing body of authoritative opinion tended to favour Aristotle on the points where the two authors conflicted'.

Aristotle hardly appears in these manuals, while Galen and his Arabic successors—Avicenna, Rhazes (c. 860–c.925), and other Arabic followers—reign supreme. In two hundred plague tracts written before 1450 I have found only eight references to Aristotle; two of these appear in plague tracts written before the Black Death[89] and three in tracts written in 1348–50.[90] The same trajectory seems also to have been the case with French plague tracts not edited by Sudhoff. While Aristotle dominated the *Urtext* from the Paris Medical Faculty in 1348, Alfred Coville found that certain authors of plague tracts later in the fourteenth century—most significantly, Guy de Chauliac—relied instead on Galen and his Arabic successors, but Coville gives no explanation for the shift.[91]

While this three-part system was the general plan for bloodletting, other doctors still working within it located the plague boils in still other places—the stomach and often near or on the chest, unusual places for a plague boil in modern plague.[92] Indeed, one plague tract from the University of Prague written for the Emperor in the early fifteenth century saw the three zones of apostemes corresponding to the three *emunctoria* as 'first under the temples or behind the ears', 'second' on or near the chest, and 'third' in the armpits.[93] The usual place of the flea-injected modern plague—the groin—was not even mentioned. But, as we have said, the plague texts rarely described individual patients with the exact locations of their boil or boils. While these manuals may not have been so theory-driven as is often assumed, they were generally prescriptive rather than descriptive. One mentioned curing a plague boil in the groin of a certain nobleman;[94] another, actually an obituary, said his patron died with two boils, one in the groin, another in a unique place at least for modern bubonic plague—up the nose.[95] But from such infrequent references, as with the chronicles, a composite picture of the plague boils cannot be drawn. Are there other sources that were patient-specific in their descriptions of these 'signs' of the plague?

*   *   *

Saints' lives and miracle cures also described the plague, its signs, and symptoms. Like the chronicles, they referred to plagues in specific times and places. The life of Saint Cyriano mentions that plague struck Gaul in 251,

[89] [81], p. 214; Thorndike, 'A pest tractate before the Black Death', *Archiv für Geschichte der Medizin*, XXIII (1930), p. 349.

[90] [106], p. 44; and 'The Report of the Paris Medical Faculty, October 1348', in Rosemary Horrox, ed. and tr., *The Black Death* (Manchester, 1994) [hereafter, Horrox], p. 159.

[91] Coville, 'Écrits contemporains', p. 347: 'Les Arabes en particulier, bien qu'influencés par Galien, étaient la principale autorité pour la peste, et s'ils ont été peu cités dans le texte de la consultation des maîtres de Paris . . .'

[92] See [5], p. 393; [63], p. 74; [5bis], p. 76; [103 and 104], p. 161; [198], p. 106; [123], p. 3.

[93] [2bis], p. 58.

[94] [24], p. 53.

[95] [150], pp. 138–9.

although says nothing of its signs or symptoms.[96] The bishop and martyred saint, Emygdio, intervened twice to save Christians from plague, once in 566 when 'glandular plague overran almost the entire world and depopulated Italy', and again in 1038. But for the latter no hints are given about its signs or any other characteristics.[97] Similarly, plague struck in 1320, when Saint Wendelino bestowed immunity on the faithful, but his miracles give no clues of what this 'peste' might have been.[98]

Further, we learn from these lives that the European plague of the early 1370s also struck places as far away as Ethiopia, and like the European epidemic, had become a plague of children.[99] In a legend of John the Baptist, his ashes spread out like an umbrella over Genoa to guard against further plague casualties in 1358 (a plague year north of the Alps but not mentioned by the chroniclers or any other source for Genoa).[100] Another plague well known for France and Germany—that of 1438—apparently reached as far south as Foggia by 1439. According to a life of Saint Michael, it entered ports on the Gargano peninsula and spread 'by commerce' through the kingdom of Naples.[101]

Yet such information at the city or regional level occurs rarely in the lives as against the chronicles. Instead, the value of the lives for the historian of plague rests on the miraculous cures, which focused on individual plague patients. At times these come close to being case histories, giving the signs and symptoms of a disease and how long the patient suffered before being cured by devotion to a saint or a blessed one. With plague, often such last-minute hope came on the third day, the same time it took plague to kill, according to most chroniclers. Such was the case of a Portuguese girl who suffered from a serious plague boil (what 'the Greeks call an anthrax') along with 'inflamed spots (*inflammatuine*)' that formed on her neck and throat. Beatus Egidius cured her by bursting her boil, allowing 'all the virulent pus to erupt from it'.[102] The Blessed Giovanna of Signa (several kilometres west of Florence) miraculously cured a man from her village on the third day of his suffering from plague in 1366.[103] In the 1451 plague at Viterbo, a twenty-four-year-old man was near death on his third day when the Blessed Rosa intervened.[104]

[96] *Acta Sanctorum, Analecta bollandiana* (Paris, 1863–1983), 67 volumes [hereafter *AS*, followed by month, volume within month, and part within volume where applicable], Octobris, II, 1868, p. 25.

[97] *AS*, Augusti, II, pp. 23–4.

[98] *AS*, Octobris, IX, p. 350.

[99] *AS*, Novembris, IV (9–10), p. 255.

[100] *AS*, Junii ,V, p. 676.

[101] *AS*, Septembris, VIII, p. 68. It also struck Cairo in February 1438; *Arabic Annals of Abu L-Mahâsin Ibn Taghrî Birdî*, IV, p. 145.

[102] *AS*, Mai, III, p. 422.

[103] *AS*, Novembris, IV (9–10), p. 286.

[104] *AS*, Septembris, II, p. 456.

But others seemed to have lingered on their deathbeds for an unusual period for plague, whether of the medieval or modern variety. Just as Guy de Chauliac lay recovering from plague (by his own account) for six weeks, a victim of the Tuscan plague of 1383 had pestilential fever and boils for five weeks before Beata Giovanna of Signa saved him. More remarkable, a man cured by the Blessed Martyr Werheri (Varnerio) of Trier[105] suffered from 'deadly pestilential pustules' on his shin for 18 years.[106] The life does not give the date of this plague, and perhaps it was not plague at all. On the other hand, boils on the shins were not peculiar to this saint's miracle. In addition to works of art that showed them there, another adolescent was cured by the fourteenth-century saint Nicolai de Rupe Anachor with three plague ulcers on his shins,[107] and at least one chronicle spotted them (*glauces*) around the arms and on the shins[108]—unheard-of as a place of modern plague sores.

Because these miracles were essential for trials of canonization, they were often reported in detail and witnessed. In northern and central Italy, on occasion public notaries recorded these events, naming the relatives or friends who attested them.[109] During the plague of 1373 the little-known Blessed Giovanni or Giovannolo, a Franciscan tertiary from Cagli in the Papal States, who died around 1370,[110] cured a lady Clara then suffering from a high fever and two plague boils in her groin. The notary recorded those who had witnessed Clara on the point of death—her mother, father, and husband: 'with their own eyes and by word of mouth they attested' that Clara had prayed for the supplication of Jesus and had gone to the church where the blessed Giovannolo was buried and offered him the clothes in which her mother and other women had dressed her for her burial.[111] A notary also drew up the testimonies in the mid-fifteenth-century plagues at Viterbo.[112]

The pattern of these miracles was roughly the same from the earliest plague miracles during the Black Death to the long list of individuals of whom Saint Rosalia of Palermo cured at Messina in 1743.[113] They identified the plague sufferer, at times giving the age, profession, and *contrada* or

---

[105] *Bibliotheca Sanctorum*, ed. by Mons. Filippo Caraffa, Istituto Giovanni XXIII, 13 vols (Rome, 1961–9) (hereafter *BS*), XII, cols 956–7.

[106] *AS*, Aprilis, II (1866), pp. 724–5.

[107] *AS*, Martii, III (1865), pp. 435–6.

[108] *Annales Francofurtani*, p. 395.

[109] Many more of these notarised miracles might be found in notarial books. For instance J. Giovanni Ciappelli, 'A Trecento bishop as seen by Quattrocento Florentines: Sant'Andrea Corsini, his "Life", and the Battle of Anghiari', in *Portraits of Medieval and Renaissance Life*, ed. by S.K. Cohn and Steven Epstein (Ann Arbor, 1996), p. 291, finds a notarised miracle for this saint not uncovered in the *Acta*.

[110] *BS*, VI, p. 639.

[111] *AS*, Aprilis, II, p. 949.

[112] *AS*, Septembris, II, p. 456.

[113] *AS*, Septembris, II, pp. 412–14: 'Caput X: Praeter Panormitanos alii quoque Siculi ipsique Messanenses tempore pestis, anno 1743.'

parish of residence. They described the symptoms—almost invariably high pestilential fever, sometimes accompanied by headaches—and gave details of the 'signs'—the plague boils or ulcers—reporting their number and position. Inevitably, the miracle maintained that no medicine could cure the patient and the doctor or doctors (on occasion even named) had given up all hope.[114] The lives show a competition with, even hostility towards the medical profession and its hubris about secular cures. Thus a miracle of Peter the Confessor scoffed at a woman with a plague boil on her neck: she had spent so much money on doctors but 'had gained so little profit from it'.[115]

Once the doctor left the patient's bedside, the patient or a family member, often the mother, turned to extra-terrestrial remedies, would make a vow, such as promising that a stricken daughter would enter a monastery at a certain age if she recovered, or would make an offering, often a painting or a wax image to a local saint. Then the patient became well almost immediately, losing all signs of the former affliction. In the plague of 1435 at Viterbo, a girl had been disfigured by three plague ulcers (*pestiferis apostematibus*) in her face near an ear, but after Blessed Rosa's cure none of her cuts or scars remained. Later, the girl, no longer disfigured (*deturpata*), was able to marry and have a family, the saint's life tells us.[116] Only in one case did any sign remain from the former illness. Saint Nicholas de Rupe Anachor was able to remove only two of three plague ulcers on an adolescent, but the remaining one became benign.[117]

Unlike the chronicles' sweeping historical surveys and the doctors' recipes, the lives have an advantage: the historian can count the cases when the buboes were multiple and tabulate where they formed on the body. The lives also have drawbacks. First, they sometimes lack chronological clarity. Although almost invariably they occurred after the saint's death, how long afterwards is not always clear. Sometimes it could be centuries as with the Renaissance's most popular plague saint (at least in art), Sebastian, who died in the fourth century. Although already active in protecting Christians against plague in the time of Paul the Deacon (ninth century)—when 'a contagious plague' struck for the summer months of July, August, and September[118]—his miracles for curing individual plague victims multiply only 1300 years after his death, in the seventeenth century.[119]

For other saints the wait was not as long, but still the post-1348 plagues could revive a little-known Blessed one, giving a new lease on life in another

---

[114] A miracle of the Blessed Rosa reported that a Matteo from Castro Vitorchino near Viterbo had received treatment from a Magister Gentile of Viterbo for his pestilential fever and plague sores and ulcers (*ex quadam fistula seu apostemate*); AS, Septembris, II, p. 453.

[115] AS, Augusti, VI, p. 645.

[116] Ibid., p. 453.

[117] AS, Martii, III, pp. 435–6.

[118] AS, Januarii, II, p. 624.

[119] AS, Januarii, II, p. 762.

era, as with the thirteenth-century Blessed Rosa of Viterbo whose plague miracles come in the mid-fifteenth century or San Gimignano's Santa Fina (born in 1238), whose first plague miracle is not until 1631.[120] Nicolaus of Tolentino, who died in 1305, came into his own as a plague saint only with the plague in Cordova in 1601–2.[121] Thus it takes guesswork to know in which 'great plague' David of Wales intervened to protect his people from a disease that 'grew from England (Anglia) killing a large number of people'.[122] Nor would we know without further research into local documents (which might prove fruitless) when Santa Francesca Romana cured a certain Jacobus de Clarellis.[123] From the Bollandists' text, all we know is that her plague miracles occurred sometime after her death in 1440.[124] In this case, however, Jacobus de Clarellis of the Campitelli neighbourhood of the Roman nobility is sufficiently well known to establish that he was still alive in 1458.[125] Perhaps her miraculous intervention came in the Roman plague of 1450.

Second, miracles for plagues become numerous only in the sixteenth and seventeenth centuries. As in painting, curiously few saints appear active during the plague's most devastating attack between 1347 and 1351. The life of San Firenze records that Perugians processed through their city with his relics to ward off plague on 2 May 1348.[126] On 7 October 1349 the people of Hanover (Saxony) processed with the relics of Saint Waldetrude during this plague.[127] And in the same year, the ancient bishop Saint Remigius of Reims, who died around the beginning of the seventh century,[128] liberated his town 'from the universal plague', from its 'harsh pestilential fever, boils, and sores'.[129] However, the only miracle cure performed for an individual plague victim in 1348 occurs in the small market village of Signa. The town's Blessed Giovanna (born in 1307) saved a fellow villager suffering from a bubo (*malam bullam*) that had formed on his chest.[130]

Specifically dated cures during later plagues of the fourteenth century increase in number but remain rare, and the great majority of them come from central Italy. Giovanna of Signa continued to work on behalf of her villagers, healing a girl with a plague boil under her left breast in 1363, a man with plague fever and boils in 1366, another with plague fever and

[120] *AS*, Martii, II, p. 238.

[121] *AS*, Septembris, III, pp. 692–706.

[122] *AS*, Martii, I, p. 47.

[123] *AS*, Martii, II, p. 217.

[124] Also see *BS*, V, cols 1011–28.

[125] Teodoro Amayden, *La Storia delle famiglie romane* (Rome, 1914), I, p. 361.

[126] *AS*, Junii, I, pp. 33–4.

[127] *AS*, Aprilis, I, p. 828.

[128] *BS*, XI, pp. 104–13.

[129] *AS*, Octobris, I, p. 187.

[130] *AS*, Novembris, IV (9–10), p. 286. Little is known of this Giovanna; see *BS*, VI, p. 559.

boils saved on 10 August 1383. Finally, she cured a fourteen-year-old boy at Scarperia while he and his mother were crossing the Apennines from Bologna to Florence, no doubt fleeing the Bolognese plague of 1362.[131] As we have seen, John the Baptist's ashes protected Genoa from plague in 1358, and Giovannolo of Cagli cured Clara in the plague of 1373. The only non-Italian saint whose plague miracle was specifically dated for the latter half of the fourteenth century was the obscure ninth-century Saint Gauderico, the confessor, from Carcassone,[132] who intervened in the plague of 1384 to save the city of Perpignan, the region of Valencia (Cerdaniam), 'and many other places', protecting 'thousands of men and women who otherwise would have died'.[133] But his actions were on the societal not the individual plane.

Unlike surviving works of art, in which depictions of plague saints (principally Saint Sebastian) begin to increase by the early fifteenth century, the collection of saints' lives and miracle cures trace no sudden increase with the Renaissance, even in Italy. Moreover, all of the Quattrocento references to saintly interventions to protect against the plague come from a circumscribed geography, even narrower than the Trecento set. For the fifteenth century they appear almost exclusively between Rome and Florence. The life of San Bernardino of Siena tells of his heroic deeds at the hospital of Santa Maria della Scala during the plague of 1400.[134] As in 1348 San Firenze again enters the streets of Perugia to end the plague of 1400[135] and then fails to appear again until the plague of 1622, after which he regularly answered the Perugini's processional calls 'contra pestem'.[136] The life of Blessed Philippa the Virgin reports plague spreading to Rome with the Jubilee of 1450, lasting till 15 October 1451; afterwards, it spread to Milan in 1452.[137] From the miracles of San Bernardino a Fossa, plague peaks in Rome in June 1458.[138] The miracles of the Episcopal Saint Giovanni Taussiniani tell of 14,000 perishing in L'Aquila during the plague of 1476.[139] Other miracles report plague striking Florence in 1480.[140] Finally, the life of Blessed Columba of Rieti records a terrible plague that struck Perugia in 1494.[141] But on the level of individuals liberated from plague,

---

[131] *AS*, Novembris, IV (9–10), pp. 284–7.
[132] *BS*, VI, col. 65.
[133] *AS*, Octobris, VII.2, p. 1116. On the societal level, a few other saintly interventions occur, such as Peter the Bishop's protection of the region around Florence during the plague of 1373, seen in the *Life of Sant'Andrea of Fiesole*; *AS*, Januarii, III, p. 609.
[134] *AS*, Mai, V, p. 120.
[135] *AS*, Junii, I, pp. 33–4.
[136] *AS*, Junii, I, p. 38.
[137] *AS*, Octobris, VII, 1, p. 92.
[138] *AS*, Novembris, III, 5–8, p. 691.
[139] *AS*, Julii, V, p. 862.
[140] *AS*, Octobris, X, p. 889. According to Ficino, *Consiglio contro la pestilenza*, p. 109, this was the worst plague in Florence in over a hundred years.
[141] *AS*, Mai, V, p. 178.

Blessed Rosa was the exception. In fact, no comparable saint or blessed one can compete with her store of plague miracles before the seventeenth century, when Nicolaus of Tolentino transposed to Cordova combated the disease,[142] or later still when Santa Rosalia of Palermo made more interventions to relieve plague sufferers than any other saint, first throughout Sicily in the 1620s, then in 1743 with the Black Death's Italian finale at Messina.[143]

Rosa of Viterbo performed 82 miracles. Unlike other saints with such a large repertoire, she operated within a narrow geography and time span. Her miracles cluster in the middle decades of the fifteenth century and affected only those of her hometown and a few of its outlying hamlets. Again, unlike those of other saints, hers were exclusively of a medical nature, curing patients from leprosy, caduco (epilepsy), pontura (insect stings), phtysicus (tuberculosis), sciatica (a disease of the nervous system), paralysis, and snake bite, but her most numerous interventions (22 cases) cured plague, almost exclusively in Viterbo from 1449 to 1552.[144]

* * *

Before considering the distribution of plague swellings and spots for the later Middle Ages, let us turn to the much more voluminous evidence collected during the bubonic plague in and around Bombay City in 1896–97. Afterwards, no such collection of individual clinical histories remains (at least published). Of the 27 hospitals in and around Bombay City that submitted reports in 1896–97 to the army officer in charge, Brigadier-General Gatacre, seven classified their clinical data according to the positions and number of plague boils that formed on their patients.[145] Of 3752 plague patients admitted to these hospitals, 2883 (or 77 per cent) developed plague boils, 58 per cent of whom (1681) had them in the groin or on the thigh—significantly less than what *Manson's Tropical Diseases* continues to report as the norm (70 per cent) or what Yersin claimed to have found from his corpses in Hong Kong, 1894 (75 per cent).[146] While Manson, his successors, and Yersin have not tabulated or quantified the positions of the plague scars, their estimates may not have been out of line with other plagues. In Glasgow in 1900 (from a much smaller number of cases than in Bombay City) 72 per cent of the boils were in the region of the groin.[147] But despite these discrepancies, the groin was certainly the principal area of swelling with modern bubonic plague.

---

[142] *AS*, Septembris, III, pp. 700–6.

[143] *AS*, Septembris, II, pp. 320–413.

[144] *AS*, September, II, pp. 413–58.

[145] Gatacre, *Report on the Bubonic Plague in Bombay*.

[146] Both the first edition (1898, p. 157) and the most recent ones of *Manson's Tropical Diseases* (19th ed., p. 593), have reported that 70 per cent of the buboes form in the groin; for Yersin's figure, see 'La peste bubonique à Hong-Kong', p. 663.

[147] Chalmers, *Report on Certain Cases of Plague*, pp. 14–15, 43–56 and 65–6.

From the Bombay City records 660 or 23 per cent formed in the armpits (*axilla*), 399 or 14 per cent in the cervical region, and only 15 or 0.05 per cent elsewhere on the body. In only two cases, both from the hospital at Cutch, did the hospitals suggest anything close to what Boccaccio, Llywelyn Fychan, and numerous chroniclers and doctors described as normal from the Black Death to the early modern period—pustules or spots of various colours that spread all over the body. But even in these two cases, the doctors used the singular, 'Plague with "black blister" '.[148] In fact, in his editorial comments, Gatacre observed that 'true carbuncles were never met with any of the Parel patients'.[149] Nor was this a peculiarity of the first plague in Bombay City, 1896–97. No such spread of pustules is seen on any of the 36 hospitalised at Glasgow in 1900.[150] By 1935 *Manson's Tropical Diseases* observed that 'carbuncles' were extremely rare in cases of bubonic plague, but neither this edition nor later ones referred to a single case of such pustules after the London plague of 1665.[151]

In addition, multiple boils were also rare (even if they did occur). In 1896–97, the vast majority of patients with swellings had a single bubo (94 per cent).[152] From the much smaller number of cases at Glasgow in 1900, the proportion was higher, but still unusual; two of the 36 had multiple boils, and in one case, both were in the groin.[153]

Of patients miraculously cured by saintly intercessions in the fourteenth and fifteenth centuries our sample size is substantially smaller than the hospital reports from Bombay City. But despite their problems and number, the saints' lives provide more individual case histories of plague than any other source I know of for the later Middle Ages at least until 1450. Of 35 datable cases of individuals miraculously cured between 1348 and 1452, 27 were described as having swellings or other scars on the body and 22 with precise indications of where they formed. Of these, as with modern bubonic plague, the most usual place of the ulcers was either the groin or the thigh (9 of 22 cases), although less than would be expected from modern plague. But these differed from the inguinal swellings of modern bubonic plague in that two-thirds of saintly-cured swellings (6) were not in a major gland at all but on the thigh (*tibia*). At Bombay those in the groin outnumbered others in the femoral region by almost five to one, and seventeen to one in the

---

[148] Gatacre, *Report of the Bombay Plague Committee*, p. 145.
[149] Ibid., p. 58.
[150] *Report on Certain Cases of Plague.*
[151] *Manson's Tropical Diseases*, 10th ed., p. 254, and the 19th ed. (1986), p. 593. Also, Craven, 'Plague', p. 1307, maintains that viscular and pustular skin lesions occur rarely but cites no cases of them.
[152] The total number of buboes (2956) is greater than the number of patients with boils because of the multiple positions of buboes in 201 cases.
[153] *Report on Certain Cases of Plague*, pp. 14–15, 43–56 and 65–6.

Glasgow plague of 1900, where the only case of a femoral boil was on a rare patient with multiple boils.[154]

Perhaps the aesthetic prevailed over the anatomical. Or was it a matter of modesty? While a strong case might be made for such decorum in painting, it seems less plausible with words. As we have seen, 'inguinial' had even become a general term of the plague in Tuscany. Moreover, the saints' lives were often explicit about the problems that the position could pose especially for young girls. One of the miracles of the sixteenth-century Saint Francis Solanis concerned the young virgin Joanna Francisca Hurtado from Cordova (Montilia), who developed two buboes in her groin. 'Out of prudery' both she and her mother tried to conceal them. However, because of the disease's contagion, within a few days, two of their servants died and the others threatened to retaliate by burning all her household goods. With this household revolt brewing and the girl on her deathbed 'with burning fever and delirium', saint Francis answered her relatives' devotion and restored the girl to health.[155]

The distribution of boils between the late-medieval and modern samples differed further. In the saints' cures, few plague boils were reported in the armpits—only three, i.e. less than one in seven—as opposed to between a fifth and a fourth of all the boils seen in the modern plague. Moreover, 20 per cent or almost double the modern proportions were in the cervical region of the neck or behind the ears. But the most significant differences between the two epochs of bubonic plague lie with those boils that did not form in any principal gland and the prevalence of multiple swellings for the later Middle Ages. While 'the other' category, outside the three principal glands, from the Bombay City hospitals were extraordinarily rare, comprising half of one per cent, miraculously cured boils of the fourteenth- and fifteenth-century plagues formed in places such as on the face, on the shins, and under women's breasts with no counterpart at Bombay City or Glasgow. After the groin, those on or under the breasts or on the chest (*mamilla, pectore*) appear as the second most prominent area for the swellings (5 of the 22 cases). Equally strange for modern bubonic plague are the saintly-cured multiple boils and sores. While little over 5 per cent of the Bombay plague victims had more than one, nearly half of the late-medieval men and women (10) had them. Several counted three or more, and in one case they numbered as many as 18. Further, six of these miracles described patients with swellings or ulcers 'in many places all over the body'.

To be sure, plague miracle cures collected and dated specifically between

---

[154] Not all the hospitals broke down their counts by femoral/inguinal. Also, for Jain Hospital either the hospital or Gatacre reversed the data between inguinal and femoral, showing just the opposite ratio as reported by the other hospitals. At Glasgow the percentage of patients with plague boils in the inguinal and femoral regions was slightly higher than at Bombay: 18 of 25 patients with boils (72 per cent); *ibid.*, pp. 43–56 and 65–7.

[155] *AS*, Julii, V, p. 906.

1348 and 1500 in the Bollandists' collections of saints' lives provide a limited sample. Their number can be increased with undated miracles performed by saints who died before 1465 and for which the texts suggest that the cure took place between 1348 and 1500. The nine saints involved—Santa Francesca Romana (1384–1440); Nicholaus de Rupe, the Anchorite († 1310); Varnerio of Oberwesel († 1136); Peter the Confessor (thirteenth century); Isidore Agricolae (1080–1130); the Portuguese beatus Aegidio of the Dominican Tertiaries (Santarèm) (1184 or 1190–1265); Vincent Ferrier (1350–1419); Saint Stanislao, bishop of Krakow (1030 or 1035–1079); Saint Francis of Paola (1416–71); and Magdalena Albrica of Como (1430–65)—were born well after the plague of Justinian and thus would not have cured any from that earlier plague. Moreover, among the datable cases I have not encountered a single plague miracle that cured an individual as opposed to a protecting a city, region, or country before 1348. Further, with the sixteenth and seventeenth centuries, when these miracles become more prevalent, almost invariably they are dated.[156] For example when the miracles of the eleventh-century Stanislao of Krakow reached the seventeenth century, they are consistently tied to specific plague years.

These saints cured 21 plague victims: for 16 the plague sores were described and for 14 the places where they formed on the body. While again limited, these descriptions are suggestive and match even less well than the datable cures the signs of modern plague. Only three of these miraculously cured victims had their swellings in the groin, and one of them also had a boil on the neck. Further, only one boil was spotted in the underarms. Instead, their swellings clustered on the neck and throat (nine cases, or two-thirds of the total), giving an impression similar to that of the authors of plague tracts. Again, the sores also crop up in strange places as far as modern plague goes—on the shins and the upper part of the throat (*fauces*).[157] Finally, multiple plague boils were even more common with this set of miracles. Of the 16 cases, only four had a single boil.

In closing, I turn to a source that may be unique for the later Middle Ages if not for plague history until the eighteenth century. It is the chance survival of a two-page insert (*cedole*) found in the diary of the fourteenth-century Lucchese doctor, Ser Iacopo di Coluccino.[158] It charts seven cases, all from just two families, describing the doctor's twice-daily visits to his patients during plague in Lucca in 1373. It includes the signs, symptoms, and days of illness before his patients died or recovered, and documents the treatments he administered. From May to November four were of the pneumonic form, which Iacopo commented were the 'most contagious' that could not be cured 'for love or money', and three showed cutaneous signs

---

[156] The one exception that I have found were miracles of the Spanish Saint Francis Solanis.
[157] *AS*, Aprilis, II, pp. 724–5; and Martii, III, pp. 435–6.
[158] *Il Memoriale di Iacopo di Coluccino*, 55–428; the cedole is on page 397.

that he called a 'male' or 'infiato'. In all three, the 'evil' was found on the neck or under an ear—not in the groin or armpits.

For more than a century,[159] historians and doctors have connected the Black Death and successive waves of medieval and early modern bubonic plague with the disease that broke out in Yunnan in the 1850s, spread to Hong Kong in 1894, then to Bombay and across to ports world-round by the first decade of the twentieth century. Their evidence for this identity has rested largely on the 'signs' of the plague taken from a handful of well-known late-medieval authors. 'After five centuries', should we remain 'reasonably comfortable' with the identity of the two as the same, as historians continue to instruct? Our examination of hundreds of chronicles, plague tracts, and saints' lives and their comparison with the signs of modern plague shows that we should not: the signs of the two diverged on one crucial count after another.

Even the most cited text on the Black Death, Boccaccio's *Decameron*, is far from being the iron-clad testimony for cutaneous identity across the centuries: after the 'gavòccioli', Boccaccio recorded buboes and then their spread along with black pustules over the entire body. Nor was his description unique, or the Black Death's first appearance a radical departure from the 'normal' signs of the disease once it became established. Other contemporary texts—chronicles, plague tracts, saints' lives, and poetry—attest to the persistence of these pustules' spread, sometimes before, sometimes after, sometimes concurrently with the swellings as big as goose eggs. Further, the medieval plague boil was neither singular, as in 94 per cent of the cases with modern plague, nor located predominantly in the groin as happens with the flea-conveyed modern plague. Instead, they often formed under the breasts, on the shins, the face and even up the nose—places not mentioned in the 3000-plus cases reported from hospitals around Bombay City during the plague years 1896–97. Mostly, these late-medieval sores formed higher up the body than those that characterise modern bubonic plague, in the cervical region, higher than a flea can possibly jump. To keep the paradigm, should we hypothesise that medieval men and women were more supine than modern Indians or Glaswegians?

Historians have cast rats and fleas as the protagonists (or antagonists) of Western civilization. Many have argued that the mid-fourteenth-century depopulation of Europe ended serfdom and gave rise to the yeomanry in England, changed class structure on the continent, was responsible for the rise of literacy and vernacular literatures, for changing the course of the Hundred Years War and English European dominance, for the

---

[159] We might even extend this identification back to I.F.C. Hecker, *The Black Death in the Fourteenth Century*, tr. by B.G. Babington (London, 1833; orig., 1832), p. 20, who maintained that the Black Death possessed 'all the symptoms of the oriental plague which have been observed in more modern times'.

Reformation, and even modernity itself.[160] Of course, evidence for these actors cannot be found in any archives or, for that matter, in any narrative source. As for the absence of rats associated with the medieval plague, historians have asked us to believe that their ubiquity made them invisible, even though they were noticed in moments other than plague. For the terrible siege of Rouen in 1418, the English chronicle of Henry V even distinguished between rats and mice, claiming that hunger led to the besieged eating 'alle thair cattis, hors, houndis, rattis, myse'.[161] The Ferrarese chronicler Delayto saw field mice in the early fifteenth century when they damaged the planting of grain.[162] The chronicler of the monastery of Zwiweltum reported mice [*mures*] running wild in 1434, counting 600 that were killed in a single field. But these were not descriptions of rat epizootics. No plague followed these rats' strange appearance as happened periodically in plague in subtropical zones and was duly observed and feared by native peoples before and after the discovery of *Yersinia pestis*.[163] Even for late-medieval Egypt, chroniclers described and counted the rats officials killed because of the damage to crops, but their increase was not associated with plague; nor did they flare up in plague years.[164]

For that other protagonist of Western civilization, the flea, more than simply the absence of evidence, the place of the medieval plague boils tells against its vital importance in the transmission of the late-medieval plagues. As we shall see, climate and other epidemiological considerations will speak even more loudly against its likelihood in fulfilling the role historians, entomologists, and other scientists have placed on it during the later Middle Ages.

---

[160] See G.G. Coulton, *The Black Death* (London, 1928); Gottfried, *The Black Death*; Herlihy, *The Black Death*; Giovanni Berlinguer, *Le mie pulci* (Rome, 1988); and Cantor, *In the Wake of the Plague*, pp. 203–8 and 218.

[161] *English Chronicle of the Reigns of Richard II*, p. 47.

[162] Corradi, *Annali delle epidemie*, I, p. 248.

[163] The next reported plague in Germany was not until 1439; *Annales Zwifaltenses*, p. 63.

[164] See the numerous examples in Hassanein Rabie, 'Some technical aspects of agriculture in medieval Egypt', *The Islamic Middle East, 700–1900: Studies in Economic and Social History* (Princeton, 1981), pp. 79–80.

|5|

Symptoms

To claim that the Black Death and modern plague were the same, some have gone beyond the bubo to descriptions of symptoms. These vary enormously. While the saints' lives often described in great detail glandular swellings and other cutaneous signs, they say less about the symptoms, reporting only headaches (*dolorem capitis*), 'atrocious pain', great or burning fevers, and on occasion an odd stench—all of which could be associated with bubonic plague but certainly are not peculiar to it, and in the case of extreme pain or consistently high fevers it was not even usual. In addition, the saints' lives report another symptom not described by the Bombay Plague Committee, the Glasgow Plague reports, the later Indian Plague Commission, or any other description of the symptomology of plague that I have found. At least three plague miracles described swellings on the throat that made their victims unable to swallow, eat, or drink.[1]

The chroniclers also described plague symptoms and on occasion in greater detail. Perhaps most famous (and longest) of these is that of the Piacentine lawyer Gabriele de' Mussis:

> For the rest, so that the conditions, causes, and symptoms of this pestilential disease should be made plain to all, I have decided to set them out in writing. Those of both sexes who were in health, and in no fear of death, were struck by four savage blows to the flesh. First, out of the blue, a kind of chilly stiffness troubled their bodies. They felt a tingling sensation, as if they were being pricked by the points of arrows. The next stage was a fearsome attack which took the form of an extremely hard, solid boil . . . As it grew more solid, its burning heat caused the patients to fall into an acute and putrid fever, with severe headaches. As it intensified, its extreme bitterness could have various effects. In some cases it gave rise to an intolerable stench. In others it brought

---

[1] *AS*, Septembris, II, pp. 453 and 454; and Mai, II, p. 243.

spitting of blood, for others, swellings near the place from which the corrupt humours had arisen—on the back, across the chest, near the thigh. Some people lay as if in a drunken stupor and could not be roused. Behold the swellings, the warning signs sent by the Lord. All these people were in danger of dying. Some died on the very day the illness took possession of them, others on the next day, others—the majority—between the third and fifth day. There was no remedy for the vomiting of blood. Those who fell into a coma, or suffered a swelling or the stench of corruption, very rarely escaped. But from the fever it was sometimes possible to make a recovery.[2]

Few were as precise about the clinical course of the disease or the succession of symptoms, and Gabriele was unique in describing that 'some people lay as if in a drunken stupor and could not be roused', which is common to modern bubonic plague. The only other source to report a similar progression towards death was the Calendar of Würtemburg: in 1349 the victims in Vienna died 'almost sleeping and with a great stench gently eased into death'.[3] In the myriad descriptions by the doctors, none mentioned this drunken stupor or the blank look that was doctors' first and most enduring impression of plague patients in India at the end of the nineteenth century.[4]

Descriptions of plague symptoms were also rare among the chroniclers, rarer even than their reports of the plague scars, and became less frequent with successive waves of plague. As with descriptions of plague swellings, those of symptoms were less common still outside of Italy. Only three of 45 English chroniclers gave any hint of the pestilential sores, and not a single one went beyond these signs to describe the plague's symptoms. Not even Geoffrey le Baker, who described in detail the plague's spread through Britain, its passage from the English to the Welsh and Scots, and eventually into Ireland, conveyed any sense of the disease's character other than mentioning boils and spots.[5]

Moreover, chronicles on the continent beyond the Alps reported and elaborated on the symptoms of plague less often and generally in less detail than that found in saints' lives. The Calendar of Würtenburg and an Annal from Frankfurt described pain 'around the head or in other places in the body' of those who fell to the plague in 1356.[6] The Chronicle of the monastery of Saint-Denis said plague victims in 1419 suffered 'severe headaches'.[7] A

---

[2] Horrox, pp. 24–5. I have made a few minor changes such as 'spitting' as opposed to 'vomitting' for 'sputum ex ore sanguineum'; text in Haeser, pp. 160–1.
[3] *Kalendarium Zwetlense*, IX, p. 692: 'et quasi dormiendo et cum magno fetore leniter decesserunt'.
[4] Gatacre, *Report on Bombay Plague in Bombay*, pp. 55–6. The Byzantine emperor, Cantacuzenos comes the closest, describing the victims as suffering from speechlessness and insensibility to all happenings'; Bartsocas, 'Two fourteenth-century Greek descriptions', p. 396.
[5] *Chronicon Galfridi le Baker*, pp. 98–9.
[6] *Annales Francofurtani*, pp. 394–5.
[7] *Chronique du religieux de Saint–Denys*, VI, pp. 269–73.

monastic chronicle from Southern Austria was one of the few outside of Italy to allude to the two forms of the plague—bubonic and pulmonary—describing ulcers and spots that formed around the genitalia along with the excretion of blood, in which case 'there was no hope of survival'. But it is not clear whether the blood exuded from the sores or from coughing.[8]

Outside Italy texts that clearly distinguished between a pulmonary and bubonic form of the plague were much rarer than historians have led us to believe. The letter from Petrarch's friend Socrates (Louis Sanctus de Beringen) was exceptional. He described three forms, but these hardly conform to modern plague's triplex variety—bubonic, pneumonic, and septicaemic—as the historian Étienne Fournial has asserted:[9]

> With the first form victims suffered in the lungs . . . no one could escape it and no one lived beyond two days. According to autopsies made by doctors in many cities in Italy and in Avignon, those who died suddenly were found with infected lungs and with the spitting of blood. Concurrent with this illness was a second from which ulcers arose suddenly under both arms and from which people died without delay. The third form was also concurrent with the previous two in which those of both sexes suffered in the groin and died suddenly.[10]

But Louis belonged to the international Italianate intellectual culture of mid-fourteenth-century papal Avignon and only a handful of other northerners pointed to pulmonary complications. For plague in Ireland, the Franciscan friar of Kilkenny, John Clyn, said 'many died with spots, boils, abscesses, and pustules that appeared on the legs and in the armpits; others had headaches that led to almost a total frenzy, and others spat blood'.[11] A chronicle of Novgorod described the first plague in Russia (1352) only in pneumonic terms[12] but described plague in 1424 'with glands and spitting blood'.[13]

Finally, a chronicler of an Olivetan abbot from northeastern Europe (Pomerania) described the plague's symptoms in much the same terms as those found in Louis Sanctus' letter. In fact, its modern editor concludes that the abbot copied Louis: the first form was infection in the lungs with the spitting of blood, from which none survived, all dying within three days; the second, with swellings under the arms, and the third, in the groin.[14]

---

[8] *Codex Novimontibus*, p. 675.

[9] Fournial, *Les villes et l'économie d'échange en Forez aux XIIIe et XIVe siècle* (Paris, 1967), p. 302: bubonic, pulmonary, and infection of the intestines. Somehow a plague boil in the groin, the most common position with modern bubonic plague is interpreted to mean 'infection of the intestines'.

[10] Sanctus, p. 466.

[11] *Annalium Hiberniae*, p. 36. In addition, the connection between Avignon and the Irish mendicants was also strong in the middle of the fourteenth century; see Aubrey Gwynn, 'The sermon–diary of Richard FitzRalph, Archbishop of Armagh', in *Proceedings of the Royal Irish Academy*, 44 (1937–8), Section C, pp. 2–66.

[12] *The Chronicle of Novgorod*, p. 145.

[13] Ibid., p. 191.

[14] *Chronica Olivensis auctore Stanislao*, p. 345.

These remarks came in the Olivetan's chapter 69 on the plague's general characteristics. When it invaded his own region the following year and three chapters later, he described no signs or symptoms.[15]

On the other hand, plague tracts commonly described the symptoms, often adding traits not seen in chronicles. The tract of the northern Italian doctor Colle from Belluno (1350) listed a long string of symptoms: 'great thirst, black and acidic tongue, anxiety, pain in the intestines, hyper-ventilation, coughing and spitting of various fluids, with the mouth always open, tumultuous delirium, rage, swirling urine that often appears black, black excrement, swarthy complexion (*adustus*), melancolic and wild countenance, black exanthema, spots and demonic buboes that spread over the body'[16]. A plague tract from Prague written in 1416 listed six 'signs': 'First, the urine is very red; second the plague patient refuses to eat; third, he does not seek out quiet places; fourth, his stomach is filled with fluids; fifth, he sweats; sixth; he coughs and spits.'[17] With the plague tracts, however, it is not always clear whether they are describing general symptoms of diseases or those particular to plague. The report from the Medical Faculty at Prague in the early fifteenth century suggests that on occasion these symptomologies were larger amalgams of epidemic diseases, not limited to the bubonic plagues of their own immediate experience: as signs of plague, the report listed 'fevers, ulcers, pustules, scabies, vomiting, coughing, headaches, pain in the throat, paralysis, gout in the feet (*podagra*), and other illnesses as common to the pestilences and epidemics that occur in the autumn'.[18]

Moreover, some wished to draw universal lessons across time and combined other maladies such as 'de herespipei', Saint Anthony's disease, 'de variola' (smallpox), and 'morbillo' (measles) in their discussion of plague.[19] Still others specialised in urine, interpreting it variously according to colour and viscosity.[20] Some described shortness of breath with a slow pulse; others claimed that the pulse sped up.[21] To be sure, the doctors were not always referring to the same disease. At the end of the fifteenth century, a doctor from Rouen who also practised in London described patients 'with a raging pestilential fever and continuous heat and sweating for twelve hours' before dying. Most likely this was a new disease of northern France and England—the sweats.[22]

More often than the chroniclers, doctors observed the pneumonic

---

[15] Ibid., p. 347.
[16] 'Ex libro vetusto Dionysii Secundi Colle', in Haeser, p. 169.
[17] [63], p. 75.
[18] [98], p. 121.
[19] [260], p. 49; [161], p. 158; *Practica Antonii Guainerii*, pp. 97v, 106v, 107r, and 111r; *Il Libro della Pestilenza di Giovanni de Albertis*, p. 198; [107], p. 52; [116], p. 125.
[20] See for instance, [123], pp. 1–2.
[21] See [177], p. 24.
[22] [267 and 268], p. 95.

complications of their plague. The most important of these tracts both for the subsequent practice of medicine and for what recent historians have concluded about the Black Death comes from Guy de Chauliac, physician to three popes in Avignon—Clement VI, Innocent VI, and Urban V—and witness to three plagues, 1348, 1358, and 1361. His was more than a plague tract. Completed soon after the second plague in Avignon of 1361, it was a textbook on surgery, *Chiurgia magna*, which remained the most important of its genre until Ambroise Paré's text of 1561.[23] Guy's had a vast manuscript tradition and 69 printed editions between 1478 and 1895.[24]

Guy's discussion of plague falls within a larger consideration of diseases with skin disorders or 'apostemes'. But with plague itself his rigorous and controlled order for discussing diseases is momentarily interrupted; for the only time in this long textbook he reflects historically, recounts his own experiences, and draws moral lessons:

> The plague (*mortalitas*) began with us in January and lasted seven months. It had two phases (*modos*). The first was for two months with continuous fever and the spitting of blood, from which victims died within three days. The second phase lasted for the remainder of the period and patients also had continuous fevers. In addition, abscesses (*apostema*) and carbuncles (*anthracitis*) formed in their extremities, namely in the armpits and the groin. And these patients died within five days. The disease was extremely contagious, especially with the spitting of blood, so that one caught it from another, not only through close proximity but also through receiving a glance from another. As a consequence, people died without assistance and were buried without priests.[25]

Historians have seen in this description the two principal forms of plague, pneumonic followed by bubonic.[26] Moreover, to account for the plague's much more deadly sweep in 1348, when communities lost upwards of two-thirds or more of their populations, historians have relied on Guy to maintain that it was the supposedly more deadly pneumonic phase that explains the vast differences in contagion and mortalities between the late-medieval and modern plagues, when no city has lost more than 3 per cent of its population in any plague year.[27]

Emmanuel Le Roy Ladurie has gone further, concluding that the plague's highest mortalities were reaped in southern regions where it first exploded

---

[23] Sarton, *Introduction to the History of Science*, III, p. 1691. Still the most complete edition of this work is *La grande Chirugie de Guy de Chauliac*, ed. by E. Nicaise (Paris, 1890).

[24] Henri Stein, 'Comment on luttait autrefois contre les épidémies,' *Annuaire-Bulletin de la Société de l'histoire de France*, LV (1918), p. 130; and Marcellin Boudet and Roger Grand, *Étude historique sur les épidémies de peste en Haute-Auvergne (XIVe–XVIIIe siècles)* (Paris, 1902), p. 25.

[25] Guy de Chauliac, *Chirugia*, Tract. II, cap. 5, in Haeser, pp. 175–6.

[26] Most recently, see Brossollet and Mollaret, *Pourquoi la peste?*, p. 51.

[27] Such judgments are not only confined to medievalists; modern historians of the plague have pointed to the earlier pneumonic character of the late-medieval plagues in general to account for the differences in mortalities; see Catanach, 'Plague and the tensions of empire', p. 157.

in the winter and supposedly in its pneumonic form; as it moved north-ward, hitting in the summer, supposedly it switched to its bubonic form with less ferocity, milder contagion, and fewer mortalities.[28] His argument rests on three points of comparison—Avignon, where the chroniclers describe the plague's mortality as catastrophic, the region of Forez, several hundred kilometres to the north, where last wills and testaments suggest that between 20 and 33 per cent of the population died, and Paris, where Le Roy Ladurie asserts that plague only scratched the city.[29]

First, his argument is counter-intuitive: why would pneumonic plague have been more ferocious in the warmer Mediterranean than in the colder north? In modern times, pneumonic plague has reached epidemic propor-tions only in cold Siberian winters. Second, were the cities of the Mediterranean hit solely or even primarily during the winter months? For places where we possess quantitative materials for 1348, nowhere in the Mediterranean or elsewhere did plague peak in winter. Marseilles was an odd case out, the only Mediterranean city, where (at least according to wills) plague peaked before summer, but even here its apex was in March.[30] For other Mediterranean cities and their regions—Barcelona, Millau, Florence, Bologna, Perugia, Arezzo, Siena, and Rome—plague was a summer event, peaking at the hottest point of the year, either in June or July.[31] Nonetheless, plague was certainly severe in these regions. According to Louis Sanctus de Beringen (Flanders), Tuscany was one of the hardest hit regions of Europe.[32]The merchant Giovanni Morelli estimated that 80,000 souls perished in 1348 in a city that had counted 120,000.[33]

Moreover, benefices vacant because of death were higher in the dioceses of Barcelona during the Black Death of 1348–49 than in any place yet exposed to this type of analysis, with more than 60 per cent perishing from May 1348 to April 1349. Not a single benefice became vacant because of the death of a clergyman during the winter months of January and February 1348; the numbers rise sharply only in June (with 25 deaths) and peak in July (104). The plague then may have lingered into the winter months of 1349 but deaths had declined to less than 15 per cent of what they had been in June.[34]

It is unfortunate that we do not possess quantitative sources for ports

---

[28] Le Roy Ladurie, 'A concept', pp. 51–9.

[29] Ibid., p. 57, based on Coville, 'Écrits contemporains', p. 390. Le Roy Ladurie ignores Coville's remarks that the plague was particularly ferocious in certain areas of Normandy.

[30] Francine Michaud, 'La peste, la peur et l'espoir: Le pélerinage jubilaire de romeux marseil-lais en 1350', *Le Moyen Age*, 3–4 (1998), p. 408.

[31] For an elaboration on this data see chapters 6 and 7.

[32] Sanctus, p. 465.

[33] Morelli, *Ricordi*, p. 209. Stefani and Boccaccio claimed the death toll of 1348 was greater: 96,000 and 100,000 respectively.

[34] Richard Gyug, 'The effects and extent of the Black Death of 1348: new evidence for cleri-cal mortality in Barcelona', *Medieval Studies*, XLV (1983): 385–98; idem, *The Diocese of Barcelona during the Black Death: register Notule Comunium (1348–49)* (Toronto, 1994).

such as Messina, Genoa, or Pisa, where the plague struck earlier, either in the fall of 1347 or the winter of 1348 or other places such as Trapani said to have been 'totally uninhabited' after the plague.[35] But none of the narrative sources, including Guy de Chauliac's for Avignon, state that the plague peaked in the winter under its pneumonic form. Furthermore, the plague's seasonality in these Mediterranean cities was not exceptional to 1348 as many historians have speculated: supposedly, an usually cool and wet summer in 1348 made possible a summer pneumonic plague.[36] As we will see, the plague in Italy recurred through its first hundred years and probably to the seventeenth century[37] with remarkable consistency during the hottest months of the year—June and July. In terms of the seasonality, 1348 was not a freak experience.

Le Roy Ladurie's second point of comparison—Forez—where supposedly the plague's lethality was in decline because the bubonic now began to predominate over the pneumonic—is also problematic. In this region, plague stretched into the winter months of December 1348 to February 1349 (according to the wills), but it was in the winter, not the summer, that its virulence softened and was more devastating in the warmer plains than in the cooler mountains.[38]

Finally, Le Roy Ladurie's claims that the plague's force weakened further by the time it reached the north and that Paris was merely grazed is less tenable still. What is his source? Perhaps it derives from the chronicler Jean de Venette, who said that in Paris 'many houses, including some splendid dwellings, very soon fell into ruins . . . though fewer here than elsewhere.'[39] But this was a comment about buildings, not people. In fact, Venette first singles out Paris, where 'the mortality . . . was so great that it was almost impossible to bury the dead'.[40] Other chroniclers, from France and elsewhere, saw Paris as one of the worst hit cities. The *Grandes Chroniques* of France noted that 800 people died in the capital 'from one day to the next, adding up to more than 50,000'.[41] Richard the Scot gave the same estimate[42] and an anonymous chronicler of Bologna described the plague's carnage across the Alps in one place alone, Paris, where 'according to his merchant reports, 1328 were buried in one day'.[43] For a chronicler of

[35] *Cronica B*, p. 584; *Storie Pistoresi*, p. 235; *Historia Miscella Bononiensis*, col. 409; *Polyhistoria fratris Bartholomæi Ferrariensis*, col. 806.

[36] See Herlihy, *Medieval and Renaissance Pistoia*, p. 108; and Le Roy Ladurie, 'A concept', p. 51.

[37] Cipolla, *Miasmas and Disease*, p. 5.

[38] Fournial, *Les villes et l'économie d'échange en Forez*, pp. 304–7.

[39] *Chronique latine de Guillaume de Nangis (Continuatio)*, II, p. 210.

[40] Ibid., p. 49.

[41] *Les grandes chroniques de France*, IX, p. 315.

[42] *Chronique de Richard Lescot*, p. 82.

[43] Cronaca B, p. 587; *Polyhistoria fratris Bartholomæi Ferrariensis*, col. 807, maintained the same.

Pistoia, Paris's monumental mortalities soared still higher: on 13 March, '1573 noblemen were buried, not counting the others of petty affairs'. Like the Bolognese, the Pistoiese cited death figures outside his own region only for Paris, because of its remarkable toll.[44]

In addition, physical evidence tells against any soft landing for Paris: towards February 1349 its largest cemetery, that of the Innocents, had reached its capacity and was closed.[45] Finally, Le Roy Ladurie ignores completely the most authoritative source of Paris's Black Death mortality— the soaring of testamentary gifts to the Parisian parish church of Saint-Germain-l'Auxerrois. Testaments rocketed from an average of five a year to 445 from June 1348 to March 1349, a 45-fold increase, which was as extraordinary as any testamentary evidence for any Mediterranean city.[46] Nor is there any reason to think that the plague's force declined as it moved still further north to Britain. Manorial rolls in Winchester, Cambridgeshire, and County Durham attest that upwards of 70 per cent of the tenants, both customary and free, died in the plague of 1349 in certain villages and town-ships.[47] I know of no quantitative evidence to show as high death counts anywhere in the Mediterranean.

Le Roy Ladurie speculates further that while the first outbreak of plague was mainly pneumonic (at least in the Mediterranean) it became wholly bubonic in the waves that followed. Again, he supplies no evidence. The most graphic descriptions of the buboes, gavòccioli, and the like, however, come from observers of the first plague and, as we have seen, from places where plague wreaked some of its heaviest casaulties. Further, chroniclers such as Johannes de' Mussis described the second plague in Piacenza (1361) in much the same terms as Guy de Chauliac used for the first strike, except that for Johannes the plague had three deadly forms instead of two: coagulations under the skin in the armpits and groin, pustules and ulcers around the head or under the ears, and the spitting of putrid blood, which was the worst sign.[48] A chronicle of Pisa continued to describe the combination of swellings (*di anguinaja, di ditelle, di male bolle, di faoni*) and spitting of blood for the fourth plague in 1383.[49] In addition, plague tracts written after 1348 and into the fifteenth century directed doctors' attention to the various forms of plague in which apostemes and other skin defects were mixed with

---

[44] *Annales Pistorienses*, col. 524.
[45] 'La Messe pour la peste', ed. by Jules Viard, *Bibliothèque de l'École des Chartes*, LXI (1900), p. 335.
[46] Michel Mollat, 'Note sur la mortalité à Paris au temps de la Peste Noire d'après les comptes de l'œuvre de Saint-Germain-l'Auxerrois', *Le Moyen Age*, LXIX (1963): 505–27, esp. p. 509.
[47] J.Z. Titow, *English Rural Society 1200–1350* (London, 1969), pp. 69–71; F.M. Page, *The Estates of Crowland Abbey* (Cambridge, 1934), pp. 120–5; and Richard Lomas, 'The Black Death in County Durham', *Journal of Medieval History*, XV (1989), pp. 129–30.
[48] *Chronicon Placentinum*, cols 506–7.
[49] Corradi, *Annali delle epidemie*, I, pp. 232–3.

pulmonary disorders.[50] In the correspondence preserved in the company archives of Francesco di Marco Datini from Prato, merchants in Avignon as late as the plague of 1398–99 described plague patients with boils that burst after four days and who also spat blood.[51]

Finally, the seven patients of the Lucchese doctor Ser Iacopo di Coluccino suggest a pattern nearly the opposite of what Le Roy Ladurie has claimed. In the third wave of plague, 1373, more (4) had the deadlier pulmonary form of plague, characterised by coughing and the spitting of blood, than had the bubonic. Furthermore, these pneumonic cases did not coincide with winter; rather they sprung up in May or slightly thereafter. If any came with colder weather, they were the three bubonic cases, which continued as late as November.[52]

* * * *

Let us return to the key text for arguments about the plague's particular duality—that of Guy de Chauliac. First, neither Guy nor any other contemporary claimed that the highest mortalities from the plague of 1348 or later came in the winter or from the pulmonary form of plague. To be sure, Guy, the Lucchese doctor Ser Iacopo, and others such Johannes de' Mussis saw the pneumonic as the deadlier sort and Louis Sanctus, the Olivetan from Pomerania, and others including Guy saw it as the more contagious and lethal of the two. For Louis the pneumonic took only two days to kill and 'no one survived'.[53] Similarly, the Egyptian chronicler Maqrīzī said the form with coughing 'took a maximum of 50 hours to kill once the coughing began'.[54] Yet diseases that kill the quickest are not necessarily the ones with the highest mortalities. As with Ebola today, some bacteria or viruses kill too quickly for their own good; their hosts die before the microbe can spread efficiently through a population.

In fact, medieval plague in its pneumonic form took longer to kill by these accounts than modern pneumonic plague. With modern plague, death occurs in as little as sixteen hours and the septicaemic with even less time.[55] While Guy recorded three days for victims in 1348 to die from the pneumonic form, Ser Iacopo's patients with the spitting of blood staggered on for four or five days after coming to the doctor for care. For the 1424

---

[50] [47], p. 338; [63], p. 75; [230], p. 155; [262], p. 63; Corradi, *Annali delle epidemie*, I, p. 275; [116], p. 125.
[51] My information on the Datini archival correspondence comes from an unpublished list of descriptions of plague drawn up by Jérôme Hayez, 'Quelques témoignages sur les épidémies à Avignon, 2e moitié XIVe siècle.' I wish to thank Docteur Hayez for giving me his list.
[52] *Il Memoriale di Iacopo di Coluccino*, p. 397.
[53] Sanctus, pp. 465–9.
[54] Maqrīzī, *Sulūk*, p. 370.
[55] See *Manson's Tropical Diseases*, 20th ed., p. 920.

pneumonic plague in Rome and Tiburtina, in which no glandular pains or boils appeared, patients took from five to eight days to die.[56]

Of course, the virulence of the bacillus may have weakened with successive waves of plague. Yet, despite a steady decline in plague mortalities over the fourteenth and fifteenth centuries (as we shall show), the bacillus (whatever it was) does not appear to have flagged with later plagues. Given the reported number of days it took to kill, it may have even become more virulent. A Florentine chronicler reported that in the plague of 1363, patients died in only ten hours after the deadly 'gavòcciolo' appeared on their bodies.[57] In the business correspondence between Datini's agents in Tuscany and Avignon, merchants continued to distinguish the plague by the rapidity of death. In the 1384 plague at Avignon, the victims died within a day-and-a-half. Yet at the height of this fourth plague, merchants reported 50 to 60, and not thousands as reported in 1348, being buried a day in Avignon.[58] Even doctors of later plagues as optimistic about their remedies as John of Burgundy insisted that treatment must begin immediately, within six hours of the first signs; after 24 hours, hope was lost.

On the other hand, while Guy de Chauliac's description of the two forms of plague is certainly not unique—some contemporaries even called the plague 'the death of swellings and the spitting of blood'[59]—it is alone in establishing a distinct seasonality separating the two forms, a winter or early spring pulmonary type followed by a summer bubonic phase. The only other commentator whose testimony survives from Avignon in 1348 contradicts the papal doctor. Louis Sanctus claimed that the three forms of the plague—the pulmonary, the bubonic in the armpits, and the bubonic in the groin—were all concurrent.

Other than the near word-for-word copying of Guy de Chauliac by the chronicler Joannis Dlugossii, a canon of Krakow,[60] the closest approximation to Guy's description of a seasonal succession of the plague forms comes from the Egyptian chronicler Maqrīzī, but his succession was the opposite of Guy's and without necessary seasonality. Maqrīzī said that first the spots and tumours formed on victims in Damascus then the 'coughing and vomiting of blood' followed 'sometime later'.[61] The Florentine Matteo Villani also saw a succession from one form to the other, but his was a geographical divide. For 'China and upper India' the plague 'began with people of every condition, age, and sex spitting blood and dying quickly in

---

[56] [230], p. 155.

[57] *Cronichetta d'incerto*, p. 183.

[58] Hayez, 'Quelques témoignages'.

[59] This comes from an unpublished chronicle of Faenza, Bibliotheca comunale, cited in Antonio Ubertelli, 'Delle cose di Faventia. Dall'anno 1310 all'anno 1474': 'appellato mortalitas gangolarum et sputi sanguinis'; see Antonio Ferlini, *Pestilenze nei secoli a Faenza e nelle valli del Lamone e del Senio* (Faenza, 1990), p. 46.

[60] *Annales seu Cronicae . . . Joannis Dlugossii*, IX, p. 252.

[61] Maqrīzī, *Sulūk*, p. 370.

two or three days'. By the time it reached Italy it maintained its ferocious contagion—'anyone who attended the sick caught the disease and died in a similar fashion'—but now with all 'at least one swelling was shown on the infected body'.[62] Other Italians, such as the Cortusii father and sons from Padua, the abbot of San Lorenzo at Cremona, the monastic scribe of a necrology from Apuleia (Friuli), and the Trentine canon Giovanni da Parma,[63] described the Janus face of the plague—the spitting of blood and formation of buboes, or other skin disorders. While the pneumonic might kill more quickly, for them the two, three, or more forms occurred concurrently. Nor did every chronicler claim that the bubonic was any less contagious. After describing the plague in Rimini as having three forms—spitting of blood, a swelling (*carbunculo*), or spots (*fistulis*), all of which killed in two or three days—Marcha di Marco Battagli described the disease's contagion by pointing to plague's bubonic form:

> And by their corruption, the ill visibly spotted the healthy, simply by mixing with them (*solum cum ipsis conversando*). From this mingling, thousands of men and women died and were buried.

Later he repeated: 'I note that this mingling among the sick lethally spotted those who were well'.[64]

For some such as the Sicilian Franciscan Michele da Piazza, the pulmonary and bubonic were not even separate forms. Rather, the pulmonary led immediately to the bubonic in the same patients (nearly unheard of with modern bubonic plague, where the pneumonic kills so fast that buboes have no time to form): 'the inhaled infection (*hanelitus inficiatione*) caused the formation of pustules like lentils to form around the thigh or the arm'. Once infected the same individuals, according to Michele, violently coughed up blood and continued to spew it for three days, without any hope of a cure.[65] In retracing the course of the disease in Catania, which peaked around April,[66] the pulmonary and bubonic were again present in the same patients but now with the sequence reversed, plague progressing from bubonic to pneumonic and taking two to three days to kill.[67]

Similarly, for the Florentine chronicler Marchionne di Coppo Stefani, the two forms were intertwined in the same season and possibly experienced concurrently by the same patients:

---

[62] Matteo Villani, *Cronica*, I, p. 9.
[63] Cortusii, *Historia de Novitatibus Paduae*, col. 926–7; *Alberti de Bezanis*, pp. 102–3; 'Fragmenta Historica', pp. 42–44; *Cronica inedita di Giovanni da Parma*, p. 50.
[64] *Marcha di Marco Battagli da Rimini*, p. 54. This testimony, Marcha proclaimed, came from direct personal experience. 'By the grace of God', he recovered trom the plague, even that form with 'the spewing of blood'.
[65] Michele da Piazza, *Cronica*, p. 82.
[66] This is the date of the death of Duke Giovanni, who roamed through the wilds of Sicily, trying to escape the plague: ibid., p. 87.
[67] Taken from Horrox's translation with minor adjustments, *The Black Death*, p. 40.

The sign was this: that between the thigh and the body in the groin or under the arm appeared a lump (*grossetto*) and fever and if perchance one spat, it was a bloody mix with saliva, and of those who spat blood, none survived.[68]

Looking back on the Black Death with the hindsight of as many as four waves of pestilence in his native Florence, Giovanni Morelli charted the course of the disease with three distinct phases:

> it began with the death of people afflicted with great pain and a rapid fever which derived from a certain swelling either in the groin, under the arms, or in the throat at the bottom of the ears; and from this they lived four to six days. Then, as the disease mounted others died in two days or less; and finally, as this poison intensified, certain tiny balls appeared on the skin in various places on the body and these were more deadly than the swellings and with less chance of a cure. And then at the heart of this disease there appeared certain red and blue bumps along with the spitting of blood, which also poured down through the nose. And this was the worst sign for which there was no cure.[69]

He then went on to tell how quickly this form of the disease spread: 'at one moment you would see people laughing and joking with their mates; at the next, they'd be dead.' While Morelli credits Boccaccio's *Decameron* as his source for the 1348 plague, nothing like it appears in the novella. Boccaccio had only two forms or phases of plague. For him, when the plague struck in Florence in the early spring, it erupted immediately with the plague boils, the *gavòccioli*. By his description, those symptoms experienced earlier in the east—bleeding from the nose—were not present in Florence, and he never mentions the spitting of blood. Instead, Boccaccio's second form was the spread of 'black spots or bruises on the arms, across the thighs and in every other part of the body', for some large and few, for others small and many.[70] The more probable source of Morelli's triplex description—including blood spitting, nose bleeding, and the terrible stench of the infected (none of which appears with Boccaccio)—was Morelli's own experience in the later plagues of the fourteenth and early fifteenth centuries. These, like 1348 at least in Florence and other places in the Mediterranean, reached their height at summer. Clearly, neither cold nor the pulmonary form was necessary for the disease's contagion or capacity to spread and execute its accelerated mortalities. In contrast to Le Roy Ladurie, Morelli stressed that plague sputtered in winter and only came to its violent fruition in summer, when the more deadly forms of small pustules accompanied by blood spitting burst forth. As with much of this merchant's account his descriptions and figures match with what we now find from the quantification of archival sources.

---

[68] Stefani, *Cronica fiorentina*, p. 230.
[69] Morelli, *Ricordi*, p. 207.
[70] Boccaccio, *Decameron*, pp. 10–1.

The doctors also commonly spoke of their patients taking either the bubonic or pulmonary form of the plague, and like the chroniclers, but unlike Guy de Chauliac, none separated these types into two seasons or even into consecutive courses. One of the earliest plague tracts, that of the Neapolitan doctor Johannes della Penna, who performed autopsies on plague victims, separated the symptoms of his plague patients:

> some had a multitude of ulcers that were internal, in the chest and on the lungs, and that from these came the spitting of blood and they died rapidly. Others had them externally, having ulcers, spots and herpes that formed under the skin in the three principal glands.[71]

By the end of the next century, an anonymous plague pamphlet from the north of Italy continued to speak in the same terms. Patients either had internal boils on the lungs which provoked coughing and the spitting of blood, or they were external, corresponding with the three emunctoria.[72]

*   *   *

These symptomologies found in various medical and literary genres across Europe, not only in 1348, but also for outbreaks through the fifteenth century show Guy de Chauliac's sharp division of the plague into a winter pulmonary disease followed by a late spring or summer bubonic one as atypical, even unique, and not the norm as historians continue to assume. Nor were the pulmonary and bubonic forms necessarily the principal division made by contemporaries. Others described various forms and courses of the disease including sleeping; some such as the humanist Louis Sanctus distinguished the phases according to where the plague boils formed—in the groin, the under-arm, or elsewhere. Still others distinguished between swellings forming on the right as opposed to the left side of the body.[73] For others, such as Boccaccio, Michele da Piazza, the Welsh poet Llywelyn Fychan, Geoffrey le Baker, the doctor Tommaso del Garbo, and later Marsilio Ficino, a distinction in two bubonic phases was more significant than a difference between pneumonic and bubonic plague. For them, the glandular swellings as big as goose eggs were less deadly than the spots (variously called *carbunculi, pustules, formicae* (ants), *anthrachi, lentiles, piccoli bolli*, and *herpes*) of a carbuncular phase that spread across the body, sometimes preceding, sometimes following, sometimes concurrent with the larger buboes. Yet despite the frequency with which chroniclers and doctors distinguished the plague by these two carbuncular phases, historians have yet to comment on them. Instead, their focus remains fixed on the bubonic/pneumonic distinction that appears so readily to confirm the late-medieval plague's identity with the modern plague experience.

---

[71] [35], p. 348.
[72] [198], pp. 106 and 109.
[73] *Cronica inedita di Giovanni da Parma*, p. 52.

THE BLACK DEATH:
EPIDEMIOLOGY

|6|

Chroniclers and doctors

Of 407 chronicles, calendars, and 'necrologies' covering the plague years from 1347 to 1450 that I have been able to read in various libraries in Britain, France, and Italy, barely 16 per cent of them (68) identified the plague by pointing to cutaneous signs—the *bubo, gavòcciolo, biscica piena di veneno, apostemata, macchie, rossorie,* or even with just the adjectival phrase, 'pestis inguinaria'.[1] Moreover, these include in essence the double counting of chroniclers such as Bower, who copied Fordun for 1349, and the two 'World' chroniclers of Cologne, who copied one another. More than half of these [35] come from Italy and one such description is found not actually in a chronicle but rather etched on the facade of a charitable institution in Venice.[2] In England, where chroniclers have been used as thoroughly to study plague as anywhere, only three of 45 mentioned apostemes or other skin disorders, and for German-speaking areas the proportion was less (nine of 117 chronicles, annals, and calendars). Further, less than a handful described boils for more than a single plague—the Florentine chroniclers, Matteo Villani and Stefani, the chronicler of Novgorod, and the Polish canon of Krakow, Joannis Dlugossii—even though some chronicles such as one from Ragusa remarked on as many as 12 plagues without once mentioning plague boils, rashes, pustules, or any other skin disorders.

---

[1] I did not count 'notae', calendars, or 'necrologies' unless they mentioned plague, but I did count chronicles and annales that covered the plague years, even when plague was not mentioned. I have not used sermons. Of those collected by Rosemary Horrox, not a single one mentioned the signs or symptoms of plague (although one, actually a plague tract, used boil as a metaphor for sin, 'the boil of his vices', Horrox, p. 149); thus the inclusion of sermons and other non-chronicle religious writings would further diminish the percentage of sources that mention plague but fail to point to its cutaneous signs.
[2] Reinhold C. Mueller, 'Aspetti sociali ed economici della peste a Venezia nel Medioevo', *Venezia e la peste, 1348–1797* (Venice, 1979–80), p. 82.

Still fewer described the symptoms or course of the disease, from headaches, sharp pains, and burning fevers to pulmonary complications. Yet an even smaller number of this small set of descriptions—those by Boccaccio, Gabriele de' Mussis, Louis Sanctus, and occasionally a few others—has formed the focus for historians' and doctors' analyses of the Black Death, providing the grist for their certainty that it and its successive waves must have been modern bubonic/pneumonic plague (*Yersinia pestis*).

More than burning fevers, the spitting of blood, or the bubo, basic epidemiological facts instead impressed chroniclers of the fourteenth and fifteenth centuries—the plague's geographic scope, the numbers killed, the speed by which it spread and killed, and its terrible contagion. Furthermore, elementary epidemiological patterns, more than the bubo, were the means by which contemporaries saw a connectedness between the plague of 1347–51 and its successive waves. First and foremost of these was the mortality, not only with the first plague of 1347–52, but of later plagues, which astonished contemporaries, even by medieval epidemic standards. Second, it was the plagues' geography, which amounted to more than isolated or local misfortunes. Contemporaries saw especially (but not only) the first plague as having engulfed the entire world ('De mortalitate universali per totum orbem').[3]

Its 'universality' struck almost all the chroniclers who reported the disease in its first outbreak. An Egyptian chronicler maintained that the plague of 1347–48:

> was without precedent, in the sense that it affected not only one region at the exclusion of another, but that it spread to all parts of the world, through the Orient as well as the West, to the North as with the South. Moreover, it engulfed not only all mankind but also the fishes in the sea, birds in the sky and wild beasts.[4]

Even the annalists with their one- or two-line descriptors distinguished the plague by the universality of its catastrophe, as did an anonymous annalist of the monastery at Friesach, Kärsten (in southern Austria):

> And in this year [1348] a pestilence struck that was so great and universal that it stretched from sea to sea, causing many cities, towns, and other places to become almost totally desolated of human beings.[5]

---

[3] A number of chroniclers called the plague a 'universal plague', or one that circulated throughout the entire known world: Stellai, *Annales Genuenses*, p. 150; *Marcha di Marco Battagli da Rimini*, p. 54; Raphayni de Caresinis, *Chronica*, p. 4; *Annales Caesenates*, col. 1179; *Cronaca di Pisa*, pp. 96–7; Michele da Piazza, *Cronica*, p. 82; *Notae Historicae Blidenstadenses*, p. 392; *Chronique et annales de Gilles le Muisit*, p. 257; *Chronique de Jean le Bel*, I, p. 222; *Ecclesia Spalatensis*, III, p. 324; *Chronique Normande*, p. 72; *Chronique de Richard Lescot*, p. 82; *Chronicon Galfridi le Baker*, p. 92; *Chronicon Elwacense*, p. 40–1; *Annales S. Victoris Massilienses*, p. 6; *Polychronicon Ranulphi Higden*, p. 355; *Chronica Monasterii de Melsa*, p. 40; 'Necrologio' di S. Maria Novella, I, p. 65, as well as those below.
[4] Maqrīzī, *Sulūk*, p. 368.
[5] *Annales Frisacenses*, p. 65.

Sometimes chroniclers further distinguished the areas worst hit. The chronicler of Perugia said the 'death spread almost throughout the world but worse in coastal regions and especially in France'.[6] Several Italian chroniclers pointed to Milan as a place that escaped the plague's initial onslaught. According to the Pisan Ranieri, no more than three families died there; their houses with all the doors and windows were then quickly walled up.[7] John of Cornazano maintained that in addition to Milan, the plague of 1348 also hit Parma less severely than elsewhere.[8] The Polish chronicler Joannis Duglosii said that although the plague's 'horrendous reign was nearly universal among Christians and barbarians', it struck in Poland in 1348 'but not so severely as in Hungary, Bohemia, Dacia [Romania], France, and Germany.[9] The Florentine Matteo Villani with his extensive network of merchant correspondents was geographically the most detailed, reporting the Black Death's spread 'from China and upper India, then through their surrounding provinces, and then to coastal places across the ocean'.[10] In charting the plague through Italy and Europe he singled out both the areas it devastated and those it merely grazed:

> In 1348 it infected all of Italy, except the city of Milan and certain outlying areas of the Alps, dividing Italy and Germany, which were only lightly grazed. In the same year it began to cross the mountains, extending into Provence, Savoy, the Dauphine, and Burgundy. By sea it invaded Marseilles and Aguamorta. It ran through Catalonia, the island of Mallorca, Spain, and Granada. By 1349 it had spread to the westernmost shores of the Atlantic (Occeano) encompassing Europe, Africa, Ireland, the islands of England and Scotland, and further western islands, all with almost the same mortality, except for Brabant, where it gave little offence. In 1350 it struck the Germans, Hungarians, Danes, Goths, Vandals, and other northern peoples and nations. And the succession of this plague lasted in each country that it struck for five months continuously.[11]

The plague's universal, cross-regional character was the single most important trait that convinced contemporaries—Guy de Chauliac, the Cortusii chroniclers of Padua, the Scot John of Fordun, the chronicler of the Grey Friars at Lynn, and others—that the Black Death was new to history.[12] Numerous chroniclers charted the origins and geographical spread of the plague from mysterious China or India to the particular paths it took once it reached and ravaged their own countries and towns.[13] The

---

6 *Cronica della città di Perugia*, p. 148.
7 *Cronaca di Pisa*, p. 97.
8 *Chronica Abreviata Fr. Johannis de Cornazano*, p. 385.
9 *Annales . . . Joannis Dlugossii*, IX, p. 252.
10 Matteo Villani, *Cronica*, I, p. 8.
11 Ibid., p. 11.
12 See chapter 9.
13 Despite these reports, J. Norris, 'East or West? The geographic origin of the Black Death', *Bulletin of the History of Medicine*, 51 (1977): 1–24, has claimed that the plague originated

Bolognese Chronicler B claimed the plague followed immediately in the wake of two infected Genoese galleys [some said there were three; others twelve] as they passed through Constantinople, Pera on the Black Sea, and then Messina, where it blazed through Sicily, killing two-thirds of the population, then to Genoa, and finally Marseilles, making it 'uninhabited'.[14] The German chronicler Heinrich Surdi of Selbach traced the plague's arrival from 'the pagans over the seas' to Venice, then across the Alps to Hungary, all of Germany, France, and finally Scotland.[15] The 'World Chronicler' of Cologne mapped the plague's progress from overseas through various provinces within Italy to Spain, France, and beyond.[16]

The English chroniclers paid closest attention to charting the origins and spread of the plague across the seas into their country. The chronicler of the Cathedral priory of Rochester pointed to its supposed origins in India 'through the whole of infidel Syria and Egypt, and also through Greece, Italy, Provence, and France' before its arrival in England.[17] Geoffrey le Baker thought it originated in eastern India and Turkey (as though they were nearby), that its first port of call in Britain was in Dorset, and from there it spread to Bristol, then to Gloucester, Oxford, London, and the rest of Anglia, and afterwards to Wales and Scotland with invading troops and war.[18] Henry Knighton called the first outbreak of plague 'A universal mortality of men throughout the world' that 'began in India, then spread to Tartary [Turkey], and then to the Saracens, and finally to the Christians and Jews'.[19] At least eleven other English chroniclers clocked the plague's arrival and progress through their island. Nor was this simply a case of one chronicler copying another: they came to no consensus about where it first touched British shores or its precise itinerary thereafter; Dorset, Devonshire, Southampton, Melcumbe, Cornwall, and Bristol were all contenders for the first port of call.[20] The chronicler John Capgrave even saw it originating in the north of England.[21]

Chroniclers after 1348 continued to see this cross-regional character as

---

in neither India, China, nor Central Asia but in southern Russia. The claim derives from no contemporary sources or new archaeological evidence. For contemporary evidence of plague in India in the 1320s, see Sarton, *Introduction to the History of Science*, III, pp. 1650–1.

[14] *Cronaca B*, p. 584; for a similar trajectory, see *Historia Miscella Bononiensis*, col. 409; and *Polyhistoria fratris Bartholomæi Ferrariensis*, col. 806.

[15] *Cronica Heinrich Surdi*, pp. 75–6.

[16] *Die Weltchronik des Mönchs Albert*, p. 109.

[17] *Historia Roffensis* in Horrox, p. 70.

[18] *Chronicon Galfridi le Baker*, pp. 98–100.

[19] *Knighton's Chronicle*, pp. 94–5.

[20] See Koenraad Bleukx, 'Was the Black Death (1348–49) a real plague epidemic? England as a case-study', in *Serta Devota in Memoriam Guillelmi Lourdaux*, ed. by Werner Verbeke (Leuven, 1995), II, pp. 106–9. In addition to the ones he lists, see 'A fourteenth-century chronicle from the Grey Friars at Lynn', p. 274; *Chronicon Abbatiae de Parco Ludae*, pp. 38–9; and *Chronicon Angliæ Petriburgense*, p. 169.

[21] *John Capgrave's Abbreuiacion of Cronicles*, p. 166.

the plague's distinctive trait in successive waves of the disease and often tracked the plague's progress. Spanish chroniclers saw the plague of 1358 originating in Africa, then erupting in Savoy, Provence, and the Dauphiné before spreading through Catalonia and Castile. They also recorded that it 'attacked Germany, Hungary, and Denmark'.[22] Even though it did not hit his own city of Florence, Matteo Villani gave finer detail to the geography and mortality of this plague, specifying places in Flanders, Brabant, Germany, and Bohemia, where it touched down as well as places it skipped over.[23] For the next plague, that of 1360, he charted its path through Damascus to Cairo.[24] Giovanni da Parma described the plague of 1361 'as spreading through the world no less than the first plague, even if fewer died from it'.[25] According to Villani, the plague of 1363 originated in Egypt and Syria and other parts of the Levant, where his merchant correspondents noted that it was 'the same pestilence with the swellings' that appeared in Florence. He further traced the disease's movement, which 'seriously damaged' Venice, Padua, Istria, Schiavonia, as well as nearly all of Tuscany.[26]

Chronicler B of Bologna saw also the plague of 1374 as spreading 'through the entire world, the Christian world, in Turkey, finally everywhere'; as with the first one 'all died from this disease within a few days'.[27] The plague doctor Raymundus Chalmelli de Vivario recorded that the plague of 1382 had spread 'through all of Syria and Greece before entering Italy, Germany, England, Scotland or Ireland (Scotia), France, Spain, and Navarra, specifying that it hit some areas more than others'.[28] Jacobo de Delayto, the Ferrarese chancellor of the Este family, along with the Venetian Sanuto considered the plague of 1399 still as 'universal', striking 'throughout the entire world'.[29] This was the last of the plagues to find such claims to universality among Italian chroniclers, but elsewhere chroniclers of later plagues, such as the annalist of the magistrates of Bratislava, the Parisian Bourgeois, and the annalist of Zwifaltena continued to see plagues in 1413, 1414, and 1419 as 'reigning throughout the world, killing innumerable thousands—so many that no one can count them'.[30]

In addition to charting origins and tracking paths, no less than seventy-seven chroniclers dated the duration of various plagues, often stating the

---

[22] *Epidemiología Española*, I, p. 85.
[23] For more on Villani's description of this plague, see chapter 9.
[24] Ibid., II, p. 506.
[25] *Cronica inedita di Giovanni da Parma*, p. 52.
[26] Matteo Villani, *Cronica*, II, p. 660.
[27] Cronaca B, III, p. 293
[28] [257], p. 39.
[29] *Annales Estenses Jacobi de Delayto*, col. 958; *Specimen Historiæ Sozomeni*, col. 1170; and Sanuto, *Vitæ Ducum Venetorum*, col. 766 (for 1400).
[30] *Annales magistratus Wratislaviensis*, p. 530; *Journal d'un bourgeois de Paris*, p. 49; and *Annales Zwifaltenses*, p. 63.

months when they began or ended. Some such as the Venetian Sanuto pointed to climatic factors, reporting that the 'great heat of August 1414' sparked plague in the Veneto.[31] Some traced the plague's temporal progression, indicating its peak months as well as the starting and ending points of a plague season as did the annalist of Floreffe (Namur, Belgium) for the plagues of 1361 and 1362.[32] Others gave still more detail as with Stefani's account of plague smouldering in early spring in Florence, 1383; first confined to only four houses on one street corner; it awaited the warmer weather to burst forth in May.[33] For the plague of 1400, the Minerbetti chronicler of Florence provided still more detail, plotting the plague's progress from April to September by body counts, which rose to 200 a day in June and more in July.[34] Already in the plague of 1347–8, the Egyptian chronicler Maqrīzī had given figures of the daily death mounts by month for Cairo and its old quarter, even if these numbers' peak at 20,000 a day may seem apocryphal.[35]

More than buboes or even the geographic scope of the plague, the numbers dying from plague during the fourteenth and fifteenth centuries commanded most contemporaries' attention, as is implied by the names they gave plague. Across Europe, it was not called 'Black Death' (as would become common only in the nineteenth century) or rarely as inguinial after the boils' position. Instead, they called it the Big Death—*la moria grande* or *grandissima*, *la mortalega grande*, *grande* or *grandissima mortalità*, *très grande mortalité*, *morbo grande*, *grande* or *grandissima pestilenzia* or *peste grande*, *magna mortalitas*, *mortalitas magna*, *maxima mortalitas*, *la gran mortaldat*, *magna pestilentia*, *magna epidemia*, *magna peste*, *magna clades pestilencie*, *grosze sterbet*, *das grosse Sterbole*, *grosze Pestilentz*, *grot Pestilencie*, *den großen Tod*, *La mortalità grande universalmente*, *gran mortandad y pestilencia*, *peligro grande*, *pestilencia de mortandad*, *huge mortalyte and deth of people*, and the like.[36]

The various titles for the 'Big Death' were not used solely for the grandest and most universal of these plagues, 1347–52; they continued to distinguish plague from other diseases through the fourteenth and fifteenth

---

[31] Sanuto, *Vitæ Ducum Venetorum*, col. 889.

[32] *Annales Floreffenses, a 471–1482*, p. 629.

[33] Stefani, *Cronica fiorentina*, p. 426. The Canto de' Morelli was at the corner of piazza Santa Croce and Borgo Santa Croce; see *Stradario storico e amministrativo della Città e del Comune di Firenze* (Florence, 1929), p. 79. San Pier Maggiore lies to the north of Santa Croce and to the west of Sant'Ambrogio.

[34] *Cronica volgare di Anonimo Fiorentino*, p. 250; the Florentine 'Libri di morti' for 1400 roughly support his claims: the daily peak in burials was just over 200 in early July.

[35] Maqrīzī, *Sulūk*, pp. 368 and 377.

[36] These are names consistently seen in the 407 chronicles, annals, and calendars that I have surveyed. Arrizabalaga 'Facing the Black Death', p. 243, finds from 105 documents issued by the Crown of Aragon in 1348 that either 'mortalitas' alone or with a modifier such as 'gran' is seen in 75 per cent of the cases.

centuries.[37] Just as non-medically-trained chroniclers used 'peste' with some discrimination, they used the terms for the 'Big Death' even more sparingly and not just for any illness that spread with epidemic force in their times, such as influenza, smallpox, a disease called *pondi*, and another called *dondi*. With few exceptions these diseases in the fourteenth and fifteenth century did not kill nearly so many, even when (as we will see) the plagues' mortalities had declined dramatically after 1400. Still, a disease that wiped out 5 per cent of a population was rightly perceived as different from other diseases, even diseases which often occurred in the summer, such as dysentery, *pondi*, and smallpox, as did plague in Mediterranean countries.[38]

The one possible exception that I have found was a smallpox epidemic in Paris in 1433, which the chronicler known as 'Parisian Bourgeois' called 'très grant mortalité'. However, he was uncertain whether it was smallpox (*de verolle plate*) or plague (*de boce*).[39] He was one of the few chroniclers even to report outbreaks of smallpox, *dondi*, or dysentery and used other expressions for them, such as 'la plus terrible maladie de la verolle' for a smallpox epidemic in 1445 and 'très mauvaise' for an epidemic of 'dando' in 1427,[40] but not 'grant mortalité', which he reserved for the plagues he lived through and recorded in 1418, 1433, and 1438.[41]

More than buboes, the chroniclers cited numbers or rough proportions

---

[37] *The Westminister Chronicle*, pp. 44 and 56 (for the plague of 1383); p. 476 for the plague of 1391; *Annales Forolivienses*, p. 68 (for 1362); 75 (1390); 85 (1416); 96 (the plague in Rome of 1450); Iohannis de Bazano, *Chronicon Mutinense*, p. 176 (for 1361); *Matthaei de Griffonibus*, p. 66 (for 1362); 70 (for 1373); 78 (1383); 88 (for 1399); 114 (for 1389, 1409 and 1423); 495 for 1374 and 525 for 1394; *Historia Miscella Bononiensis*, *Die Chronik Erhards von Appenwiler*, p. 251 (for the plague of 1439); *Die Grösseren Basler Annalen*, p. 32 (for the plague of 1381); *Chronicon Moguntinum*, p. 168 (for 1364), and p. 183 (for plague in Avignon in 1371); p. 184 (for plague in Hesse and Westphalia in 1371); p. 192 (for plague in Avignon in 1374); 202 (for plague in 1379); p. 209 (for plague in Saxony and Eastphalia in 1383); *Chronique du religieux de Saint–Denys*, I, p. 475 (for plague 1387); *Detmar-Chronik*, p. 556 (for 1376); and 563 (for 1378); *Continuatio Claustroneoburgensis*, V, p. 736 (for the plague of 1370); p. 737 (for 1409); *Annales Matseenses*, p. 834; *Chronicon Elwacense*, p. 45 (for 1439); *Annales magistratus Wratislaviensis*, p. 530 (for plague in Silesia in 1460); *Annales Mechovienses*, p. 671 (for plague in Poland in 1379); *Eulogium ... a Monacho quodam Malmesburiensi*, pp. 339 (for 1374) and 369 (for 1390); *Thomas Walsingham*, pp. 309 (for 1369) and 409 (for 1379); *Chronicon Angliae*, pp. 64–5 (for 1369); Stefani, *Cronica fiorentina*, p. 289 for 1374; and p. 426 for 1383; *Chronique des Pays–Bas*, p. 396, for 1426; Matteo Villani, *Cronaca*, for 1360 among the Saracens.

[38] For instance, for an epidemic of *pondi* in 1390, one of the few non-plague epidemics to be recorded by the meticulous Florentine chroniclers (in this case Minerbetti), deaths were less than 15 a day (the total number of burials) in July, when the disease peaked; Carmichael, *Plague and the Poor*, p. 46.

[39] *Journal d'un bourgeois de Paris*, p. 295.

[40] Ibid., p. 379. Also see pp. 175, 222–3, and 379.

[41] Ibid., pp. 111, 295, and 342. Such tags were used only exceptionally for other calamities such as famines. *Chronica Abreviata Fr. Johannis de Cornazano*, p. 355, written at the end of fourteenth century referred to a famine of 1085, when mothers ate their children, as 'Magna Mortalitas'.

of populations suddenly to fall to the plague's rage. The estimates ranged from claims about world mortality to more precise counts of those who perished in an author's village or monastery. No less than 97 chroniclers cited such figures. Many such as the chronicler of Mainz and one from Ragusa estimated the death figures for several plagues. Some, such as the Florentine Stefani, the Gatari of Padua, Friar Francesco of Viterbo, and an anonymous scribe of Parma, said their figures derived from official counts gathered by local communes or the archbishop, reflecting new administrative practices brought on by the plague.[42]

While only three English chroniclers mentioned skin disorders for any plague, at least ten tallied the horrifying death tolls of the plague. Eight of them—Geoffrey le Baker, John of Reading, *The Brut*, Thomas Walsingham, the *Chronicon Angliae* from St Albans, the Bristol Calendar, the Annals of Bermundesia, and John Capgrave—reported that 'scarcely a tenth of the population survived' the first plague.[43] While this may seem an outlandish exaggeration, at least in one case it was grounded in local knowledge, that of the abbey of St Albans, where in its dependent houses of every 20 monks two survived.[44]

The English were not the only ones to make extraordinary claims for the plague's death counts. The chronicler of Saint-Denis came to the same conclusion—'of twenty hardly two remained'[45]—as did a chronicler from Orvieto—'nine of every ten succumbed'.[46] The anonymous annalist of Pistoia, whose chronicle ends abruptly in 1348, estimated that eight of every ten died across the world with many countries becoming completely abandoned. By his figures 'more than 120,000' died in Avignon in three months. Closer to home his estimates were less exaggerated; for Pisa he claimed that more than 25,000 died—a figure that was about half the city's population on the eve of the plague. By several reports Pisa was heavily hit by pestilence, and by the Catasto of 1427 its population had fallen to less

---

[42]   According to Stefani, in October 1348 the Signoria of Florence and the bishop drew up an ordinance to count how many people had died in the plague; the number Stefani cited was 96,000, not far from Boccaccio's estimate of 100,000, which historians take as a gross exaggeration, but perhaps the area under consideration was the diocese of Florence. His references to this official gathering of statistics continues until the plague of 1383, the last one he recorded. For Parma, 1361, see *Gravina: Additamenta*, col. 751; for Viterbo, 1400, *Le croniche di Viterbo scritte da Frate Francesco*, p. 362; for Padua, 1404, Gatari, *Cronaca Carrarese*, p. 560.

[43]   See Bleukx, 'Was the Black Death (1348–49) a real plague epidemic?', pp. 106–9. This useful article, which purports to cite all the English and Welsh narrative sources written before 1400 that mention the Black Death, fails to include the chronicle of John of Reading, the *Westminister Chronicle*, 'Chronicle from the Grey Friars at Lynn', Thomas Stubb's chronicle of the Church of York, *The Chronicle of Louth Park Abbey*, *Historia Roffensis*, 'Chronicle of William Gregory, Skinner', *The Great Chronicle of London*, *The Chronicles of London*, *Scalacronica*, and the *Peterborough Chronicle* (see Appendix II).

[44]   *Chronicon Angliae*, p. 27.

[45]   *Richardi Scoti Chronicon*, p. 82.

[46]   *Discorso Historico*, p. 25.

than 8000.[47] Here, the chronicler may have even underestimated the plague's toll.

Others expressed the plague's horror by numbers. The Irish chronicler John Clyn reported that the plague of 1347–48 killed 40 million 'as it swept through the Saracens and the unbelievers'.[48] The report from a chronicler of Erfurt was more vague but even gloomier: in many regions, cities, towns, and villages especially in Gaul not a single man remained by 1349'.[49] Jean Froissart was more judicious, reporting that a third of the world's population perished in the first wave of plague[50]—an estimate that (for whatever reason) is often accepted by historians today.[51]

Such global, even national, figures, however, were the exceptions. Most instead counted burials or funerals within their own regions, cities, or smaller localities. For the city of Valencia, its chronicler claimed that 300 died a day in June.[52] John Clyn claimed that 14,000 died in his nearest big town, Dublin, between August and Christmas 1348.[53] For Vienna, a monastic annalist claimed that 500 funerals had taken place in the city in a single day in 1349.[54] The chronicler of Perugia estimated the death of a 100,000 for the city and *contado* of his city.[55] Ranieri Sardo estimated that four of every five died in the five months of plague in Pisa.[56] The chronicler in verse of Mantua estimated that 50,000 died there.[57] And the list can be continued for Orvieto, Venice, Bologna, Paris, Avignon, Tournai, and many other cities.[58] The highest estimates for any city came from Egyptian and Syrian chroncilers who estimated that at the height of the plague in Cairo and its old quarter the daily number of deaths reached 20,000 in December. During the months of ša'bān and ramadān (November and December), 900,000 are said to have died in the city. Damascus was not far behind; in October its daily count reached 13,000.[59]

In Germany and Poland the numbers were considerably lower. For

---

[47] *Annales Pistorienses*, col. 524; for Pisa as place of heavy plague mortalities in 1348, see Chronica A of Bologna, p. 583; Chronica B, p. 584; and *Storia della città di Parma*, p. 12; for its 1427 population, see Herlihy and Klapisch-Zuber, *Les Toscans*, p. 238.
[48] *Annalium Hibernae*, p. 35
[49] *Chronicon Elwacense*, p. 40.
[50] *Chroniques de J. Froissart*, p. 100.
[51] See almost any textbook on Western civilisation for the Middle Ages, also, Zeigler, *The Black Death*. Henry of Herordia, *Chronikon Henrici de Hervordia*, p. 284, made the same estimate for the plague of 1350 in 'all of Germany (*Theutonia*)'.
[52] *Epidemiología española*, p. 81; and *Chronique Catalane de Pierre IV d'Aragon*, p. 272.
[53] *Annalium Hibernae*, p. 35.
[54] *Kalendarium Zwetlense*, p. 692.
[55] *Cronica della città di Perugia*, p. 148.
[56] *Cronaca Pisana*, p. 97
[57] 'Aliprandina', p. 133.
[58] *Discorso Historico*, p. 25; Sanuto, *Vitæ Ducum Venetorum*, col. 614; Cronica A, p. 585; *Richardi Scoti Chronicon*, p. 82; *Les Grandes Chroniques de France*, IX, p. 315; Sanctus, pp. 467–8; *Chronique et annales de Gilles le Muisit*, p. 257.
[59] Maqrīzī, *Sulūk*, p. 368, 374, and 378; and 'Récit d'Ibn Iyās', p. 384.

Frankfurt, its local chronicle claimed that 2000 died in the 72 days of plague in 1349.[60] The chronicler of Limburg estimated 2400 died in his town, not including children.[61] For the village of Engelberg, its chronicler reported that 20 houses, particularly in the valleys, remained empty in 1349.[62] In Poland, where the plague appears to have skipped over large areas and the death tolls remained low at least for the first wave, a chronicler reported 1500 funerals in a day in Avignon, but did not mention anything for his own region.[63]

Other chroniclers, even outside the statistically-minded merchant city-states of northern Italy, analysed their data by various categories. At Ragusa the city's annalist divided the death figures by class: 170 counts, gentlemen, ladies, and their children; 100 *popolani* (middling sorts), and over 1000 of the *povolo menudo* (workers and artisans).[64] The Augustine canon at Leicester, Henry Knighton, broke down the town's death statistics by parish.[65] Monastic chroniclers in particular also reported the small but terrifying death figures from their own houses as well as at others often hundreds of miles away. The German chronicler Johann of Winterthur reported that 'in a brief space of time' 30 of the 60 Minor friars died in the plague of 1348 in Messina.[66] Henry Knighton enumerated precise death figures (their accuracy of course might be questioned) for houses over a thousand miles away, claiming a count made by the pope as his source: 358 Dominicans in Provence died during Lent [March-April 1348]; at Montpellier only seven of 140 friars survived; at Magdelaine also only seven of 160; of 150 friars at Marseilles 'only one remained to tell the tale'; of the Carmelites 66 perished at Avignon 'before the citizens knew what was happening' and of the Augustinians at Avignon not one survived.[67] It is not that these estimates were accurate or unreasonable—certainly both were true for different places and different chroniclers. Rather, they show the preoccupations of contemporaries, the ways they imagined plague and distinguished it from other diseases and epidemics.

This tendency to report the numbers who died, were buried, or remained continued with other waves of plague through the first half of the fifteenth century. For German chroniclers the practice became more common after the first plague. For the first one, they often skipped from harbingers of disruption, such as the earthquakes on Vespers 25 January, 1348, to the

---

[60] *Acta aliquot Francofurtana*, p. 433.
[61] *Die Limburger Chronik*, p. 8.
[62] *Annales Engelbergenses*, p. 281.
[63] *Rocznik Miechowski*, p. 885.
[64] *Annales Ragsuni*, p. 39.
[65] *Knighton's Chronicle*, pp. 98–9.
[66] *Die Chronik Johanns von Winterthur*, p. 276.
[67] *Knighton's Chronicle*, pp. 96–7. Similar counts of one's brothers and those in other orders are seen in *Chronica Monasterii de Melsa*, p. 36; and by Clyn, *Annalium Hiberniae*, p. 36.

death tolls of Jews burnt in many German cities in 1349 or the chiliastic enthusiasm and bloodletting of the flagellants, without mentioning the plague at all. For instance, the chronicler of Mainz made no estimates for the first wave of the plague, but for the second of 1364 claimed that 6000 died in his city; in 1373 3000 in the province (in Maguncia); and in the plague of 1398 more than 30,000 in the region of Cologne.[68]

In other places, chroniclers such as the Florentine Stefani, continued to report plague deaths from what he claimed were government registers for successive strikes even though the numbers were usually considerably less than those taken by the original onslaught. An exception was the plague of 1405 in Padua, which according to the Gatari chroniclers killed 300 to 500 persons a day from the first of July to the middle of August, amounting to 44,000 deaths in the city alone. Perhaps suspecting that those afterwards might think that his father, then on his deathbed from this plague, might be guilty of gross hyperbole, the son added: 'In this I describe in truth; every day the bishop by the orders of the town council (*Signoria*) have kept an account [of the dead]'. For the plague of 1400 in Pistoia, the chronicler Ser Luca Dominici could rely on his own statistics as head of the hospitals in the city. He recorded that 4000 or half the city perished in that plague. For the same plague a chronicler of Viterbo put the dead at 6663, a number that he maintained came from the new collecting of vital statistics prompted by the plagues. From then on Viterbo's bishop was required to count the plague dead.[69] No other disease of the later Middle Ages received such statistical scrutiny or was pinned with such high figures. In fact, among the chroniclers I know only one who estimated the numbers dying from a disease that was not plague. Again the exception was the Parisian Bourgeois, who claimed that that smallpox epidemic of 1445 infected 6000 in the capital and many died from it.[70]

* * *

Beyond numbers, contemporaries were struck by the speed of the disease's spread, the brevity of what we now would call its incubation period, and its virulence or how quickly it killed its victims. As the anonymous chronicle of Orvieto put it: 'in the morning they were healthy, the next morning they were dead'.[71] Morelli was more vivid:

> It took little time for them to fall, grandees and commoners alike, from one day to the next: at one moment you'd see them laughing and joking with their

[68] *Chronicon Moguntinum*, pp. 168, 189, and 233.
[69] For 1383 Stefani, *Cronica fiorentina*, pp. 289 and 426; Padua: Gatari, *Cronaca Carrarese*, p. 560; Pistoia: *Cronache di Ser Luca Dominici*, I, p. 233; *Le croniche di Viterbo scritte da Frate Francesco d'Andrea*, p. 362.
[70] *Journal d'un bourgeois de Paris*, p. 379.
[71] *Discorso Historico*, p. 26.

mates; the next you'd see them dying! And it happened so quickly that many died in the streets or on benches, abandoned, without help or any comfort.[72]

Outside Italy the stories were much the same. Before mentioning the buboes, the apostolic notary at Rouen, Pierre Cochon, reported that 'on one day they'd all be together, but when they woke the next morning, some would be dead, others ill, and some still in good health . . . and when they felt the buboes (*boces*), they would call for the priest but soon would be dead.'[73] The chronicler of Meaux saw the plague as so virulent that men and women dropped dead as soon as they walked into public squares.[74] When the plague reached Bristol, Henry Knighton described it snatching away the population 'by sudden death . . . few kept their beds for more than two or three days, or even a half day'.[75]

Nor was such astonishment confined to 1347–51. For the second plague, Jean de Venette sounded a refrain heard from the first: 'A very striking fact was that a man who was well and happy one day would be dead two or three days later.'[76] Doctors also were astonished by the plague's speed. A century after John of Burgundy said that treatment of plague must begin within 24 hours of the first signs, [77] a doctor from Reichenbach in northern Germany made the same point: doctors could not neglect the patient in the first day of illness; after 24 hours, the disease uncared for was incurable.[78]

Others, as we have seen, continued to chart the number of days it took the plague victims to die. Saints' lives, medical tracts, and chronicles generally reported the same span of two or three days to kill with estimates ranging from ten hours to eight days. According to Morelli, if the patient were stricken only with the buboes and not the more deadly pustules, death would come in seven days.[79] Even if the plague's force declined as measured

---

[72] Morelli, *Ricordi*, p. 207; Also see *Cronaca Senese attribuita ad Agnolo di Tura del Grasso*, p. 555.
[73] *Chronique Normande*, p. 72.
[74] *Chronica Monasterii de Melsa*, p. 72.
[75] *Knighton's Chronicle*, pp. 98–9.
[76] *Chronique latin de Guillaume de Nangis (Continuatio)*, II, pp. 325–6.
[77] [27 and 28], p. 67.
[78] [125], p. 9.
[79] *Knighton's Chronicle*, p. Morelli, *Ricordi*, p. 207. *Marcha di Marco Battagli da Rimini*, p. 54, reported that plague victims 'expired in the first, second or third day'; *Brevi annali della Città di Perugia*, p. 68, claimed that none of those striken with plague lasted beyond two days; Angelo Pezzana, *Storia della città di Parma*, p. 50, reported that 'almost no one lived beyond the third, fourth or fifth day'; *Chronique de Jean le Bel* (p. 222) reported that patients died in three days; the Cortusii brothers, *Historia de Novitatibus Paduae*, said it usually took one to two days, and 'that it was very rare for there to be any hope after the third day' (col. 927); Dominici de Gravina, *Chronicon de rebus in Apulia*, p. 49, said 'the plague killed within two days and three at the latest.' Sanctus, p. 465, said that with the pneumonic form no one lived more than two days and, with the bubonic, all died 'immediately'. The *Fritsche (Friedrich Closener's) Chronik*, p. 120, of Strasbourg reported that the plague in 1349 killed in three or four days. *Cronica Heinrici Svrdi*, p. 75, reported that the plague of 1347 took from six to eight days to kill its victims, but Heinrich was then far from where it was raging.

by the proportions of populations killed, not much changed as regards the numbers of days it took. For the plague of 1356, the Frankfurt annals said plague patients died 'in about three days'. Sanuto reported three days to kill in a plague in Friuli in 1360, and the chronicler of Istria, even less time: two to three days. Filippo Villani reported that the plague of 1363 took five days to kill his uncle, Matteo. The *Cronichetta d'incerto* of Florence gave the victims less time for the second plague, less in fact than in 1348: once the '*gavòcciolo* appeared, the patient had ten hours of life left'. But two to three days remained the norm for plague in Milan in 1374, for Trent in the same year, and for plague in Tuscany in 1390.[80] For the virulent plague of 1400 in Tuscany, the time to kill may have sped up, at least this what the meticulous statistics-gatherer Ser Luca Dominici observed when as chief-officer of Pistoia's hospitals, he was in a position to know: 'those stricken with plague died in one or two days'.[81]

The chroniclers were also astonished with the plague's speed in another sense, the quickness by which it spread from one city or country to the next as it circumnavigated the then known world. As we have seen, this rapid, worldwide transmission was not limited to the first plague. From his merchant contacts, Matteo Villani chronicles a plague in 1361 that spread throughout Britain and which at about the same time also cut through Provence, Avignon, then in Lombardy, first Como, then Pavia, Milan, Venice, the Romagna, Gubbio, the Alps of the Ubaldini (north of Florence) to Mallorca, which lost three-quarters of its population—all in less than a year.[82] According to Villani, the source of Florence's plague in the following year was in Egypt and Syria, where pestilence broke out in the same year, spreading first to other parts of the Levant, Venice, Schiavonia (Slovenia), Istria, and Padua.[83] According to chronicle A of Bologna, the plague of 1374 came from Turkey in the same year.[84] Such transmissions from north Africa or Asia Minor across Europe in less than a year without the assistance of the steamship or railways is remarkable and certainly of a different character from the so-called Third Pandemic of bubonic plague, which took 40 years to creep the far shorter distance from the Yunnan peninsula to Hong Kong .[85]

---

[80] *Annales Francofurtani 1306–1358*, p. 394; Sanuto, *Vitæ Ducum Venetorum*, col. 644; Mons. Gasparo Negri, 'Memorie storiche della città e diocesi di Parenzo', *Atti e memorie della società istriana di archeologia e storia patria*, III (1887), p. 136 (a summary of the *Cronaca Dolfina*); Matteo and Filippo Villani, *Cronica*, II, p. 663; *Cronichetta d'incerto*, p. 183; *Annales Mediolanenses Anonymi auctoris*, col. 756; *Cronica inedita di Giovanni da Parma*, pp. 53 and 50; *Cronica volgare di Anonimo Fiorentino*, p. 88.
[81] *Cronache di Ser Luca Dominici*, I, p. 232. For further examples see chapter 5.
[82] Matteo Villani, *Cronaca*, pp. 514–15.
[83] Ibid., p. 660.
[84] Chronica A, III, p. 293.
[85] On this movement, see Benedict, *The Bubonic Plague*, pp. 36–48 and Pollitzer, *Plague*, p. 14.

Connected with the plague's transmission was its lightning contagion, which chroniclers reported with astonishment when the Genoese carriers first landed at Messina, Pisa, and Genoa. As the Pisan chronicle Ranieri remarked:

> at the beginning of January two Genoese galleys arrived from Romania and when they reached the fish market someone began to talk with them and immediately he fell ill and died; others who talked with them also became ill as well as any who were touched by those who had died . . . and thus was sparked the great corruption that killed everyone.[86]

Nor was this speed of transmission and contagion confined to the ports initially struck by plague during the winter of 1347 or 1348 or to the supposed pneumonic form of the disease. When plague broke out later in inland Siena, Agnolo di Tura saw the disease communicated simply through conversation: 'And they died almost at once: with the swelling under the arms and in the groin, they fell dead while talking (*favellando*)'.[87] Others saw the mingling of sick and healthy as the means of the plague's rapid spread, and again this held for the bubonic form as clearly as for pneumonic plague. The chronicler of Jean le Bel saw sheer proximity as enough for the plague's rapid dissemination: 'if there were those wounded with the plague in a street or in a hostel, one would take the disease from another, and because of this no one dared to assist or visit the sick'.[88] The Scottish chronicler Walter Bower described those who 'fearfully shunned the contagion as they would flee from before a serpent'.[89]

The chroniclers along with town councils and other governing bodies[90] saw touch as another mode by which plague spread directly from person to person.[91] As with Gabriele de' Mussis, who told of the disease having been sparked by infected lobbed corpses, others such as John Clyn said the disease was 'so contagious that those who touched the dead or the sick were infected immediately and died'.[92] The Florentine chronicler Stefani saw gravediggers because of their contact with the plague dead as being the profession most likely to die in times of plague.[93]

Others, as in Boccaccio's story of the pigs that dropped dead after tossing the rags of the infected, saw the plague spreading through articles left behind by the plague victims—their clothes, even their money, which the

---

[86] *Cronaca di Pisa*, p. 96.

[87] *Cronaca Senese attribuita ad Agnolo di Tura*, p. 555.

[88] *Chronique de Jean le Bel*, p. 223.

[89] Bower, *Scotichronicon*, VII, p. 273.

[90] Giuliana Albini, *Guerra, Fame, Peste: Crisi di mortalità e sistema sanitario nella Lombardia tardomedioevale* (Bologna, 1982), pp. 56, 84 and 86; Testa, 'Alle origini dell'Ufficio di Sanità, pp. 376–86.

[91] See for instance, *Cronaca Aquilana*, p. 181.

[92] *Annalium Hiberniae*, p. 36.

[93] Stefani, *Cronica fiorentina*, p. 231.

Pisan chronicler remarked were left untouched along with the dead on their beds, left without funerals or even burials.[94] The chronicler of Jean le Bel observed that 'no one dared use or even touch the clothes of the plague-stricken.'[95] The message of the Neuberg chronicler was the same: 'The goods and chattels bequeathed by the dead were given a wide berth by all, as if they too were infected.'[96] Some of the chroniclers' stories may reflect fears more than medical reality. The Egyptian Maqrīzī told of a washer-woman in 1347 or 1348 who while preparing a woman's corpse for funeral grazed the plague-victim's pimple. The washer woman let out a scream and died immediately; on one of her fingers was discovered a plague bump the size of a bean.[97] He further tells of fishermen on the lake of Buhayrat (Syria) filleting fish infected with the plague 'spots'. Along with the fish, they caught the plague, and pimples spread all over their bodies.[98]

Chroniclers of later plagues continued to see touching the infected and their belongings as a sure means of catching the plague, as the Parisian Bourgeois cautioned with the plague of 1414.[99] In describing the plague of 1448, the Perugian chronicler said 'the disease continued through touching, which terrified everyone'.[100] Further, the doctors were convinced that the disease spread by touching or inhaling the fumes given off by the bodies, clothing, and other possessions of the plague-afflicted.[101] Such perceptions are also clear in plague legislation from 1348 through the early modern period. In Venice, Milan, Ragusa, Valencia, and elsewhere, governments passed emergency measures to destroy infected merchandise and the goods of the plague dead and to clean the streets of their corruption.[102] Special plague laws were passed against the used goods trade and in particular used-cloth and clothing.[103] By the plague of Marseilles, 1720, goods were

---

[94] *Cronaca di Pisa*, p. 97; also, see 'Fragmenta Historica', p. 43;
[95] *Chronique de Jean le Bel*, p. 223.
[96] Horrox, p. 60.
[97] Maqrīzī, *Sulūk*, p. 377.
[98] Ibid., p. 373.
[99] *Journal d'un bourgeois de Paris*, p. 49.
[100] *Cronica della città di Perugia*, p. 600.
[101] See for instance the tract of Ibn Khātimah summarised by Campbell, *The Black Death*: 'Almost as harmful as the air breathed out by the sick, if not entirely so, are the fumes from their bodies, pieces of clothing, beds, and linen on which the sick lay, if they are used again. The author has observed that the inhabitants of a portion of Almeria, where the clothing and bed linen of the sick were sold, died almost without exception, while dealers in other markets under the same conditions fared as other people' (p. 56).
[102] See *Cronache di Ser Luca Dominici*, I, p. 131; Carmichael, *The Plague and the Poor*, p. 113; Ferlini, *Pestilenze nei secoli a Faenza*, p. 65.
[103] For Pistoia, see A. Chiappelli, ed., 'Ordinamenti Sanitari del Comune di Pistoia contro la pestilenzia del 1348', *ASI*, ser. 4, XX (1887), pp. 8–22. For legislation in Pisa and Lucca, see Gian Maria Varanini, 'La peste del 1347–50 e i governi dell'Italia centro-settentrionale: un bilancio', in *La Peste Nera*, p. 293; for Valencia, Rubio, *Peste Negra*, pp. 76–81 and 119; for Venice in the early modern period, see Patricia Allerston, 'The market in second-hand clothes and furnishings in Venice, c. 1500–c. 1650', Ph.D thesis, European University Institute (1996), ch. 6; for the Netherlands, M.A. van Andel, 'Plague regulations in the Netherlands', *Janus*, 21 (1916), p. 435.

seen as 'the greatest Danger' for the spread of plague from place to place. In addition to clothes, which 'harbour the very Quintessence of Contagion', the plague tract of Dr Richard Mead listed cotton, hemp, flax, paper, books, silk of all sorts, linen, wool, feathers, hair, and all kinds of skins as of danger in retaining the infection. Curiously, the one commodity not listed—grain—is the one through which modern plague is disseminated.[104]

In addition to touch, the anonymous author of the Aquilea necrology saw the plague infecting some by sight and others by air (*alii vero ex oculo-rum aspectu, alii autem ab aere*);[105] Matteo Villani saw 'the plague's infection spreading by sight and touch, and thus when a husband, wife, or their children knew that one of them was ill with the swellings, they would abandon the sick'.[106] For Jean de Venette the plague's contagion was so speedy that it came 'ex imaginatione'.[107] Even the medically trained saw the disease disseminated by sight.[108]

At least 22 chroniclers used the word 'contagion' to express the rapid communication of the disease from person to person both in its pulmonary form and its various cutaneous manifestations. In his brief letter, Louis Sanctus used it three times. It was used for 1348 and for subsequent plagues through my analysis, which ends in 1450, even in Egypt and Syria, where Moslem law outlawed the notion.[109] To breath, touch, and sight, others added stench as the mechanism for the plague's contagion.[110]

Nor did doctors shun the concept of a person-to-person transmission of plague or the words contagion and infection in their tracts as Andreina Zitelli, Richard Palmer, and Ann Carmichael have charged.[111] Instead, both the concept and the words are omnipresent in the plague tracts from the outset in 1348 through the fifteenth-century;[112] it is difficult to find a plague tract that did not use one or both terms. Although Melissa Chase has gone too far in claiming that contagion was a novelty of the Black Death

---

104 For a synopsis of Mead's tract, see Winslow, *The Conquest of Epidemic Disease*, p. 189.
105 'Fragmenta Historica', p. 43.
106 Matteo Villani, *Cronica*, p. 11.
107 *Chronique latine de Guillaume de Nangis (Continuatio)*, II, p. 211.
108 [64], p. 92: '. . . est morbus contagiosus et vadit ab vno homine ad alium, ymmo solo anhelitu unus inficit alium et iacens uns cum alio inficit alium . . . . quod sola ymaginacio pestis hominem facit pestilenticum'. [98], p. 132; [113], p. 71; [114 and 115], p. 76. Also a doctor of Montpellier who wrote his tract in May 1349 (Coville, 'Écrits contemporains', p. 359) and Guy de Chauliac thought the plague was spread by sight.
109 For the 1429 plague in Genoa, *Cronice de Ianue*, p. 367; the 1439 plague in Florence and Livorno, *Ricordi de me Sere Perizolo da Pisa*, p. 387; the plague of 1399 in the territory of Piacenza, Johannes de' Mussis, *Chronicon Placentinum*, p. 559; the 1419 plague in Paris, *Chronique du religieux de Saint–Denys*, VI, p. 270. For the plagues of 1347–8 in Syria and Egypt, see Maqrīzī, *Sulūk*, p. 369: 'The contagion conquered all the regions of the Orient.' For Moslem law on contagion, see below.
110 *Chronique du religieux de Saint-Denys*, VI, p. 270.
111 Zitelli and Palmer, 'Le teorie mediche sulla peste', esp. p. 24; for Carmichael, see chapter 3.
112 See Sudhoff and for the Montpellier ones he did not edit, see Chase, 'Fevers, posions, and apostemes', p. 155.

plague tracts that distinguished them from earlier discussions of epidemics by Avicenna,[113] 'it was', according to Charles-Edward Winslow, 'the Black Death which at last taught the communicability of disease beyond any peradventure'.[114] Some, such as an anonymous fifteenth-century tract from southern Germany, began by defining plague as 'a contagious disease (*est morbus quidam contagiosus*)'.[115] Others, such as the doctor of King Martin of Aragon recommended in his tract of 1406 that the infected be separated from the healthy, even if they belonged to the same household, 'because the disease was so contagious.'[116] Still others, such as the mid-fifteenth-century Saladino da Ascoli, Jacobus de Manderano (Monterone) in 1440, and Johann Vinck of Southern Germany in the latter half of the fifteenth century, distinguished the plague as being more contagious than any other 'putrid fever'.[117]

Even Moslem plague tracts that for religious reasons had to deny that diseases were infectious, showed nonetheless that plague was contagion as in the plague tract of Ibn Khātimah, which illustrated it through observations on neighbourhood and household dissemination of the disease. For the Christian world, on the other hand, it was accepted 'almost without discussion', as Ann Campbell showed 70 years ago.[118] According to Antonia Pasi Testa, by the end of the fourteenth century 'no one any longer doubted that the plague was a contagious disease.'[119] I would add that in the plague tracts it was never doubted; at least no one has shown any evidence to the contrary or even that European doctors debated it in 1348. To be sure, doctors had various ideas of the means by which plague passed from person to person—its 'modus invasionis'. Much the same as the chroniclers, they saw it transmitted by breath, touch, sight, speech, sweat, through communal eating and even working together in close proximity.[120] Others pointed to the infectivity that came from the stench of human faeces and decaying bodies.[121] As a consequence, the plague doctors advised in

---

[113] Ibid.; Avicenna in his *Canon of Medicine* certainly had a notion of person-to-person contagion; see Winslow, *Conquest of Epidemic Diseases*, pp. 94–5.

[114] Ibid., p. 96. As early as 1860 L.A. Michon, *Documents inédits sur la Grande Peste de 1348, Thèses de l'Ecole de Médicine* (Paris 1860), had concluded much the same: 'Was the plague contagious? All the authors of the time, medical and non-medical, are in unanimous agreement on this point'. (Cited by Winslow, p. 99.)

[115] [198], p. 104.

[116] [273], p. 112.

[117] Simili, 'Saladino Ferro da Ascoli', p. 40; [238], p. 172; [109], p. 57.

[118] Campbell, *The Black Death*, p. 59. Dols, 'The comparative communal responses to the Black Death in Muslim and Christian societies', *Viator* 5 (1974), p. 279, maintains that in contrast to the West, thinkers in the Middle East did not support a belief in the contagious nature of plague.

[119] Testa, 'Alle origini dell'Ufficio di Sanità', p. 378.

[120] See for instance, [9], p. 214; [23], p. 43; [24], p. 50; [38], p. 356; [47], p. 339; [56], p. 371; [2bis/23], pp. 60–1; [64], p. 92; [98], p. 132; [198], p. 105; [234], p. 165; [258], p. 42.

[121] See for instance, [20], p. 423.

times of plague that their readers avoid mixing with others and congregating in public places—graveyards, public baths, communal dwellings (*stubarum*), markets, businesses, taverns, and churches.[122] The doctor of a Benedictine monastery in the Südtirol even recommended to his holy patrons that they avoid church along with markets and other places 'where crowds gather'.[123] And at least one doctor advised that governments shut down and politicians shut up during plague, since the disease spread through speech.[124]

There was no conflict in these medical tracts between a theory of disease that was spread by air, water, and stench and its capacity at the same time to spread directly from person to person.[125] Miasmic theory's bout with person-to-person contagion sprouted later in the eighteenth and nineteenth centuries.[126] Early on, a follower of Gentile da Foligno remarked 'because of the advent of putrid air, the disease is communicated from one to another with continual breathing as the contagion progresses with the circulation of people from one part of a city to another.[127] After a long theoretical discussion of the corruption of air and causes of plague, doctor Johan Lochner of Nuremberg advised his patients: 'as far as is possible, you should avoid pestilential air and infected and pestilential persons along with crowds'.[128] In a plague tract of the early fifteenth century, Dr Johannes Aygeis of Korneuburg saw the plague spreading through the mixing in crowds not only through breath but also by touch, speech, and occasionally sight.[129] This doctor and many others repeated the refrain, 'it only took one in a crowd to spread the disease to many others.'[130]

---

[122] Tommaso del Garbo, *Consiglio contro la pistolenza*, ed. by Pietro Ferrato (Bologna, 1866), p. 21; [20], p. 423; [46], pp. 329–30; and [74], p. 180; [117], p. 136; [119], p. 159; [24bis], p. 33; [183], pp. 49–50; [190 and 191], p. 62; [232], p. 158; and [140], pp. 93–4; [153], p. 145; Savonarola, *I Trattati in volgare della peste*, p. 7.

[123] [83], p. 243.

[124] [140], p. 93.

[125] As Vivian Nutton, 'The seeds of disease: an explanation of contagion and infection from the Greeks to the Renaissance', *Medical History* 27 (1983), p. 1, has charged: to deny that doctors of antiquity had no knowledge of contagion on the grounds that they had no theory of seeds of disease or of germs 'is to confuse an appreciation of contagion *qua* contagiousness' with an explanation of its mechanics. Also see Henderson, 'The Black Death in Florence', pp. 136–41; and Arrizabalaga, 'Facing the Black Death', p. 260.

[126] See Winslow, *The Conquest of Epidemic Disease*, p. 115, the conflict between 'contagionistic' and 'miasmatic' theories arose later; also see his chapter on 'the last of the plague tractates', by Dr Richard Mead in 1720, esp. pp. 181–3. None of the essays in the recent *Contagion: Perspectives from Pre–Modern Societies*, ed. by Lawrence Conrad and Dominik Wujastyk (Aldershot, 2000), deals with the Black Death and the plague tracts, which followed; nor do any of the authors seem to know the excellent work of Winslow.

[127] [34], p. 338.

[128] [138], p. 87.

[129] See for instance [56], p. 371; for others who saw the spread of plague by speech as well as by other means, see [38], p. 356; [113], p. 72; [198], p. 105.

[130] In addition to the citations in the previous note, also see [64], p. 92; [57], p. 373; [151], p. 141; [153], p. 145; *Practica Antonii Guainerii*, 97r.

Further, because of the risk of contagion, the plague tracts advised a battery of methods by which doctors might escape contagion while administering treatment to plague patients: use of various scents and ointments, keeping windows open and covering the nose and mouth during examinations.[131] Suspicion of contagion through water led one tract after another to counsel patients not to take baths in plague time and especially not to share the bath water.

For several chroniclers the concept of contagion also carried theoretical overtones of a general 'corruption' of nature or air, although they are rare with merchant chroniclers. Matteo Villani described the plague of 1357 as 'an epidemic of corrupt air' and used the same terms to explain the origins of the glandular plague of 1362.[132] Such notions were more prevalent with monastic chroniclers. Michele da Piazza, the anonymous author of the Apuleian necrology, Richard the Scot and other chroniclers of Saint-Denis, Jean de Venette, Gilles le Muisit, Henricus Dapifer of Diessenhoven, those at Westminster, and at St Albans in the late fourteenth century pointed to vapours and atmospheric corruption to explain the plague's speed.[133] But, again these concepts did not conflict with person-to-person contagion as the plague's *modus operandi*. As with the doctors, corruption of the air and contagion were mutually reinforcing.

Among all these writers such notions of contagion were not theory-driven but instead came from empirical observation of the plague's course and its patterns of morbidity and mortality. To them, the clearest sign of this person-to-person contagion was the elementary epidemiological observation that if one person in a household came down with plague, the rest soon became infected. As the Cortusii put it: 'Just as one sheep would infect the rest of the flock, so if one in a household caught the plague it would spread, killing the rest even down to the household's dogs'.[134] Merchant chroniclers—Stefani, the anonymous annalist of Forlì, and the chronicler of the German town of Erfurt[135]—as well as a wide range of religious writers, the author of Pope Clement VI's life (who died soon after the first plague), Michele da Piazza, Gilles le Muisit, the author of the Austrian *Codex Novimontibus*, Thomas Walsingham, the chroniclers of Cologne, and others,[136] observed the same and drew the same conclusion about the

---

[131] See for instance [74], pp. 179–81.

[132] Matteo Villani, *Cronica*, II, pp. 118 and 585.

[133] Michele da Piazza, *Cronica*, p. 277: 'et human corpora corruptione aeris infecit'; 'Fragmenta Historica', p. 43; *Richardi Scoti Chronicon*, p. 82; *Chronique du religieux de Saint–Denys*, II, pp. 696 and 690; *Chronique latine de Guillaume de Nangis (Continuatio)*, II, p. 213; *Chronique et annales de Gilles le Muisit*, pp. 195 and 257; *Henricus Dapifer de Diessenhoven*, p. 65; *The Westminister Chronicle*, pp. 190 and 438; *The St Albans Chronicle*, p. 11.

[134] Contusii, *Historia de Novitatibus Paduae*, col. 926.

[135] Stefani, *Cronica fiorentina*, p.230; *Annales Forolivienses*, p. 85; *Chronicon Elwacense*, p. 40.

[136] *Vita Clementis VI ad annum 1348*, ed. by Baluze-Mollat, 1 (Paris 1914), p. 251; Michele da Piazza, *Cronica*, p. 82; *Chronique et annales de Gilles le Muisit*, p. 257; *Codex*

plague's new and remarkable levels of contagion. From England to Poland, chroniclers commented on these household patterns and not only for 1348. For Louis Sanctus the clustering of plague deaths reached beyond the household to larger kin groups; 'if one family member died, almost all the rest followed'.[137]

Although the doctors' texts are certainly far more riveted with theoretical explanations of contagion—putrification, odours, the corruption of nature, the effect of planetary configurations and above all else the corruption of air—they too observed the plague's mortalities clustering within households because of contagion. In a plague tract of 1371 doctor Henricus of Bratislava even derived his theory of the plague's spread from the observation that all who lived in the same household with the infected tended to die; from fetid breath, one infected another, 'so that all thus die in the same household or curia'. He further speculated that those who share the same food and water tend to infect one another, and thus pestilential fevers can derive from fetid water and 'the fruits of the land' as well as from bad vapours.[138] In a text of the fifteenth century that borrowed from Henricus, the author made it clear that these principles of inner household infection derived from observation and experience (*sicut nos vidimus ad experienciam*).[139] The doctors even used this epidemiological feature of the plague's household clustering to distinguish it from all other diseases, which they saw as less contagious.[140] Against the moral preaching of the chroniclers such as Matteo Villani, who was alarmed at the inhumane and cowardly fleeing from the plague and especially the abandoning of stricken family members, the doctors advised their patients and readers to do just that: 'cito, longe, et tarde' as many plague tracts repeated; flee the plague quickly, go far way, and return as late as possible.[141] Some, as we have seen, such as King Martin's doctor, even advised abandoning their own families because of the tendency for deaths to cluster in households.

Like the chroniclers,[142] the doctors also saw this pattern of mortality clusters operating in larger 'households'. The doctor Saladino Ferro da Ascoli asked at the end of his plague treatise: 'Why are prisoners and nuns sometimes able to avoid the plague's offence entirely, yet at other times, they all die from it?'[143] In contrast to the 1348 reports of exceptional and

---

Novimontibus, p. 675; *Historia Anglicana*, p. 409; *Continuatio Mellicensis*, p. 513; *Annales Mechovienses*, p. 670; *Die Kölner Weltchronik*, p. 92; *Die Weltchronik des Mönchs Albert*, p. 280.

[137] *Breve chronicon Flandriae*, p. 467.
[138] [9], p. 214. Also see [57], pp. 373–4.
[139] [9bis], p. 85, built on the theory of the contagion and infection of a region or city from the model of infection within a household.
[140] See for instance [258], p. 40; [265], p. 80.
[141] [19], p. 420.
[142] *Chronique du religieux de Saint-Denys*, II, p. 693.
[143] Simili, 'Saladino Ferro da Ascoli', p. 40. Also, see [98], p. 130.

massive mortalities within the cloistered orders, by the early fifteenth century one tract even thought that nuns were less susceptible to plague than others and raised 'a doubt' about the general theory of breathing corrupt air in enclosed places.[144] Further, Bartolomea Riccoboni's remarkable chronicle of the deaths of her 49 sisters cloistered in the Dominican house of Corpus Domini in Venice gives some support for these observations. Over the plague-ridden years from 1400 to 1436, not a single sister died of plague. Only one died quickly (within three days); most were long-drawn-out affairs, winning Bartolomea's praise for longsuffering and patience.[145] Instead of any special immunity, their protection no doubt had to do with the plague's epidemiology. Corpus Domini happened to be a house in which no nun caught or came to the house with plague; thus the nunnery remained plague-free. Had one nun caught it, its demographic history would have no doubt been entirely different. By the second half of the fifteenth century officials in Mantua took the clustering of deaths within households as one of the most consistent signs of plague,[146] and by the sixteenth century at least one plague tract—that of Filippo Ingrassia—found this epidemiological feature—not the buboes or other skin disorders—to be the crucial test for judging whether an epidemic was 'true plague'.[147]

Can we go beyond these perceptions to test the degree of household clustering quantitatively? From the testaments of Pierre Clarion drawn up on 18 March 1349 and his widow's six days later in Forez (southwest France), Fournial was able to determine that within that period two of their four children had died and both parents were on their deathbeds; thus one might presume that four out of a household of six had been deadly attacked by the plague.[148] From the notarial business of the Roman Paulus de Serromanis, a father and his two sons made testaments on their deathbeds from the 15 May to 11 June during the plague of 1363.[149] But without time-consuming family reconstructions, probably impossible with any set of testaments before the early modern period, these sources like the chronicles can only supply examples. On the other hand, burial records, which list deaths from day to day, would also require painstaking family reconstruction, and often the records, particularly of children's deaths, do not provide enough identifiers for one to sort out with confidence to which families or

---

[144] [258], p. 40.

[145] B. Riccoboni, *Cronaca del Corpus Domini*, pp. 257–94, in B. Giovanni Dominici OP, *Lettere spirituali*, ed. by M.-T. Casella and G. Pozzi, Spicilegium Friburgense, 13 (Friburg, 1969). I wish to thank Daniel Bornstein for bringing this text to my attention.

[146] Carmichael, *Plague and the Poor*, p. 24.

[147] Irma Naso, 'Individuazione diagnostica della "pesta nera". Cultura medica e aspetti clinici', in *La Peste Nera*, p. 371.

[148] Fournial, *Les villes et l'économie d'échange en Forez*, p. 310.

[149] Archivio Capitolino, Section I, tome 649, vol. 6 (1363), 3r–4v, 11v–13r, 13r–14v, and 14v–15v.

households they belonged. From the burial records of Florence, few died in the same household at least on the same day during periods of plague, and although the numbers went up slightly with the plague months of 1400, the differences were negligible.[150]

Giovanni Dominici's chronicle of the plague in Pistoia in 1400 gives us a rare, if not unique, opportunity to gauge quantitatively the household speci-ficity of mortality during a late-medieval plague.[151] Obsessed with all manner of statistics from the numbers of men and animals taken hostage by the Cancellieri rebels during mountain raids of 1402 to daily weather reports,[152] Dominici as officer in charge of Pistoia's hospitals listed by parish those to fall from plague in 1400. The organisation of these lists varies (perhaps reflecting what the parish priests happened to submit to him). Most of the dead are registered by the death day as in the burial records, but for two large parishes, San Piero in Strada and San Vitale, the plague-stricken 'bodies' are grouped according to household over the entire plague period of 1400, from January to August.

The impression given by these statistics is wholly different from the slim chance of multiple household deaths occurring on the same day. In San Piero 139 died of plague (according to the doctors who examined the bodies) from 50 households. Of these two-thirds (33) came from a house-hold in which another had died of plague; in five households, six family members died.[153] For San Vitale the per centages were almost as high: 218 plague victims came from 111 households; plague killed more than one member in 64 of these houses. These figures are of mortalities only.[154] Even if the plague was as virulent as the chroniclers claimed, the cases of plague per household would have been higher: we know of doctors and others infected who escaped death; by Raymundus Chalmelli's account, the proportions of survivors increased rapidly over time.

Like chroniclers and plague doctors of the later Middle Ages, the modern plague researchers in India also employed this elementary lesson in epidemi-ology to understand their current plague and were astonished to find the very opposite: 'the great majority of the patients whose history was accu-rately known had had no contact with previous plague sufferers . . . in the great majority of instances not more than one person became infected per house'.[155] Moreover, when they occurred (again unlike those of the later

---

[150] Before the increase of plague deaths in 1400 (January 1398 to May 1400) only 0.8 per cent of the households showed more than one death on a given day (23 cases out of 2721); when the plague reached its peak in July 1400, it increased to 1.6 per cent of households (53 of 3359) on the same day—a significant but hardly impressive change.

[151] *Cronache di Ser Luca Dominici*, I.

[152] On Dominici's numeric fascination, see Cohn, *Creating the Florentine State*, pp. 127–30.

[153] *Cronache di Ser Luca Dominici*, I, pp. 242–5.

[154] Ibid., pp. 245–8.

[155] Pollitzer and Meyer, 'The ecology of plague', pp. 472–3.

Middle Ages), they were simultaneous, within hours of one another.[156] For
the plague of 1900 in Sydney, instead of two-thirds of plague victims residing in the same households, only ten of 276 households or 3.6 per cent were
multiple cases of plague infection (and not deaths).[157]

*   *   *

Another sign of the plague's contagion was the professions most exposed
and killed by it. For the plague at Messina, Michele da Piazza observed that
'many priests, judges, and notaries' refused to attend to the plague-stricken,
to hear confessions or draw up wills. On the other hand, those of his order
(the Minor Friars) answered the cries of the stricken and, as a result, caught
the disease and died, 'so that hardly any now remained in their cells'.[158]
Gilles le Muisit maintained that certain chaplains and parish curates, those
who heard confessions and administered the sacraments, died in inordinate
numbers, since they were the ones who visited the plague-stricken.[159] In a
single phrase, the Irish chronicler John Clyn illustrates the connectedness
between the speed of contagion and the clergy's especial risk: 'the confessor
and confessed were led together to the grave'.[160] The chronicler of Mainz
for plague in 1361 and Jean de Venette for 1363[161] continued to point to
clerics as the heaviest-hit. For the plague of 1418 the Parisian Bourgeois
claimed that so many priests died that as many as eight household heads
would be buried with only one mass sung for all of them.[162] In addition to
'almost all the friars and priests of Trent dying' in 1348, Giovanni da Parma
pointed to doctors, adding that 'the best' died in even greater numbers
(presumably because like Guy de Chauliac they risked their lives to treat the
plague-stricken).[163] According to the Parisian doctor Simon de Couvin, all
the doctors of Montpellier perished in the plague of 1348, despite the fact
that because of its medical school a greater number resided there than elsewhere in France.[164]

---

[156] See the classic article by Simond, 'La propagation de la peste', p. 637, and Thompson, 'On
the epidemiology of plague', *JH*, 6 (1906), p. 566. Curiously, Roger Schofield, 'An Anatomy
of an Epidemic: Colyton, November 1645 to November 1646', in *The Plague Reconsidered*,
p. 102, asserts the opposite: that diseases such as bubonic plague cluster in households but
airborne infections do not. His claim (and denial of hundreds of years of common sense and
epidemiological research) is not, however, based on any new epidemiological findings; no note
follows it, but perhaps because of Schofield's reputation as a demographic historian and his
quantitative skills, others have followed blindly: see Bradley, 'Some medical aspects of plague,'
11–24, ibid.; and Benedictow, *Plague in the Late Medieval Nordic Countries*, p. 174.
[157] Thompson, 'On the epidemiology of plague', p. 540.
[158] Michele da Piazza, *Cronica*, pp. 82–3.
[159] *Chronique et annales de Gilles le Muisit*, p. 257.
[160] *Annalium Hiberniae*, p. 36.
[161] *Chronicon Moguntinum*, pp. 164–5; *Chronique latine de Guillaume de Nangis
(Continuatio)*, II, pp. 325–6.
[162] *Journal d'un bourgeois de Paris*, p. 111.
[163] *Cronica inedita di Giovanni da Parma Canonico di Trento*, p. 51–2.
[164] Cited in Campbell, *The Black Death*, p. 31.

Another profession disproportionately exposed to the infected were gravediggers—the 'gavoti'—whom Stefani in Florence[165] and Louis Sanctus in Avignon claimed were among the worst hit in 1348 'because of the infectious contagion'.[166] Boccaccio maintained that the plague gave rise to the gravediggers as a profession. Neighbours, kinsmen and, in particular, kinswomen, out of fear of contagion, abandoned their traditional roles of preparing the bodies, accompanying the dead to their graves, and ensuring that they received honourable funerals. In their place, the most miserable sectors of society, often immigrants from the mountains, filled the vacuum for what Boccaccio and Stefani claimed were extortionate sums.[167]

Other evidence points to other professions that demanded close contact with the dead and who thus died in disproportionate numbers. For Perpignan, Richard Emery has calculated that between 58 and 68 per cent of notaries died in 1348.[168] In February 1349, the Commune of Montevarchi on the Arno south of Florence petitioned the Florentine *Signoria* to let stand those wills redacted during the plague by non-matriculated notaries. They argued that the plague had there wiped out the entire profession, leaving them no alternative.[169] Another profession that may have disappeared altogether in the first plague was the wax chandlers of London. In addition to supplying candles for funerals, they embalmed bodies and prepared them for funerals.[170]

Finally, soldiers sometimes figured among those worst hit by plague. For the plague of 1350, Henry of Hervordia claimed that along with clerics, soldiers (*militaribus*) died in greater numbers throughout Germany.[171] Matteo Villani also saw them dying in the greatest numbers at Pisa during the plague of 1362 as well as outside of Brescia in July and August of that year when fighting was particularly fierce against soldiers of the Lombard League.[172] For the same plague, a year later, the *Cronichetta d'incerto* also singled them out.[173] These chroniclers did not explain why soldiers should have died disproportionately, but presumably as with other contagious diseases it would have spread amongst those sharing closed quarters and enduring unhygienic conditions.

By contrast, plague researchers of the late nineteenth and twentieth centuries did not single out any of these professions. Instead, early on they

---

[165] Stefani, *Cronica fiorentina*, p. 231.
[166] Sanctus, pp. 467–8.
[167] Stefani, *Cronica fiorentina*, p. 231; *Decameron*, pp. 15–16.
[168] Richard W. Emery, 'The Black Death of 1348 in Perpignan,' *Speculum*, XLII, 4 (1967), pp. 614–17.
[169] Cohn, *Creating the Florentine State*, p. 228; ASF, Provisioni Registri, no. 36, 54v.
[170] I wish to thank Richard Percival, Assistant Clerk to the Company of the Wax Chandlers Guild, London, for this communication, and see *The Worshipful Company of Wax Chandlers* (privately published, 2001), p. 6.
[171] *Liber de Rebus Memorabilioribus*, p. 284.
[172] Matteo Villani, *Cronica*, II, p. 585.
[173] *Cronichetta d'incerto*, p. 183.

discovered that modern plague, whether bubonic or in its occasional pneu-monic form, was not a particularly contagious disease. They repeated often with astonishment: 'the safest place during plague was the plague ward of hospitals'.[174] Instead of priests, doctors, morticians, and others who dealt with the plague sick and dying, one profession stood out clearly as dying disproportionately from modern plague—those who dealt with grain. Late medieval chroniclers made no connections between grain dealers or bakers and plague; as we will see, with good reason.

Another lament of the chroniclers was the absence of a decent burial for the plague dead, which resulted not only from the unprecedented task of burying such vast numbers, but also from fear of the disease's contagion. As in Siena, Pisa, Venice, and Trent, the chronicler of Perugia decried: 'No one could be found to bury the dead.'[175] In Messina, 'bodies remained alone in their own houses without any priest, son, father, or kinsman daring to enter; instead porters were paid unusual sums to carry them off.'[176] In Rouen, 'new cemeteries sprang up'.[177] The ecclesiastical chronicler of Erfurt reported that 'such was the multitude of burials in cemeteries every-where that two or three had to be put in each grave, and afterwards, eleven giant ditches were dug in the cemetery of Nuzezse near Erfurt, where 12,000 bodies were placed.'[178] In Vienna, 'because of the contagion, horror and stench . . . the plague dead were brought to a common place outside the city called the field of God, where five ditches were dug to bury them.'[179] In England, existing cemeteries were 'insufficient' and 'fields were elected to bury the dead'.[180] Stefani compared the plague's rushed mass burials in 1348 to the layering of lasagna, a light scattering of dirt served as the cheese that separated the next layer of bodies.[181] For some, the threat of burial without sacraments or decency rivalled, even surpassed, the horrors of the plague's painful illness and its mass death. Thus, the Sienese Agnolo di Tura ended his account of the plague of 1348:

> I'll not write about the cruelty that took place in the countryside (*contado*), of the wolves and other wild animals, which ate the bodies of those poorly buried, and of other atrocities which would be too sad for anyone to read.[182]

---

[174] See Bannerman, 'The spread of plague in India', p. 180: of 533 plague cases treated at the plague hospital at the Old Government House at Parel (1896–7) there was not a single instance of the plague spreading from the patients to the nurses or attendants.
[175] *Cronaca Pisana*, p. 114; *Cronaca Senese attribuita ad Agnolo di Tura*, p. 555. *Cronica inedita di Giovanni da Parma*, p. 51; Sanuto, *Vitæ Ducum Venetorum*, p. 615; *Cronica della città di Perugia* p. 148.
[176] Michele da Piazza, *Cronica*, p. 83.
[177] *Chronique Normande*, p. 73.
[178] *Cronicae S. Petri Erford. cont. III* , p. 381.
[179] *Codex Novimontibus*, p. 675.
[180] *Chronicon Galfridi le Baker*, p. 98.
[181] Stefani, *Cronica fiorentina*, p. 231.
[182] *Cronaca Senese attribuita ad Agnolo di Tura del Grasso*, p. 555.

For later plagues, these problems did not altogether disappear. During the plague of 1374—Milan's second major plague—its anonymous annalist claimed that 'hardly anyone could be found who would carry the bodies to the grave' and that 'in a single ditch, ten, twenty, even thirty bodies would be piled up'.[183] The Gatari ended their woeful story of the plague of 1405 in Padua with what they thought was the most upsetting news of all—an ignominious death without an individual burial or funeral that properly honoured one's station in life:

> And you the reader should note the way in which people were buried. In the morning, carts gathered the dead and each carrying 16 to 20 bodies; at the head was only one priest with a cross fit on the cart's rudder and a lighted lantern. Every day a large ditch was dug in the churchyard and in every ditch 200 or even 300 were thrown, one over the other, covered little by little with dirt. And these were citizens and bourgeois, who were not to be buried in their family tombs (*casate*). Some carried their fathers on their shoulders to the grave; some their sons in their arms, husbands, wives; wives, husbands; brothers, sisters, with such anguish, screams, and cruel cries that could be heard in heaven. And after the crying, with tears still in their eyes, their hearts closed with grief, our citizens were forced to turn to arms and iron to defend the city day and night from enemies who desired our blood. What more can one say? I am of the opinion that after the destruction of Jerusalem or the great city of Troy by the furore of the Greeks, no city in the world could be as full of sadness as this, our city of Padua.[184]

Finally, in the plague of Paris in 1418 'the Bourgeois' also noted with a spirit of poetic license usual for this matter-of-fact chronicler: 'so many people died so fast towards the end of the month that they had to dig great pits in the cemeteries of Paris and lay 30 or 40 in at once, in rows like sides of bacon, and then a bit of earth scattered over them'.[185]

Along with these observations came others which show that not only the chroniclers but those they chronicled understood and treated the plague as a poison transmitted rapidly person-to-person. Numerous chroniclers reported the same lament but in different words. As the *Annales Pistorienses* put it:

> the father abandoned his children and the children the father and mother, and one brother the other, so that none could be found to help the sick or carry the dead to the grave; neither friar nor priest attended those wishing their services, because the disease spread from the sick to the well.[186]

Moralists such as Matteo Villani were astounded that Christians could possibly be so callous:

---

183 *Annales Mediolanenses*, p. 756.
184 Gatari, *Cronaca Carrarese*, p. 560.
185 *Journal d'un bourgeois de Paris*, p. 111.
186 *Annales Pistorienses*, p. 524.

This cruel inhumanity of mothers and fathers abandoning their children, children their fathers and mothers, one brother the other brother and other relatives, began with infidels. Faithful Christians detested cruel and astonishing behaviour, strange and against human nature, but they soon followed the barbaric nations, practising the same cruelty.[187]

Later, the humanist chancellor Coluccio Salutati castigated his fellow Florentines for fleeing the city and their republican obligations in plague time. As can be seen in the missing sessions of the *provvisioni* for Florence and other cities, the plague brought governments to a standstill and not only in 1348.[188] During the plague of 1374, Florence also could not muster a quorum required of its two major chambers to pass laws. In response to the exodus of its ruling classes, it passed laws requiring the departed to return or face penalties up to 500 lire as well as losing their rights to hold political office (*divieto*), but, as Stefani suggests, it was to no avail.[189] With the plague of 1383, the humanist Leonardo Bruni lamented the evacuation of the city by its best citizens, leaving behind the plebs, for which reason the elitist Bruni concluded there was nothing worth writing about for that year.[190]

By contrast, doctors advised their clients to act in the very fashion merchant and republican moralists condemned,[191] and it was their pragmatism, not the priests' or republicans' moralism, that prevailed. By the fifteenth century and increasingly into the early modern period, governmental reports advising citizens where to flee in plague time became standard summer reading for the ruling classes of Italy.[192] Yet the widespread abandonment of family members appears to have been largely confined to the plague's first horrific appearance. Even the disapproving Matteo[193] saw light at the end of the tunnel in the human condition of his fellow Florentines after the worst of the plague of 1348. In Florence, he maintained, 'people without suspicion began to help and serve one another, from whence many were cured, and people were secure in helping others'.[194]

---

[187] Matteo Villani, *Cronica*, p. 11.
[188] See above pp. 146–7.
[189] Stefani, *Cronica fiorentina*, p. 289.
[190] Bruni, *Historiarum Florentini*, p. 236. He also sees them leaving in droves during the plague of 1400 (p. 280).
[191] See [22], p. 41; [24], p. 51; [26], p. 57; [5]; [19], p. 420; and many others.
[192] Cipolla, *Cristofano and the Plague: A Study in the History of Public Health in the Age of Galileo* (London, 1973), pp. 118–19.
[193] The most often cited section of Villani's chronicle is undoubtedly, Book I, chapter VI: 'Come li uomini furono piggiori che prima', pp. 15–17, which painted a gloomy picture of the moral after-effects of the plague. Millard Meiss, *Painting in Florence and Siena after the Black Death* (Princeton, 1951), pp. 65–8; G. G. Coulton, *Five Centuries of Religion*, IV (Cambridge, 1950), p. 456, and Raymond Crawfurd, *Plague and Pestilence in Literature and Art* (Oxford, 1914), p. 117, commented extensively on this section but, as with other historians, noted little else of what this remarkable chronicler had to say about the plagues.
[194] Matteo Villani, *Chronica*, I, pp. 9–10.

There may have been some truth in his observation. Except for one occasion, a plague in Perugia in 1448,[195] such descriptions of family abandonment in the face of plague, even when conditions became as bleak as those described at Padua in 1405, disappear from the chronicles.

Not that the plague lost its contagion with subsequent strikes; rather, contemporaries found ways, even rules, for behaving in plague time that led less to panic and more to what they saw as efficacious remedies both on the societal as well as the individual plane—as the mounting production of plague tracts with specific recipes, treatments, and preventatives attests. The change in mentality can be seen with both the chroniclers and the doctors. It rested no doubt with contemporaries' horror and incomprehension of the first outbreak, which caused them to jump to the stars and other extraterrestrial explanations. But the social explanations for the later plagues may in fact reflect a change in the epidemiology of the plagues. As social historians have recently argued, the first wave of plagues may not have been socially prepared by hard times, unusually unhygienic conditions, social injustice and inequalities, 'a culture of poverty, dirt and promiscuity' as historians Le Roy Ladurie and David Herlihy once argued and introductory texts still proclaim with great confidence.[196] Instead, Barbara Harvey, Bruce Campbell, and a later David Herlihy have seen the plague of 1348 as a 'grand exogenous variable', a new pathogen that invaded from outside the European ecology and for which personal hygiene or health had little bearing.[197]

The narrative sources lend support to this revised thinking. Various chroniclers claimed that the first wave of plague hit populations indiscriminately, regardless of age, sex, or social class.[198] Gilles le Muisit asserted that 'neither the rich, the middling sort (*mediocris*), nor the pauper was secure; each had to await God's will'.[199] While Matteo Villani suggested that the poor were among the first victims, he called the first plague 'a pestilence among men of every condition, age and sex'.[200] The Paris Medical Faculty, Geoffrey le Baker, the Abbot at Tournai, and Henry of Hervordia even saw the first plague striking down the strong and rich in greater

---

[195] *Cronica della città di Perugia*, p. 600.

[196] Le Roy Ladurie, 'A concept', pp. 48–51; Herlihy, *Medieval and Renaissance Pistoia*, p. 114; and, most recently, Prosperi, *Dalla Peste Nera*, p. 43; and Aberth, *From the Brink of the Apocalypse*, p. 112.

[197] Harvey, 'Introduction: The "crisis" of the early fourteenth century', in *Before the Black Death: Studies in the 'Crisis' of the Early Fourteenth Century*, ed. by Bruce Campbell (Manchester, 1991), pp. 1–24; Herlihy, *The Black Death*, ch. 1.

[198] See for instance *Chronica antiqua Conventus Sanctae Catharinae*, p. 541 and Stefani, *Cronica fiorentina*, p. 232.

[199] *Chronique et annales de Gilles le Muisit*, p. 257.

[200] Villani, *Cronica*, I, pp. 9 and 14. Also, an anonymous German plague tract of the 1370s made the same point, that 'the poor and common people die first' and the better off, later; Horrox, p. 179.

numbers than the weak and ill.[201] Ragusa's loss of most of its ruling council in 1348 gives such claims some credence.[202]

Others from the British Isles saw it differently. The chronicler who continued the *Polychronicon* of Higden commented that hardly any of the lords or magnates died in this plague, but he was probably referring to the second one,[203] and the Scottish chronicler John of Fordun thought the plague struck 'the middle sort and commoners but rarely the magnates'.[204] This alternative view of the class bias in mortality, moreover, might be supported by the great rarity of agricultural and skilled labour in the plague's aftermath, as seen in the rocketing rise of the prices of basic commodities decried by numerous chroniclers and writers—Henry Knighton, the chronicler of Rochester Priory, William Langland, Matteo and Filippo Villani, Stefani, the anonymous chronicler of Milan, and the chronicler Maqrīzī of Egypt[205]—along with the enactment of labour legislation in England, Aragon, Castile, Ragusa, and many city-states in Italy.[206] At least one modern historian, Raymond Cazelles, has claimed that from the beginning the Black Death was 'a proletarian epidemic' but more convincingly others, such as Geneviève Prat and Edouard Perroy, relying on local studies with land registers and fiscal records, have corroborated the message heard from the mass of the chroniclers: initially the Black Death was egalitarian in its onslaught[207].

For subsequent plagues of the fourteenth century chroniclers still pointed to the high numbers of notable citizens. For 1358, the historian of Orvieto emphasised that it was the 'good and notable citizens of Orvieto who received the greatest damage'.[208] For the same plague in Germany, Guy de Chauliac reported that it began with commoners (*populares*) but ended by killing more of the rich and nobility.[209] The chronicler of the Grey Friars at Lynn called the plague of 1361 'a great pestilence . . . of children, adolescents, and the wealthy'.[210] The Sienese Donato di Neri pointed to fathers,

---

[201] Horrox, p. 183; *Chronicon Galfridi le Baker*, pp. 98–9; *Chronique et annales de Gilles le Muisit*, p. 257; *Liber de Rebus Memorabilioribus*, p. 284.

[202] *Monumenta Ragusina: Libri Reformationum*, II; ed. by Fr. Racki (Zagreb, 1882), p. 27.

[203] *Polychronicon Ranulphi Higden*, p. 355.

[204] *Johannis de Fordun Chronica*, p. 369; Bower, *Scotichronicon*, VII, p. 273, repeated Fordun for 1349.

[205] Knighton and the chronicler of Rochester Priory, Horrox, pp. 69–75; William Langland, *Piers the Ploughman*, trans. J.F. Goodridge (Harmondsworth, 1959), pp. 89–90; Matteo Villani, *Cronaca*, I, p. 392; Filippo Villani, ibid., II, p. 668; Stefani, *Cronaca fiorentina*, p. 232; *Annales Mediolanenses*, col. 756; and Maqrīzī, *Sulūk*, p. 380.

[206] See Charles Verlinden, 'La grande peste de 1348 en Espagne: Contribution à l'Étude de ses conséquences économiques et sociales,' *Revue belge de Philologie et d'Histoire* 17 (1938): 103–46; Maxim Kovalevsky, 'Die wirtschaflichen Folgen des schwarzen Todes in Italien', *Zeitschrift für Sozial- und Wirtschaftsgechichte* III (1895): 406–23; for a fuller discussion and bibliography, see my 'Labour legislation after the Black Death' (forthcoming).

[207] Carpentier, 'Famines et épidémies', pp. 1069–70, summarises this historiography.

[208] *Discorso Historico*, p. 84.

[209] *Chirurgia*, Trat. II, cap. 5 in Haeser, p. 176.

[210] Horrox, p. 86.

heads of households, grand citizens and merchants as the ones who died in the plague of 1363 at Pisa.[211] For the next one in 1374, he singled out the grand: ten cardinals at Avignon and at Siena, the *podestà*, his son, six judges, all his knights, notaries, and police so that hardly anyone in his service was left.[212] *The Anonimalle Chronicle* maintained that the plague of 1374 'killed a great number of the citizens of London, the best sort and the richest of the city, including many valiant officers of the Chancery, Common Pleas, and the Exchequer'.[213] Thomas Walsingham said the plague of 1379 rapidly stripped England of its best men: 'of the middling groups (*mediocribus*) nearly every house had been evacuated so that hardly any remained'.[214] Others such as the anonymous chronicler of Tournai continued to see the plague as lacking any distinct class bias even as late as the plague of 1400:

> And this plague began by killing agricultural labourers and manual workers (*gens mécaniques*), who gained their living by the day or otherwise. As for the bourgeois and rich merchants, they were said to be on their guard, and thought that the death would only take drinkers of cheap beer and ale (*buveurs de ambours*[215] *et de goudale*). But, soon afterwards, the plague struck the drinkers of fine wines (*ypocras* and *Malevisée*), neither sparing the bourgeois, canons, priests, vicars, chaplains, nor other churchmen, nor all other sorts of people. It killed the genteel along with the vile, and included doctors and physicians among its numbers.[216]

This class bias of the plague towards the rich (or absence of it towards the poor) may have resulted from the chroniclers' concern and desire to commemorate their own; hence the Bolognese chronicler Matteo Griffoni recorded the plague in 1399 as 'killing many good citizens, among whom was Lord Jacobus de Griffonibus'.[217]

After the first plague, others began to suggest that the plague mortalities may have been mounting against the poor. The chronicler who continued Higden's *Polychronicon* maintained that by the second plague of 1362: 'few or hardly any lords and magnates died in this plague.'[218] The difference may have arisen as much from economic as biological advantage; the rich had the resources to follow the plague-tracts' recommendation to leave and stay away as long as possible. As Stefani reported in 1374: 'most with their wives and children left Florence to live in the countryside, leaving behind only those who had no means and could not leave (*e niuno era, che avesse di che fare le spese, che non se ne andasse*). Yet,

---

[211] *Cronaca senese di Donato di Neri*, p. 604.
[212] Ibid., pp. 654–5.
[213] *Anonimalle Chronicle*, p. 77.
[214] Walsingham, *Historia Anglicana*, p. 319.
[215] A beer made in Hamburg.
[216] *Chronique des Pays-Bas*, p. 332.
[217] *Matthaei de Griffonibus*, p. 88.
[218] *Polychronicon Ranulphi Higden*, p. 355.

for the first hundred years of plague I have found no chronicler who considered the plague principally a disease of the poor (even if a few, such as the chronicler of Tournai, MatteoVillani, and Giovanni Morelli,[219] saw it originating with them). None yet recommended special measures against them to protect the rich and middling classes from infection. Such attitudes, however, were on the horizon and became manifest with special plague legislation against beggars in places such as Châlons-sur-Marne by the second half of the fifteenth century,[220] in Florence by the end of the fifteenth century,[221] and in England by the sixteenth.[222] In Chapter 8 we will turn to other sources that reflect on the changing social composition of the plague dead.

* * *

Another epidemiological fact of the plague that may have changed over time was its gender bias. As we have seen, along with class, contemporaries thought the first plague struck down men and women in equal numbers,[223] as the verse-chronicler Andrew Wyntoun saw for Scotland in 1349:

> Before that tyme wes neuir sene
> pestilence in our lande sa keyne:
> Bath men, and barnnys, and women,
> It sparit noucht for to keyl then.[224]

At least four chroniclers saw the first plague killing more women than men—Giovanni da Parma, the Venetian Lorenzo De Monacis, an anonymous Venetian chronicler, and the Egyptian Maqrīzī. For some it was women's supposed weaker nature that explained the difference.[225] Although a law to attract new labourers to Ragusa in 1348 suggests the opposite: '[only] a modicum of people, especially of men, had survived the plague'.[226]

For the next plague, however, several chroniclers saw the sex bias swing in the opposite direction. For Germany and northern countries, Guy de

[219] Morelli. *Ricordi*, p. 211.

[220] Sylvette Guilbert, 'A Châlons-sur-Marne au XVe siècle: un conseil municipal face aux épidémies', *Annales: E.S.C.* 23, (1968), p. 1288.

[221] Luca Landucci, *Diario fiorentino dal 1450 al 1516 continuato da un anonimo fino al 1542*, ed. Iodoco del Badia (Florence, 1883), p. 175; also Henderson, 'Epidemics in Renaissance Florence', pp. 168–86.

[222] Slack, *The Impact of Plague in Tudor and Stuart England*.

[223] In addition to the above, the chronicler of the priory of Rochester, Geoffrey le Baker, and others commented only on the equal numbers of men and women struck down in 1348–49; see Horrox, p. 70; *Chronicon Galfridi le Baker*, p. 98.

[224] *The Original Chronicle of Andrew of Wyntoun*, VI, p. 197.

[225] *Cronica inedita di Giovanni da Parma*, p. 52; Mueller, 'Aspetti sociali ed economici della peste', p. 73; Naso, 'Individuazione diagnostica della "pesta nera"', p. 362; and Maqrīzī, *Sulūk*, p. 374.

[226] *Monumenta Ragusina: Libri Reformationum*, II, p. 27.

Chauliac observed that in contrast to the rich, nobles, and 'an infinite number of children', few women died in this plague.[227] For England at least seven chronicles were in agreement that the second plague of 1361 killed more men than women—John of Reading Thomas Walsingham, the *Anonimalle Chronicle*, the *St Albans Chronicle*, the chronicler who continued Higden's *Polychronium*, the Chronicle of Louth Park Abbey, and the anonymous Canterbury chronicle.[228] The chronicler of Louth Abbey said it was chiefly of young men and boys and said it was commonly called 'the boys' pestilence'.[229] From this demographic change, John of Reading drew further moral conclusions that he charged derived from the resulting sexual imbalance:

> Widows, forgetting the love they had borne towards their first husbands, rushed into the arms of foreigners or, in many cases, of kinsmen, and shamelessly gave birth to bastards conceived in adultery. It was even claimed that in many places brothers took their sisters to wife . . . [They] no longer worried about sexual lapses; now fornication, incest, and adultery were a game rather than a sin.[230]

But no such resounding consensus can be found on the continent.[231] I have found only one chronicler, Jean de Venette for the plague in Paris in 1363, who saw a later plague as killing one sex over the other. As in Britain more men than women died.[232] If the second plague killed more men than women in Tuscany (as one might have thought, since it began with soldiers fighting in the wars between Florence, Pisa, and San Miniato), the statistically minded chroniclers—Matteo Villani, Stefani, and later Minerbetti—left no hint of it. While they made distinctions in mortalities according to class and especially age, they either did not mention sex or asserted that men and women died in equal numbers in the plagues after 1348.[233] Other chroniclers in other regions of Italy and France—Orvieto's chronicler for 1358;[234] Pistoia's Sozomenus for 1400;[235] the Parisian Bourgeois for 1438 and 1445—maintained the same: men and women died in equal numbers.[236] Further, no British chronicler saw the mortalities of any later

---

[227] Haeser, p. 176.

[228] John of Reading, p. 150; Walsingham, *Historia Anglicana*, I, p. 296; *The Anonimalle Chronicle*, p. 50; *Chronicon Angliae ab anno Domini 1328*, p. 50.

[229] *Chronicon Abbati de Parco Lude*, pp. 40–1.

[230] Horrox, pp. 87–8.

[231] Immediately following the plague of 1348, the *Cronaca Aquilana*, p. 85, claimed that widows quickly remarried so that a man of 90 could marry a saucy young girl (*la citola pilliose*).

[232] *Chronique latine de Guillaume de Nangis (Continuatio)*, II, pp. 325–6.

[233] Such were the conclusions of Matteo Villani for the epidemic in the countryside of Florence in 1357, *Cronica*, II, pp. 118–19; and of Stefani for the plague in Florence of 1383, *Cronica fiorentina*, p. 426.

[234] *Discorso Historico*, p. 84.

[235] *Specimen Historiæ Sozomeni*, col. 1170.

[236] *Journal d'un bourgeois de Paris*, pp. 342 and 379.

plague of the fourteenth or early fifteenth century with a sexual profile similar to that of 1361.[237]

In contrast to class and sex, chroniclers across Europe, from Scotland to Poland, observed in unison a profound change over the plague's first hundred years according to another social category—age. As we shall see, the second plague, which the English called the children's plague, was not a particularity of that plague, as some historians have thought. Rather, from the narrative sources as well as areas that can be studied quantitatively, children as the plague's chief victims continued to mount disproportionately through the second half of the fourteenth century.

The chroniclers described still other epidemiological features of the plague. Even if they did not see rats, mice, or other rodents during plague and certainly no prior rat epizootic, they often saw a thin line separating the disease from themselves and the wider animal world. For the most part, it is impossible to know the direction of transmission between humans and other animals. For the plague of 1348, Stefani listed 'dogs, cats, chicken, oxen, donkeys, and sheep' as plague victims. Like humans, they also showed 'the signs', swellings in the groin and armpits and few survived.[238] Similarly, Henry Knighton, in perhaps the most cited of plague epizootics, gives no sense of whether the death of animals came before or after the human plague:

> In the same year there was a great plague (*lues*) amongst sheep everywhere in the realm, that in one place more than 5000 died in one pasture, and they so rotted that neither beast nor bird would touch them.[239]

Others saw the disease spreading from themselves to other animals and not vice versa. As we have seen, the Cortusii brothers described the disease raging through households, first killing its people, then its dogs.[240] To dogs, Gilles le Muisit added cats,[241] and Michele da Piazza 'all other animals existing in the household'.[242] But is not clear whether such phrases were literary devices for emphasizing high contagion or if the death of the odd household pet did indeed indicate an epizootic. The English chronicler John Capgrave (writing 70 years after 1348) maintained that the 'moreyn of bestis' followed the plague of 1348.[243]

---

[237] While Walsingham saw the plague of 1361 as killing more men, he saw the next one of 1375 as killing the sexes in equal numbers, *Historia Anglicana*, p. 319. For the seventeenth century in England, the picture seems mixed as well; Mary F. Hollinsworth and T.H. Hollingsworth, 'Plague mortality rates by age and sex in the parish of St Botolph's without Bishopsgate, London, 1603', *Population Studies*, 25 (1971): 131–46.

[238] Stefani, *Cronica fiorentina*, p. 230.

[239] *Knighton's Chronicle*, pp. 100–1.

[240] Contusii, *Historia de Novitatibus Paduae*, col. 926.

[241] *Chronique et annales de Gilles le Muisit*, p. 257.

[242] Michele da Piazza, *Cronica*, p. 82. Also, see Sanctus, p. 467.

[243] *John Capgrave's Abbreuiacion of Cronicles*, p. 166.

On the other hand, others suggest that the disease started with the animal world and spread to humans. The chronicler of Salona on the Dalmatian coast said the Black Death began with large animals (*in brutis animalibus*):

> Mange and rashes (*scabies et leprae*) overwhelmed totally horses, oxen, sheep, and goats. And as the hair pealed from their backs, they fell, became emaciated and weak, and after a few days died. From this began the rabid plague, which raged throughout the world, debilitating, killing, and sending into misery men everywhere.[244]

In reporting the plague of 1350 the German chronicler Henry of Hervordia also saw a prior epizootic but again of mostly large mammals; the first to catch the disease were dogs, wolves, birds, and oxen.[245]

In seeing the connectedness of plague between humans and animals the Egyptian and Syrian chroniclers went the furthest. As we have seen, Maqrīzī saw the plague as engulfing the human and animal worlds. For him the plague originated from a murrain of pasture animals in Uzbekistan, which broke out in 1341: 'the wind transmitted their stench around the world'.[246] When it spread to the Franks in Cyprus it struck animals first, then children and adolescents. He further implicated animals not seen in the Western sources as plague carriers. At Burullus and Nastarāwah, plague was spread by fishermen who caught the infected fish then the disease, their odour causing a pimple 'all black and of the size of a hazelnut' to form on the fishermen's heads.[247] The disease also afflicted crows, kites, and other birds, which also formed boils the size of hazelnut.[248] Relying on a Palestinian source, Maqrīzī reported that in Baysān and other cantons nearby (Uzbekistan) the disease slew wild animals: lions, wolves, hares, camels, onagers, wild boar 'all lay dead in fields afflicted with the boil'.[249] For the plague of 1430, the chronicler Ibn Taghrî Birdî, based on Maqrīzī, added crocodiles in the Nile and wolves and gazelles in the desert to the plague dead.[250] Along with dogs, cats, camels, the Syrian chronicler Ibn Iyās said that the boils formed under the paws of wild animals and added ostriches to Maqrīzī's list of birds so afflicted.[251]

Unlike continental chroniclers who reported these connections only for the first plague,[252] the English found them also after 1350. The continuation

---

[244] *Ecclesia Spalatensis*, p. 324.
[245] *Liber de Rebus Memorabilioribus*, p. 285.
[246] Maqrīzī, *Sulūk*, p. 368.
[247] Ibid., pp. 370, 372–3.
[248] Ibid., p. 378.
[249] Ibid., p. 379.
[250] *Arabic Annals of Abu-L-Mahâsin Ibn Taghrî Birdî*, IV, p. 70.
[251] 'Récits d'Ibn Iyās', p. 384.
[252] Also other evidence points to a preceding and accompanying epizootic of sheep and cows with the first plague in parts of Hainault; see Gérard Sivéry, 'Le Hainaut et la Peste Noire', *Société des artes et lettres du* Hainault, 79 (1965), p. 439.

of Higden reported 'a great plague of men and large animals' for the second and third waves of plague in 1369 and 1374; as did Walsingham, two of the St Albans chronicles, and *The Brut*.[253] But only one of the St Albans chronicles indicated the contagion's direction—animals followed men—and in every case the animals were large ones. No one smelled a rat.

In contrast to some chroniclers, many of the doctors saw plague as a human disease that spared the animal kingdom, both large and small. These observations in fact conflicted with their theories of a general corruption of air, by which they reckoned all sharing the same air—both animals and men—should fall equally prey to any disease. But instead of slavishly following antique doctrine, they raised these observations as 'doubts' and 'questions'.[254] Ficino may have been original in thinking that dogs and cats carried the disease 'from house to house' where it spread among humans, but he observed these animals did not become ill.[255]

The only mention of rats coming out of their holes before the late-medieval plagues (but not dying) is found in the plague tracts. Historians of the late-medieval plagues have yet to fish out this information to support their insistence that late-medieval plagues had to have been the rat-borne bubonic disease discovered at the end of the nineteenth century (and I would here say with good reason). As a sign of the corruption of the world and the inverted order of things, several doctors repeated a cliché of natural philosophy that goes back at least to Avicenna if not before.[256] The tractatus of Henricus of Bratislava cited the 'signs of plague' taken from Avicenna, of which the fourth was when mice and dormice (*mures et glires*) are seen above ground as they have been this year and as well in another year when plague followed. However, he also said other animals that lived underground—toads and moles—fled their homes in the ground because of the earth's corruption. This discussion came within the context of plagues in general founded on the Galenic principles of the triple corruptions or causes of plague, the first being 'bad constellations'.[257] Others added frogs, snakes, snails, bugs (*cimice*), scorpions, and 'similar things' to the list of subterranean animals that surfaced to announce the coming of plague.[258]

Despite Henricus's claim that he spoke from observation as well as theory, no chronicler confirmed such happenings in the animal world. As we have seen, they mentioned mice but in connection with crop failures, not

---

[253] *Polychronicon Ranulphi Higden*, pp. 418 and 438; *Chronica Monasterii S. Albani*, p. 292; and *Chronicon Angliae*, p. 64; *Thomae Walsingham*, p. 309; and *The Brut*, p. 321.
[254] [109], p. 57; [116], p. 124; [190 and 191], p. 62; Simili, 'Saladino Ferro da Ascoli', p. 39
[255] Ficino, *Consiglio contro la pestilenza*, pp. 57–8.
[256] Several doctors credited Avicenna with the observation.
[257] [9], p. 211. Also see [9bis], p. 83.
[258] Ficino, *Consiglio contro la pestilenza*, p. 57; Savonarola, *I trattati in volgare della peste*, p. 8. 'I libri italiani della pestilenza', p. 165. Also, see [52], p. 353; and *Il Libro della Pestilenza di Giovanni de Albertis*, p. 200; [52], p. 353; [98], pp. 120 and 128; [41], p. 394; [258], p. 40; Simili, 'Saladino Ferro da Ascoli', p. 40. [116], p. 125.

plague. Moreover, with the doctors these topsy-turvy movements in the animal kingdom came not as an immediate cause of plague but in the theoretical sections on remote signs of 'future plagues', heavily laden with citations to Galen, Avicenna, Rhazes, and others.

Only one doctor—Magister Johannes of Saxony—gave what may have been evidence of rats associated with a plague. When plague struck Strasbourg, where he was practising sometime around the middle of the fifteenth century, he claimed that in a household of his neighbourhood all but two of ten children died from bubonic plague (*ex bocio pestilenciali*) within eight days. On his advice the two were removed to another house where they remained healthy, but in the house, where the others had died, mice could be seen scurrying about fifteen days later. Even here, however, we have no description of an epizootic of rodents; the mice were still alive.[259] Moreover, the household specificity of death, the death of children, and not the adults, is (as we shall see) consistent with the highly contagious plague of the late Middle Ages, which by the fifteenth century had evolved into mostly a childhood disease; neither trait was characteristic of modern bubonic plague. The same goes for the more theoretical descriptions of 'reptiles' (which included mice) leaving the underground. They remained alive and, as one German plague tract averred, 'many of them were afterwards caught'.[260]

*   *   *

In contrast to historians' preoccupation with the Black Death's signs and symptoms, contemporary chroniclers spent more space describing and discussing epidemiological aspects of the plague from the numbers it killed and the speed of its contagion to traces of human immunity. Although they may have contradicted themselves on points such as the social and sexual composition of plague victims or whether epizootics of large animals preceded or followed human plague, they provide us with new epidemiological clues that historians have yet to follow.

As we have argued, the implicit link between the plague of 1348 and subsequent waves of plague was their unusual levels of mortality. In addition to the words 'pestilence' and 'big death', chroniclers such as Henricus of Hervodia in 1350, Morelli in 1363, and Stefani in 1383 could be more explicit, seeing subsequent strikes of the plague as linked to the first in 1348.[261] As the *Annales Matseenses* reported in its single-line entry for the 'magna pestilentia' of 1369: 'it began with the plague of 1349'.[262] The

---

[259] [177], p. 25.
[260] [97], p. 70.
[261] See for instance Morelli's description of the plague of 1363 in Florence (*Ricordi*, p. 216); Stefani's of 1383 (*Cronica fiorentina*, p. 426); and Henricus of Hervodia's of the plague in Germany of 1350 (*Liber de Rebus Memorabilioribus*, p. 285).
[262] *Annales Matseenses*, p. 834.

Franciscan Fratre Bartolomæo Della Pugliola acknowledged that the 1362 plague in Bologna showed the signs 'of swelling under the arms and in the groin', but he linked this plague to 1348 by turning to an elementary epidemiological factor, the numbers who died: 'it [1362] was a death of so many people, who died as with the other one, which was in 1348'.[263]

Furthermore, not every epidemic or disease was called plague, as some modern historians have claimed. Rather, after 1348 it was used sparingly within the chronicle literature to refer to the 'big death' of plague. Even those few who used the term 'peste' or 'pestilentia' as a generic term for epidemics of various sorts made distinctions between different pestilential epidemics. Thus the early-fifteenth-century chronicler from Mainz, who recorded in 1371 the outbreak of disease in the Hessian towns of Fritzlar, those in Westphalia, and in Argentina, which he called an epidemic of dysentery (*pestilentia dissenteriarum*),[264] also used pestilence for plagues of animals, as with the pestilence of chickens (principally in Frankfurt) in 1380.[265] John de Waurin called a disease *la pestilence de flux de ventre* (dysentery) that struck down 2000 among the English army in its siege of Rouen in 1415.[266]

Other laymen of the late fourteenth and early fifteenth centuries without university medical training could and did make distinctions between diseases and used the term 'peste' or 'mortalitas magna' more sparingly than the Mainz chronicler. On occasion, they might discriminate even more finely than those in the medical profession, as did the Florentine Minerbetti, who described a sudden change in temperature in the winter of 1386, which he maintained set off a disease with fever in which many died.[267] But for this illness that reached epidemic proportions and 'did great damage to the city', Minerbetti did not use the terms he and his contemporaries reserved for plague—'peste' or, more often, 'the big killer'. Similarly, for 1390, he described in vivid detail the spread and horror of a disease called *pondi*:[268]

> At the end of July the disease *pondi* began in Florence, which doctors say is related to plague. But this malady was long lasting, taking more than a month to run its course, even though most died from it. The disease was filthy (*sozzo*) and disgusting, throwing off blood everywhere and stinking up the house wherever the ill go. It brought great pain to the body and aroused great and sorrowful torments. Many men, women, and children died from it, and it lasted past the middle of September.[269]

---

[263] *Historia Miscella Bononiensis*, col. 466.

[264] *Chronicon Moguntinum*, p. 184

[265] Ibid., p. 203.

[266] *Recueil des chroniques et anchiennes istories de la Grant Bretaigne*, II, pp. 183 and 187.

[267] Minerbetti, *Cronica volgare*, p. 23.

[268] On this disease, see Carmichael, *Plague and the Poor*, p. 48, who calls it dysentery, but from Minerbetti's description, which Carmichael says is the fullest, it is not clear why she has diagnosed it as such. Minerbetti talks of disgusting and foul smells but mentions the excretion of blood, not diarrhoea.

[269] Minerbetti, *Cronica volgare*, p. 110.

It would have been easy to have simply called this disease plague or the great killer but Minerbetti did not do so. Moreover, his distinction did not rest on the disease's signs—the apostemes (which may have misled the doctors into confounding it with plague). Instead, his judgement turned on epidemiological grounds, the fact that this was a slow killer, taking a month instead of a matter of days to kill its victims. Such a distinction would have taken especial care and perception in 1390, since this was also a plague year in Tuscany:

> And also at this time, some began to have certain pestilential ulcers and these died in a few days. This aposteme disease lasted until November and many died. And this mortality spread into the Florentine countryside, killing many in the same way.[270]

Also, the merchant chronicler Matteo Villani distinguished between epidemic diseases. After describing in detail the spread of plague through Flanders, Brabant, Germany, and Bohemia in 1358 he noted that

> at the same time, a general illness as in the previous year struck those in our country in the Valdelsa, Valdarno di sotto, and the Chianti [roughly the rural zones south of Florence]. It was tertiary, quartene and other fevers; like plague, one caught it from others and it left spots.

But Villani did not call this plague; like Minerbetti's, his distinction rested on epidemiological grounds: 'this was a long illness and few died from it, and the people of the Valdelsa and Chianti marvelled at the similarities [between the two diseases] and no one knew the reason for it.'[271]

Nor was this ability to distinguish concurrent diseases with similar, even the same, physical manifestations peculiar to the Florentines. The anonymous chronicler of Tournai reported a plague of 1413, which 'killed many in that city both young and old. At the same time another disease flourished from February to May, which was a throat infection, people called "le heuquette" [hiccup, rhume], but unlike plague few died from it.'[272] The Scottish chronicler Bower described a summer disease in 1420 with high fevers, eye inflammations, and dysentery that killed 'not only magnates but numberless men of the people' but which commoners called 'qwhew', not plague or 'the great death'.[273] In England *The Brut* described a 1369 epidemic that combined smallpox and plague. Like Minerbetti, the Englishman distinguished between the two, not by signs but again on epidemiological grounds, in this case the levels of contagion and the speed of the death: With 'pestilens' people went to bed healthy, 'hool and in good poynt', and 'suddenly they died'; whereas smallpox (an illness that men callen 'the pokkes') was 'much slower to infect both men and women'.[274]

---

270 Ibid., p. 110.
271 Matteo Villani, *Cronica*, II, p. 273.
272 *Chronique des Pays-Bas*, p. 343.
273 Bower, *Scotichronicon*, VIII, p. 117.
274 *The Brut*, p. 316.

Another layman to distinguish between diseases that rose to epidemic levels was the so-called Bourgeois of Paris, who ironically was most likely a cleric. He recorded waves of plague, smallpox (*varioli*), 'dondi', and other illnesses from 1414 to 1445. All of these arose with the heat of summer and in the case of smallpox and plague had similar signs. Both by the fifteenth century attacked principally children and might arise concurrently as in August 1433.[275] Unfortunately, the Parisian, unlike Minerbetti and *The Brut*, was not explicit in revealing how he distinguished these diseases, but given the similarity in the signs, especially between smallpox and plague, his judgements must have rested on differences in contagion, periods of illness, and rates of mortality—in other words, differences in epidemiology.

I conclude with two unusual epidemiological descriptions of plague, the first from the north of Europe, the second from the Mediterranean. Neither, to my knowledge has ever been cited by a historian of the Black Death. The first comes from an anonymous chronicler of Tournai:

> In 1400 in the month of May a terrible epidemic of pestilence began in the city of Tournai and at the same time in several other towns and regions, and it soon spread everywhere. And in Tournai this pestilence began in the street of Le Val, outside the gate of Cocqueriel. It then entered at the Cow Market and expanded through the parish of St Marguerite and St Jacques. In the beginning of this plague only farm workers and mechanics died, those who earned their living by the day or otherwise.[276]

The second comes from Matteo Villani, whose chapter on the moral consequences of the plague has been cited time and again by historians, but whose remarkable comments on the plague's epidemiology have yet to be examined. Unlike other chroniclers, who claimed that the plague was universal, striking 'all parts of the world', Matteo noted also the places plague failed to strike—in 1348 Milan and the Alps dividing Italy and Germany; in 1349 Brabant.[277] In charting the plague that swept through many parts of northern Europe in 1358 he noted that it struck with unusual virulence those very areas it failed to touch in 1348/49:

> it did not touch Flanders, where previously it had been very serious, and therefore Brabant felt it much more; and for similar reasons plague struck in Germany and at Basel, and in other cities and hamlets in Bohemia and Prague, which had not been seriously infected by the first plague.[278]

For the 'glandular plague', which spread through Friuli and Schiavonia in the following year, Villani gives further clues about the character of the spread which go beyond other descriptions of its cross-regional, lightning-fast

[275] *Journal d'un bourgeois de Paris*, p. 295.
[276] *Chronique des Pays-Bas*, p. 333.
[277] Matteo Villani, *Cronaca*, I, p. 11.
[278] Ibid., II, p. 273.

contagion. Again, the plague did not strike all parts of cities and hamlets alike; rather 'it struck in the way of a hail storm, leaving one area intact while destroying another'.[279] For the plague of 1362, the second to hit Tuscany, his survey of the plague's pattern of hits and misses emphasised the same random character of its spread:

> In these times, June and July, the accustomed pestilence of the glandular swellings swept through the city of Bologna, causing great damage, and occupied the entire Casentino, except for certain hamlets that it skipped over . . . striking this, that, and the other field but skipping over another in the middle; the effect was similar to the way corrupt air comes through the sky, similar to early thin clouds through which rays of sunlight appear, casting light here but not there'.

He went on to describe this pattern of the plague's ragged spread through Romagna, the Florentine Alps, and beyond into other city-states. With the spread of the plague to Brescia and the Arno town of Figline, his focus narrowed still further: in the former 'it did considerable damage, but in one quarter it did little, and in others, nothing at all'. For the latter, 'it began in one street (*ruga*) but did not touch others'.[280]

Similarly, doctors such as Saladino da Ascoli, Mariano di Ser Iacopo from Siena, and a doctor Johanns Rosenbusch from northern Germany were impressed by the plague's seeming randomness, striking some zones, skipping others.[281] Saladino also had a sense of some individuals' immunity to plague and even recognised the special immunity given to infants who were still being suckled. He suggested other epidemiological characteristics of plague, such as its having an incubation period, even if it were brief.[282] Often these doctors listed their 'doubts' and 'questions' about classical theories and their explanations of the plague's complexities. The fifteenth-century Sienese doctor Mariano di Ser Iacopo observed that some died immediately from plague, some were not affected at all, and some were infected but could be cured, even though all had breathed the same corrupt air. Without using the terms or inventing new ones for it, he too sensed that humans could acquire immunity to the plague. He marvelled at the gravediggers, who he said were rarely struck by plague or died from it by his day (the mid-fifteenth century), despite their constant exposure to the venomous and corrupt vapours of plague corpses.[283]

Many of the epidemiological points brought out by contemporary chroniclers and doctors do not square with what we know about modern bubonic plague. They describe the striking speed of the disease's spread. Not only in

---

[279] Ibid., p. 301.
[280] Ibid., II, pp. 585–6
[281] Simili, 'Saladino Ferro da Ascoli', p. 40; [223], p. 143; [152], p. 143.
[282] Simili, 'Saladino Ferro da Ascoli', p. 40.
[283] [223], p. 143.

1348 but also later: it took only a matter of months to spread over large tracts of Asia and Europe. Its contagion seemed so fast and omnipresent that sophisticated doctors such as Guy de Chauliac saw it spreading by sight. Unlike with modern plague, one medieval chronicler after another observed the household clustering of plague victims. Some even hinted at the possibilities of natural and acquired immunity among special occupations or populations in general. Yet at the same time Villani's metaphors of random hits and misses (heretofore unnoticed by historians) suggests one similarity between the late-medieval plagues and the rat-based bubonic disease discovered at the end of the nineteenth century, even if this trait was not unique to plague, past or present.

Further, this curious topography of the late-medieval plagues matches enigmas found in local studies of plague in Cambridgeshire and at St Flour in the Auvergne: some cantons lost only 5 per cent, while neighbouring ones lost as much as 76 per cent of their populations.[284] Exactly what do these patterns mean: could it have been a disease first triggered by rodents? Was it a disease common to other mammals? Was there an insect vector? Was it a bacterium or a virus? Some of these questions might be answered on the basis of descriptive materials left by the chroniclers and doctors; others must await further study by zoologists, immunologists, and those better acquainted than I am with large numbers of epidemic diseases in both the human and zoological worlds. But to proceed we should not assume that 'medieval writers on plague left few comments pertinent to epidemiology'.[285] Instead, the blinkered focus on signs and symptoms—the bubo and blood spitting—and the assumption that the epidemiology of medieval and modern plague was the same have blocked from view vital clues found in contemporary accounts.

---

[284] See Page, *The Estates of Crowland Abbey*, pp. 120–5; and Ada Elizabeth Levett, *Studies in Manorial History*, ed. by H.M. Cam, M. Coate, and L.S. Sutherland (Oxford, 1938), pp. 249–50, and 253; Dubois 'La dépression', p. 321.
[285] Ell, 'Immunity as a factor', p. 874.

|7|

Climate

This chapter and the next follow Sir Macfarlane Burnet's advice—diseases in the past must be studied not just by their signs and symptoms but by their epidemiology. From the narrative sources I now turn to the archival. For certain data, such as last wills and testaments drawn up in time of plague, our databases could be extended but principally in the countries where I have already taken numerous samples from such documents in northern Germany, parts of France (especially the south), Flanders, and northern Italy. For other sources, such as burial records, especially before 1400, we may not be able to go much beyond the data presented in this chapter. In addition to confirming or contradicting the claims of chroniclers often caught in the trauma of their own lives and class-bound experiences, this data will shed new light on epidemiological aspects of the plague and raise new questions that do not emerge from the narrative sources alone.

In analysing the plagues of the supposed 'Third Pandemic', what first struck researchers in India was the seasonal consistency of the plague cycles in any given place—its appearance, peaks with rats, then humans, its decline, and disappearance from one year to the next. It was from these climatic regularities that researchers began to hypothesise that the modern bubonic plague depended on an insect vector and in particular the flea.[1]

A reading of the chronicles might suggest that the medieval bubonic plague had no season and could strike at any time throughout the varied ecozones of Europe. According to the chroniclers, it flared in places such as Messina, Genoa, Pisa, and Marseilles as soon as the Genoese galleys happened to arrive, regardless of season. In Messina it was late autumn

---

[1] See chapter 1 on Ogata, Simond, Hankin, and Thompson.

(October, 1347),[2] in Pisa[3] and Genoa the coldest month of the year, January (by some accounts), [4] in Marseilles by November, and Avignon by the end of January with a peak in deaths on 14 March.[5] According to Cronaca A of Bologna, the plague months of Pisa, Lucca, and Venice were the same, from February to June.[6] *Les Grandes Chroniques de France* reported plague already in Provence by 1347, ahead of Pisa and Genoa.[7]

For Florence, and probably most of inland northern and central Italy, the plague of 1348 came later and lasted longer. According to Matteo Villani, it arrived in Florence in April and lasted to the beginning of September.[8] For Stefani, it arrived in March,[9] coinciding with Bologna's first plague according to Cronaca A and the *Historia Miscella Bononiensis*,[10] but not by Matteo Griffoni's account, which dated its arrival at Bologna to May and said it lasted an entire year.[11] In Perugia, further inland and further removed from seaports and especially from Pisa, where the plague entered central Italy, the dates of infection were about the same as at Florence, from 8 April to the end of August.[12] However, in Rimini and the lands of the Malatesta only slightly further north but on the Adriatic Sea, its chronicler maintained that the plague entered on 15 May and lasted to the first of December.[13] According to a stone plaque erected by the Minor Friars at their church in Rimini, the plague arrived even later, beginning in June and lasting to the first of November.[14] Similarly, with Siena, though in constant contact with Florence, plague came later than to its northern neighbours, entering the city in May.[15] In other places in Italy even closer to the sea and nearer to the first entry point in Sicily, it took even longer to arrive. It did not reach Naples until June and lasted to Christmas.[16]

According to an anonymous chronicler from Pistoia, the plague

[2] Michele da Piazza, *Cronica*, p. 82.

[3] *Cronaca di Pisa*, p. 96: '1348, alla intrata di gennaio'.

[4] The chroniclers of Genoa are not specific about the month when the plague arrived but report its plague for the entry of 1348, Stellai, *Annales Genuenses*, p. 150. Genoa's calendar begins with Christmas. A. Cappelli, *Cronologia, Cronografia e Calendario perpetuo*. 7th ed. (Milan, 1998), p. 9.

[5] For Marseilles see various chroniclers and the plague tract of Jacme d'Agramont, [278], pp. 120–1; for Avignon, Sanctus, p. 467, suggested that the plague peaked on 14 March when 11,000 bodies were buried (out of 62,000 to die in the three months from 25 January).

[6] Cronaca A, p. 585.

[7] *Les Grandes Chroniques de France*, p. 313.

[8] Matteo Villani, *Cronaca*, I, p. 13.

[9] Stefani, *Cronaca fiorentina*, p. 232.

[10] Cronaca A, p. 585; the Bolognese friar gives the same dates, *Historia Miscella Bononiensis*, col. 409.

[11] *Matthaei de Griffonibus*, p. 56.

[12] *Cronica della città di Perugia*, p. 148.

[13] *Cronache Malatestiane*, p. 17.

[14] Ibid., note 4, p. 17.

[15] *Cronaca Senese attribuita ad Agnolo di Tura*, p. 555.

[16] *Annales Caesenates*, col. 1179.

peaked in Paris on 13 March 1349.[17] Closer to home, the Saint-Denis chronicler Richard the Scot estimated the Parisian death toll but said nothing about its seasonality or duration.[18] In Normandy, the dates of new plague hospitals and permission for canons to disperse at Bayeux suggest that the plague was an autumnal epidemic, flaring at the end of July and peaking in Bayeux and Rouen in October or November, but the chroniclers are of no assistance here.[19] Also for German-speaking areas, the chroniclers generally gave the year but not the months or duration of the first plague.

Several chroniclers dated the plague's arrival in England. According to Geoffrey le Baker, it reached Bristol on 15 August. The chronicler of the Monastery of Bermundeseia (Bermondsey) dated the plague's appearance in London to the feast of St Michael (29 September) and said it lasted until the feast of St Peter ad Vincula (1 August) of the following year;[20] *The Brut*, *The Chronicle of William Gregory*, *The Great Chronicle of London*, and another based on the *Great Chronicle* specified the same time-span;[21] Le Baker gave it the same starting date, but Robert of Avesbury saw its arrival as more than a month later (All Saints' Day).[22] Contemporary chroniclers dated the height of the plague in Valencia, Barcelona, and parts of Aragon to June, but further south, in the Cortes of Zaragoza, it was not until the beginning of October[23] and did not hit still further south, around Gibraltar, until 1350.[24]

For later waves of plague, the chroniclers were more specific about the plague's timing across Europe. Jean de Venette tells us that the second epidemic in Paris raged from July to the feast of St Luke (18 October).[25] The chronicler of Saint-Denis said the plague of 1399, which ran through Burgundy, the Loire, the Seine, Champagne, and Paris, endured from May to November.[26] The anonymous chronicler of the Low Countries reported the plague of 1367 lasting at Tournai from Easter to Christmas, while its plague of 1426 was more a summer disease with a duration of four or five months.[27] The plague of 1379 erupted in Mainz in the autumn[28] and about

---

[17] *Annales Pistorienses*, col. 525.
[18] *Richardi Scoti Chronicon*, pp. 82–4.
[19] Roger Jouet, 'Autour de la Peste Noire en Basse-Normandie au XIVe siècle', *Annales de Normandie*, 22 (1972), p. 268.
[20] *Annales Monasterii de Bermundeseia*, p. 475.
[21] *The Brut*, p. 303; *The Great Chronicle of London*, p. 38; *Chronicle of William Gregory*, p. 83; *Chronicles of London*, p. 12.
[22] *Chronicon Galfridi le Baker*, p. 100.
[23] *Epidemiología Española*, pp. 80–2.
[24] Lopez de Ayala, *Crónicas de los Reyes de Castilla*, I, p. 8.
[25] *Chronique latine de Guillaume de Nangis (Contiuatio)*, II, pp. 325–6.
[26] *Chronique du religieux de Saint-Denys*, II, p. 693.
[27] *Chronique des Pays-Bas*, pp. 240 and 396.
[28] *Chronicon Moguntinum*, p. 202.

the same time at Mechovie (Makov), Poland.[29] In 1401 it struck this city and its district again in the autumn.[30]

The chronicler of Ragusa dated several plagues: the second of 1361 began on 15 January and lasted a year; the third, 1363, on 15 March and lasted three-and-a-half months; the fourth, 1374, a year; the sixth, 1391, on 15 May and lasted six months; the sixth, 1400, on 20 February and lasted two years.[31] Several English chroniclers also dated later plagues. The Grey Friars said plague hit London on Michaelmas (29 September) 1360.[32] The *Anonimalle Chronicle* reported the fourth plague (1378) in London just before Michaelmas.[33] On the other hand, the plague of 1375 coincided with scorching hot weather, and in 1379 (in the north country) and in 1389 (Cambridge) plague struck in summer.[34] For Scotland, Bower dated the plague of 1362 as beginning and ending in winter months, from the feast of the Purification of Our Lady (2 February) to Christmas.[35]

As with the first plague, the Italian chroniclers give the most exacting information on dates and duration for later ones. We in fact learn more about the plagues at the end of the 1350s and early 1360s in Flanders, England, Germany, Rhodes, and Mallorca from the Florentine Matteo Villani than from any native chronicler I know of. For 1358 he reported a late autumn plague (October and November) that 'ripped through' Brussels, Antwerp, Leuven, and other towns of Brabant.[36] The following year, again in autumn, plague struck parts of Brabant and the Rhineland. In the winter of that year until March of the next it passed through Friuli and parts of Schiavonia but 'was not too deadly even though it was the sort with swellings under the arms and in the groin'.[37] According to Villani (and his merchant correspondents) the English plague of 1361 broke out in April and May and ran through June, reaching its peak in London on San Giovanni day (June 24) with 1200 dead 'on that day and on the following'. In May and June of the same year it struck Lombardy—Como, Pavia, then Milan.[38]

In 1362, Villani recorded plague in Bologna, the Casentino as far as Dicomano, the lands of count Robert (Ubertini) in the Romagna, Modena, Verona, Pisa, Lucca, the northernmost mountains of the Florentine *contado*, Pisa, and the Island of Rhodes. For the months of July and August it spread to other parts of Lombardy, first north of Brescia and then into

29 *Annales Mechovienses*, p. 671.
30 Ibid., p. 673.
31 *Annales Ragsuni*, pp. 41–2, 49, and 54.
32 Horrox, p. 86.
33 *The Anonimalle Chronicle*, p. 124.
34 Ibid., pp. 79 and 124.
35 Bower, *Scotichronicon*, VII, p. 319.
36 Matteo Villani, *Cronica*, II, p. 273.
37 Ibid., II, pp. 300–1.
38 Ibid., II, pp. 514–15.

that city. In October, it reached Figline (southeast of Florence), and finally Florence in November, but perhaps because of the winter 'it struck only in one or two houses until it disappeared in December.'[39] Finally for 1363, when Matteo himself died of plague, he first reported that by June the plague was in full bloom in Egypt, Syria, the Levante, Venice, Padua, Istria, Schiavonia, Florence, and all of Tuscany and lasted three months.[40]

Other Italian chroniclers were less geographically expansive but gave dates of plagues in their regions and neighbouring places. Sozomenus recorded the plague of 1362 as beginning in June and lasting to December.[41] The plague of 1400, which infected this author but from which he recovered, lasted from April to October in Tuscany.[42] For Bologna and its territory, Griffoni dated it from May to the end of October.[43] While the surviving Genoese chroniclers provide little information for the first plague, they dated later ones: in 1372 it began in April and lasted a year; in 1384 it began on the feast day of Mary, 25 March; in 1411 it began in July, and in 1429 at the beginning of August, lasting through the autumn.[44]

Numerous chronicles dated the plague of 1373–74: in Florence, the *Cronichetta d'incerto* from March to November;[45] Stefani, from March to September or October.[46] For Rimini it came in March and lasted to Christmas. Its chronicler also saw it as rampant throughout the territories of Rome, Puglia, the Marche, and Tuscany to Parma for the same period.[47] For Bologna, both Cronaca A and B reported it as lasting two years, beginning and ending in January.[48] For the Trentino, it was the same.[49] For Milan, however, its chronicler dated it as lasting only from March to July.[50]

Unfortunately, less information of a descriptive or statistical nature comes from Italy south of Rome. A necrology for a confraternity at Salerno mentions plague only once, for 1368 (although it could have been a scribe's or printer's inversion of A.D. MCCC°LXVIII° for MCCC°XLVIII°). At any rate the plague's peak is clear: 'in June the mortality became general'.[51]

The list of dates and periods of plagues recorded by Italian chroniclers (at least for the northern and central regions) could go on. In addition to the number and frequency of such entries, several Italian chroniclers also began to comment on the mortality trends within a given period of plague,

---

[39] Ibid., pp. 585–6.
[40] Ibid., pp. 661–2.
[41] *Specimen Historiæ Sozomeni*, col. 1066.
[42] Ibid., col. 1170.
[43] *Matthaei de Griffonibus*, p. 66.
[44] Stellai, *Annales Genuenses*, pp. 165 and 190; and *Cronice de Ianue*, pp. 303 and 367.
[45] *Cronichetta d'incerto*, p. 191.
[46] Stefani, *Cronica fiorentina*, p. 289.
[47] *Cronache Malatestiane*, p. 35.
[48] *Corpus Chronicorum Bononiensium*: Cronaca A, p. 291; Cronaca B, p. 495.
[49] *Cronica inedita di Giovanni da Parma*, p. 52.
[50] *Annales Mediolanenses*, col. 756–7.
[51] *Necrologio del Liber Confratrum di S. Matteo di Salerno*, p. 79.

presumably between the first known cases and when it wound down or disappeared altogether. For instance, for the plague of 1374, the Bolognese chroniclers recorded that it lasted two years but added that it was in full force from June to October 1374.[52] For the next plague of 1383, Stefani's analysis gives another dimension to the plague's character; once it arrived, plague no longer appears to have burst on the scene at full force as chroniclers reported for 1347–48; rather, its arrival in Florence in March was confined to about four houses in the Canto a Monteloro and around the church of San Pier Maggiore—'hardly anyone in Florence knew about it through April'. In May it picked up momentum, becoming vicious in the summer months until September.[53] For the plague of 1400, the Florentine patrician of the Minerbetti family no doubt consulted the new government registers of burials in Florence, from which he charted the plague's monthly progress. While it lasted from April to September, he showed numerically that it rose quickly to its apex in June and July.[54] Finally, Giovanni Morelli, addressing his future heirs on how to defend against plague, looked back over the late-Trecento plague experience in Florence and probably elsewhere in northern Italy:

> From me I wish you to have this bit of advice . . . in the winter before a plague you will hear some whispers of plague in the *contado* or on the periphery of our territory. It would be correct to assume that the disease must also be somewhere in Florence. And if you know this in February, others in the city will begin to know of it. In June, the deaths will mount and will peak by mid- July, afterwards there will be fewer deaths but of the better sort.[55]

From these varied observations made by the chroniclers, three or four conclusions can be drawn. First, plague could occur at any time of year and could last through the year in places with wide variations in temperature and humidity. According to the chroniclers, no month was plague free. It could strike and endure through the coldest as well as the warmest times of year in areas as diverse as the Alps of Friuli, the city of Florence, and the countryside of northern England or Scotland. While some chroniclers pointed to the plague flagging with winter (for example, Villani and Morelli for Florence), others saw it continuing through January in the colder climes of England, Friuli, and Germany. This seeming lack of a seasonal specificity, not only for 1348 but for successive plagues as well, does not follow any known pattern for modern plague, of either the bubonic or pneumonic form. Not only do these patterns fail to implicate the rat-flea or any other flea with their period of activity

---

[52] Cronaca A, p. 291; Cronaca B, p. 495.
[53] Stefani, *Cronaca fiorentina*, p. 426.
[54] *Cronica volgare di Anonimo Fiorentino*, p. 250.
[55] Morelli, *Ricordi*, pp. 210–11.

dependent on narrow temperature and humidity ranges; they do not suggest the reproductive cycle of any insect I am aware of.

On the other hand, it is difficult to rely on many of these reports for a useful picture of the plague's seasonality. For one thing, they tend to contradict one another, but more importantly, they fail to distinguish whether they are describing the plagues between the first and last cases known to them or only when plague attained extraordinary levels of mortality. Only a handful of Italian chroniclers distinguished between these two senses of the plagues' duration and only by the third plague of 1374. As we know from Morelli, Stefani, and Minerbetti, plague might arrive in late winter or early spring but sputter with only a few cases until May, when suddenly the death counts would soar.

Despite such reservations, a general pattern possibly emerges from these accounts: autumn plagues in the colder northern and central parts of Europe as well as the northernmost areas of Italy and summer ones in the warmer zones of the Mediterranean. The plague tracts give a similar impression. Those written in Bratislava, Prague, Berlin, Elbinger, Erfurt, and Southern Germany referred to plague as starting in the late summer or later[56] and coming to full force in autumn.[57] By contrast, John of Naples writing in 1348 thought that the plagues were mostly summer occurrences;[58] the 1382 tract of the Florentine doctor Niccolò da Borgo called plague a summer event;[59] an anonymous plague tract from Padua in the second half of the fourteenth century predicted that plagues would recur in the summer and advised his patients to be prepared to flee the city in that season.[60] Finally, after three bouts of plague, the Florentine doctor Franceschino de Collignano reasoned that they occurred in summer 'because of the heat' and 'could not begin in the autumn because temperatures were too frigid'.[61] Similarly, it was mostly in the summer months in 1348 that town councils in central Italy shut down because of plague. The Council of Elders in Lucca did not meet from March to mid July. Siena's government came to a complete halt from the first of June to the beginning of August with no sessions of the town council or the judiciary.[62] Orvieto's town council did not sit from 5 July to 21 August, [63] and in Florence its two

---

[56] [9], p. 213, said that the time of plagues [in Bratislava] was the end of the summer towards autumn, around the feast of Saint Lawrence (10 August) or the Assumption (15 August); doctors at Prague said that the plagues in 1406 and 1407 came in autumn; see also [109], p. 57; [113], p. 71, asserted that 'many die of the disease with the aposteme in autumn'; [114 and 115], p. 76; [119], p. 148, reported that the plague of 1410 in Lübeck began 20 July and ran through to the end of the autumn.

[57] [198], p. 108. It is unclear where this tract conserved in Latin and German in Berlin was written; [173], p. 5.

[58] [35], p. 343.

[59] [38], pp. 356 and 358.

[60] [47], p. 335.

[61] [39], 369–70.

[62] Varanini, 'La peste del 1347–50', pp. 297–9.

[63] Carpentier, *Une ville devant la peste*, p. 128.

legislative bodies, the Popolo and Commune, failed to convene from 11 April to 23 August.[64]

*   *   *

Archives across Europe provide other possibilities for charting the season-ality of the plague, particularly when mortality began to soar above normal levels. Even the less devastating plagues of the late fourteenth and early fifteenth centuries matched or surpassed any experience of mass death at least since the Great Famines of 1314–22, if not before. These sudden changes in mortality can be seen in a variety of sources: (1) last wills and testaments and other similar documents, such as gifts to churches and kin known as 'causae propter mortem'; (2) 'necrologies', obituaries, and 'chronicae' that recorded the deaths in monastic communities and lay confraternities; (3) vacant benefices; (4) manorial death taxes (*heriots* in England) and inheritances that revert to lords because of death (*bersteften*) in Holland; and (5) burial records of monastic communities, lay parishes, and finally entire cities.

Like the chronicles, these sources are not without problems. First, none of them express the cause of death systematically before the 1420s, and then the Florentine burial records stand alone until after the second half of the fifteenth century.[65] Before, the best source for knowing whether the cause of death was plague was the Dominican 'necrologies', especially the first and largest of these, kept at Santa Maria Novella in Florence. These marked plague years and often identified the brother first to die from a plague.[66]

On the other hand, a more common source—last wills and testaments and 'causae propter mortem'—almost never revealed the cause of death. From over three thousand wills from six city-states across Tuscany and Umbria, I have not seen one referring to plague or any other disease, even though these documents consistently stated whether the testator was in good health or mortally ill. Those for the Lyonnais were somewhat excep-tional in that 'peste' was cited in twenty-six wills in 1348.[67] Elsewhere in

---

[64] ASF, Provvisoni, registri, nos. 35 and 36.

[65] See Giuseppe Parenti, 'Fonti per lo studio della demografia fiorentina: I libri dei morti', *Genus*, 5–6 (1943–9): 281–301; Carmichael, *Plague and the Poor*; Carlo Cipolla, 'I Libri dei morti,' in *Le fonti della demografia storica in Italia* (Rome, 1972), II., pp. 851–66.

[66] See especially 'Necrologio' *di S. Maria Novella*, I, p. 65, which begins the plague deaths of 1348 with a long description of the disease, its signs, and symptoms; also *Chronica antiqua Conventus Sanctae Catharinae de Pisis*, p. 541, began its entries for certain years with 'anno mortiferae pestis', 'anno dirissimae pestis' and the like; for an entry no. 140, the chronica of Orvieto, Jean Mactei Caccia, *Chronique du couvent des prêcheurs d'Orvieto*, p. 147, related that the brother, who died on 11 April 1348, 'made his last confession after four days in extreme pain from the contagion'.

[67] Jean Canard, *Les pestes en Beaujolais, Forez, Jarez, Lyonnais du XIVe au XVIIIe siècle* (1979), p. 9.

Europe for the fourteenth and fifteenth centuries perhaps a handful of cases might be collected. But even for the region adjacent to the diocese of Lyon, the county of Forez, with an even larger number of surviving wills, only one testament has surfaced that refers to 'pestis sive mortalitas'.[68] Nonetheless, in plague years these documents soared to new levels not seen before 1348. At Bologna and Millau (Aveyron, south-central France), they increased during the plague months of 1348 more than a hundred-fold over the average monthly rate before the plague (Figs 7.1 and 7.2).

The second problem with these various death documents is their relative rarity; unlike the chronicles, they concentrate in a few areas of Europe. The best of these sources is the most rare—burial records. Before the late sixteenth century and the last act of the Council of Trent, which required parishes to collect vital statistics in Catholic regions, burial records remained rare.[69] For the fourteenth century, I know of only a few: one for the parish of Ste-Maurice, in the Swiss canton of Valais that runs from 8 April, 1348 to 8 June 1349;[70] another, for Givry in Burgundy (near Chalon-sur-Saône) from 1342 to 1349;[71] at the urban parish of St-Nizier in Lyon, which registered just over two years of burials, 1346–48, but unfortunately ceases with the plague's crescendo in June, 1348;[72] the poor at the hospital of Saint-Julien in Cambrai,[73] though they begin only in 1377; the parish confraternity of S. Frediano (Florence), which ends in May, 1348;[74] the Dominican cemetery at Camporeggio, Siena;[75] the Dominican cemetery of Florence, Santa Maria Novella;[76] those organised by the city-wide confraternity of the Misericordia of Arezzo, which begin in 1373 but which have serious gaps until the plague of 1390;[77] and the first certain city-wide collection of burials, the death books (*Libri dei morti*) in Florence, which start in 1385 and continue until 1786.[78] Of these, only two span the plague history from 1348 to the early fifteenth century—the Dominican burials at their parishes of

---

[68] Fournial, *Les villes et l'économie d'échange en Forez*, p. 302.

[69] Parish registers were instituted in England a generation earlier in 1538.

[70] Benedictow, *Plague in the Late Medieval Nordic Countries*, pp. 62–3.

[71] P. Gras, 'Le registre paroissial de Givry (1334–1357) et la peste noire en Bourgogne', *Bibliothèque de l'École des Chartes*, C (1939), 295–308.

[72] *Inventaire du Trésor de St-Nizier de Lyon 1365–1373: Listes des sépultures de la paroisse 1346–1348*, ed. by Georges Guigue (Lyon, 1899).

[73] See note 158 in this chapter.

[74] For these records, see Henderson, 'The parish and the poor in Florence at the time of the Black Death: the case of S. Frediano, *Continuity and Change*, 3 (1988): 247–72.

[75] *I Necrologi di Siena di San Domenico in Camporeggio*.

[76] 'Il "Libro dei Morti" di Santa Maria Novella (1290–1436)', ed. by C.C. Calzolai, *Memorie Dominicane*, ns XI (1980), 15–218.

[77] *L'Archivio della fraternità dei Laici di Arezzo*, ed. by Augusto Antoniella. Inventari e cataloghi toscani, 17, 2 vols (Florence, 1989), 'Libri dei morti 1373–1888', p. 881 ff.

[78] On these see Carmichael, *Plague and the Poor*, pp. 28–30; Calzolai, 'Il "Libro dei Morti" di Santa Maria Novella', p. 20. One break occurs for the period 5 to 14 July 1400, the height of the plague, in 1400. According to Herlihy and Klapisch, *Les Toscans*, pp. 448–9 these become more fragmentary after 1412.

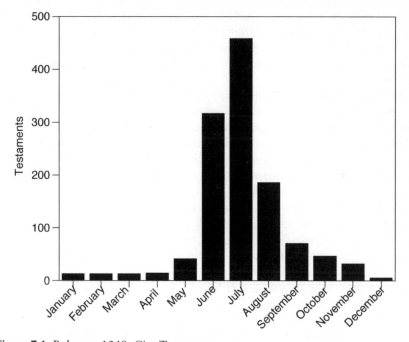

Figure 7.1 Bologna, 1348: City Testaments

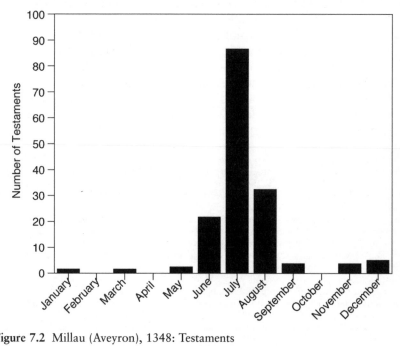

Figure 7.2 Millau (Aveyron), 1348: Testaments

Camporeggio in Siena and Santa Maria Novella in Florence. Further, as we shall see, these also have problems, especially for 1348. At this crisis moment, as the chroniclers bewailed, burial counts were lost as wagons gathered bodies en masse, funerals were curtailed, and corpses dumped in ditches.

Various records kept by monks, nuns, friars, and occasionally lay confraternities[79] were certainly more numerous. The earliest of these are the obituaries of monastic communities and can be found all over Europe, but they are almost entirely useless for demographic analysis of plague years, their cycles and seasonality. To remind their communities to pray for the souls of past members, they recorded precisely the month and day of death but rarely bothered to record the year. In addition, monasteries kept other books of the dead called *Libri mortuorum*, which were more meticulous in recording the day, month, and year of dead brothers and sisters, but I know of only two that have been published, both Dominican, one at Siena, the other at Florence. Finally, the best of these monastic sources, the 'croniche' of the friars, misleadingly called necrologies,[80] celebrated the lives of all those brothers born within a territorial province, such as Florence, with short biographies. These sources, however, were restricted to the Dominicans; only six survive (if one counts the biographies for the Dominican nuns of Corpus Domini in Venice).[81] Of these, only four recorded the year of death consistently, and only two stretched from the Black Death of 1348 to the fifteenth century, those for Siena and Florence, where we also possess Dominican burials of the laity.[82]

By far the most numerous and widespread of archival documents that reflect on death and cover the early plague years are last wills and testaments. They can be found in substantial numbers for places in France, Spain, Flanders, Germany, and especially Italy. For this study I have collected either through published works or with new archival research 24,509 wills from France (three regions): Flanders (2); Germany (4);

---

[79] On these see Calzolai, 'Il "Libro dei Morti" '; and especially Emilio Panella OP, 'Cronica fratrum dei conventi domenicani umbro-toscani (secoli XIII–XV)', *Archivum Fratrum Praedicatorum*, LXVIII (1998): 223–94. For obituaries of lay confraternities that cover the plagues of the latter half of the fourteenth century and in which members' deaths were dated by year as well as by month and day, I know of only three: the Franciscan confraternity of Orvieto in Biblioteca Vittorio Emanuele, Roma, Codice, V.E. no. 528 that of the jugglers of Arras (Roger Berger, *Le Nécrologe de la confrérie des jongleurs et des bourgeois d'Arras [1194–1361]* [Arras, 1970]), which recorded the year of death but arranged the commemoration around three feast days of the year and ceases before the second plague; and, thirdly, those of the brothers of the hospital of St John at Bruges.

[80] Panella, 'Cronica fratrum'.

[81] Riccoboni, *Cronaca del Corpus Domini*, pp. 257–94.

[82] In addition to those from Pisa, Orvieto, and Florence cited above, there are ones from Perugia (*La Cronica di S. Domenico di Perugia*); and Siena (*I Necrologi di Siena di San Domenico*), which contain both the Dominican burials in their cemetery and the obituaries of the brothers from the territory of Siena.

England (3)[83]; and Italy (8). Thus, even if they remain local studies of cities or regions, they provide a sampling of Mediterranean and northern European plague patterns. Further archival research could certainly build on this set of documents, but, with the exception of Spain it would be difficult to expand it into countries not examined here.[84]

While the testaments are the most numerous, they are also the most problematic of these sources for drawing conclusions about the plagues' mortalities. First, while most may have been redacted on the deathbed, they could be and were drawn up at various stages of life. The Tuscan, Umbrian, and southern French testaments almost invariably stated whether the testator was in good health (*sanus*) or on the deathbed (*licet corpus egritudine*); those for northern Europe, however, supplied this information less consistently or not at all.

Second, despite the church's desire for all good Christians to write wills from the twelfth century on, it was a practice of the propertied and in some regions, especially before 1348, of the rich. Third, children, even the propertied, rarely made wills, and I know of not a single will of an infant. Fourth, in most parts of late-medieval Europe men wrote wills more readily than women. In Florence and Arezzo, less than a third of the late-medieval testaments came from women, and for the Court of Husting (London) they accounted for barely ten per cent.[85] Pisa was exceptional in that the numbers for men and women were about the same. And in Venice, at least among patricians, women will-makers even outnumbered men.[86]

---

[83] In addition to the Court of Husting wills for London, I considered two other sets of calendared or published wills: Lincolnshire wills, *Calendar of Lincoln Wills*, vol. I., ed. by C.W. Foster, British Record Society, XXVIII (London, 1902), pp. 1–17, lists 232 wills before 1401. However, none of the fourteenth-century plagues left an imprint on these records: no wills were recorded for 1348, only one for 1349, one for the plague year 1361, none for 1362, three for 1369, one for 1374, four for 1375, eight for 1382, nine for 1383, and four for 1400. Yet, according to Ziegler, *Black Death*, p. 185, testaments from the Burwarmote Book (Lincoln) shows a sharp peak of 105 wills disposing of burgage tenements in 1349. Secondly, in the *Testamentary Records in the Archdeaconry Court of London*, I., ed. by Marc Fitch, British Record Society, 89 (London, 1979) few fourteenth-century wills survive.

[84] Ragusa (Dubrovnik) might be a possibility.

[85] From the earliest surviving will (1259) to 1425, women wrote 392 of 3450 wills. These data were taken from the summaries made in *Calendar of Wills: Court of Husting, London, 1258–1688: The Archives of the Corporation of the City of London at the Guidhall*, ed. by Reginald R. Sharpe, 2 vols (London, 1889); from 1258 to 1425, 3058 testators were men and 392 women; by their end in 1688, they numbered just over 4000. For the problems and deficiencies of this source, see Derek Keene, 'Tanners' widows, 1300–1350', in *Medieval London Widows 1300–1500*, ed. by Caroline M. Barron and Anne F. Sutton (London, 1994), pp. 1–27; Vanessa Harding, 'Burial choice and burial location in later medieval London', in *Death in Towns*, pp. 119–35; and Gwyn A. Williams, *From Commune to Capital* (London, 1963), pp. 315–16. On the Court of Husting itself, see Williams, *From Commune to Capital*, p. 36. Other large repositories of wills, such as those from the diocesan Exchequer Court of York with 4700 wills dated 1389 to 1475, begin after the major plagues of the fourteenth century; see Christopher Daniell, *Death and Burial in Medieval England 1066–1550* (London, 1997), p. 97.

[86] See Stanley Chojnacki, 'Patrician women in Early Renaissance Venice', *Studies in the Renaissance*, 21 (1974): 176–203, esp. 196.

Fifth, the popularity of will-writing changed over time, especially after the Black Death; almost everywhere plague boosted testaments. In Besançon (Franche-Comté, western France today), the 'officialité' of the cathedral registered 1725 testaments from the earliest will of 1255 to 1348, 18.5 per annum; afterwards to 1450, 3204 were registered, 31.4 per annum, even though the Black Death and successive waves of plague cut the population in half.

With Tournai the increase was more impressive. As with a number of Flemish towns, Douai, Valenciennes, Mons, and towns in northern France,[87] the échevins or town councillors registered wills at Tournai in two copies called chirographs, one for the testator or his family, the other to be kept in the town hall archives. They go back to 1194 and were inventoried at the beginning of the twentieth century. Although the chroniclers said the plague reached Tournai in 1348 (which certainly may have been the case), the wills show that it waited to the following year before taking its devastating toll, rising eight-and-a-half times, from 69 in 1348 to 582—by far the highest annual number seen for Tournai. Before 1349, 2752 were listed, 17.75 per annum, afterwards to 1425, 5592 were registered, 73.58 per annum, a more than fourfold increase for a city whose population had shrunk by as much as half. Thus per capita the post-plague increase may have been eight times or more.

Finally, for Mediterranean Florence, where no such 'officialité' or registry of wills existed, I have collected 652 testaments from 1260 to 1425 scattered through the notarial archives and copies originally held in monastic and mendicant archives. The Black Death's divide was as dramatic here as in Tournai: before 1348, I found 171 testaments or 1.94 a year; afterwards, 408 or 5.37 per annum, an almost three-fold increase for a city population that we know with some confidence had declined from a pre-plague peak of 120,000 to under 40,000 by 1400 and rose only slightly in the ensuing decades. Will-writing may have increased per capita by as much as twelve times.

For other cities in Europe the trend was presumably similar. In addition to the church, the impetus came from the individual, no doubt more conscious after 1348 of the need to prepare the legal mechanisms for ensuring a decent burial, the last rites, and the allocation of property. In Ragusa as well as other places, the state played a part in the increase in will writing as well as their survival. On 21 June 1348, the city required its notaries to announce (*debeat gridari per civitatem . . .*) that everyone in the city and countryside was obliged to write a will, which from then on would be preserved in separate notarial books for wills alone.[88]

---

[87] On the places where these records were preserved, see Robert Jacob, *Les époux, le seigneur et la cité: coutumes et pratiques matrimoniales des bourgeois et paysans de France du Nord au moyen âge* (Brussels, 1990), ch 1.

[88] *Monumenta Ragusina: Libri Reformationum*, II, p. 29.

Despite these uncertainties, last wills and testaments uncover consistent patterns of the plagues' mortalities and seasonality from place to place and plague to plague within various regions of Mediterranean Europe. First, they chart the Black Death's unprecedented demographic impact. Will-writing in six city-states (Arezzo, Assisi, Florence, Perugia, Pisa, and Siena) whose records I studied for an earlier study (henceforth called 'the six cities')[89] shows the soaring mortality of 1348—a 17-fold increase over the annual average of the previous decade (from 19.5 per year to 340 in 1348). For Bologna, where all wills were registered in its *Libri memoriali*[90] the increase in 1348 was more remarkable: in the plague months June and July, wills increased 400 times over those of the preceding winter months (Figs 8.3 and 7.1).

Before 1348 the highest number of wills also came in a year of disease, 1340, with 31, or less than 10 per cent, of the 1348 toll. The chroniclers have left little record of the signs, symptoms, or epidemiology of this mysterious disease other than to say that it caused high fevers and coincided with a severe famine.[91] The chronicler Della Tosa claimed that in Florence 80 a day were buried in May.[92] Giovanni Villani reported that the illness began in March and continued to winter, with 15,000 buried in the city of Florence alone, and was worse in the city than in the countryside.[93] Later, Leonardo Bruni added a thousand to Villani's figure and remarked that not just adolescents but those in the fullness of life (*provectos aetate*) and thus of service to the republic died.[94] An anonymous chronicle of Pistoia charted the 1340 disease most fully, seeing its spread 'in Pisa, Lucca, Prato, Venice, parts of Lombardy, Romagna, and all of Tuscany, where it was especially severe in Florence'. He claimed that 24,000 perished in that city and Pistoia lost a quarter of its urban population.[95]

The severity of this plague is also seen in the burial records of Santa Maria Novella. In fact, their numbers almost doubled those recorded for 1348 (120 vs 68): against the evidence of chronicles and testaments should we conclude that the epidemic of 1340 was more devastating than the Black Death? Instead, the comparison testifies to the horror stories told by

---

[89] These were collected for *Death and Property in Siena: Strategies for the Afterlife* (Baltimore, 1988) and *The Cult of Remembrance and the Black Death: Six Renaissance Cities in Central Italy* (Baltimore, 1992; and 1996).

[90] Martin Bertram, 'Bologneser Testamente. Erster Teil: Die urkundliche Uberlieferung', *Quellen und Forschungen aus italienschen Archiven und Bibliotheken*, 70 (1990): 151–233, has quantified these wills only for 1348.

[91] *Chronicle of the Villa di Santa Maria Maddalena*, p. 167; *Cronichetta d'incerto*, p.178; *Annales Pistorienses*, p. 476; *Petri Azarii, Liber gestorum in Lombardia*, p. 35; *Chronicon Estense*, p.110.

[92] See Corradi, *Annali delle epidemie*, I, p. 179.

[93] Giovanni Villani, *Cronaca*, Lib. XI, cap. CXIII, pp. 232–5.

[94] Bruni, *Historiarum Florentini populi*, p. 157.

[95] *Storie Pistoresi*, p. 162.

Boccaccio, Agnolo di Tura, and others when in 1348 cemeteries, churches and state administrations, overwhelmed by mass death and fearful contagion, lost count of the dead, failed to bury them, or dumped them into mass graves. In addition, the number of burials recorded at Santa Maria Novella during the second plague of 1363 also outstripped those of 1348 (90). But from the chroniclers we know the second plague killed far fewer—at most a quarter of the city of Florence as opposed to as many as 80,000 claimed by the meticulous Morelli for 1348 or 96,000, which Stefani said he drew from the official count taken by Florence's archbishop for the town council (but may have covered the larger jurisdiction of Florence's diocese).

A single plague tract survives for the 1340 plague but gives even fewer clues than the chroniclers of its character. Instead of reporting signs and symptoms, the Augustinian lecturer at the University of Perugia faulted the medical community for not paying close enough attention to the stars. He then described the 'bad constellations' that presaged 1340's coming.[96] But whatever the disease, its timing was slightly earlier than plague in 1348 or the plagues thereafter. By both the chronicles[97] and the Dominican burials, the 1340 pestilence burst forth in late-spring and had virtually disappeared by July; burials dropped from a peak of 52 in June to three in July, and there were only two more for the remainder of the year.[98]

Further, unlike 1348, this plague was not 'universal'; it appears to have been mostly confined to central and northern Italy, principally Florence, Pistoia, Siena, Bologna, Romagna, Lombardy, and Venice. I know of only one chronicler north of Bologna who referred to disease in 1340—Henry Knighton—but the one he described was different. It was 'terribly painful and caused men to bark like dogs'. But unlike the Italian disease, which took as much as a quarter of city populations,[99] the English one was not a killer.[100]

* * *

To return to 1348 and its seasonality: no place in central Italy where I have quantified the wills—Arezzo, Bologna, Assisi, Florence, Perugia, Pisa,

---

[96] Thorndike, 'A pest tractate before the Black Death'.

[97] *Chronicon Estense*, p.110, dated it later to June and July.

[98] These are my calculations based on Calzolai's edition of the burial records, which like the monastic 'necrologies' were organised by month, and day (but here the year is also included). The same seasonality is seen from the burial records of the parish confraternity of San Frediano (principally the poor); see Henderson, 'The parish and the poor', pp. 252–3.

[99] *Annales Pistorienses*, p. 476.

[100] *Knighton's Chronicle*, p. 37. Perhaps, the disease did spread to northern places with less virulence. From the necrologies of the Confraternity of Jugglers and Bourgeois at Arras, more deaths were recorded for 1340 than any other year (101) from 1194 to 1361, more than doubling the average number of deaths in the 1340s and 1350s; Berger, *Le Nécrologe de la confrérie des jongleurs*, I, p. 175.

Siena, or Rome—shows the bi-modal pattern described by Guy de Chauliac and taken later by historians to be the norm—a winter pneumonic peak followed by a less severe late spring–summer bubonic one. Instead, plague in central Italy was markedly a summer event, rising rapidly in May or June, peaking in June or July and disappearing by the end of September, if not earlier. In none of these cities did the plague wreak unusual death tolls in either winter or spring. In contrast to some chroniclers' reports of plague lasting six months or more (which may have been the case with relatively low levels of infection and mortality), the wills cast another picture: one of soaring mortalities lasting for only three months followed by a rapid decline (Figs 7.1, 7.3–7.9). The peak may have been in late winter in Pisa, where chroniclers say it arrived in January. Unfortunately, few wills survive there for 1348 (14); nonetheless, they show May as the peak, and, according to Dominican obituaries, its first Pisan brother did not die of plague until March.[101]

Summer was the plague's season for other places in the south of Europe in 1348, despite hundreds of miles separating one place from another. The middling-size market town of Millau has preserved a remarkable number of last wills and testaments for the fourteenth century. While I was able to collect only 73 testaments in 1348 from the rich notarial archives of Florence with its pre-plague population of 100,000 or more, for Millau, which had an immediate post-plague population of less than 4000,[102] I have collected 155 testaments for 1348 and another 20 for the second plague of 1361.[103] The seasonal distribution of these testaments resembles Tuscany's, though in Millau the rise was even more sudden. Only three wills were drawn up in this market town before June, then they soared to twenty-three, followed by eighty-six in July. By September the plague had withered; testaments fell precipitously to three (Fig. 7.2).[104] Further to the south, at

---

[101] *Chronica antiqua Conventus Sanctae Catharinae*, p. 541. Forty died from plague during the year, which constituted a large though incalculable proportion of the house.

[102] J. Colussi, 'Population de Millau 1280–1363: Étude démographique', typescript of 91 pages, (Toulouse, 1955), found in the Archives départementales de l'Aveyron [hereafter AA], AA 157–21. According to a tax survey (rôle des tailles) drawn up in 1353, Millau had 918 hearths (p. 85).

[103] To compile this chart I consulted the following notarial books: AA, Archives Notariales de l'Aveyron, série 3E, 11979, 11763, 11530, 11752, 11751, 11531, 11532, 11842, 11447 and 11843.

[104] The only other place with surviving testaments from 1348 in the notarial archives of Aveyron is the tiny agricultural hamlet of Saint-Côme in the northern part of the region. Its three surviving testaments are nonetheless suggestive; all were drawn up on the Thursday and Friday after the feast of Peter and Paul (29 June), that is, in the first week of July (AA, Saint-Côme E 1216, fols 28v, 34v, and 35r.) For other towns covered in the archives of Aveyron, I was unable to find testaments for 1348. Most prominent among the towns is the centre, Rodez, with six notarial books that cover the period of the Black Death—E 965 1333–57, E 966 1334–86, E 967 1318–66, E 1221 1338–1360, 1222 1347–8, E 968 1344–50; Unfortunately, E1221 was missing at the time of my visit to the archives.

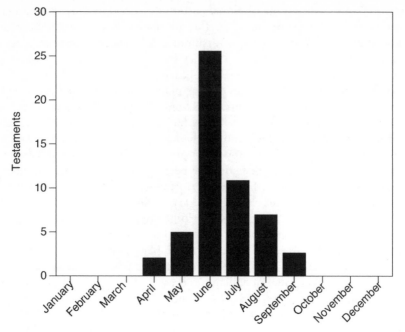

Figure 7.3 Siena, 1348: testaments

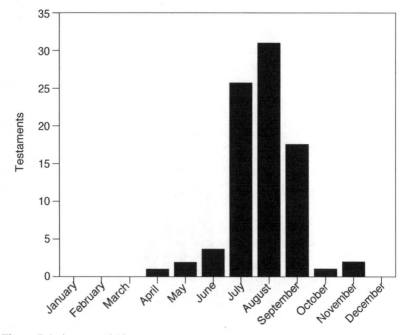

Figure 7.4 Arezzo, 1348: testaments

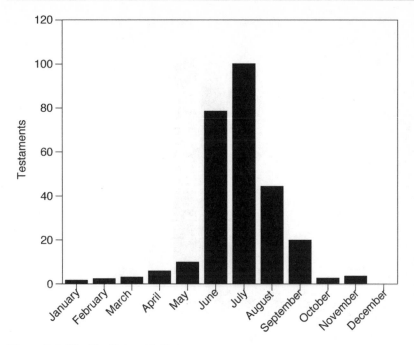

Figure 7.5 The Six Cities, 1348: testaments

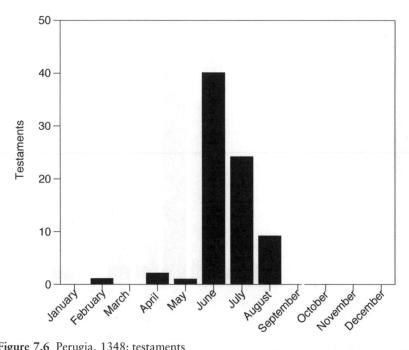

Figure 7.6 Perugia, 1348: testaments

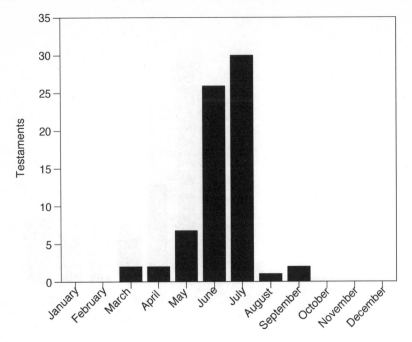

Figure 7.7 Florence, 1348: testaments

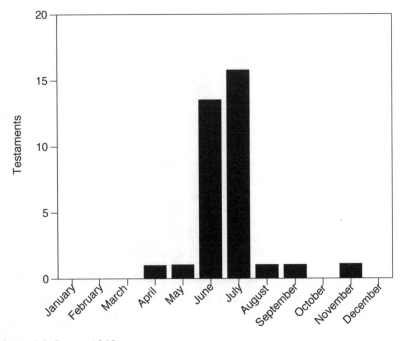

Figure 7.8 Rome, 1348: testaments

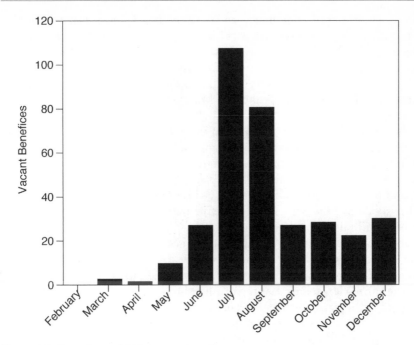

Figure 7.9 Barcelona, 1348: vacant benefices

Perpignan and its surrounding villages, Black Death wills also peaked in the summer months.[105]

The survival of large numbers of testaments for Barcelona would allow the historian to estimate the seasonal distribution of deaths, but to my knowledge no one has carried out that research. At Valencia, however, with 48 surviving wills for 1348, again the peak was a sharp mid-summer one, with 31 or two-thirds of them drawn up in June.[106] Further, for Barcelona Richard Gyug has analysed parish benefices that became vacant because of the death of the clergy in the diocese of Barcelona in 1348 (Fig. 7.9). As with Tuscany, Umbria, Bologna, and southern France, a similar pattern emerges: the absences begin to rise only in May and then soar in July. After

---

[105] Emery, 'The Black Death of 1348 in Perpignan,' *Speculum*, 42 (1967), pp. 611–23. Unfortunately, Emery has not shown the monthly distribution of the testaments but says those from Perpignan clustered in late April, May, and June (63 testaments) and from the village of Pia (75 testaments) in late May, June, and July, thus following the pattern seen in Tuscany and Umbria. For the plague of 1361, he says the Perpignan wills clustered from April to November (p. 618). This goes against his claims that the plague died out with the heat and dryness of the Mediterranean climate; instead, at least for Pia, where his documentation is best, it was when they soared and peaked.

[106] Rubio, *Peste Negra*, pp. 26–7. The sharp rise in wills corresponds with the chronicle report of the plague beginning in May and peaking in June, *Chronique Catalane de Pierre IV d'Aragon*, p. 272.

August, they tumble but linger on to December. Gyug suggests that the persistency was, however, an accident of the source; with such massive losses it took the bishop time to fill the vacancies created by the summer's disaster.[107] The one exception to this pattern for places in the Mediterranean south with surviving last wills or other death documents is Marseilles. Its testaments peaked in March—still not in winter,[108] as the chroniclers suggest.[109]

To explain the odd juxtaposition of a contagious, supposedly pneumonic plague occurring in summer, historians have speculated that 1348 was a bizarre year with an unusually cool and wet spring and summer. But 1348 was not an odd year in terms of the plague's recurring seasonality. For the second plague in central Italy (1362 in Pisa and Bologna and 1363 in the other six cities), the wills show the same pattern as in 1348, rising steeply in June and falling off by August[110] (Figs 7.10–7.14). In Millau, its town council claimed that five of six councillors died in the second plague of 1361[111] and its surviving testaments show plague again peaking in mid summer; by September its traces had disappeared altogether (Fig. 7.15).

The chroniclers tell us that the third and fourth plagues, 1374 and 1383, dragged on in places such as Florence and Bologna for longer periods without any marked seasonality, enduring for two years. The wills tell another story, repeating the same summer plague pattern. As Stefani describes for Florence in 1383 and Morelli more generally, a handful of cases may have sputtered before summer and lingered on afterwards, but the plague's course remained one of a quick summer rise although it may not have been as steep as for other plagues[112] (Figs 7.16 and 7.17 and 7.27). For 1400, curiously few testaments survive for most of these towns, but for Perugia with 28 and Rome with 39, again they rise sharply and peak in both places in June (Figs 7.19–7.20). The same is seen when the six cities are combined—a dramatic rise in June, followed by a slight decline in July and a return to normal levels already by August. This summer consistency can be seen from the much larger samples preserved at Bologna from its town registry of wills, the *libri memoriali*. As in 1348, plagues thereafter peaked

---

[107] Richard Gyug, 'The effects and extent of the Black Death', p. 390.

[108] Michaud, 'La peste, la peur et l'espoir', chart 2a, p. 408. It would be interesting to know if Marseilles's monthly pattern changed with successive plagues, but no one to my knowledge has quantified these later wills.

[109] Some say the plague reached here as early as November, 1347 (Biraben, *Les hommes et la peste*, I, p. 54); others said January, 1348 (*Breve chronicon Flandriae*, p. 14).

[110] For Assisi, only five testaments survive for 1363.

[111] *Archives Historiques du Rougergue* VII: *Documents sur la ville de Millau*, ed. Jules Artières (Millau, 1930), p. 118. The testaments come from one notary, AA, 3E. 11851 (1361).

[112] For Rome, only two wills survive for 1374 (both from the same notary, Biblioteca ApostolicaVaticana, Sant'Angelo in Pescheria, I, 8, 31r–2r, and 71v–2r; from the IMAGO parchment database and those kept in the Archivio di Stato, the Archivio Capitolino, and the Vatican twelve testaments survive for 1383; its peak is in July (four wills) and August (the same).

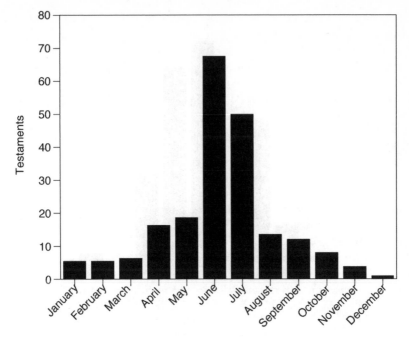

Figure 7.10 The Plague 1363: Six Cities

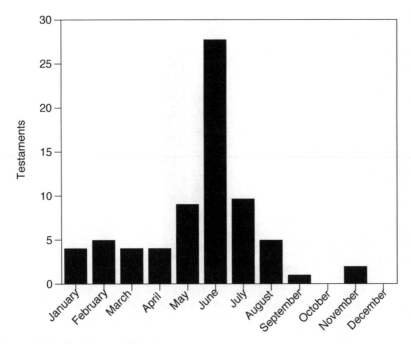

Figure 7.11 The Plague 1363: Arezzo

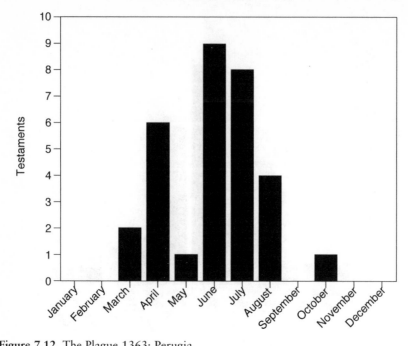

Figure 7.12 The Plague 1363: Perugia

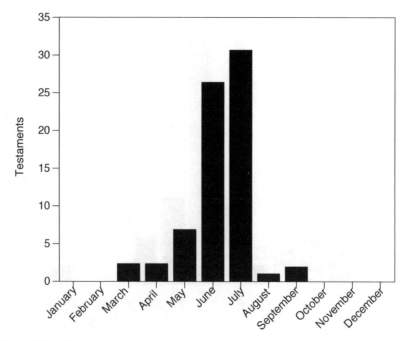

Figure 7.13 The Plague 1363: Florence

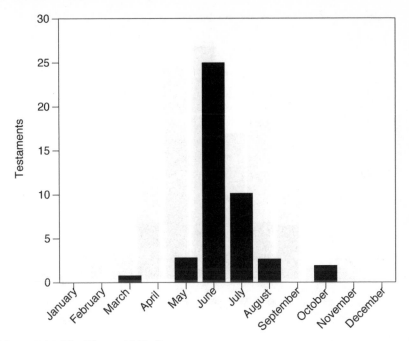

Figure 7.14 The Plague 1363: Rome

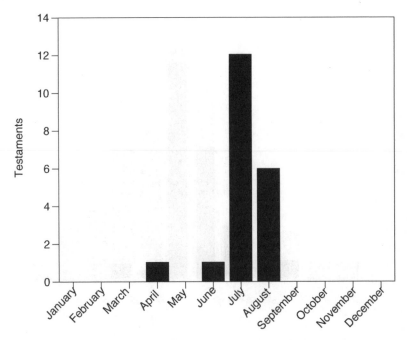

Figure 7.15 The Plague 1361: Millau

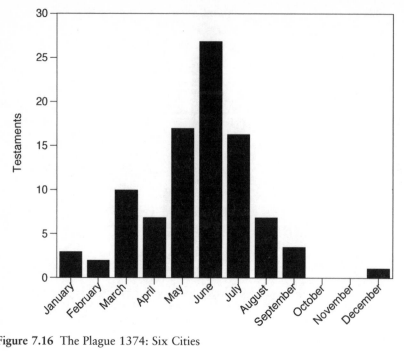

Figure 7.16 The Plague 1374: Six Cities

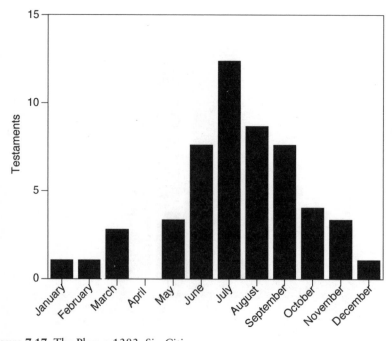

Figure 7.17 The Plague 1383: Six Cities

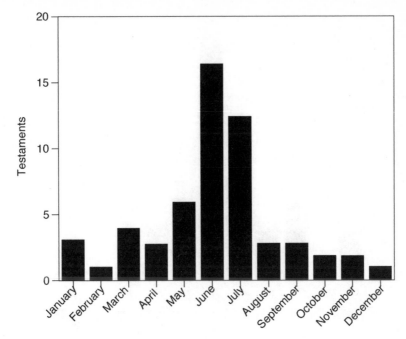

Figure 7.18 The Plague 1400: Six Cities

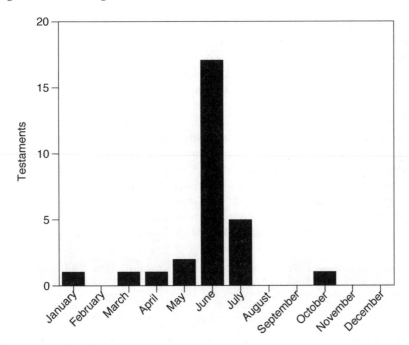

Figure 7.19 The Plague 1400: Perugia

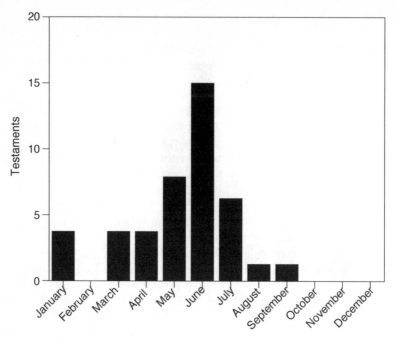

Figure 7.20 The Plague 1400: Rome

in the city of Bologna in June, July or August with every plague to the early fifteenth century: 1362, 1374, 1383, 1389, and 1423.[113]

Given the observations of Matteo Villani, Giovanni Morelli, and the anonymous chronicler of Tournai that plague struck first the poor and then the better-off, testaments might reflect a second wave of the plague after it had left the alleyways of the poor, where it may well have made its biggest killing. In Florence and Siena, however, other sources replicate the same seasonal patterns reflected by the wills in plague time. First, large numbers of them along with 'causae propter mortem' gifts were drawn up and preserved by the major hospitals of these two cities, Santa Maria Nuova in Florence and Santa Maria della Scala in Siena.[114] This group of testamentary gifts reflects a lower clientele than can be captured from the more or less random survival of testaments in the notarial books usually redacted in homes of the testators and especially the more elite wills preserved in

---

[113] I have tallied these testaments from the plague years 1362, 1374, 1383, 1389, 1399, and 1423. Archivio di Stato Bologna, Ufficio dei Memoriali, Liber memorialium contractuum et ultimarum voluntatum, for 1362 (vols 269 and 270), 1374 (294 and 295), 1383 (312 and 313), 1389 (316), 1399 (319), 1409 (320), 1423 (321). On the first three plagues see Cronache A and B, pp. 66, 70, 78, and 80; *Matteo Griffoni*, p.114; and *Historia Miscella Bononiensis*, cols 466, 495, and 525. The wills show no evidence of a serious plague in 1399.

[114] Both sets of records are now preserved in their respective state archives, the former in the ASF, Diplomatico, Santa Maria Nuova; the latter in the ASS Santa Maria della Scala, Spoglio.

parchment by the monasteries and friaries. For the most part, the hospital wills were of poor inmates with little or no disposable property. Yet, as with the other wills, these rose steeply only with the summer months, peaking either in June or July for all the plagues I have sampled: 1348, 1363, and 1383 (Figs 7.21–7.26).

Still other quantitative sources show the same summer pattern. The Black Death of 1348 wiped out 81 Dominicans born in the territory of Florence. For this community the peak in deaths was even more pronounced than that seen from the last wills and testaments. Eight-three per cent of the brothers died in three months (May, June, and July) with a peak in June. By August, the plague had spent its force with only three casualties (Fig. 7.27). For the second plague, 1363, again death peaked in June; two-thirds died in June and July alone (11 of 17 deaths).

For those buried at Santa Maria Novella (mostly the laity) the peaks for 1348 and 1363 did come slightly later, in July for 1374 and August in 1383. This parish and those outsiders who had to pay extra to be buried there represented a wide social spectrum, from an ironmonger to the members of the Strozzi family, but it certainly was a wealthier community than the testators who died in hospitals or those whose wills happen to survive in the notarial books.

For Siena, the Dominican death-book chronicle (misleadingly called a

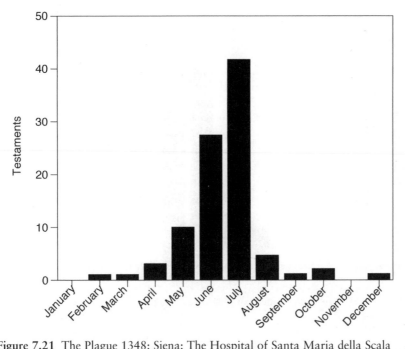

Figure 7.21 The Plague 1348: Siena: The Hospital of Santa Maria della Scala

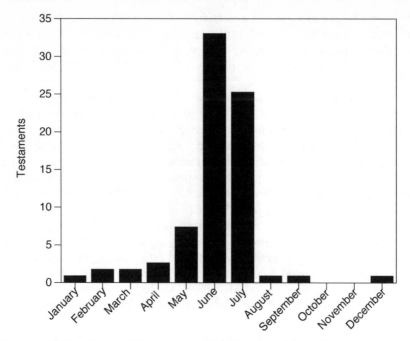

Figure 7.22 The Plague 1348: Florence: The Hospital of Santa Maria Nuova

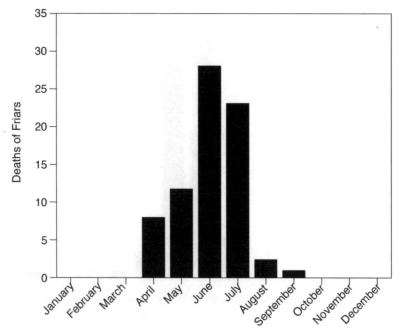

Figure 7.23 The Plague 1348: Florence: The 'Necrology' of Santa Maria Novella

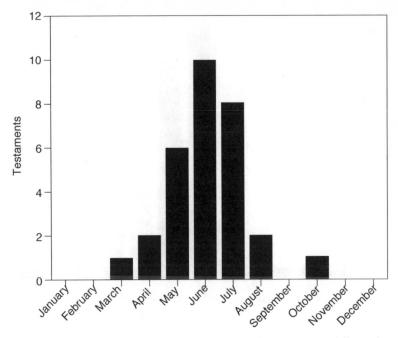

Figure 7.24 The Plague 1363: Siena: The Hospital of Santa Maria della Scala

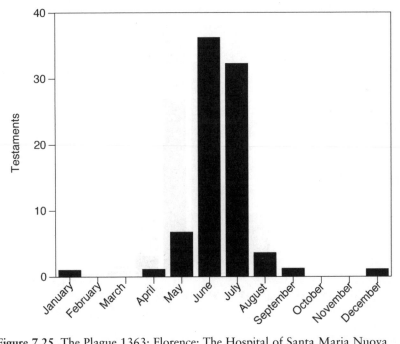

Figure 7.25 The Plague 1363: Florence: The Hospital of Santa Maria Nuova

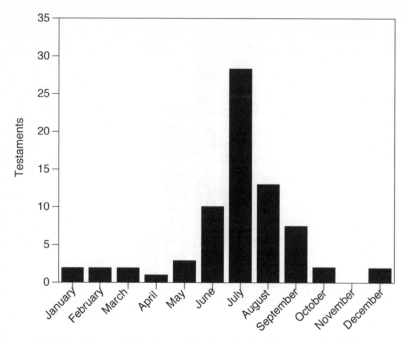

Figure 7.26 The Plague 1383: Siena: The Hospital of Santa Maria della Scala

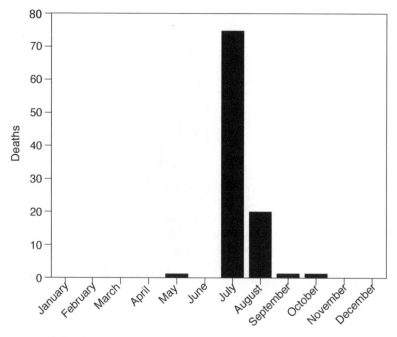

Figure 7.27 The Plague 1348: Orvieto: The confraternity at San Francesco

necrology) recorded 50 brothers dying in the plague of 1348 but did not list their month and day of death. The next plague, 1363, was far less severe for the community; only five died but all in July (3) and August (2). For the third plague, four of the six listed with their dates of death died in June, July, or August; and for 1383, four of the five died in these summer months. Until 1449, the last year of this death chronicle, only one year registered more than five deaths: in 1449 seven died, five in June and one in July.[115]

For burials of the laity in Dominican grounds at Siena, the figures for 1348 show the same seasonal trajectory: they mounted in May, jumping from seven to 54, and continued to climb in June (66 burials), but for July the scribes ceased their reporting, perhaps turning to unrecorded mass graves or dying themselves. When the register was resumed in August, its count had returned almost to normal (6). For the second plague (1363), the burials again jumped in May, peaked in June (76) but this time remained high through August (72), before falling sharply to only two burials in September.

Finally, more than any data from any source that I have seen, the meticulous recording of the deaths of the lay brothers who belonged to the society of Santa Maria at San Francesco in Orvieto highlights the plague's steep climb in mortalities at the hottest time of year in 1348. Two-thirds of the members (64) died in July and nearly 90 per cent died in June or July[116] (see Fig. 7.27). Moreover, this did not reflect a single diseased quarter of the city as the Dominican parish records might have; instead the confraternity dead came from all the city's districts.[117]

For a true cross-section of a late-medieval city-state's pattern of plague mortality, however, we must wait until the plague of 1390 at Arezzo, whose burials were recorded by that town's one city-wide confraternity, the Misericordia or Fraternità dei Laici.[118] Here, in contrast to the middling-to-upper-crust representation of families found in Orvieto's lay confraternity or the burial grounds of Santa Maria Novella, all the city's parishes and *contrade* are represented (more than 41) along with women and children. Further, of those listed by occupation, lower-class ones—*trecche* (greengrocers) and other vendors of cheap everyday utilities, barbers, servants (*fante, fancello, fameglio dei frati, donzelli di signori*), and a *donna di soldieri* (prostitute?)—were predominant. In the plague of 1390, 1075 died in a town that may not have then been much larger than 5000; its burials increased from a normal monthly load of 24 in March to 146 in May. But the big surge came in June when 437 were buried. After July the burials

[115] *I Necrologi di Siena di San Domenico*, 'Necrologio dei Religiosi', p. 5ff.

[116] Codice, V.E. no. 528, and Mary Henderson, 'La Confraternità e la catastrofe: La Confraternità francescana di Orvieto e la peste nera', in *Bollettino dell'Istituto Storico Artistico Orvietano*, xlviii–xlix (1992–3) (Orvieto, 1999), pp. 89–127, tab. IV, pp. 123–5.

[117] The records also give the brothers' parish of residence.

[118] Archivio di Fraternità dei Laici (Arezzo), Libri di morti, no. 882.

quickly slipped back to manageable numbers and had returned to normal by September. In other words, the pattern of these deaths matches closely that seen from the more elite death records of friars, confraternity members, and testators—a rapid summer rise and fall, peaking at the hottest and driest time of year, in June (Fig. 7.28).

For 1400, plague at Arezzo was minor by comparison; the confraternity buried less than a third the number they interred in 1390, and the pattern was different with a peak in August and epidemic levels continuing through October. This was exceptional not only against the backdrop of other plagues, but also in comparison with Florence, where plague in that year killed between 10,000 and 12,000 residing within the city walls. Here, similar to previous years and with other death documents, the peak came in the last week of June or first days of July, when as many as 202 were buried in a single day. In July alone, 5002 or almost half of that year's dead were buried[119] (Fig. 7.29).

Given the rarity of testaments redacted during this plague in Florence

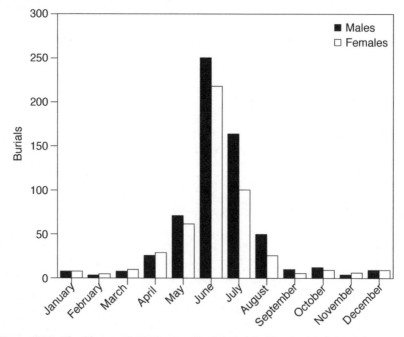

Figure 7.28 The Plague 1390: Arezzo: Burials by the Fraternità dei Laici

---

[119] ASF, Libri dei morti, no. 187. 1400 is the first plague for which these records survive. In this register the folios from 143r to 192v are missing, but this does not reflect a breakdown in the commune's burials or their recording as happened in 1348 with other registers; the numbers continue, showing that between 5 and 14 July, 1694 individuals were buried—around 170 a day.

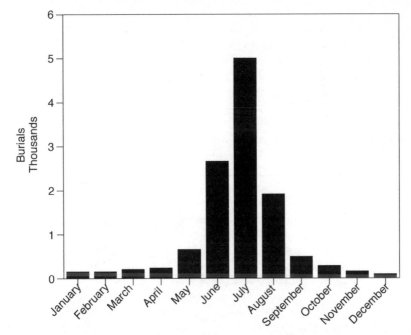

Figure 7.29 The Plague 1400: Florence: Burials, *Libri dei morti*

and other cities in Tuscany, it may have been the first to kill principally the poor. During the plague months relatively few with family names or upper guild professions appear, and the parishes which bore the brunt were the larger and poorer ones on the periphery of the city—San Frediano, Santa Maria in Verzaia, Santa Lucia Ognissanti, San Pier Maggiore, and Sant'Ambrogio—as opposed to the wealthier ones within its first rung of Roman walls (see map).[120] Yet the seasonality of plague, essentially among Florence's relatively poor, plots the same curve as seen with testaments and the obituaries of the privileged.

In summary, the death data from six cities in Tuscany and Umbria, plus Bologna, Rome, Barcelona, and Millau chart a pattern that differs from impressions given by chroniclers. By their accounts, plague occurred at almost any time of year, often dragging on for six to nine months or more without a sharp seasonal delineation, and with the plagues of 1374 and 1383 crossing all seasons. Certainly, the chroniclers are not to be dismissed, but the testaments and other death documents add another dimension, showing when plague unfurled its sails, peaked, and declined. The monthly distributions traced by these quantitative sources give plague a more

---

[120] On the class geography of fifteenth-century Florence, see Cohn, *The Laboring Classes*. For the statistics from the death books, see chapter 8.

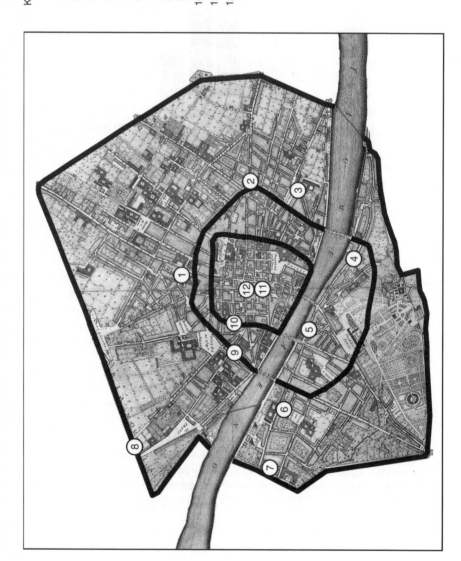

KEY:

1 S. Lorenzo
2 S. Pier Maggiore
3 Canto a Monteloro
4 S. Lucia de' Bardi
5 S. Iacopo Sopr' Arno
6 S. Frediano
7 S. Maria in Verzaia
8 Third city walls
9 Second city walls
10 Roman walls
11 The Grain Market
12 Orsanmichele

compact and explosive force than seen with chronicles and show a greater consistency in occurrence across time and across the northern shores of the Mediterranean. Most likely, this pattern of plague flaring at the hottest moments of the year continued past our analysis. In 1461 Pope Pius II called plague 'that summer contagion'.[121] Further, if the early twentieth-century doctor and plague researcher Georg Sticker is correct, the plague's seasonality was similar on other shores of the Mediterranean. Without giving his sources, he maintained that in 1348 plague peaked in July in Damascus, Aleppo, Cairo, and Babylonia as it had done the previous year at Constantinople.[122] However, contemporary chroniclers in Egypt and Syria give another picture with plague peaking in Damascus at the end of October 1347 and in Cairo in December.[123] On the other hand, in 1419 plague in Egypt was in springtime, arising on 28 March and abating by 2 May.[124] The plague of 1429–30, which the chronicler Ibn Taghrā Birdī assessed as even more deadly than that of 1348, hit Syria in May but raged through Egypt in winter.[125] He later alleged that this had been a freak occurrence, 'previously plagues had been witnessed only in spring'.[126]

Yet, the differences between different shores of the Mediterranean, the recurrence of the plague in Mediterranean Europe at the same time of year roughly in every instance from 1348 to 1450 and probably later shows a pattern that was even more consistent in its seasonality than modern bubonic plague in India, where plague might strike at either side of the hot months of the year, when it abruptly ended. By high temperatures, the plague commissioners pointed to limits certainly not beyond Mediterranean summers: 80°F or even 78°[127] marked 'the threshold at which plague usually cannot maintain itself in epidemic form'.[128] Further, these ranges pertained to the relatively humid summers of northern India.

---

[121] Aeneas Silvius Piccolomini (Pope Pius II), *I Commentarii*, ed. by Luigi Totaro (Milan, 1984), I, p. 1615. From the plague of 1430 to the sixteenth century, Alan Morrison, Julius Kirshner, and Anthony Molho ('Epidemics in Renaissance Florence', *American Journal of Public Health* 75 (1985), p. 532–3) find that the major epidemic peak (all diseases) for young girls was summer, followed by a second peak in autumn.

[122] Sticker, *Abhandlungen*, I, pp. 45–6.

[123] 'Relation d'Ibn Katir', p. 383; and Maqrīzī, *Sulūk*, pp. 374–5. Summers in Cairo and Damascus are warmer than in Florence but they are also more humid; see *Washington Post Historical Weather Data website*.

[124] *Arabic Annals of Abu L–Mahasin Ibn Taghrā Birdī*, III, pp. 64–7.

[125] Ibid., IV, p. 69.

[126] Ibid., IV, p. 181.

[127] 'On the seasonal prevalence of plague in India', *JH*, 8 (1908), p. 275.

[128] 'Digest of recent observations on the epidemiology of plague', *JH*, 7 (1907), p. 717; Kunhardt and Taylor, 'Epidemiological observations in Madras Presidency', pp. 713–51; Ralph St. John Brooks, 'The influence of saturation deficiency and of temperature on the course of epidemic plague', *JH*, 12 (1912): 881–9; Hirst, *The Conquest of Plague*, p. 263. In some areas of India, the plague peaks with average temperatures as low as 58°F when levels of humidity are favourably high; see 'Epidemiological observations in the United Provinces of Agra and Oudh', *JH: Plague Supplement V* (1917); Otten, 'The problem of the seasonal prevalence of plague'.

As far as climate goes, the historiography of the late-medieval and early modern plagues has turned on the problems of fleas and rats surviving northern European winters. The sense that plague generally (though not always, as we have seen) disappeared with winter reinforced views of the Black Death as modern bubonic plague. But no one has pondered the problems of European summers, even in the warmer Mediterranean. Although Florentine winters are much colder than those of Bombay City, little difference separates them at midsummer. The maximum average highs for Bombay City over the past twenty-one years have been 85°F, while for Florence, they have in fact been higher, 89°F.[129]

In addition, the Mediterranean summers were particularly inhospitable to fleas for another reason. As found in India, the combination of dryness and high temperatures limits flea fertility, cuts short 'the life of free-wandering fleas', hampers the bacillus's survival, and curtails its infectivity.[130] Plague researchers of the second decade of the twentieth century even found humidity as more important than temperature for predicting plague. In comparison with a relative humidity in Bombay City at over 80 per cent in the summer, in Florence it is around 60 per cent, meaning that plague in epidemic form would decline and disappear at lower temperatures in such climes. Commensurate with these conditions, researchers of the early twentieth century found that the season for the rat flea (*X. cheopis*) in the region of Marseilles, southern France, and most of Italy was September and October, after the rains of the early autumn and the cooling off at the end of the summer.[131] For Italy's most common rat flea, *C. fasciatus*, which is more adaptable to cold than *X. cheopis*, peak fertility comes even later,[132] that is, several months after the late-medieval plagues regularly peaked and a month or more after they had lost all their epidemic force. Indeed, plague for most of Italy and the Mediterranean peaked at the hottest and driest time of year, June and July, at or near the low-point in the rat flea's population. Even January would have been a more likely month had the disease been modern rat-based plague.[133]

At no time in the fourteenth century did any of these Italian towns (except Pisa in 1362 and possibly in 1348, based on insubstantial numbers)

---

[129] *Washington Post* Historical Weather Data website.

[130] Hirst, *The Conquest of Plague*, pp. 227, 280; *JH*, 8 (1908), 'The mechanism by which the flea carries itself of plague bacilli' p. 262.

[131] 'Some recent observations on rat fleas', *JH* 13 (1913), pp. 7–9; Chick and Martin, 'The fleas common on rats', p. 125; Hans Zinsser, *Rats, Lice, and History* (London, 1935), p. 93; J.C. Gauthier and A. Raybaud—'Des variétés de pulicidés trouvés sur les rats à Marseille', *Comptes rendus hebdomadaires des séances et mémoires de la société de biologie*, 67 (1909): 196–9—found that for Marseilles between 1906 and 1909, with 10,000 collected fleas on rats, June was the absolute low-point in flea numbers (p. 198).

[132] 'A study of the bionomics of the common rat fleas', *JH: Plague Supplement III* (1914), p. 642; Chick and Martin, 'The fleas common on rats', pp. 122–36; Rothschild, 'Note on the species of fleas', pp. 483–5.

[133] Gauthier and Raybaud, 'Des variétés de pulicidés', pp. 196–9.

show plague peaking either in spring (even as late as May) or autumn, as would be expected had the disease depended on the flea. Even for a much milder climate, that of San Francisco, plague at the opening of the twentieth century did not strike in summer but waited until September before reaching its peak.[134] Reflecting these entomological and ecological realities, the only bubonic plague for Italy observed by Pollitzer in his survey of the distribution of plague in the twentieth century (Taranto, 1945) occurred between September and November.[135]

Nor has recent global warming changed matters; instead, temperatures in the Mediterranean through the first half of the fourteenth century may have been +1°C warmer than when Lamb constructed his historical weather maps in the 1970s.[136] Evidence from chroniclers and doctors also points to hot, even unbearable summers in the late fourteenth and fifteenth centuries. For Venice in 1414, Sanuto reported a heat wave in August (*grandissimi caldi*) and reasoned that plague raged as a consequence.[137] In 1420, the papal doctor Antonio Guainerio said the heat was so intense at the end of June and first days of July in Lombardy that farm labourers dropped dead in the fields.[138] In the plague year 1457 a Genoese chronicler recorded that the summer was 'caldissima' and that from mid-June to mid-September it had not rained—conditions that would have been unimaginable for an outbreak of modern plague, yet in this year plague was 'grandissima'.[139] Plague in Parma also spread with a summer heat wave reported as 'grandissimo' in 1468.[140] Finally, a chronicler in Rome described plague in 1485, which peaked in June, as 'multiplying with the rising heat'.[141]

In addition to problems of climate, the similarity in monthly peaks among places separated by mountain ranges and distances of over a thousand kilometres does not accord well with historians' attempts to plot out the plague's pace or, more to the point, the slow overland travel of modern bubonic plague, dependent on the homey rat: overland, the latter travels no more than eight miles a year. The nearly simultaneous outbreak of plague between places as far removed as Bologna and Assisi or even Rome and Valencia suggests a highly contagious disease like influenza, where the same variant of flu may irrupt in places separated by thousands of miles at the same moment, even before mass airplane travel. In fact, the name 'influenza,' derived in seventeenth-century Italy

---

[134] Blue, 'Anti-plague measures in San Francisco', p. 7.
[135] R. Pollitzer, *Plague*, p. 30.
[136] Lamb, *Climate*, II, p. 436, table 17.1.
[137] Sanuto, *Vitæ Ducum Venetorum*, p. 889.
[138] Corradi, *Annali delle epidemie*, I, p. 259.
[139] Ibid., p. 296.
[140] Ibid., p. 306.
[141] Ibid., p. 261.

because of this trait of springing forth 'universally' at the same moment.[142]

* * *

If not the flea, then could the disease's vector have been another bug, whose fertility cycle and survival were more conducive to warmer and drier conditions? If dryness and heat were the necessary conditions for the plague's explosion, then we might expect that the plagues should have been primarily a Mediterranean disease, more devastating the further south one went, as in fact Le Roy Ladurie concluded for 1348. After all, according to chronicle lore, two of the worst-hit cities of the first wave were Trapani in Sicily and Marseilles.[143] Other cities prominently pinned for their terrible mortalities were also predominantly southern—Pisa, Genoa, Florence, Avignon. Yet, as we have seen, northern cities figured as well—Paris, London, and Dublin—and more recent historians have found in places such as Cambridgeshire mortalities mounting to over 70 per cent of village populations. Nor do later plagues appear to have been any less devastating in the north than in the south. The second plague of the late 1350s was principally a northern plague with heavy mortalities in Brabant, parts of Flanders, northern Germany, and Bohemia, and the next round of pestilence in 1361 started in London (according to Villani) with little devastation to the south until 1362.[144]

Even more confounding for any theory of an insect as the vector of the Black Death and its successive waves is the seasonality of plague in the north of Europe. Finding large numbers of wills north of the Alps is more difficult than in Italy. Except for the Roman-law south of France, traditions of the public notary were weak and the collections for the north come almost exclusively from places where the bishop or a town council kept wills, as in Besançon, where the bishop registered them from 1255 to the end of the seventeenth century. Before the French Revolution, this collection contained over 8000 testaments with the bulk of them (5005) written before 1450. The majority of these, however, have disappeared. Except for the hundred-odd wills of prominent citizens that the Abbé Guillaume ran off with to Paris,[145] we now have only the list compiled by the Abbé in the mid-eighteenth century, containing the name of the testator and year of registration.

Another story of northern destruction, this time from another epoch, regards the largest collection of parchments (chirographs) found north of

---

[142] Crosby, 'Influenza: in the grip of the grippe', in *Plague, Pox and Pestilence*, p. 148.

[143] See for instance the chroniclers of Bologna, *Cronaca B*, p. 584; *Historia Miscella Bononiensis*, col. 409; *Annales Pistorienses*, p. 524; and *Polyhistoria fratris Bartholomæi Ferrariensis*, col. 807.

[144] See previous chapter.

[145] I wish to thank Jack Warwick for this information.

the Alps: those registered by the town council of Tournai, which were reduced to ashes by a German bomb in May 1940.[146] At the beginning of the twentieth century inventories of this deposit's testaments were compiled with 8344 survivals from its earliest parchment of 1155 to 1425. Like Besançon's, this one also did not record the day or month of the testament.[147]

Other collections kept by municipalities or regional courts have better stood the test of time, including those at Forez, Lyon,[148] Douai, Lübeck, and London. The wills of Forez are different from those of the cities considered above in that its urban centre, Montbrison, was not the dominant contributor. The majority came from a variegated countryside of plains, mountains, and small castle villages, and perhaps partially as a result, its distribution of wills at the time of plague contrasts with what we have seen for the warmer and drier south. First, its Black Death stretched over both years, 1348 and 1349. In 1348 wills peaked in September, two to three months after peaks in Mediterranean cities. Third, the plague's decline was not as sharp as in the south; instead at Forez they persisted at more than double the normal levels through the winter of 1349 without an appreciable drop until the next spring.[149] Nor were these characteristics of the first plague alone. The second in 1360 peaked even later, in November—four or five months after that of Florence and other Mediterranean cities[150]—and like Forez's first one, continued into the following year. According to Fournial, the plague of 1361 'was particularly virulent during the hottest months', but he has not analysed the wills' monthly distribution.[151] By my tallies, the wills peaked in August (25) with the same number in September as in July (11), and unlike the Mediterranean wills, instead of dropping steeply with the advent of autumn, they lingered on through the early winter.[152]

The cloth town of Douai in Flanders along with others in the region such

---

[146] See H. Platelle, 'Chirographes de Tournai retrouvés dans un fonds de la Bibliothèque de Valenciennes, *Revue du Nord*, XLIV no. 174 (1962): 191–200; and R. Jacob, *Les époux*, p. 77.

[147] Adolphe Hocquet, 'Table des Testaments', *Annales de la société historique et archéologique de Tournai*, ns 6 (1901): 284–99; 7 (1902): 81–161; and 10 (1906): 1–197.

[148] The testaments at Lyon have been the subject of an excellent study by Marie-Thérèse Lorcin, 'Clauses religieuses dans les testaments du plat pays lyonnais aux XIVe et XVe siècles, *Moyen Age*, 78 (1972): 287–323; and *Vivre et mourir en Lyonnais à la fin du Moyen Age* (Paris, 1981). Between 1300 and 1510, 1145 wills were preserved for the city (far less than at Besançon, Forez, or Douai). For the plagues of 1348, 1361, and 1392, 376, 206, and 91 wills respectively have been preserved in this archive (p. 11). Unfortunately, neither Lorcin nor anyone else to my knowledge has shown the monthly distribution of these plague wills.

[149] These data are based on Fournial, *Les villes et l'économie d'échange en Forez*, p. 303.

[150] Ibid., p. 312; further, 44 per cent of that year's testaments were drafted in October or November.

[151] Ibid., p. 313.

[152] All these wills come from Archives départementales de Loire, B 1865 (1348–62); other wills for 1361 might be found scattered throughout booklets, but this one contains the vast majority of them (143 wills from 1361 of which I could date 90).

as Lille and Arras[153] had a plague experience unlike most towns in Europe. No evidence points to the Black Death in these towns from 1347 to 1352; for Douai, not a single testament survives for these years, neither from the voluminous chirograph archive of wills registered by the town counsellors nor in collections kept by hospitals and other ecclesiastical houses and corporations.[154] Further, no greater number of city aldermen died in 1348 than in previous non-plague years.[155] The first major plague was not until 1400. Jean-Pierre Deregnaucourt has assumed that plague struck in 1382, because the wills trebled in that year (a small jump for a first plague as seen elsewhere), but no narrative source confirms it.[156] If Deregnaucourt is correct, its plague season, like that of Forez, was later than in warmer Mediterranean cities: the peak in testaments for this year came in August with a second peak in October.[157] For the first big plague—that of 1400— eighty-two testaments survive, eight times the previous yearly averages, on par with the jump as seen with first-plague testaments elsewhere. But the build-up did not begin until July and peaked in September, two to three months after the southern plague season (Fig. 7.30).

Douai's plague season is corroborated by nearby Cambrai. The burial records of the poor at the hospital of Saint-Julien register fifteen outbreaks of plague from 1377 to 1473. Even though the poor were presumably the first to catch the plague, consistently, their plague burials began in late summer and ran through the autumn, with peak mortalities in September.[158] Thus the peaks for other portions of the population may have come even later. With fewer records to rest a quantitative argument, the surviving documentation further west in upper Normandy shows a similar plague season. According to grave choices at Caen and deathbed gifts to the Dominican friary at Coustance, the plague peaked in November and

---

[153] Martine Aubry, 'Mortalités lilloises 1328–69', *Revue du Nord*, 65 (1983): 337–60. Based on rents not paid because of death, 1360 may have been the first plague year in Lille. But, if so, it appears not to have been as catastrophic as the first year of plague in other cities and regions; here, the number of such rents increased by less than three-fold, from around 13 or 14 a year to 35. The necrology of the Confraternity of Jugglers and the Bourgeois of Arras lists the deaths of 11,300 members between 1194 and 1361. Neither 1348 nor 1349 registers an increase in deaths: for 1345, 52 were listed; 1346, 32; 1347, 48; 1348, 48; 1349, 36; 1350, 22. Nor were there any increases for the plague years 1357 (48), effectively, the last year of this necrology; Berger, *Le Nécrologe de la confrérie des jongleurs*, pp. 174–80.

[154] *Inventaire général des chartes . . . appartenant aux hospices et au bureau de bienfaisance de la ville de Douai*, ed. by Félix Brassart (Douai, 1839).

[155] G. Dhérent, *Historie sociale de la bourgeoisie de Douai*, Thèse d'École des Chartes (1981), p. 111.

[156] The *Chronique des Pays-Bas,* which reported on events and plagues within Flanders, makes no mention of plague here before 1400.

[157] Deregnaucourt, 'Autour de la mort à Douai: Attitudes pratiques et croyances, 1250–1500', 2 vols, Thèse, Université Charles de Gaulle (Lille, 1993), I, p. 60. Also see Archives Municipales de Douai [AMD], FF. 864 1381–5.

[158] Hugues Neveux, 'La mortalité des pauvres à Cambrai (1377–1473)', *Annales de démographie historique* (1968), p. 79.

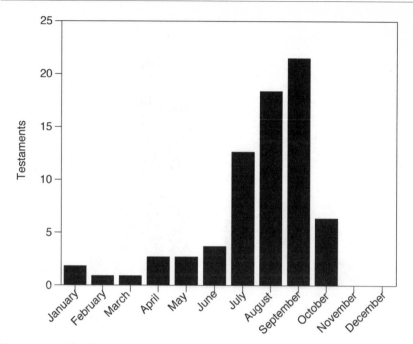

Figure 7.30 The Plague 1400: Douai

lingered through the winter of 1349.[159] To the southeast in Besançon (Franche-Comté) the few surviving wills dated by month suggest that the first plague may have been slightly earlier than in Normandy or Flanders, peaking in August or September, but still two months after the Mediterranean season.[160] Finally, according to testamentary gifts to the parish of Saint-Germain-l'Auxerrois in Paris the Black Death rose abruptly in August and probably peaked either in September or October; the scribe's grouping of gifts makes it impossible to know precisely.[161]

The wills registered in the Hanseatic town of Lübeck by its town council (of which more than a thousand survive from its earliest exemplum to 1363) also manifest this later northern plague time. When plague arrived in 1350, its wills did not rise appreciably until July and peaked in August;

---

[159] Jouet, 'Autour de la Peste Noire', p. 270. Further north in Holland few quantitaive or narrative sources record the plagues' first onslaught in 1349–50, but later ones of the four-teenth and early fifteenth centuries are etched in church records such as commemorative books of Saint Pancras at Leiden. For the two plagues that Dick de Boer, *Graaf en grafiek: sociale en economische ontwikkelingen in het middeleeuwse 'Noordholland' tussen 1345 en 1415* (Leiden, 1978), pp. 84 and 89, has analysed by month (1382 and 1411), plague deaths peaked in September followed by October.

[160] Roland Fiétier, *La cité de Besançon de la fin du XIIème au milieu du XIVème siècle: Étude d'une société urbaine* (Paris, 1978), I, p. 338.

[161] Michel Mollat, 'Note sur la mortalité à Paris', p. 509.

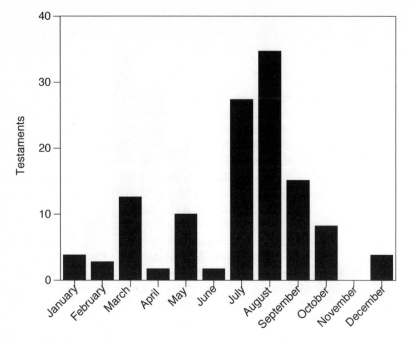

Figure 7.31 The Plague 1350: Lübeck

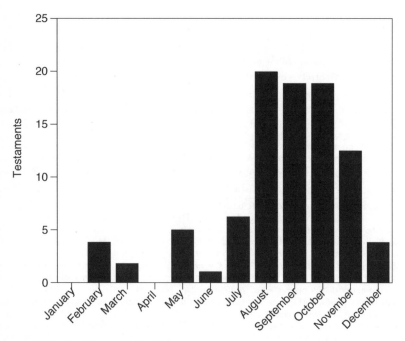

Figure 7.32 The Plague 1358: Lübeck

further, as in Forez, they persisted at high levels to October (Fig. 7.31). For its next plague, 1358, the wills again peaked in August but remained at roughly the same high level until October, declining only slightly in November (Fig. 7.32).[162]

Finally, the wills proved and preserved in abbreviated form by the London Court of Husting show a third pattern. The plague, which according to the narrative sources, arrived in London as early as July 1348 did not, according to the wills, begin to build steam until the winter of 1349, peaking in spring. Lawrence Poos has maintained that this seasonal pattern was general throughout southern England[163] (see Fig. 7.33). A similar pattern is found for Coventry according to the less precise death markers of deeds and property transfers, mounting in February and peaking in May 1349.[164] On the manor of Farnham (Surrey), according to Pipe rolls and indications of failure to pay rents because of *defectus per pestilentiam*, plague arrived in October 1348 declined in the winter, and rose again in the late spring, 1349.[165] According to Shrewsbury, plague in Hampshire peaked in May.[166] Other than distant Marseilles (for 1348) in a completely different ecosystem of Europe, these are the only spring plague peaks I have seen with the quantification of death records of various sorts—property deeds, vacant benefices, wills, and burials.[167]

In London, where wills survive in substantial numbers for successive

---

[162] These testaments have been edited in abbreviated form in Regesten der Lübecker Bürgertestamente des Mittelalters, ed. A. von Brandt, 2 vols (Lübeck, 1964). Wills from three other northern German towns have been edited—Lüneberg, Hamburg, and Braunschweig; Lüneburger Testamente des Mittelalters 1323 bis 1500, ed. by Uta Reinhardt (Hanover, 1996); Hans–Dieter Loose, Hamburger Testamente 1351 bis 1400 (Hamburg, 1970) Testamente der Stadt Braunschweig, ed. by Dietrich Mack (Göttingen, 1988–93), 5 vols. The wills of Lünenburg show no evidence of the plague at all. Before 1412, the maximum number in a year was five, climbing to 11 in 1421 (the high-point before the series end in 1440). Hamburg shows a climb in wills to 20 in 1350 and to 19 in 1351, but in the first instance only 11 can be dated by the month and these do not show a distinct peak. The same goes for the plague year of 1358. Finally, the surviving testaments at Braunschweig show no evidence of plague in 1348–50 but increase from three or four a year to 17 in the plague year of 1358, with increases for 1365, 1366 and 1426. However, it is only for 1426 that most of the wills are dated by month. In that plague year, the peak comes in September with over a third of the wills drawn up in that month.

[163] Poos, 'Population and resources', p. 380.

[164] A. Goodes, 'Coventry at the time of the Black Death and afterwards', in *The Black Death in Coventry*, ed. by M. Hulton (Coventry, 1998), pp. 29–39.

[165] E. Robo, 'The Black Death in the hundred of Farnham', *English Historical Review*, XLIV (1944), p. 562.

[166] Shrewsbury, *A History of Bubonic Plague*, p, 91, but for other areas—Gloucester, Worcester, Hereford, Norfolk, Suffolk, Cambridgeshire, York, and Durham—the plague came in the summer of 1349; pp. 64, 68, 70, 99, 106, 111, and 114.

[167] For later plagues, springtime was even rarer; the only case that comes from my survey of death documents or others that I know of was for Forez in the plague of 1397–8; Fournial, *Les villes et l'économie d'échange en Forez*, p. 319. The chronicler Maqrīzī, *Sulūk*, p. 378, says plague peaked at Gaza between 2 April and 4 May with 25,000 deaths, supposedly according to a government report.

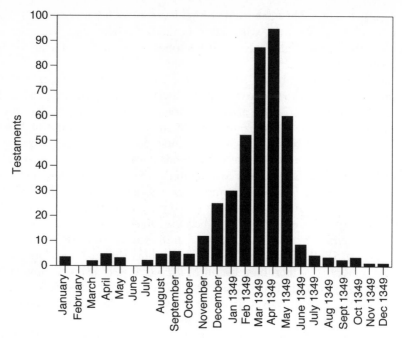

Figure 7.33 The Plague 1348–9: London: The Court of Husting

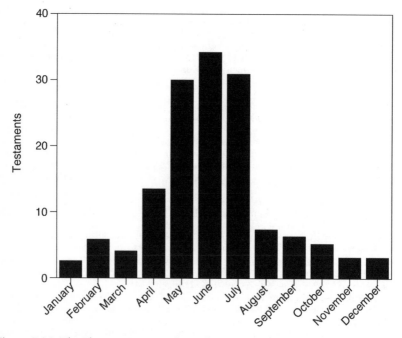

Figure 7.34 The Plague 1361: London: The Court of Husting

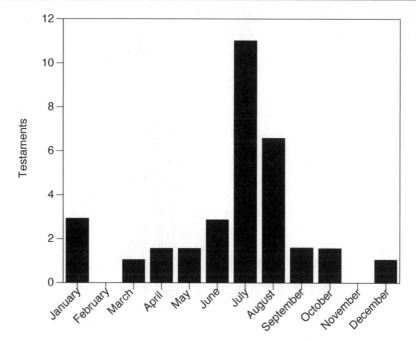

Figure 7.35 The Plague 1375: London: The Court of Husting

plague waves, this spring pattern did not persist. For the next two plagues, they appear to follow the Mediterranean course, peaking in June in 1361 and in July in 1375 (see Figs 7.34 and 7.35).[168] On the other hand, by the sixteenth century at Bristol, the plague season resembled that of northern France, Flanders, and Germany, peaking in late autumn,[169] while for seventeenth-century Colyton in Southwest England, plague was a summer event.[170] Despite the difference, but similarity in climate, the authors— Slack and Schofield respectively—came to the same conclusion: plague mortality 'follows the classic seasonal pattern' of modern bubonic plague.

In Ireland, according to the sermon diary of Richard FitzRalph, Archbishop of Armagh, plague reached Drogheda about August 1348 and peaked in autumn, resembling the northern continental seasonality.[171] The

[168] These statistics have been compiled from the abbreviations edited by Sharpe, *Calendar of Wills: Court of Husting*, I and II. For Lincolnshire testaments also peaked in July, 1349; according to Zeigler, *The Black Death*, p. 185.
[169] Paul Slack, 'The local incidence of epidemic disease: the case of Bristol 1540–1650', in *The Plague Reconsidered*, p. 51.
[170] Schofield, 'An anatomy of an epidemic: Colyton, November 1645 to November 1646', ibid., pp. 101 and 119.
[171] Gwynn, 'The Sermon-Diary of Richard FitzRalph'; and idem, 'The Black Death in Ireland', *Studies: An Irish Quarterly Review of Letters, Philosophy and Science*, 24 (1935), p. 29.

Franciscan John Clyn reported the same arrival date for Dublin and said it continued to Christmas. For his own village of Kilkenney, however, the mortalities mounted later in the winter of 1349.[172] The chronicler who continued John's work also noted 1349 and not 1348 as the year of the plague's first Irish strike. The English chronicler Geoffrey le Baker remarked that plague did not reach the Irish mountains until 1357, but he does not specify the month.[173] According to the continuation of Clyn's chronicle, the *Annals of Loch Cé*, *Annals of Connacht*, *Annals of Clonmacnoise*, and *Annals of the Kingdom of Ireland by the Four Masters* the dates of the fourteenth- and early fifteenth-century plagues correspond closely with those on the continent: 1349, 1362, 1373, 1382, 1391, 1398, 1400, 1406, 1408, and 1431.[174] But none gave any indication of these plagues' seasons; nor are there quantitative sources that I know that mark them.

Thus testaments and other death documents that can be quantified for judging the seasonal character of the plagues in northern Europe show a pattern that was less consistent than that for Mediterranean Italy, Spain, and southern France. But in general the plague took off and peaked in these colder climes between September and November or even later, at about the time they should have peaked in the warmer Mediterranean had the disease been the rat-based, flea-transmitted bubonic plague, whose seasons turn tightly round the reproductive cycle of the rat flea. By contrast, for northern Europe, a better timing would have been the mid-summer Mediterranean one because of the north's higher summer humidity and lower temperatures. But by October and certainly November in places in northern Germany, France, Flanders, and Ireland, when the late-medieval plague peaked and persisted at high levels, temperatures would have been in the 40s (°F), at or below the limits of the rat-flea's capacity to survive, especially with the plague's best vector, *X. cheopis*. To say the least, it would not have been an ideal time for modern bubonic plague to blossom.

Does this curious pattern of plague seasons in the different ecozones of Europe prove that the plague had no insect vector? Could the plague's difference in seasonality reflect its upward spread from a southern Mediterranean base? For the first plague such a hypothesis might be reasonable, but, as we have seen, the second wave of plague began in the north, in 1357 and again in 1358, and travelled southward, reaching Genoa, Orvieto, and grazing parts of Tuscany, the Romagna, and Umbria. The same north–south trajectory was also true for the next plague's course in

---

[172] *Annalium Hibernae*, p. 36.
[173] *Chronicon Galfridi le Baker*, p. 100.
[174] *Annalium Hiberniae*, p. 38; *Annals of the Kingdom of Ireland*, III, pp. 595, 623, 763; *The Annals of Clonmacnoise*, pp. 301, 308, 322–3, 325, 328; *Annála Connacht*, pp. 303, 377, 397, 403; *The Annals of Loch Cé*, II, pp. 3, 59, 73, 89, 117, 125, and 153.

1361, which by Villani's reckoning originated in England, crossed the Channel to France, then Provence, Avignon, Lombardy (Como, Pavia, Milan), Venice, Romagna, the Marche, Gubbio, finally reaching the Island of Mallorca.[175]

Further, by the second plague, the disease no longer had a single source or a simple single itinerary. Instead, it could flair at about the same time in places as far removed as Brabant and Bohemia in 1358, and Florence and Egypt in 1362. But season mattered and may explain why the plague of 1362 resulted in infecting only 'a house or two' in Florence. Although this plague executed heavy mortalities in Bologna, Pisa, Lucca, the Casentino, and Figline, for some reason, it did not penetrate Florence's gates until December. But when summer returned in 1363, the plague blazed forth, that is, at the same time as it had in 1348 and would do so again in numerous other summers to the seventeenth century.[176]

We close this chapter with more evidence against the flea as one of Western Europe's protagonists. As important, we leave new questions for entomologists, zoologists, and epidemiologists to solve given the plague's enigmatic seasonality. What sparked the plague's consistent sharp rise during the hottest and driest months of the year in the Mediterranean from Rome to Barcelona? Why north of the Alps did it not depend on similar climatic factors but instead awaited cooler, wetter weather from August to early winter? If the disease had been dependent on an insect vector, could it have been an insect like the mosquito with different species in different places having radically different breeding seasons?[177] If not temperature or humidity, what were the critical variables that conditioned the plagues' rise and fall in these different ecosystems of Europe's temperate zone?

---

[175] Matteo Villani, *Cronaca*, II, pp. 514–15.
[176] Ibid., II, p. 586.
[177] On the different species of mosquito determining different seasons of malaria in different parts of the world, see Winslow, *Man and Epidemics* (Princeton, 1952), pp. 168–79 and idem, *The Conquest of Epidemic Disease*, pp. 351–2.

8

Cycles and trends

Last wills and testaments, monastic obituaries, and burial records allow us to chart cycles and trends of the plagues in different parts of late-medieval Europe. Historians and epidemiologists have alleged that the cycles of modern plague resembled those of the late-medieval past in that both recurred at five- to ten-year intervals. In fact, the cycles of the two diseases are wholly different. Modern bubonic plague in India and more recently Brazil, Cambodia (1946 to 1952), Thailand (1944 to 1952), Vietnam (1961 to the 1970s), and other places charted by Pollitzer for the twentieth century[1] struck annually in a locality with varying levels of severity for five to as many as 20 years or more without missing more than one or two plague seasons. For the late Middle Ages, especially before 1450, plague rarely struck two years or more running with more than a single plague peak. Instead, it would disappear altogether for intervals of between five to 15 years. For instance in Florence (as in most places in central Italy) the plague years were 1348, 1363, 1374, 1383, 1390 (a weak presence), 1400, 1411, 1417, 1423–24, 1430, 1438, and 1450.

It may have been slightly different elsewhere. At Trent, its chronicler referred to 1373–74 as a 'biennium' plague.[2] In London the chroniclers reported that the first plague endured for two years, 1348 and 1349, but the distribution of wills shows one plague season covering no more than seven or eight months, which crossed the winter divide of these two years.

---

[1] Pollitzer, *Plague*. After low mortalities from plague in the opening years, the number of fatal cases climbed to 1,328,249 in 1905 and continued at more than million deaths per annum until 1908. Between 1904 and 1908, 4,325,237 in India died of plague; Hirst, *The Conquest of Plague*, pp. 105 and 300. In Vietnam, deaths climbed from 8, 32, 110, 242, to 4503 from 1961 to 1965 with already 2649 deaths in 1966 before the onset of the worse months of the plague season; Marshall, *et al.*, 'Plague in Vietnam'.
[2] *Cronica inedita di Giovanni da Parma*, p. 52.

The testaments from Besançon suggest that its second plague of 1360 (195 testaments) may have been followed by a lesser bout the following year when the wills (92) amounted to three times the normal 30 per annum. Finally, plague in the region of Forez may have lingered for as long as five years, 1397 to 1402, but not necessarily striking the same villages over this variegated terrain.[3]

These consecutive repeats were the exceptions, though, at least for the first hundred years of the plague. Later the character of the disease may have changed. In Geneva plague struck four years running from 1473 to 1476, for five years, 1481 to 1485, and by the early sixteenth century, for the nine years, 1502 to 1510.[4] Historians and scientists have yet to explore, or even comment on, these possibly long-term shifts in the plagues' epidemiology.

Other long-term trends of the late-medieval plagues are less enigmatic and separate the medieval and the bubonic disease discovered in 1894 more decisively than any of the medical characteristics we have thus far examined. After 20 years of repeated plague strikes in India, with the third worst season late in 1917–18, the plague researcher Norman White took stock of the disease's characteristics: 'of the many interesting epidemiological features that have characterised the disease in India during the last two decades, perhaps the two most noteworthy are: (1) the remarkable variation in intensity and diffusibility [sic] that have distinguished the outbreaks of different years; (2) the constancy of the seasonal prevalence of the disease in the worse infected areas ... '[5] The second of these we have already commented on. In part, we have in fact seen a similarity on this score between the two plague epochs, at least within the warmer climes of the Mediterranean. Even if their seasons were wholly different, both possessed a consistent seasonality. White's first observation, however, forms an even sharper divergence between the two plagues.

When plague struck Bombay in 1896 it made no difference that the disease was new to the population. No cataclysmic first explosion of morbidity or mortality occurred, nor afterwards do we see the normal pattern with infectious diseases—declining levels of morbidity and mortality as a host population adapts to its new parasite either through individual exposure to the disease or through a Darwinian selection whereby those with resistant genes survive, passing on their genetic armour to successive generations. Instead, in India the plague continued building a head of steam for at least its first nine years and for the next ten fluctuated almost randomly from year to year depending on climatic conditions; greater than

---

[3] Fournial, *Les villes et l'économie d'échange en Forez*, p. 319.
[4] Dr William Naphy, 'Learning to live with plague: the development of Genevan Plague Regulations, c.1400–c.1530', Seminars in the Wellcome Unit, University of Glasgow, 15 February 2000.
[5] White, 'Twenty years of plague in India', pp. 190–1.

normal levels of rainfall and higher relative humidity brought heavier plague casualties.[6] A decline in cases and mortality began in the second decade of the twentieth century resulting not from human immunity, but from the bacillus's preferred host, the rat, acquiring it[7] (see Figs 8.1 and 8.2). This curve of modern plague was not peculiar to the so-called Third Pandemic's first invasion of the early twentieth century. Rather, it is seen again when epidemic levels of plague returned in India at the end of the 1930s, in Vietnam in the 1960s, and in other places, even after DDT, implementation of rat controls in strategic places, and effective antibiotic treatment.[8]

Such random jumps in modern plague cases and mortality result from a characteristic of *Yersinia pestis*, that is not unique to this bacterium[9] but is rare among the agents of infectious diseases that have struck European populations from the Middle Ages to the twentieth century—human inability to acquire immunity to it. This epidemiological fact distinguishes modern plague from a medley of other diseases more tellingly than the appearance of buboes in lymph nodes. Moreover, it is a medical feature that

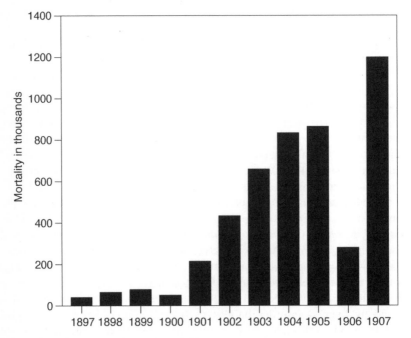

Figure 8.1 Plague in India, 1897–1907

---

[6] Ibid., pp. 96–7.

[7] Ibid., p. 215, and see chapter 2. Unfortunately, Ell, 'Immunity as a factor' does not distinguish between the immunity possessed by rats and that of humans.

[8] See chapter 2.

[9] See Introduction, p. 3.

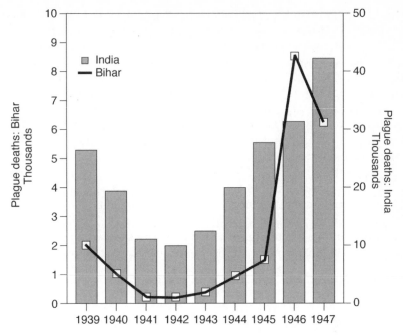

Figure 8.2 Plague Mortality in India, 1939–1947

needs no microscope to detect. In fact, it is best seen historically and statistically on the macro-level of cases of infection or figures of mortality.

By contrast, the figures given by chroniclers and doctors and the
evidence from the data I have assembled from late-medieval wills, obituaries, and burials show a sharp and progressive decline in plague mortalities.
The trends portray a disease in which pathogen and host rapidly adapted to
one another through acquired immunity or natural selection. After having
survived four plagues, the papal physician Raymundus Chalmelli de
Vivario, reflected: 'In 1348, two-thirds of the population were afflicted, and
almost all died; in 1361, half contracted the disease, and very few survived;
in 1371, only one-tenth were sick, and many survived; in 1382, only one-
twentieth became sick, and almost all survived.'[10]

For Bologna, the numbers of testaments registered in the *libri memoriali*
declined by over two and a half times from 1348 (1235) to the second
plague in 1362 (478). The third plague of 1374 afflicted the countryside
more than the city (with only 67 wills registered from citizens). In 1383 the
urban plague mortality returned to high levels (275 wills) but the overall
downward trend continued from the perspective of 1348 and 1362.
Afterwards, no plague year as recorded by the chroniclers (1389, 1399,

---

[10] Zinsser, *Rats, Lice, and History*, p. 89.

1409, 1423) appears to have inflicted great losses in the city, at least among
that class and those age groups that drew up last wills. The numbers barely
rose above the annual averages (posting 25, 43, 18, and 62 wills respectively). The plague of 1423 produced a fifth of the wills written in 1383, an
eight of those in 1362 and one-twentieth that of 1348. Though it took
longer, the decline was not far off those claimed by the optimistic Avignon
doctor in 1382 (see Fig.8.3).[11]

Surviving testaments taken from the six cities in Tuscany and Umbria
show an even steeper and more consistent decline, sinking from 340 in
1348 to three-quarters that figure in 1363 (241), to less than a third in 1374
(102), to a fifth in 1383 (71); further, no plague of the first quarter of the
fifteenth century exceeded the 1383 number (see Fig.8.4). This trend might
even underestimate the steepness of the decline in plague mortalities, especially between the first and second plagues. At Florence, hardly any difference in the surviving numbers of testaments arises between the two, even
though Morelli tells us that in 1363 the plague did not amount to even a

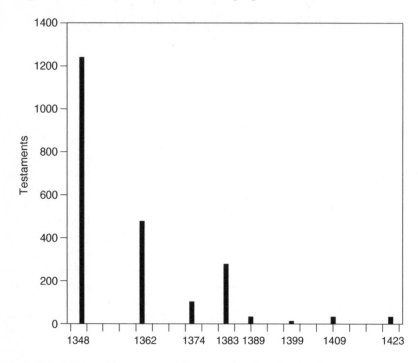

Figure 8.3 Bologna: Plague Years, Testaments, *Libri Memoriali*

---

[11] Archivio di Stato, Bologna, Libri Memoriali, vols 226, 269, 294–5, 312, 316, 319–21. For
the plague years 1409 and 1423, only the second semester wills survive. I have doubled the
numbers for these years, which probably overstates the number of wills, since in all other
plague years more wills were drawn up in the second half of the year than the first.

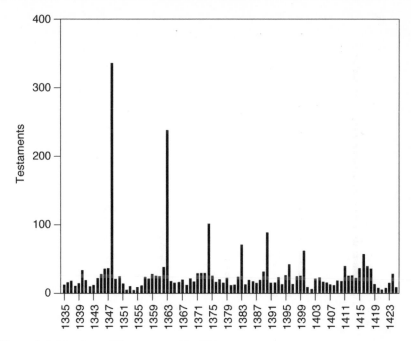

Figure 8.4 Number of Testaments: Six Cities

quarter of the damage it inflicted in 1348.[12] The second time around, citizens were better prepared to address the horrors of mass death, ready to draw up their wills before plague struck them. As the appeals from the commune of Montevarchi attest and chroniclers such as John de Cornazano of Parma proclaimed, notaries were hard to come by during the plague months of 1348, so that many died without last rites or the opportunity of drafting a testament.[13] Further, finding a witness was even more difficult than finding a notary, according to Morelli.[14] The figures of dead friars drawn from Santa Maria Novella's 'chronica' charts a more realistic picture of the downward thrust in the plague's mortality at Florence, more closely corroborating Morelli's estimate: 1363 took only a third the number who died in 1348. Afterwards, the downward trend traced by the Dominican obituaries continued along the lines traced by the testaments. For this brotherhood the fall was almost as steep as that claimed by Raymundus: already by the third plague of 1374 only little more than a twentieth (5) of the 1348 figure perished, and after 1400 no plague felled more than five brothers (see Fig. 8.5).[15]

---

[12] Morelli, *Ricordi*, p. 305.
[13] *Chronica Abreviata Fr. Johannis de Cornazano*, p. 386.
[14] Morelli, *Ricordi*, p. 208.
[15] I have compiled these figures from Orlandi, *'Necrologio' di S. Maria Novella*. Rather than

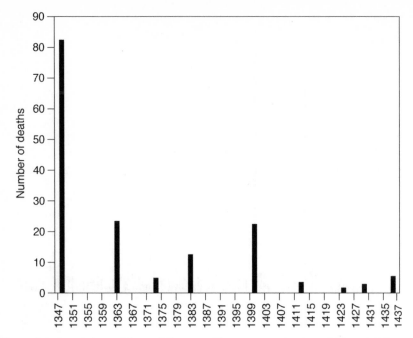

Figure 8.5 Dominicans friars of Florence: Plague-years deaths, 1348 to 1437

This same downward thrust was as pronounced for another community in another central Italian town—that of the lay confraternity of San Francesco in Orvieto. The plague of 1348 killed off 109 lay brothers, more than seven times that of any previous year (1336) and 36 times more than the annual average since the society's foundation in 1337. From the survival of a matriculation list alongside this death book, it is possible to calculate that nearly two-thirds of the confraternity perished in 1348.[16] With the second plague of 1363, the number of victims rose above any previous non-plague year (22) but was a fifth of the 1348 toll, and by the third and fourth plagues, 1374 and 1383, the numbers of deaths (8 and 9) tumbled to just over one-twentieth the plague's first strike. However, plague rebounded here in 1384 with greater force (16 deaths). Nonetheless the downward turn of the plague's mortality remained steep, showing no upswings with the plague years, 1390 or 1400 (see Fig.8.6).

---

being a 'necrology' of the friars and *conversi* at Santa Maria Novella (as Orlandi and others have assumed), the 'Chronica' collected brief obituaries of all those Dominican friars and *conversi* who belonged to the Province of Florence, that is, who were born in Florence's territory, regardless of where they resided at the time of their death; see Panella, 'Cronica fratrum'. According to these obituaries, the plague of 1437 was the most severe after 1400, when only five brothers or *conversi* died as opposed to 81 in 1348.

[16] Codice, V.E. no. 528; and M. Henderson, 'La Confraternità e la catastrofe', p. 116, which tallies the deaths and matriculations only for 1348.

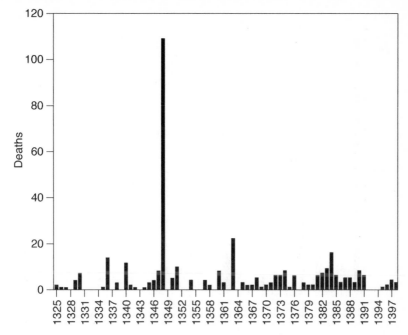

Figure 8.6 Orvieto: Confraternity at San Francesco

On the other hand, the records of the laity buried at the Dominican cemetery of Camporeggio in Siena on first observation appear to deviate from the
patterns traced above (see Fig.8.7). There, the peak death rate came in 1363,
not 1348. But this discrepancy stems from the cessation of records caused by
the pervasive fear and overwhelming magnitude of the task faced by the
friars and civil authorities in 1348. As Boccaccio and many chroniclers and
doctors across Europe lamented, fathers abandoned sons, wives husbands,
friends one another, etc., resulting in mass burials, corpses left to rot or to be
eaten by dogs as Siena's principal chronicler, Agnolo di Tura, described. At
the end of June, the scribes ceased recording the burials and did not resume
until the plague had abated in August. According to Agnolo di Tura, it was
at this time that the plague peaked, killing three of every four in Siena.
Reflecting the breakdown in social organisation, he ended his lament on
1348 by recalling that with his own hands he buried all five of his children;
no individual or insitution came to assist him.[17]

---

[17] *Cronaca Senese attribuita ad Agnolo di Tura*, p. 148; The burial records of S. Frediano
show a similar deterioration in record keeping as the plague heated up in April and May, no
longer specifying names or the sex of those buried. Either overwhelmed by the task or killed
by the plague, the scribes of this confraternity ended their recording of burials on 18 May; see
Henderson, 'The parish and the poor', p. 257.

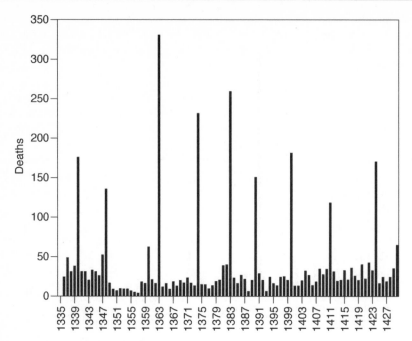

Figure 8.7 Burials, 1335–1430: Among the laity at San Domenico, Siena

Afterwards civil and religious authorities in various places adjusted to the sudden increase in burials demanded in plague time, and institutions such as the Florentine Grascia recorded and regulated burial across all the parishes within cities, even in years of grave crisis such as in 1400. In Florence, Ragusa, Viterbo, and probably other cities, governments required more from their civil servants and the church in plague time; for one, they demanded that their bishops record and count deaths from plague.[18] After 1348 the Dominicans at Siena, instead of abandoning their registers when plague raged, added extra details such as the addresses of the dead, perhaps attempting better to understand the plague's spread. But despite this increased scrutiny, from 1363 on, the numbers interred at Camporeggio show a decline in the plague's 'triumph of death'. By 1430, the plague's toll was one-sixth that of 1363, perhaps a twentieth or less of what it had been in 1348.

* * *

The testaments in northern Europe also show a decline in the plague's ferocity over the late fourteenth and fifteenth centuries. For London, the decline

---

[18] See chapter 6, note 73.

charted from the Court of Husting is more dramatic than that seen anywhere in the Mediterranean. From 356 wills in 1349 the number dipped to 127 with the second plague of 1361 and to 33 for the fourth in 1375. The third one of 1368 did not even reflect unusual mortalities. According to the Peterborough chronicler, plague did strike London in that year but those who died were mostly foreigners (*et maxime alienigenarum Londoniae fuit*) perhaps these ones did not write wills or at least register them at the Court of Husting.[19] Nonetheless, after 1372 to 1425, no plague significantly dented these registers (see Fig.8.8).

For other northern places the decline was neither so steep nor steady. At Tournai, registered testaments dropped by less than half from the first to second plague (582 in 1349 to 245 in 1360), and half again in the third plague of 1381 (126). But in 1400, they rose to 373—higher than for any plague except the first. With the fifth plague the numbers dropped to 186 and did not surpass that figure through the 1430s (see Fig.8.9). At Besançon, the wills declined from 311 in 1349 to 195 in 1360 to 97 in 1400 to 62 in 1418 and rose only slightly to 75 in 1439—a steady decline, if less steep than in southern Europe. Instead of a twentieth, as seen with the early fifteenth-century plagues in the Mediterranean, 1418 in Besançon took a

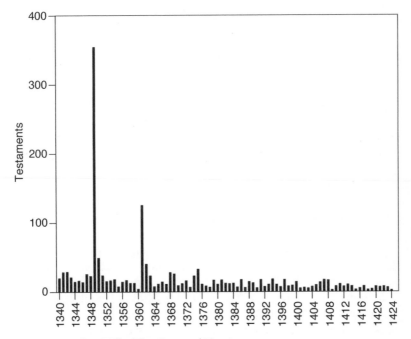

Figure 8.8 London Wills: The Court of Husting

---

[19] *Chronicon Angliæ Petriburgense*, p. 173.

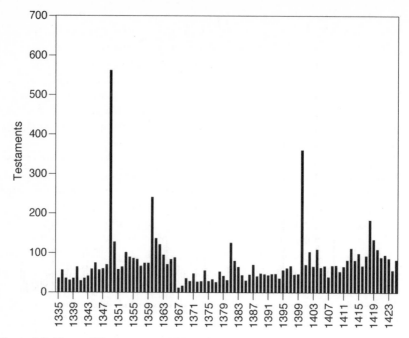

Figure 8.9 Tournai Testaments, 1335–1425

quarter the number killed in 1348 (see Fig.8.10). In Lübeck, where published wills provide data only for first two plagues, the testaments dropped only slightly, from 131 in 1350 to 93 in 1358, but, as we shall see, because of changes in the tradition of will-writing, the relative decline in deaths here was most probably steeper.

Wills from the region of Forez and Douai also reflect a less steep and steady downward spiral in the plagues' mortalities. In Forez, they halved from the first and to the second plague, from 296 to 151 wills. But the plagues of 1398 to 1400 brought a new peak of 368 wills, topping even the Black Death's first strike. For Douai, the trend depends on assumptions about when the plague first appeared. Certainly, 1400 was the first big plague in this medium-sized Flemish cloth town. From various sources 1348–49 shows no evidence of infecting the city, but plague may have struck Douai in 1377 and 1382. In 1377, wills more than doubled the previous year (9 to 21), and in 1382, they increased by a third (21 to 31 wills). By contrast they increased eight-fold in 1400 (82) and then fell with the next plague in 1415 to 33.

Are these downward trends an artefact of data that need to be placed in larger and more complex demographic contexts? Were the plagues' mortalities declining relative to the surviving populations after each bout of plague? Unfortunately, we know little about the precise population trends

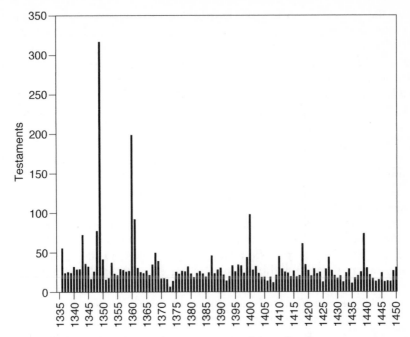

Figure 8.10 Besançon, 1335–1450: Testaments of the Officialité

of these towns after each strike of plague. On the other hand, particularly for larger cities—the places reflected in our data—countervailing forces pushed against the assaults of plague. Populations responded with increased fertility as can be seen from the moralistic comments in sermons and chroniclers as well as in baptismal records to the seventeenth century.[20] Further, migrants from the countryside flooded cities after plagues, quick to realise the new opportunities opened by the dead. At least in the fourteenth century, urban decline was not as great as the plagues' death tolls might lead us at first to suspect. For instance, Charles de la Roncière has estimated that in 1362, on the eve of the second plague, Florence's population was around 70,000,[21] meaning that it had sprung back with remarkable speed

---

[20] See the comments of religious chroniclers such as John of Reading and Jean de Venette (*Chronique latine de Guillaume de Nangis (Continuatio)*, II, p. 214) who decried the lewd habits and multiple births that followed in the wake of the Black Death. Also, see Herlihy and Klapisch–Zuber, *Les Toscans*, p. 426–7, for the increased fertility of 1427 following from the plague of 1423–4 and the tallies drawn by Marco Lastri, *Recerche sull'antica e moderna popolazione della città di Firenze* (Florence, 1775), from Florence's baptismal registers, which consistently show bumper fertility years following plague years. For sermons and songs that decried against lechery, incest, rape, adultery following plague, see Horrox, pp. 127, 141–2, and 146.

[21] Charles-M. de La Roncière, *Prix et salaires à Florence au XIVe siècle (1280–1380)* (Rome, 1982), p. 676; also see Alessandro Stella, *La révolte des Ciompi: Les hommes, les lieux, le travail* (Paris, 1993), p. 149.

from the aftermath of the Black Death, when the population had stood at 40,000. And after the second plague, which took around a third of the population, Florence sprung back again, amounting to 60,000 or more on the eve of the third plague of 1374. After this plague, Florence's population rebounded again: by the tax (*estimi*) of 1379, the city tallied 13,779 households. Given a conservative household multiplier of four (less than that for 1427) Florence must have recouped almost all its pre-1374 losses in five years only.[22]

These urban recoveries came largely from immigration. Across Western Europe demographic historians have shown a new post-Black Death demography: regional populations tended to cluster in greater concentrations in urban places. Peasants flocked to towns and small townspeople to larger regional capitals.[23] Such was the pattern in late-fourteenth- and fifteenth-century Holland with Gouda, Delft, Leiden, and Haarlem gaining at the expense of the surrounding countryside as well as from smaller towns.[24] The demographic dominance of Florence in northern Tuscany by the Catasto of 1427 uncovers a similar pattern: this regional capital now had become more than five times larger than the next largest town in its territory, Pisa, which at the beginning of the fourteenth century had been a close rival with a comparable population.[25]

In addition, as we have seen, plague stimulated will-writing in Tuscany and Umbria as well as in almost every other place where these records survive in bulk; from the rich the practice slid down the social hierarchy. This social change was most dramatic at Lübeck. In the decade before the Black Death, only 11.5 testaments were registered per annum; for the interval between the two plagues, they increased by more than three times to 38.6 per annum, despite the decline that ensued from plague.

To control for demographic shifts and the offsetting factors of emigration and increased fertility, I have charted the plague figures as ratios of the preceding intervals of non-plague years. By these means, the steady downward thrust of plague mortality is even more striking than that shown by the raw figures. By the testamentary evidence from the six cities in Tuscany and Umbria, the third plague's mortality (1374) relative to the preceding non-plague years was less than a quarter of 1348's onslaught and that of 1400, one-sixth of 1348 (see Fig. 8.11). Similarly, the demand to be buried

---

[22] Cohn, *Women in the Streets: Essays on Sex and Power in Renaissance Italy* (Baltimore, 1996), p. 22.

[23] See Karl F. Helleiner, 'Population of Europe from the Black Death to the Eve of the Vital Revolution', in *The Cambridge Economic History of Europe*, IV, ed. by E.E. Rich and C.H. Wilson (Cambridge, 1966), pp. 14–15; for London, John A.F. Thomson, *The Transformation of Medieval England, 1370–1529* (London, 1983), pp. 48–9; and for Tuscany, Herlihy and Klapisch-Zuber, *Les Toscans*, pp. 229–31.

[24] Boer, *Graaf en Grafiek*, pp. 135–68 and 343–4.

[25] Herlihy, *Pisa in the Early Renaissance: A Study of Urban Growth* (New Haven, 1958), pp. 113 and 185–6.

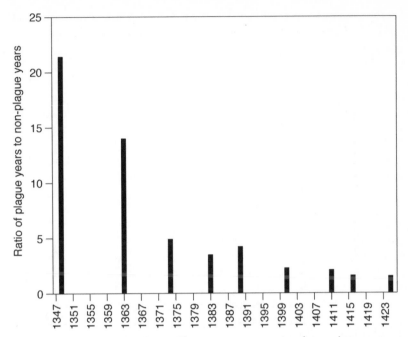

Figure 8.11 Testaments, Six Cities: Plague years as a ratio of non-plague years

in Siena's Dominican cemetery also appears to have risen in tandem with the rising prestige of the Dominicans in post-plague Siena, as illustrated in the pious choices of the laity in their last wills and testaments.[26] What appeared as a rather ragged decline from the raw numbers buried appears from the ratios as a steady and steep fall. The death toll from the plague of 1374 amounted to half the relative mortality of the preceding plague of 1363 and by their last recorded plague of 1430, its mortality relative to non-plague years had fallen to around a tenth of that scored by second strike of pestilence in 1363 (see Fig. 8.12).

A matriculation list that accompanies the obituaries of the lay brothers at Orvieto provides the one case with a solid demographic backdrop for viewing the decline in plague mortalities over the plague-ridden fourteenth century. Here, 1348 emerges not only as an extraordinary year for death, it was equally remarkable in the numbers of new members who joined the community: while 109 died, 110 joined. Forty-eight of the new members were among those to perish in the plague. Were they already ill, enrolling just before death to insure against the odds of mass death? With a certain Tura di Cecco, this may have been the case; he entered and was interred on the same day. On the other hand, his case may illustrate exactly what the

---

[26] Cohn, *The Cult of Remembrance*, p. 37.

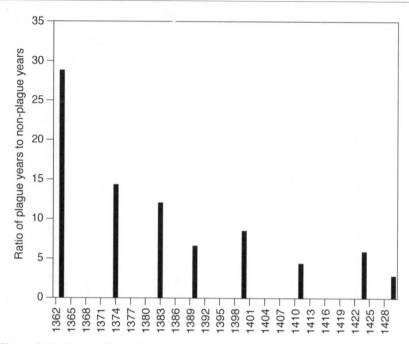

Figure 8.12 Sienese Plague Burials: Plague years as a ratio of non-plague years

chroniclers such as Giovanni Morelli said—at one moment they might be 'laughing and telling jokes'; the next they were lying amongst the plague corpses. The dates of entry and burial for the others who died in 1348, however, were separated by at least two weeks, probably beyond the period of incubation and certainly the first signs of plague by all the chronicle accounts. At any rate, the new entrants did not boost the Black Death's mortality rates: 44 per cent of the new members died in 1348 as opposed to 55 per cent of the old members (34 of 62).[27]

In the following two years the confraternity continued to attract larger numbers of new entrants than in any year before the plague, and this general upward trend continued to the end of the fourteenth century. Clearly, the plagues had enhanced the confraternity's popularity. Most likely, it hinged on its role in ensuring the spiritual and corporeal services for the dead. But regardless of the reasons, with this lay community—exclusively adult men—we can be sure that the decline in subsequent plague mortalities was not offset by a decline in the community's population. Instead, the decline in the plagues' mortalities was steeper than what the raw death figures tell.

---

[27] My calculations differ slightly from those of Henderson, 'La Confraternità e la catastrofe', p. 103. I have used the deaths and entry of new members for the entire year, 1348, and not what she has considered to be the plague months.

concentrate in the city's large parishes on its periphery. Nonetheless, by 1400 the process had begun certainly with the city centre being more desirable than the periphery. Florence was not the ideal-typical medieval city, where each neighbourhood had its tower elite and class structure was divided vertically rather than horizontally. Instead, the 'better' neighbourhoods clustered within the 34 small parishes once encircled by Florence's Roman walls, along with certain parishes within the second rung of walls, such as Santa Trinità, Santa Maria Novella, and the sopr'Arno parishes with palaces that lined the Arno and the via Maggio (San Jacopo sopr'Arno and Santa Felicità), and to the east of the Ponte Vecchio, Santa Lucia dominated by the Bardi family.[34] Other parishes, such as San Lorenzo, the city's largest with nearly a seventh of its population, were mixed with patricians near the streets of Palazuolo, where workers lived in poverty (see map).

A comparison of the mostly elite parishes within the city's former ancient Roman walls with the larger and more impoverished parishes of the periphery[35] shows the class nature of the plague and its progression over the disease-ridden months of 1400. From May 1398 (when a new register of the *Libri dei Morti* begins) to April 1400 (before the mortalities began to mount) 43.5 per cent of the burials came from the parishes on the periphery and 16.27 per cent from within the ex-Roman walls. By contrast, in June 55 per cent came from the poorer periphery and less than 11 per cent from the richer inner city.[36] Then, after the disease had passed its peak in August (1947 burials as opposed to 5002 in July), the proportions of elites burials began to mount with those from the centre now exceeding even its pre-plague proportion.[37]

As we saw earlier, because of the different habits of different classes and in particular to their practices of storing food and grain, modern plague in India also had a clear class dimension. But, a certain level of poverty or at least an iron-deficient diet may even provide protection against the modern plague, given *Yersinia pestis*'s need of 'exogenous iron for growth and replication'.[38] Further, does this movement of the plague from periphery to centre correspond with what we should expect had the disease been the rat-based *Yersinia pestis*? As we have seen from research in India, Vietnam, and elsewhere, grain and its depositories were the explosive sources of modern

---

[34] On the social composition of these areas see Cohn, *The Laboring Classes*, ch. 5; and Stella, *La révolte des Ciompi*, pp. 125–43.

[35] These large parishes with concentrations of labourers and the poor are San Frediano, Santa Maria in Verzaia, San Felice in Piazza, San Pier Gattolino, Santa Lucia Ognissanti, San Paolo, Sant'Ambrogio, and San Pier Maggiore.

[36] Of 2697 burials, the numbers are 1476 from the periphery and 285 from within the Roman walls.

[37] The 38 per cent (734) from the periphery and 20 per cent (392) from within the Roman walls.

[38] Ell, 'Immunity as a factor', p. 873.

plague. The first and heaviest mortalities came from where grain was stored and were the epicentres from where infection spread. As White concluded after 20 years of plague in India, grain was 'the dangerous trade', which as much as any variable accounted for the plague's spread from one area to another.[39]

If the late-medieval plague had been modern bubonic plague, fourteenth- and fifteenth-century Florence would be blessed from the researcher's point of view. Here, strict legislation demanded that only one grain depository, located in one well-defined spot, exist for the entire city.[40] First it was at Florence's famous church of Orsanmichele; then in 1367 it was moved less than 60 metres to the new Mercato del Grano also called the Mercato Nuovo.[41] The Commune required with heavy penalties that bakers and pastry makers from every neighbourhood of the city purchase their grain from this depository alone. If the plague had been the modern one, it is from here that the earliest cases and heaviest mortalities should have surfaced.

The Mercato del Grano is not dominated by a single parish but instead straddled by two—Santissimi Apostoli and San Biagio (also called Santa Maria sopra la porta).[42] Santa Cecilia and Orsanmichele were on its borders and given the small size of these parishes' territories and popula- tions I have grouped the burials for all four.[43] In the year and a half before 1400, the Grascia recorded only 25 burials from these parishes, represent- ing just 1.1 per cent of the city's burials. With the first signs of increased mortality in April, 1400, they show no signs of being the explosive epicen- tre of what was to follow; only one person was buried here of the city's 194—half of one per cent. Nor with the mortality take-off in May (705) or in June and July (6105 in the surviving burial records) did these four parishes figure with striking rises above their pre-plague proportions. For May their proportion was almost exactly what it had been before 1400 (nine burials or 1.2 per cent). Even more surprisingly, for June and July, with plague raging ferociously throughout the city and burials climbing to almost one hundred times the non-plague monthly norms, the parishes around Florence's grain market experienced just the opposite of what should have been happening had the disease been modern bubonic plague. They appear as a protected haven, with deaths remaining near pre-plague levels. With only 17 burials for these two months, they accounted for less than 0.03 per cent of the city's deaths.

---

[39] White, 'Twenty years of plague', p. 212.

[40] On these laws, see *Statutum Bladi Republicae Florentinae (1348)*, ed. by Gino Masi (Milan, 1934), pp. 153–6. Further, Masi has shown that the laws of 1348 had already been enforced since the Statuti del Capitano of 1322 and were repeated in 1355, 1378, 1408, and 1415.

[41] Henderson, *Piety and Charity*, p. 222.

[42] *Stradario storico*, p. 75.

[43] On these parishes, see Cohn, *Laboring Classes*, p. 116

The impressions given by the topography of the dead is supported by their occupations. In India, one researcher after another pointed to grain dealers, along with their families, as the first victims and those bearing the highest mortalities. In Florence, where around 20 per cent of those buried were identified by occupation, not a single grain dealer was so identified in the first month of full-blown plague (May) and only 12 in the peak months of June and July, which represented half of 1 per cent of those identified by occupation. Nor did the bakers loom large: before the plague they comprised 3.38 per cent of the deaths by occupation; with the rise of the plague in May, their proportion fell (2.33 per cent), and in June and July it rose back only to around its pre-plague level (46 burials, or 3.95 per cent).

In fact, no profession was strikingly over-represented in the plague months of 1400. For the plague of 1456, Ann Carmichael found deaths clustering within two families of carpenters residing in two neighbour-hoods, but this connection I would speculate had more to do with family ties than occupation. More to the point, neither she nor any other historian has found that the mortalities of those who handled grain or lived near the granaries shot up significantly when plague flared.[44]

For Arezzo, where the burial records identified fewer by profession, the same impressions are nonetheless given for the plague of 1390. In a town of between 5000 and 7000 its city-wide confraternity, the Fraternità dei Laici, buried 1075 in that year, 89 per cent (956) of whom were buried in the plague months, May to August. [45] By the plague's peak, the monthly average of burials jumped by nearly 32 times, from 15 in the winter to 476 during the second week of June. But despite this ferocity, the percentage of dead grain-dealers and bakers instead of rising, declined in the plague months.[46] Nor do the burials from plague-stricken Arezzo in 1390 or Florence in 1400 lend credence to assertions by Biraben and others, who have claimed without citing any evidence, that wheelwrights, barrel-makers, and blacksmiths were spared in plague times, because 'the noise made the rats flee'.[47] In a source not cited by these historians, a Parisian doctor of the early fifteenth century maintained that blacksmiths (*fabri*)

---

[44] Carmichael, *Plague and the Poor*, p. 80.

[45] L'Archivio della fraternità dei Laici di Arezzo, Libri dei morti, no. 882. Although these records begin in 1373, they are spotty until 1390; burials for the plagues of 1374 and 1383 are not recorded. On this source, see Lorenzo del Panta, 'Cronologia e diffusione delle crisi di mortalità in Toscana', *Ricerche Storiche*, 7 (1977): 293–343.

[46] Before the plague months grain dealers represented 8 per cent of those identified by occu-pation; during the plague they disappear altogether. Bakers also comprised 8 per cent of occu-pations before and after the plague months but only 2.86 (5) per cent during the plague. On the other hand, the death of gravediggers and notaries became more prevalent in plague but only just.

[47] Biraben, *Les hommes et la peste*, II, p. 34; idem, 'Les temps de l'Apocalypse', in Jean Delumeau and Yves Lequin, *Les malheurs des temps: Histoire des fléaux et des calamités en France* (Paris, 1987), p. 190; and Giampaolo Moraglia, 'Introduzione' to Ficino, *Consiglio contro la pestilenza*, p. 40.

died less than others, but his reasoning for their special protection stemmed from the fires purifying the air rather than from noise.[48]

Further, in Arezzo and Florence by the end of the fourteenth century, either doctors, notaries, priests, and gravediggers had acquired special immunity to the plague (as the fifteenth-century doctor Mariano di Ser Iacopo of Siena observed for gravediggers)[49] or they had by then learnt how to protect themselves against their plague. At any rate, they do not appear to have continued to die disproportionately as chroniclers lamented in 1348 and as sources such as the testaments of Besançon suggest.[50] Perhaps some, taking heed of the doctor's first advice, had simply fled.[51] Others such as notaries may have learnt lessons from the plague's contagion and redacted the wills of the plague-stricken by standing in the street beneath the victim's window along with the judges and witnesses as had become the practice in Parma by the plague of 1484.[52]

As early as the second plague in Florence, Tommaso del Garbo had advised notaries, doctors, and priests to enter the rooms of patients only with the doors and windows open, to wash their hands with vinegar and rose water, and to cover their mouths and noses. He further advised priests to take deathbed confessions with the room cleared of all servants and visitors so that plague patients could confess loudly and 'not mouth to mouth' with the priest as was customary.[53] Michele Savonarola was even more elaborate in his instructions to priests and friars in plague time: first they should disinfect or fumigate the patient's room, then take confession at a distance below the patient, with a sheet soaked in vinegar and water stretched between them. During the exchange, the confessor was to keep a disinfectant called a 'zedoaria' in his mouth and brush his teeth with tiriarca before entering.[54]

Similar to the notaries, doctors may have cured patients at a safe distance shouting out instructions to barber-surgeons, as was later the method of care for patients in Lazzaretti during the early modern period.[55] Further,

---

[48] [265], p. 80.
[49] [223], p. 143.
[50] Fiétier, *La cité de Besançon*, I, pp. 339–41.
[51] Some followed this lesson from the start as did the Sienese notary Ser Francesco, who in 1348 fled his city for a summer vacation on the coast at Talamone; see Bowsky, 'The impact of the Black Death upon Sienese government and society', *Speculum*, XXXIX (1964), pp. 18–19. In Venice so many notaries and official clerks fled that the Senate passed legislation demanding their return on 5 July, 1348; see Mueller, 'Aspetti sociali ed economici della peste', p. 72.
[52] Corradi, *Annali delle epidemie*, I, p. 330. For doctors' advice for such practices, see Castiglioni, *Il Libro della Pestilenza di Giovanni de Albertis*, p. 184.
[53] Del Garbo, *Consiglio contro la pistolenza*, p. 22.
[54] Savonarola, *I trattati in volgare della peste*, p. 10.
[55] Cipolla, *Cristofano and the Plague*, p. 26. Plague tracts such as that of the Montpellier doctor Johannes Jacobi, writing in 1373, advised 'doctors and their servants to keep far away from plague patients and to face open doors and windows'; [256], p. 25.

doctors advised their colleagues to wash their hands after examining plague patients with vinegar and rose water, to turn their noses and mouths away from the patients towards an opened window or door, to cover their mouths and noses with masks soaked in vinegar and rose water, and to examine patients only in well-ventilated rooms with windows and doors open.[56] The Montpellier doctor Johannes Jacobi claimed that such practices enabled him to visit numerous victims during the plague of 1373 without catching the disease, much to the amazement of his colleagues.[57] Other plague tracts recommended that their patients and readers follow similar sanitary practices. The personal doctor of the Milanese Visconti, writing in 1378, advised covering their noses and mouths while near plague patients, to expel mucus from these orifices, and to wash their faces with warm water after coughing and defecating.[58] Tommaso del Garbo gave other simple rules of sanitation—frequent changes of underwear and keeping the body and head clean.[59] In plague time, Ficino advised his readers to keep drinking vessels and plates separate from one another and not to share bed linen, especially the sheets. Although he thought that animals did not become sick in plague, he saw them as 'repositories of plague poison' and advised his patients to be 'very cautious' around horses, sheep, and other animals as well as their equipment during an epidemic.[60] Of course, had the disease been modern bubonic plague, none of these precautions would have made any difference, but if it were a fast-spreading air-borne disease passed person-to-person as almost every chronicler and doctor described, these sanitary regimes and prophylactics may not have been so pointless as modern historians such as Carlo Cipolla would now lead us to believe.

* * *

If not the grain market, where did the plague of 1400 find its first sparks in Florence? Curiously, it was exactly in one of the two neighbourhoods where Stefani had spotted it smouldering in the late winter and early spring of 1383.[61] In 1400, the parish to show the most extreme jump in burials during the plague's first month (April) was San Pier Maggiore, the most populous parish in the Santa Croce district, comprised largely of labourers and artisans. In the year and a half before 1400, the dead of this parish comprised 7.59 per cent of the city's burials (161 or less than 10 per month). In April, its monthly death toll soared by more than four times (39 burials), accounting for over 20 per cent of the city's dead. With the escalation of

---

[56] [24], p. 50; [26], p. 57 (which summarised lessons from the earlier Montpellier doctor Johannes Jacobi); [41], p. 394; [140], p. 94.

[57] [26], p. 57.

[58] [45], p. 322. Also, see [46], ibid., p. 330.

[59] Del Garbo, *Consiglio contro la pistolenza*, p. 32.

[60] Ficino, *Consiglio contro la pestilenza*, p. 110.

[61] Stefani, *Cronica fiorentina*, p. 426.

plague in May, its burials almost trebled (99), and those from its neigh-bouring parish, San Michele, rose from 38 or two per month (1.79 per cent) to 23 in April alone, a more than ten-fold increase.

By May, another area of the city began to show far higher numbers of burials relative to the rest of the city. In Florence's poorest parish, Santa Maria in Verzaia, located across the Arno in the city's southwest corner, as far from San Pier Maggiore as is possible within Florence's city walls, the numbers buried jumped from 1.65 per cent of the dead before 1400 (35) to 5 per cent in May 1400. In June and July, those from its neighbour San Frediano joined the cortège of mass death; relative to its population, its burials now climbed higher than those of any other parish, from less than ten burials a month before 1400 (167) to 746, over 12 per cent of the city's totals at the plague's height. As with the frontrunners Santa Maria in Verzaia and San Piero, this sopr'Arno parish possessed high concentrations of wool workers and other low-paid artisans.[62]

Other than poverty, what was the connection between these two areas of the city? Could it have been common places of work in the wool industry? Was it the sources of water or was it simply the subsoil of unhygienic and crowded places that gave rise to plague and its spread? Was it mere coinci-dence that both the plagues of 1383 and 1400 began almost exactly in the same spot? It calls to mind the cholera epidemics of the early and mid-nine-teenth century, the Broad Street pump, and Dr John Snow's discovery of the disease's source by tracing its neighbourhood recurrence and diffusion to communal sources of water.[63] But other diseases can originate from bad water or peculiarities of place, some of which may now be extinct. I leave these questions to epidemiologists. For the moment, let's stay on the safe side: the plague of 1400 resembled diseases of poverty such a typhus and cholera and not modern bubonic plague with its close ties to rats and their food—grain.

*   *   *

The burial records from Florence and Arezzo also support several chroni-clers' hints that, after 1348, men may have died in greater numbers than women from plague. For Florence, the sex-ratios in the months leading up to the plague of 1400 were almost perfectly even, suggesting the care and precision taken by the Florentine scribes and the city's administration. Indeed, the slightly higher figure for men, 52 per cent of the burials (1417 of 2729) from May 1398 to April 1400 may reflect the general sex ratios

[62] See Cohn, *The Laboring Classes*, pp. 115–28, and Stella, *La révolte des Ciompi*, pp. 125–43; Henderson, 'The parish and the poor'.

[63] Christopher Wills, *Plagues: Their Origin, History and Future* (London, 1997), pp. 109–16; and Charles S. Rosenberg, 'Cholera in nineteenth-century Europe: a tool for social and economic analysis', *Comparative Studies in Society and History*, 8 (1965–66): 459–62.

found later for Florence in documents such as the Catasto of 1427, where men outnumbered women by even more.[64] The first month of full-blown plague, May, however, reversed the sex imbalance; women were the first to die with 54.75 per cent of the deaths (386). Yet when the plague peaked in June and July, the imbalance shifted again; now women resisted better than men: 54 per cent of the burials were men (3297 vs 2808). In the last phases of the plague (August and September), the imbalance became further accentuated, 60 per cent were of males (1503 vs 999).

The Aretine experience of 1390 matched Florence's for 1400. Before the onslaught of plague, Arezzo's burials were evenly distributed by sex—57 males and 56 females. As in Florence, the first month of plague (April) took more women than men (31 as against 28), but when plague exploded, May to August, it showed the same appetite for men as in Florence; 58 per cent of the burials were male (552 vs 404). Again, the sex imbalance peaked during the last month of the plague's ferocity, August; dead men now more than doubled dead women (51 vs 21).

Further, lay burials at Siena's Camporeggio bear out even more forcefully the same patterns. In 1348, men and women were buried in almost equal numbers, the same as in non-plague years.[65] But, with the plagues of 1363, 1374, 1383, 1400, and 1411, women consistently fared better than men, accounting respectively for 43, 45, 42, 42, and 43 per cent of the burials,[66] and in the last of the plagues recorded by the Dominicans, their proportion slipped still further with women comprising only 39 per cent of the dead.[67] Nor did this shift reflect a change in Dominican burial practice. For the next five non-plague years burials of women (I imagine because of their better fortune in plague time) exceeded men in every year, accounting for 56 per cent of the burials.[68] Finally, English wardship rolls point in the same direction: the disparity between male and female orphans fell for the first 50 years following the Black Death.[69]

---

[64] On the reasons for the predominance of men over women in Florence, see Herlihy and Klapisch-Zuber, *Les Toscans*, pp. 326–32. Carmichael, *Plague and the Poor*, p. 135, finds that women were generally 'underrepresented' in the Libri dei Morti at Florence from 1385 to 1409, but was this an 'under-representation' or a reflection of the imbalance of the sexes in the city of Florence? The imbalance was less pronounced in the Libri dei Morti than in the Catasto.

[65] *I Necrologi di Siena di San Domenico*, 66 of 136 were female, or 49 per cent.

[66] In 1363, 143 of 331 were women; in 1374, 104 of 233; in 1383, 110 of 260; in 1400, 78 of 182; and 52 of 120 in 1411.

[67] Sixty-eight of 173. In addition to the number of burials bulging far beyond normal years, the Dominican scribes signalled each of the years above as an 'annus pestilentie', 'fuit peste', or 'peste percussus'. They even indicated the months of heavy plague deaths by marginal comments, such as 'mortalitas generalis inguinarie' with the July burials of 1363.

[68] Sixty-eight of 121 burials from 1425 to 1429.

[69] Barbara A. Hanawalt, *Growing up in Medieval London: The Experience of Childhood in History* (New York, 1993), p. 58. Moreover, evidence for the plagues of 1603 and 1625 in London shows a similar tendency for more men than women to die from plague; see Biraben, *Les hommes et la peste*, I, p. 223; and Hollingsworth and Hollingsworth, 'Plague mortality rates', pp. 135, and 144–5.

Why were women the first victims of plague but then fared better than men as the disease heated up:[70] biology or social practice? Did men die in greater numbers because they sent their women and children to the countryside, while they minded government and business in the perhaps more lethal cities? Such an explanation might work for the elites, but, as we have already seen, later plagues at least in Florence had assumed a class bias, killing much greater numbers of the poor, who were less likely to skip town. Was it because men tended to work away from the home in crowded places such as the shops of the wool industry? Did it rely on diet and iron deficiency as Stephen Ell has argued?[71] Or did it rely on differences in genetic resistance? At any rate, these sex ratios of the late-medieval plagues do not replicate the Indian plague experience, where women died in greater numbers than men—57 per cent of plague deaths in Bihar and 62 per cent in Shahabad were female in the Indian plagues of the early twentieth century, despite the underreporting of female deaths. The census report of 1921 in Bihar and Orissa attributed the difference to 'the habits of women': they swept floors and handled grain more than men and simply stayed more at home and thus were 'more exposed to the attacks of the rat flea'.[72]

* * *

More than class or sex, the most persistent and consistent change with late-medieval plague across Europe was the age of its victims. Like many other infectious diseases, medieval plague, after striking virgin-soil populations, tended to kill those who had not been previously exposed to it the next time around. As a consequence, after several strikes, it became domesticated as a disease largely of children. By contrast, to repeat, modern *Yersinia pestis* is unusual: humans have no natural immunity to it and cannot acquire it. As a result, no such change in the age structure of its victims ensues.

The records of Camporeggio (Siena) are the only ones I know to record the burials of the laity across the plague experience from the Black Death of 1348 to the fifteenth century. Here, we witness a remarkable transformation. Of 136 Sienese buried in the Dominican cemetery in 1348, only 12 or under 9 per cent, were identified as children (simply *filii* or *filie* without their own names).[73] With the second strike in 1363, their proportion increased to 116 of 331, over a third of the plague burials. The change corresponds with what

---

[70] One chronicler, Maqraīzī, *Sulūk*, p. 374, commented that women were the first to contract the disease in 1348.

[71] Ells, 'Immunity as a factor', p. 874.

[72] White, 'Twenty years of plague', p. 211. In general, Pollitzer, *Plague*, p. 504, has concluded that mortality from bubonic plague has been about the same for both sexes. On the other hand, Ell, 'Immunity as a factor', p. 871, has argued that adult males died in more than twice the numbers as adult females. For the figures above and citations, see Sheels, 'Bubonic plague in south Bihar', pp. 434, 436, and 441.

[73] Similarly, Creighton, *History of Epidemics in Britain*, p. 122, found that the plague of 1348–49 in England carried off able-bodied young adults and not the young, weak, or elderly.

chroniclers across Europe were saying. As we saw earlier with sex and social class, they emphasised the plague's indiscriminate killing in 1348. Matteo Villani called it 'a plague among men of every condition, age, and sex'.[74] The same was perceived north of the Alps. The chronicler in verse Androw Wyntoun described the plague when it reached Scotland:

> Befor that tyme was neuir seyn
> pestilence in our lande sa keyne:
> Bath men, and barnnys, and women,
> It sparit noucht for to keyl then.[75]

The chronicler of Cologne noted that 'there was no disparity in sex or age, taking men, women, the old, the young, plebs and nobles, paupers, the rich and powerful, priests and the laity.'[76]

On the other hand, with the second plague (1361) numerous chroniclers in Britain—the *Anonimalle* chronicler, Thomas Walsingham, Henry Knighton, the Chronicle of Louth Park Abbey, the Grey Friars of Lynn, the anonymous Canterbury chronicler, John of Reading, the Peterborough chronicler, and John of Fordun[77]—noted that it struck down greater proportions of children than the first, so much so that they called it 'the children's plague (*la mortalite des enfauntz*)'.[78] Historians of Britain have sometimes assumed that their second plague was the odd one out. Thus the famous medievalist V.H. Galbraith reckoned that *The Anonimalle Chronicle* had taken a stock phrase from 1361 and applied it to the next plague of the 1370s falsely thinking that the third was also unusually fatal to children.[79] But other British chroniclers such as the Westminster Chronicle for the plagues of 1381 and 1382 in London, 1383 in Norfolk, 1387, 1389, and 1390 'in various places in England', Adam Usk for 'for all of England' in 1400, and Wyntoun for the plague of 1401 in Scotland, saw the same:[80] after 1348–49 the plagues had become largely a disease of children.

Nor was the experience peculiar to Britain. The chronicler of Orvieto along with Guy de Chauliac had already noted that 'especially the young' (*spetialmente cituli et giovani et giovane*) were the victims of the second plague in 1358.[81] Joannis Dlugosi noted that children were the chief victims for the second plague in Poland[82] as did Jean de Venette for Paris, 1363,

---

74 Matteo Villani, *Cronica*, I, p. 9.
75 *The Original Chronicle of Andrew of Wyntoun*, VI, p. 197.
76 *Die Weltchronik des Mönchs Albert*, pp. 254–5.
77 *The Anonimalle Chronicle*, p. 50; *Thomae Walsingham*, p. 294; *Chronicon Angliae Petriburgense*, p. 171, and Horrox, pp. 85–88.
78 *The Anonimalle Chronicle*, p. 50.
79 Ibid., p. 191.
80 *The Westminister Chronicle*, pp. 20, 28, 44, 204, 402, and 438; *Chronicon Adae de Usk*, p. 46; and *The Original Chronicle of Andrew of Wyntoun*, VI, p. 396.
81 *Discorso Historico*, p. 84; Haeser, p. 176.
82 *Annales . . . Joannis Dlugossii*, IX, p. 301.

adding that children caught it first and passed it on to their parents.[83] For 1383, Stefani observed that the 'young and children (*fanciuli*) died more readily than 'men and women'.[84] For the plague of 1389 the chronicler of Mainz claimed that infants and adolescents were the 'most infected'.[85] In Valencia, chroniclers pointed to the plague's age discrimination in 1362 and 1394.[86] The Parisian Bourgeois found its toll still marked against children with the plagues of 1418, 1432, and 1433.[87] For the plagues of 1430 and 1438 in upper Egypt, Ibn Taghrā Birdī claimed that they began with children, in fact female children who were slaves.[88] In Italy, the chroniclers could be more precise and more emphatic. For the plague of 1360 the Venetian Sanuto said 'for the most part, the young under twelve' were the ones who perished in Friuli and Istria.[89] The Pisan chronicler Ranieri maintained that by the third plague, in 1374, 80 per cent of the deaths were among those 12 or younger.[90] The Bolognese chronicler reported that the plague dead of that year were mostly ten or younger.[91] In Trent, Giovanni da Parma reckoned that among infants and children only one in ten survived this plague.[92]

Similarly, with the second plague and later, doctors such as Johannes of Tornamira, writing either at the time of the third (1372) or fourth plague (1382), Raymundus Chalmelli de Vinario writing in 1382, Johannes de Penna at the beginning of the fifteenth century, the medical faculty of Prague in 1406, a doctor from Lübeck in 1411, Saladino Ferro da Ascoli in the mid fifteenth century, Master Johannes de Saxonia writing in Strasbourg around the middle of the fifteenth century, a doctor from Bohemia at the same time, and Marsilio Ficino in 1480 saw children as the plague's chief victims. [93] As with the chroniclers Jean de Venette and Ibn Taghrî Birdî, some of them also saw it starting with children. From 'almost thirty years of practice', a doctor from Lübeck commented in 1411, plague began with children under six, spread first to 'the young, that is those over six, and then to the old, that is those over 30 or 40'.[94]

The burials at Camporeggio in Siena lend further credence to the claims of the *Anominalle* chronicler and numerous others as well as to the more precise proportions claimed by the Pisan Ranieri. Instead of 1361 being

83 *Chronique latine de Guillaume de Nangis (Continuatio)*, II, pp. 325–6.
84 Stefani, *Cronica fiorentina*, p. 426.
85 *Chronicon Moguntinum*, p. 222.
86 Rubio, *Peste Negra*, p. 29; and *Epidemiología Española*, p. 92.
87 *Journal d'un bourgeois de Paris*, pp. 111, 228, and 295.
88 *Arabic Annals of Abu L-Mahasin Ibn Taghrā Birdī*, IV, pp. 73 and 145.
89 Sanuto, *Vitæ Ducum Venetorum*, col. 644.
90 *Cronaca Pisana*, p. 186.
91 *Cronaca A*, III, p. 291; and *Historia Miscella Bononiensis*, p. 495.
92 *Cronica inedita di Giovanni da Parma*, p. 52.
93 [24], p. 48; Hoeniger, p. 176; [234], p. 162; [98], pp. 127 and 130; [108], p. 55; and [119], p. 148; Simili, 'Saladino Ferro da Ascoli', p. 40; [177], p. 22; [161], p. 159; Ficino, *Consiglio contro la pestilenza*, p. 59.
94 [119], p. 155.

exceptional, the burials plot this second plague on a trend-line of increasing proportions of childhood deaths through the fourteenth century. In the third plague of 1374, the death of children in Siena increased from a third to over a half (136 of 233). With the fourth plague in 1383, it rose yet again, claiming a staggering 88 per cent of that year's victims (230 of 260).[95] Afterwards, in the lesser plagues of 1390 and 1400, the proportion fell to 67 of 151 and 62 of 182, lower than in 1383 but still above the proportions struck down in the supposed children's plague of 1363.[96]

For the plague of 1400 at Florence the consequences for children are again telling. The gravediggers identified two-thirds as 'infans', 'pueri', 'puellae', 'filii', or 'filie'.[97] On the other hand, those called *iuvenis* or young adults between around 20 and 30 years old[98]—the ones most susceptible to new diseases in general[99] and to modern bubonic plague in particular,[100] accounted for only a tiny proportion (about 1 per cent). By the time of the 1423–24 plague in Florence, when the gravediggers began to mark those who they diagnosed as dying of plague with a 'P', the proportion of children remained high at 69.1 per cent.[101] Other sources for other places point in the same direction. In England the per centage of orphans failing to reach the end of their wardship jumped from 18 per cent before the Black Death to 27 per cent in the first 50 years afterwards and continued to climb during the fifteenth century.[102]

Perhaps as with smallpox in late nineteenth-century Britain, the levelling off and slight reversal in the high proportions of plague victims as children reflects a cyclical pattern found with many infectious diseases. As microbes and hosts begin to adapt to one another, thus reducing the severity and frequency of a disease, adults become more exposed and less protected against the pathogen, renewing the cycle with greater numbers of victims coming from adults.[103] While the plague may never have

---

[95] Unfortunately, ages are not reported in these documents.

[96] *I Necrologi di Siena di San Domenico*. The reversal in the proportion of children recorded in plagues after 1383 may have resulted from the record keepers' more precise terminology with terms such as *puer parvulus* and *parvulus et innocens* sometimes replacing the vaguer entries of *filius* or *filia* without first names.

[97] Occasionally, the notary supplied the ages of those they called children (*pueri* or *puellae*); they ranged from those who died stillborn to a maximum of nine years old.

[98] I have not yet found any *iuvenis* to be identified by age, but in other documents those so listed tended to be the unmarried and aged between the late teens and early thirties; see Michael Rocke, *Forbidden Friendships: Homosexuality and Male Culture in Renaissance Florence* (Oxford, 1996), p. 39.

[99] See Burnet, *Natural History of Infectious Disease*, p. 205.

[100] See Pollitzer, *Plague*, p. 516; and Gatacre, *Report on the Plague in Bombay*, p. 101.

[101] Herlihy and Klapisch-Zuber, *Les Toscans*, p. 463.

[102] Hanawalt, *Growing up in Medieval London*, p. 57.

[103] Burnet, *Natural History of Infectious Disease*, pp. 206 and 228. By the eighteenth century, 90 per cent of all deaths from smallpox in London were among children under five. Also, see Anne Hardy, *The Epidemic Streets: Infectious Disease and the Rise of Preventive Medicine, 1856–1900* (Oxford, 1993), p. 128; and for Sweden, Peter Sköld, 'The history of smallpox and

become a childhood disease to the extent that smallpox, whooping cough, or measles did by the eighteenth or nineteenth century in Britain or Sweden, it was fast approaching that reality by the late fourteenth century. By contrast, modern plague has never been a childhood disease; the ages of its victims remain highest amongst the most fit, those between 20 and 40, and has shown no notable differences over place or time.[104] In marked contrast to late-medieval plague, White found after twenty years of plague in India that 'infants and young children appear to enjoy a certain degree of immunity'.[105] The same was also seen in Manchuria with modern pneumonic plague.[106]

The age structure of the victims of later plagues helps explain at least in part why towns in Central Italy such as Florence and Siena were quick to restore significant portions of their populations immediately after the first three plagues but failed later, when in fact the plague's mortalities had declined. Those who would have replenished their numbers—the young— were the ones cut down in overwhelming proportions.[107]

The particularities of the plagues' mortalities affected culture as well. The evidence from the plague-ridden late-fourteenth and fifteenth centuries strikes against the logic offered by historians of a generation ago (Lawrence Stone, Edward Shorter, Le Roy Ladurie, and to a lesser extent Philippe Ariès), that the general high levels of mortality in the medieval and early modern periods conditioned parents to invest less emotionally in their children than in the modern period, when child mortality began to decline. Instead, in the aftermath of plague and particularly by the end of the fourteenth century when the disease had become established as principally one of children, various sources in different parts of Europe illustrate the opposite. In early Renaissance Florence, the blossoming of diaries and books on

its prevention in Sweden', paper at the 19th International Congress of Historical Sciences (Oslo, August, 2000). This shift in the cycle may be seen in data from Florence for the second half of the fifteenth and sixteenth centuries: Morrison *et al.*, 'Epidemics in Renaissance Florence', p. 533, find that 'the burden of epidemic mortality' did not then fall most heavily on the young. However, their reliance on data from the Florentine dowry fund precludes any comparison with the mortality rates of the general adult population. The bulk of their data regards girls under sixteen years of age. On this problem more can be done with the Florentine *Libri dei Morti*.

[104] 'The epidemiological observations made by the commission in Bombay City', *JH*, 7 (1907), p. 763; J.D. Gimlette, 'Plague in Further India,' *JH*, 9 (1909), p. 62; also see the data from Bombay, 1897, Gatacre, *Report on the Plague in Bombay*, vol. 2: *Temperature Charts*.

[105] White, 'Twenty years of plague', p. 211.

[106] Pollitzer, *Plague*, p. 515: 'In the Manchurian plague of 1920–21, 78.1 per cent of the cases were among those aged 21 to 40.'

[107] On the death of children and the prolongation of demographic recovery during the first half of the fifteenth century in the village of Valréas (south of France), see Monique Zerner, 'Une crise de mortalité au XVe siècle à travers les testaments et les rôles d'imposition', *Annales: E.S.C.* 34 (1979), p. 584. Also,John Hatcher, *Plague, Population and the English Economy 1348–1530* (London, 1977), pp. 57 and 61, suggests that the change in age-specific mortality from plagues of the second half of the fifteenth century helps explain the failure of the English population to recover.

'governing the family' show new levels of concern with educating children, preparing them for business, politics, and their spiritual well-being.

In addition, increasing numbers of nobles, merchants, and their wives commissioned priests and friars to write manuals on the proper behaviour for their sons and daughters, producing by the fifteenth century manuals such as the Dominican Dominici's family rules[108] and Geoffroy de la Tour-Landry's *The Book of the Knight of the Tower* on bringing up children.[109] Perhaps the *Urtext* of this new genre was written in the mid-thirteenth century, the *Tre trattati* by the north Italian jurist Albertano da Brescia, but significantly it was aimed at grown sons, already established in professional life. In fact elsewhere the thirteenth-century manuals on child rearing, such as the one by the English cleric Bartholomew Glanville, anticipated the sharp increase of these works in the late fourteenth and early fifteenth century. Yet, as Nicholas Orme has observed, these earlier manuals 'were not yet wholly devoted to the bringing up of young children'.[110]

Furthermore, moralists of the late fourteenth and early fifteenth centuries such as William Langland[111] and Jean Gerson[112] struck out against what they saw as the decline of discipline after the Black Death, a new pampering and indulgence of children. But their calls for the rod (untender as they were) also expressed new levels of concern with children's education and upbringing, which David Herlihy has highlighted as an increased investment in children, both economically and emotionally.[113] At the same time, other humanists and educators of the early fifteenth century such as Matteo Palmieri and Maffeo Vegio argued for the first time since Quintilian that such corporeal discipline impeded education.[114] However, regardless of the argument, both groups were concerned with getting the best from their progeny.

The Black Death and its successive waves also provoked a new concern for foundlings and orphans. In Orvieto, special legislation to protect orphans was promulgated after the plague;[115] the earliest hospitals to specialise exclusively in helping orphans arose in Paris in 1363[116] and then

---

[108] *Regola del Governo di cure familiare*, ed. by Donato Salvi (Florence, 1860). See Herlihy, 'Medieval children', in *Women, Family and Society in Medieval Europe: Historical Essays, 1978–1991* (Providence, R.I., 1994), p. 230.
[109] *The Book of the Knight of the Tower* (London, 1971).
[110] *From Childhood to Chivalry: The Education of the English Kings and Aristocracy 1066–1530* (London, 1984), pp. 14–15.
[111] Langland, *Piers the Ploughman*, p. 62: 'The more you love the child the more you must correct him.'
[112] See Philippe Ariès, *Centuries of Childhood: A Social History of Family Life*, tr. by Robert Baldick (New York, 1962; Paris, 1960), p. 106; and Herlihy, 'Medieval children', p. 237.
[113] David Herlihy, 'Medieval children', pp. 229–42.
[114] Ibid., p. 235.
[115] Carpentier, *Une ville devant la peste*, pp. 190–1.
[116] Herlihy, 'Medieval children', p. 233.

in Florence at the beginning of the fifteenth century.[117] Testaments in Rome during the last decades of the fourteenth century show a surge in individual donations to orphanages.[118]

Moreover, by the second strike of plague (and not the first), testators in north-central Italy began to craft a new Renaissance sense of piety, one that sought 'fame and glory' in the celestial and terrestrial spheres through the survival of their sons and preservation of the male line. It was an ideology of family remembrance effected through funnelling property to sons and their future progeny, protecting the property interests of future families *ad infinitum*.[119] The steady mounting of contingency clauses in wills from the late fourteenth century on were aimed at preventing the draining of property from family lines by the untimely and premature death of heirs. The plague's fear of sudden death had stamped on one generation after another the vulnerability of survival even though mortalities from it were in decline.

While this ideology of the male bloodlines may have jeopardised the property rights and prerogatives of women, girls too became the focus of new notions of charity: poor relief both at the level of individual gifts and institutional directives changed after the Black Death. From indiscriminate gifts to 'the poor of Christ', by the last decades of the fourteenth-century in Florence and other early Renaissance cities, poor relief became focused by age and sex. Increasing numbers of dowry funds in testaments as well as the donations of parishes such as San Frediano and Florence's largest charitable organization, Orsanmichele, directed their pious sums at benefiting poor but 'deserving' girls, those who would have been between 12 and 16 years of age.[120]

The post-Black Death milieu sparked a new concern with keeping the family and its name alive. To do so, it invented new investments in children of both sexes. In addition to new concerns for orphans, setting up sons as heads of households, dowering young girls, and educating both sexes, poetry, letters and imaginative literature express a new emotional investment in children. Again, the break came with the Black Death or more probably with the recurrence of plague once it had settled as primarily a childhood disease. The remarkable Welsh poems of grief over children lost in plagues cluster in the later decades of the fourteenth century. Only one precedes the Black Death and that one, according to its editor, Dafydd

---

[117] Ibid., p. 233; and Volker Hunecke, 'Findelkinder und Findelhäuser in der Renaissance', *Quellen und Forschungen aus italienischen Archiven und Bibliotheken*, 72 (1992): 123–53.
[118] See the extensive business of Paulus de Serromanis (Archivio di Capitolino, section I, vols 649–50), whose notarised testaments extend from 1348 to 1389. Bequests to orphans begin to appear with increasing frequency only by the 1370s.
[119] See Cohn, *Death and Property* and *The Cult of Remembrance*.
[120] See Cohn, *Women in the Streets*, ch. 5; and Henderson, 'The parish and the poor', pp. 264–5; and idem, *Piety and Charity*, 6.

Johnston, was more of a tribute than a lament. He concludes that the plague gave rise to this, an essential new genre of poetry. [121] Boccaccio's letter grieving the death of Petrarch's five-and-a-half-year-old daughter, Eletta, comparing her demeanour, laughter, hair, and love with those of his own daughter finds no earlier parallel in late-medieval literature. It was written in 1366, after the second plague.[122] And finally, no earlier psychodrama can be found comparable to Giovanni Morelli's angst over the loss of his nine-year-old son at the beginning of the fifteenth century as he climbed Monte Morello reliving his son's childhood and his own failed parenthood.[123] Louis Haas's sustained attack against those who claim that fathers paid little attention to their infants and young children before the eighteenth century has drawn on a rich panoply of literature from Humanist tracts to merchant account books in Florence, but only one of his examples predates the second plague of the 1360s.[124] As this one epidemiological aspect of plague suggests, the character of a disease (and not just its sheer levels of mortality) can shape in specific ways subsequent demographic, cultural, and psychological history. The last chapter will examine further this juncture between disease and culture.

---

[121] Johnston, *Poet's Grief*, pp. 25–7.

[122] For a translation of the letter, see Louis Haas, *Renaissance Man and his Children: Childbirth and Early Childhood in Florence, 1300–1600* (London, 1998), p. 1.

[123] Many have written on this passage in Morelli's chronicle diary; see Richard Trexler, 'In search of father: The experience of abandonment in the recollection of Giovanni di Pagalo Morelli', *History of Childhood Quarterly*, 3 (1973): 225–8; and Haas, *Renaissance Man*, pp. 171–2.

[124] The only example I find is that of Francesco da Barberino's advice on wet nursing, Haas, *Renaissance Man*, p. 92. Francesco da Barberino died in 1348.

CONCLUSION

|9|

Culture and psychology

William McNeill's now classic survey of the interaction of culture and disease, *Plagues and Peoples*,[1] uncovered a rich array of diseases in history but at the same time presented a one-dimensional appraisal of the historical relation between disease and culture. Despite their various ways of killing, weakening, or coexisting with their hosts, parasites in past time transformed the culture and psychology of the populations they invaded, turning virile, secular, this-worldly mentalities, such as Confucianism or the paganism of the late Roman Empire into pessimistic, transcendental religiosities; hence Hinduism, Buddhism, and Christianity followed in the wake of great plagues. The one contradiction of his book was its centrepiece—the Black Death and the Renaissance that followed it.

McNeill might have turned to the historiography of northern Europe, which through the anti-Renaissance lens of Johan Huizinga has seen the Renaissance's cultural revival, secularism, and optimism as at best Italian and involving only a handful of intellectuals, whose literary activities thinly covered larger worlds of despair. According to Jean Delumeau, the general population of Europe did not awake from its late-medieval nightmare until the eighteenth-century Enlightenment or later.[2] But McNeill turned instead to Jacob Burckhardt and the standard story of Renaissance optimism and individualism, making no allowances for what this chronological succession—Black Death,

---

[1] McNeill, *Plagues and Peoples* (New York, 1976).
[2] See the trilogy of Jean Delumeau, *La peur en Occident (XIVe–XVIIIe siècle: Une cité assiégée* (Paris, 1978); *Le péché et la peur: la culpabilisation en Occident (XIIIe–XVIIIe siècles)* (Paris, 1983); and *Rassurer et protéger: le sentiment de sécurité dans l'Occident d'autrefois* (Paris, 1989). On the general culture of despair, see also J. Verger, 'Nouveaux fléaux, nouveaux recours', in *Les malheurs des temps*, pp. 209–34.

Renaissance—meant for his general thesis of plagues provoking long-term shifts to despair.[3]

After McNeill, two interrelated questions arise: must all epidemics have had the same cultural and psychological consequences, perhaps varying only in degree with the severity of the mortalities they wreaked? Need the reactions to any particular disease have been the same everywhere it struck, or might societies react in totally different ways to the same or similar epidemiological catastrophes? The first sweep of plague provoked as close to a universal chorus as one hears in history, resounding through various layers of intellectual activity and across Europe. First, commentators judged the first plague as entirely new to world history. To substantiate the point, Guy de Chauliac interrupted his rigorous Galenic survey of ailments from remote causes to immediate ones and from preventive to curative regimes to reflect on the world history of plagues. Similarly, the Cortusii chroniclers of Padua went back to the Pharaohs, David, Ezekiel, and Gregory the Great to claim (perhaps incorrectly) that while previous plagues had been regional, the one of his own time, 1348, was worldwide. Others, such as the Scottish chronicler John of Fordun, after describing the plague as 'being general throughout the entire globe', proclaimed that 'so great a plague has never been heard of from the beginning of the world to the present day, or been recorded in books'.[4] The chronicler of the Grey Friars at Lynn, perhaps lacking the historical sophistication of university-trained doctors or Italian merchant writers, simply called it an 'unheard-of epidemic illness called pestilence'.[5] Only one chronicler—Henry Knighton—pointed to a precedent that in any way approximated the calamities of his present:

> There was no memory of so unsparing and savage a plague since the days of Vortigern, king of the Britons, in whose time, as Bede records in his history of the English, there were not enough left alive to bury the dead.[6]

For other writers, such as the verse-chronicler Buccio di Ranallo of Aquila or the German chronicler of Nuremberg the only precedent was the great flood of the Bible.[7]

Gentile da Foligno, whose plague tract commissioned by Perugia's city

---

[3] McNeill was certainly not the first to see a single cultural pattern resulting from plague or waves of other epidemic diseases. The theme of plague and the demoralisation of society goes back at least to Thucydides and afterwards became a commonplace among historians; see Raymond Crawfurd, *Plague and Pestilence in Literature*, p. 39 and Johannes Nohl, *The Black Death: A Chronicle of the Plague Compiled from Contemporary Sources*, tr. by C.H. Clarke (London, 1926, 1961 ed), preface. In addition, McNeill has had his followers; see Crosby, *Ecological Imperialism*.

[4] *Johannis de Fordun Chronica*, p. 368. The same was repeated by Bower, *Scotichronicon*, VII, p. 273.

[5] Horrox, p. 63; also see *Annalium Hiberniae*, p. 36.

[6] *Knighton's Chronicle*, pp. 100–1.

[7] *Cronaca Aquilana*, p. 180; *Die Chronik des Mathias von Neuenburg*, pp. 263–4.

council was among the first to be written after the Black Death's first appearance, remarked even before it had reached him in central Italy that 'no pestilence of comparative malignance had ever been seen before.'[8] In another report made soon afterwards for the college of doctors of Genoa, he reiterated: 'this pestilence, as the Pisans call it, or epidemic or whatever you wish to call it, is more awful than anything heard or seen before in books.'[9] Finally, Francesco Petrarch's observation is perhaps the most poignant: 'Consult the historians: silence. Interrogate the scientists: you get a blank. Question the philosophers: they shrug their shoulders, wrinkle their brows, and put their fingers to their lips to demand silence.'[10]

In addition to its cross-regional spread and unprecedented mortalities, it was a disease for which medical science, both ancient and present, had few solutions. Contemporaries called it 'incurable'; 'doctors knew no remedy'.[11] As Guy de Chauliac maintained, reflecting back on the plague of 1348: 'for previous plagues there were some remedies; for this one, nothing.'[12] Jacme d'Agramont, author of perhaps the earliest Black Death tract (24 April 1348), ultimately concluded that the best remedy was 'to recognise, to repent, and to confess our sins before the holy Roman Church and its representatives, as well as to do penance'.[13] In the plague poem of around 1350 by the doctor Simon de Couvin, the Black Death had 'miffed all doctors; the art of Hippocrates was lost'.[14]

As might be expected, the chroniclers were more forceful than the doctors in their doubts about medicine's utility in 1348. According to Siena's Agnolo di Tura, 'people thought it was the end of the world and no medicine or other remedy was of value; any remedy tried only brought a quicker death.'[15] The anonymous author of the Aquilean necrology suggested that the 'gathering of medical authorities, Hippocrates and others, was of no avail', since 'such an epidemic had never been seen before.'[16] Matteo Villani maintained that 'of this pestilential illness, doctors from all over the world, neither with natural philosophy, physics, nor astrology, had any remedy or effective cure. Doctors visited the sick only to make money; their medicine was nonsense (*fitta*) and led only to quicker

---

[8] [30], p. 84.
[9] [31 and 32], p. 332.
[10] Petrarca, *Le Familiari,* ed. by Vittorio Rossi, II (Florence, 1934), VIII, 7, pp. 174–9.
[11] Contusii, *Historia de Novitatibus Paduae,* col. 927.
[12] Guy de Chauliac, in Haeser, p. 175.
[13] As with the Paris Medical Faculty, d'Agramont tried to uphold the professions's exclusive prerogative on advising on curative measures but suggested that all preventive measures could safely be followed without medical help', see Arrizabalaga, 'Facing the Black Death', pp. 270–2 and [278], pp. 120–1.
[14] 'Opuscule relatif à la peste', p. 233.
[15] *Cronaca Senese attribuita ad Agnolo di Tura,* p. 555.
[16] 'Fragmenta Historica', p. 43.

death'. For Boccaccio, 'neither the advice of physicians nor strength of any medicine was of any value or had any effect.'[17]

Yet as early as the second plague the beginnings of a new sense of medical progress can be sensed. At the end of his section on plague in *The Great Surgery*, written in 1363, after the second bout of plague in Avignon, Guy's pessimism had turned to optimism. Instead of leaving all to God, he offered recipes and remedies—bloodletting, syrups, and ointments applied to the buboes. These he attested had been tried and tested, first on himself when infected with 'continuous fever and an ulcer in the groin'. Lying ill with plague for six weeks 'with all of his colleagues believing he was about to die', he cured his ulcer and thus 'evaded God's judgement'.[18] Similarly, the Florentine chronicler Stefani, who reflected on 1348 from the perspective of the later epidemics of the fourteenth century, contended that 'neither doctors nor medicine had been of any use, since no one yet understood these illnesses. Doctors had never studied them and there appeared to be no solution.'[19] The implication was that from his perspective, the late 1380s and after three plagues, this was no longer the case. Writing around 1415, after six waves of plague had swept through Florence, Morelli was more explicit:

> As we have said, [in 1348] no one had any remedy or cure, and the plague was so great and fierce that none could help in any way, and for these reasons people died without any relief. Yet today because of the present plague and many others that we have lived through, there are now cures. Even if disasters still occur, I truly believe that some remedies work. Doctors' advice and their preventive rules provide a weapon to defend against this disease's poison. It is not that one who is well armed cannot die from it, but he who is given a lance or an arrow has a better chance of survival.[20]

He then went on, stressing more positively that good remedies could be found and advised his children and future progeny on what he meant by being 'well armed': they were to seek out and observe 'diligently the remedies of valiant doctors'.[21] He continued with two pages of detailed recipes and other advice, which he believed had guarded him against the plague. For a chronicle, this was a new departure. Gross generalizations such as that made by Caroline Walker Bynum regarding the late-medieval plagues—'Medieval people did not see disease primarily as something to be cured'[22]—surely must be revised.

Chroniclers and doctors alike saw the first plague as originating from four causes—the configuration of the planets, monstrous events in the East,

[17] Boccaccio, *Decameron*, p. 11.
[18] Haeser, p. 176.
[19] Stefani, *Cronica fiorentina*, p. 230.
[20] Morelli, *Ricordi*, pp. 209–10.
[21] Ibid., p. 209.
[22] Bynum, 'Disease and death in the Middle Ages', *Culture, Medicine and Pyschiatry*, 9 (1985), p. 102.

earthquakes across the world, and God. As with the Report from the Medical Faculty of Paris, many of the chroniclers began their accounts of the plague by calling on the confluence of Jupiter, Saturn, and Mars in 1345[23] or simply the 'reign of Saturn' on the eve of the plague.[24] Of the monstrous events in the East, merchant chroniclers such as Gabriele de' Mussis reported the 'appalling weather of Saturn ... poisoning ships'. The anonymous chronicler of Pistoia described a dragon at Jerusalem like that of Saint George that devoured all who crossed its path. In the region of Tana a city of 40,000 called Lucco was totally demolished by the fall from heaven of a great quantity of worms, big as a fist with eight legs, which killed all by their stench and poisonous vapours.[25] Others, such as the Dominican friar Bartolomeo of Ferrara, told stories of

> massive rains of worms and serpents in parts of China (*Catajo*), which devoured large numbers of people. Also in these parts fire rained from Heaven in the form of snow, which burnt mountains, the land, and men. And from this fire arose a pestilential smoke that killed all who smelt it within twelve hours, as well as those who only saw the poison of that pestilential smoke.

Some, such as the Ferrarese chronicler, maintained that this calamity was confirmed by merchant accounts and written testimony (*fu raccontato e scritto pe' mercatanti*).[26] Nor were such stories merely the introductory grist of naive merchants and possibly crazed friars on the edges of Europe as with the Olivetan from Pomerania.[27] Petrarch's closest friend, Louis Sanctus (Socrates), before embarking on his careful reporting of the plague—its signs, symptoms, and mortality figures for Avignon—claimed that in September floods of frogs and serpents throughout India had presaged the coming to Europe in January of the three pestilential Genoese galleys.[28] For the most part, such fantastic tales related to distant Eastern lands, but the English chronicler Henry Knighton found such events even within mainland Italy:

> at Naples the whole city was destroyed by earthquake and tempest, and the earth opened suddenly as though a stone was thrown into water, and everyone perished with the friar who was preaching except one other friar, who fled and escaped into a garden outside the town.[29]

Numerous chroniclers reported earthquakes around the world, which prefigured the unprecedented plague. Most narrowed the event to Vespers,

---

[23] See for instance 'Fragmenta Historica', p. 43 or *Detmar-Chronik von 1101–1395*, p. 513.

[24] *Marcha di Marco Battagli da Rimini*, p. 54.

[25] *Storie Pistoresi*, p. 236.

[26] *Libro del Polistore*, col. 806; also see *Continuatio Novimontensis*, p. 168.

[27] *Chronica Olivensis auctore Stanislao*, p. 344.

[28] Sanctus, p. 465.

[29] *Knighton's Chronicle*, pp. 96–7.

25 January 1348,[30] especially German chronicles.[31] Of these earthquakes that 'destroyed many cities, towns, churches, monasteries, towers, along with their people and beasts of burden',[32] the worst hit was Villach in southern Austria (Kärnten). Chroniclers in Italy, Germany, Austria, Slavonia, and Poland said it was totally submerged by the quake with one in ten surviving.[33]

Finally, all of the above were manifestations of God's ire, but some chroniclers were more explicit than others, such as the chronicler of Ragusa who said the plague of 1348 was not plague at all but the 'wrath of God'[34] and a chronicler of Viterbo who called it: 'a divine plague from which no doctor could possibly liberate the stricken'.[35] John of Reading explained the first plague 'because of man's sins . . . God allowed the human race to be poisoned and to perish'.[36] At least two chroniclers of the first wave of plagues (Geoffrey le Baker and Henry Knighton) interpreted it as 'God's wrath against the Scots',[37] and according to Knighton and le Baker, the Scots saw it 'as the avenging hand of God' against the English.[38]

Historians often draw this picture of the plague's fantastic and religious origins as imagined by writers of all genres from university-trained doctors and natural philosophers to itinerant friars.[39] What they fail to report is just how fast this 'aetiology' of plague faded with successive strikes of it through the fourteenth and fifteenth centuries. After 1350, we hear no more of the floods of snakes and toads, black snows that melted mountains, or the presage of earthquakes, and little of astrology or even God. The meticulous Matteo Villani was one of the very few to turn to God or astrology to explain a post-1350 plague. Perhaps in an effort to show off his scholastic learning, he explained the cause of the epidemic of 1360, which began in Damascus and Cairo: 'the cause came from God alone . . . the natural necessity, which springs from the heavens and the stars and gives place to

---

[30] See for instance *Chronicon Regiense*, p. 66; 'Cronaca B', p. 584; *Libro del Polistore*, col. 806; *Ragmenta Chronici Forojuliensis*, col. 1228.

[31] *Chronicon de ducibus Bavariae*, p. 145; *Continuatio Lambacensis*, p. 561; *Notae Petri Passerini a. 1343–64*, p. 222; *Annales Windebergenses*, p. 525; *Annales Zwetlenses*, p. 684; *Continuatio Zwetlensis IV*, p. 685; *Kalendarium Zwetlense*, p. 692; *Continuatio Mellicensis*, p. 513.

[32] *Continuatio Mellicensis, 1124–1564*, p. 513; and *Rocznik Miechowski*, p. 885.

[33] See for instance 'Cronaca B', p. 584; *Libro del Polistore*, col. 806; *Continuatio Mellicensis, 1124–1564*, p. 513; *Annales Matseenses, 1327–1394*, p. 829; *Annales Frisacenses*, p. 67; *Annales Wratislavienses Maiores, 1230–1371*, p. 532; *Rocznik Miechowski*, p. 885.

[34] *Annales Ragsuni Anonymi*, p. 39: 'Fu a Ragusa una gran peste. Non fu peste, ma ira di Dio.'

[35] *Notae Veronenses, 1328–1409*, p. 475.

[36] *Chronica Johannis de Reading*, p. 110.

[37] *Chronicon Galfridi le Baker*, p. 100.

[38] *Knighton's Chronicle*, pp. 100–1.

[39] See Monique Lucenet, *Les grandes pestes en France* (Paris, 1985), pp. 71–7, and most recently Cantor, *In the Wake of the Plague*, pp. 17, 23, and 120–1; and Aberth, *From the Brink of the Apocalypse*, pp. 2–4.

the necessary explanation that proceeds from God's will.'[40] With the spread of plague in the following year through England, France, Provence, Lombardy, and Mallorca, Matteo concluded: 'As is seen from manifest experience in all parts of the world where the plague has spread, it is because of God's judgment'.[41] Bower told the story of 'a certain Franciscan friar called John who prophesised that a disaster would come to pass because of man's sin', which explained the second plague of 1362.[42] The chronicler of the Dukes of Bavaria saw the plague of 1372 as originating from Saturn's path passing through the first point of the Capricorn.[43] The anonymous chronicler of Milan explained the plague of 1374 as 'the Lord Jesus Christ, wishing to correct the ways of men by example'[44] Thomas Walsingham saw the summer plague of 1379 as resulting from 'a hostile configuration of the planets'.[45] The chronicler of Saint-Denis explained the plague of 1387 as 'God's wrath correcting the sins of man'.[46]

But these were the exceptions. While Matteo Villani may have seen sin as the origin of the plague's return in 1357–58, he also understood it in terms of human immunity, observing that it struck most vigorously those areas such as Brabant and Bohemia that had not been infected the first time around. Others turned to social and political causes to explain the origin and spread of the disease. In addition to corrupt vapours spreading from decaying corpses, war forced peasants and their animals into cities, causing overcrowding and unhygienic conditions to ignite the plague. The humanist chronicler of Pistoia Sozomenus saw the plague of 1362 arising in Bologna, the Casentino, and Parma: 'where the army of the League of Liguria was and did its work . . . disease travelled with them to Naples and Pisa'.[47] Johannes de' Mussis argued that the 'cause' of the plague of 1374 was 'war and dearth, which [first] weakened half or more of the people living in the city and Episcopate of Piacenza'.[48] Bower hinted that the third plague of 1380 sprung from the siege of Penrith along with the drunken behaviour of the Scottish soldiers who stayed behind.[49] Even religious chroniclers explained later plagues by pointing to the social pre-conditions as opposed to astrological signs or God's need to punish. The verse chronicler of the Praemonstarian abbey of Floreffe in Namur explained the plague of 1437 'because of' the war in Liège, Namur, and Hainault, which

---

[40] Matteo Villani, *Cronaca*, II, p. 506.
[41] Ibid., II, pp. 514–15.
[42] Bower, *Scotichronicon*, VII, p. 317.
[43] *Chronicon de ducibus Bavariae, 1311–1372*, p. 147.
[44] *Annales Mediolanenses Anonymi auctoris*, col. 756.
[45] Walsingham, *Historia Anglicana*, I, p. 409.
[46] *Chronique du religieux de Saint–Denys*, I, p. 475; also VI, p. 269 for the plague of 1419.
[47] *Specimen Historiæ Sozomeni*, col. 1066.
[48] *Chronicon Placentinum*, p. 520.
[49] Bower, *Scotichronicon*, VII, p. 381.

gave rise to high prices, grain shortages, and famine.[50] God was not mentioned.

Perhaps the most incisive and detailed of such attempts to understand the rise of plague in human terms was that of the Gatari chroniclers of Padua for the plague of 1405. Their reasoning is closer to the nineteenth-century understanding of crowd diseases than it is to the Black Death mindset of floods of frogs:

> It was because of the crowding (*la stretura*) in the city of Padua, the plague-ridden war having caused the peasantry to enter the city with goods and animals, creating such a mass of people that every house was full with three or four families as well as the churches, monasteries, and warehouses; everything was full. The streets and gates, where a great multitude of peasants now slept, were full of animals of all kinds. Having lost their beds, they lay on straw on the ground. And for many days they continued in this way. As we know from experience, when everything is so scarce, including hay for the animals, many [beasts ?] begin to die and silently fall into ditches. Manure and mud beyond measure filled the city outside as well as within houses, and the stench was so great that it putrefied the air, corrupting the entire city. And there was a dearth of basic necessities beyond measure, not because of any crop failure but because of the great demand, causing bread prices to soar . . . along with all other necessities. And these conditions combined with other forces of darkness sparked a ferocious plague in the city of Padua with little nuts forming on some around the throat, on others, on the arms, and on some, on the thighs, along with an intolerable and burning fever with discharges of blood. With this illness the victims lived two or three days at the most and died.[51]

While some doctors held on more firmly to astrological explanations of the plague, their plague tracts show also a trajectory similar to that of the chroniclers. As with the Report from the Medical Faculty of Paris, other tracts of the first plague concentrated on the constellation of planets and in particular the conjuncture of Saturn, Jupiter, and Mars.[52] Even Gentile da Foligno, who may have enjoined his colleagues to stop their stargazing and to the get on with the curing of plague victims, paid a similar tribute to these remote causes outside the human plane in his own plague tracts.[53] But afterwards, at least until the mid-fifteenth century,[54] the vast number of

---

[50] *Chronique de l'Abbaye de Floreffe*, pp. 147–9.
[51] Gatari, *Cronaca carrarese*, pp. 559–60.
[52] According to Arrizabalaga, 'Facing the Black Death', pp. 248–9, these universal, cosmological causes of plague were 'unquestionable' in 1348. For all six of the early plague tracts, he analyses, the planets exercised great influence. The same is seen in the early tracts from Montpellier, see Chase, 'Fevers, poisons, and apostemes', p.155.
[53] [30], p. 83; and Campbell, *The Black Death*, p. 11.
[54] For post-1450 see for instance [194], pp. 95–102, which concentrated on the movements of the moon for predicting plague; [175 and 176], pp. 12–20; [182], p. 36; Ficino, *Consiglio contro la pestilenza*, p. 56.

tracts practised what Gentile had preached: they began head on with the immediate bodily signs of plague, treatments, and recipes. As Domenico Panebianco has commented in looking at the plague tract of Cardone de Spanzotis of Milan (1360), 'it is particularly curious for this time, that he left totally aside any discussion of the supernatural origins of the plague and did not speak of averting them through prayers, abstinence, or other religious practices.'[55] 'For this time' it may have been unusual as far as the general intellectual culture is concerned, but for the doctors, at least by the second plague, the numerous plague tracts edited by Sudhoff and others show that Cardone's practice was fast becoming a commonplace.[56]

Furthermore, those few who continued to preface their remedies with 'the remote' philosophical and astrological causes, also began to point to more immediate causes within the human realm, seeing a relation between famine, war, and plague.[57] Doctors such as Heinrich of Bratislava and Johannes Jacobi of Montpellier in the 1370s,[58] Niccolò of Udine in 1390,[59] the Medical Faculty at Prague in 1406,[60] an anonymous doctor from Lübeck writing in 1411,[61] a doctor from the diocese of Besançon in the fifteenth century,[62] and a doctor from Bern in the second half of the fifteenth century[63] saw the carnage of war and unburied corpses sparking the spread of putrid and infectious vapours, and famine as the cause of corrupt and poisonous food and water.[64] Ficino claimed that the ferocity of war in the spring of 1480 was the principal cause of that year's plague in Italy, the worst, he maintained, in a hundred years.[65] By the fifteenth century, doctors also saw famine and the corruption of food as the reasons why the poor died in greater numbers than the rich.[66] Dr Johann Vinck, writing from southern Germany during the second half of the century, explained psychologically the connections between war and plague: he asked, 'why does plague come after war and scarcity (*caristias*)?' and

---

[55] Panebianco, '"De preservatione a pestilencia" di Cardone de Spanzotis de Mediolano, del 1360', *Archivio Storico Lombardo*, CII (1977), p. 353.

[56] God, the stars, and attention to the plague's remote causes experiences a slight revival in tracts of the second half of the fifteenth century and early sixteenth century; see for instance [202], p. 114; [233], p. 162; [193], p. 79; and [194], pp. 96–102.

[57] When authors of the plague tracts written in 1348, such as Gentile da Foligno and Jacme d'Agramont, referred to wars or famine, they did so in the abstract, referring to the Galenic principles of winds and putrefying corpses that brought on plague; Arrizabalaga, 'Facing the Black Death', p. 255.

[58] [9bis] p. 86; and [256], p. 24.

[59] [55], p. 362.

[60] [98], p. 130.

[61] [119], p. 149.

[62] [262], pp. 55 and 57.

[63] [190 and 191], p. 61.

[64] On famine as a cause of plague, see [39], p. 368; [193], p. 79; [213]., p. 124; [259], p. 44; [265], p. 81.

[65] Ficino, *Consiglio contro la pestilenza*, p. 109.

[66] [265], p. 81.

answered, 'because in times of struggle men suffered enormously from anxiety, worry, fear, and want'.[67]

Reactions to plague in the social realm changed as well as in the intellectual. While the Black Death provoked large-scale massacres across German-speaking areas, the Swiss cantons, parts of Spain, France, and the Low Countries[68] and may have initiated a new phase in the history of Jewish persecutions as David Nirenberg has recently argued for late-medieval Spain and Anna Foa for Europe more generally,[69] I know of only one instance of an outbreak of plague for the next hundred years that sparked a massacre of the Jews. It came from Poland in 1360, where at least for Krakow and its surroundings this plague was its first major one.[70] By the mid-fifteenth century, rather than being the targets, Jews participated alongside Christians in processions to placate God and forestall the plague.[71] After 1348, even doctors such as Heinrich Rybinitz of Bratislava, who pointed to Jews as possible sowers of plague did so by pointing only to the first plague of 1348. Others who thought that Jews died in greater or fewer numbers than Christians did not explain the difference either by accusing the Jews of poisoning wells or as being singled out for especial punishment by God as had been the case in 1348 to 1350. Instead, they turned to social differences: Raymundus Chalmelli thought they died in greater proportions than Christians in the plague of 1382 because they lived in dirty quarters; the fifteenth-century German physician Primus of Görlitz thought they died less often because of their life style and diet.[72]

---

[67] [109], p. 58.

[68] The literature on the Jewish pogroms, 1348–1350, is large; for a recent summary, see Carlo Ginzburg, *Ecstasies: Deciphering the Witches' Sabbath*, tr. by Raymond Rosenthal (London, 1991), pp. 63–88. For persecutions in the Low Countries (often left out in these surveys), see Sivéry, 'La Hainaut et la Peste Noire', pp. 444–5.

[69] Nirenberg, *Communities of Violence*, pp. 231–49. Foa, *The Jews of Europe after the Black Death*, tr. by Andrea Grover (Berkeley, 2000), pp. 13–6. On the other hand, for Maurice Kriegel, *Les Juifs à la fin du Moyen Age dans l'Europe méditerranéenne* (Paris, 1979), the Black Death does not even figure in the changing relations between Jews an Christians at the end of the Middle Ages. For Spain, Angus Mackay, 'Popular movements and pogroms in fifteenth-century Castile', *Past & Present*, 55 (1972): 33–67, argued that matters for Jews and *Conversi* improved from the persecutions of 1391 to 1449.

[70] For 1349, the *Annales Mechovienses*, p. 670, describes the plague in Hungary but does not mention it as afflicting Poland. On the pogroms of 1360 in Poland and especially around Krakow where it was most severe, see p. 671. Also Biraben, *Les hommes et la peste*, I, p. 104, maintains that no source mentions the plague in southern Poland during its first wave, 1347 to 1351.

[71] Nirenberg, *Communities of Violence*, p. 249. By the mid-sixteenth century (Udine, 1556) accusations against the Jews for spreading plague erupted again, see Carmichael, 'The last past plague: the uses of memory in Renaissance epidemics', *Journal of the History of Medicine and Allied Sciences* 53 (1998): 132–60, esp. 135; scapegoating plague spreaders (*untori*) go back at least to the beginning of the sixteenth century, but except for the Jews as poisoners of wells, 1348–50, I know of no such tales for the latter half of the fourteenth and fifteenth centuries.

[72] Guerchberg, 'The controversy over the alleged sowers of the Black Death', pp. 217–20. She then alleges that with growing anti-Semitism in the fifteenth century the conviction that Jews were immune to the Black Death became firmly rooted but gives no evidence to support this view.

Similarly, successive plagues of the fourteenth and early fifteenth centuries did not set off flagellant movements of the sort that had frightened churchmen in 1349 and 1350, provoking Clement VI to promulgate a bull against them; nor did any processions encircle Europe with long-distance wanderings as they had done in 1349 to 1350. Instead, later local movements such as those of the semi-nude flagellants at Liège, who attacked simoniacs and fornificators in 1376, had no relation to plague,[73] and others that were associated with later plagues were tamed events organised top down by town councils or the church.[74] Some have supposed that the Bianchi movement which processed through parts of Italy in 1399 and early 1400 revived the religious hysteria of 1348,[75] but insofar as this movement was associated with plague, it represented just the opposite relation, as Daniel Bornstein has recently demonstrated: the Bianchi were a form of popular orthodoxy sanctioned by the church and praised by it and the laity for their orderliness. They posed no threat to ecclesiastical or secular authorities; in fact their mission was the preservation of public order.[76]

* * *

The change with successive strikes of plague was not just one of silence, with the causes and reactions that had dominated thinking about the first plague experience extracted from the chronicles or doctors' tracts for the next ones. Doctors and chroniclers believed increasingly that something could be done about the plague. One manifestation of the new confidence was the mushrooming of what was effectively a new genre in late-medieval writing, the plague tractatus. Mainly doctors but also clerics (and in one case a school teacher) wrote two sorts of tracts, often combined within a single tract—one gave instructions to prevent plagues, the other to cure

---

[73] Francis Rapp, *L'église et la vie religieuse en Occident à la fin du Moyen Age* (Paris, 1971), p. 158. Carmichael, 'Tarantism: the toxic dance,' in *Plague, Pox and Pestilence*, pp. 166–9, supposedly following J.F.C. Hecker, 'The dancing mania' in *The Epidemics of the Middle Ages*, tr. by Babington (London, 1844), pp. 79–174, asserts that the wild St Vitus dancing in the towns of the Rhineland and into the Low Countries in 1374 and later were a repeat of the convulsive guilt-ridden acts of expiation exhibited in the immediate wake of the first plague. But neither Hecker nor the Latin and German chroniclers he cites show any relationship whatsoever between plague and these dances in 1374 or at any other time. In fact, none of these sources mentions the plague striking these towns in 1374. Instead of plague, Hecker speculates that for Cologne flooding of the Rhine and Maine in 1374 along with military operations in the hinterland may have led to mass hunger and may have been the cause of these public displays of uncontrolled emotion (p. 96).

[74] The chroniclers and other sources, literary as well as artistic, point to numerous examples of such processions organised by a local bishop or town council at the time of plague from the late fourteenth to the seventeenth century. For examples in late fourteenth- and fifteenth-century Italy, see Daniel E. Bornstein, *The Bianchi of 1399: Popular Devotion in Late Medieval Italy* (Ithaca, 1993), pp. 22 and 61.

[75] Benjamin Kedar, *Merchants in Crisis: Genoese and Venetian Men of Affairs and the Fourteenth-century Depression* (New Haven, 1976), pp. 113–17.

[76] Bornstein, *The Bianchi*, esp. pp. 165–9.

them. They prescribed long lists of recipes—herbs and foods to eat and not eat, ointments to apply to plague sores, instructions for lancing boils, and elaborate instructions about which veins to tap when letting blood, depending on the position of the boils, the age of the patient,[77] the season of the plague, and in one case the social class of the patient.[78] Although plague tracts antedated 1348—one is known for the plague of 1340 and at least two others from earlier in the century—this genre takes off only with the plague of 1348 and explodes in number afterwards with the successive strikes of pestilence from the 1360s on. A survey of this genre has yet to be taken, but while between twelve and twenty are known in the West for the first plague,[79] over 200 have been listed or edited for the plague's first hundred years, some with numerous manuscripts now found across Europe.

Few historians have bothered to track change through these sources. In fact, many continue to see them as monotonous repetitions of an *Urtext*, the *Compendium of the Medical Faculty of Paris* of 1348, even into the seventeenth century.[80] Others such as Carlo Cipolla in glancing at them have judged that it was not until the seventeenth century that doctors would tear themselves free from the 'scientia' of ancient authorities.[81] Instead, far from slavishly following abstract ancient theories,[82] the doctors of plague tracts from the second half of the fourteenth century on relied on their experience and experimentation from their own practices. The Moslem doctor Ibn Khātimah looked to his neighbourhood in plague time and saw 'from observation and experience' what he considered proof of the plague's contagion: 'a well man did not remain long with a sick one without being attacked by the disease'. He further observed in the neighbourhood of Almeria, where the clothing and bed linen of the plague-infected were sold,

---

[77] [113], p. 73.

[78] [193], p. 88.

[79] Campbell, *The Black Death*, pp. 9–33, lists sixteen tracts she reckons were written between 1348 and 1350; however, two of these are by Eastern doctors, written in Arabic, and two—the poem of Simon de Couvin and 'Is it from Divine Wrath That the Mortality of the These Years Proceeds (c. 1350)?'—are not plague tracts. Guerchberg, 'The controversy over the alleged sowers of the Black Death', claims there are 20 survivals between 1348 and 1350 but does not list them or cite more than a handful in her text.

[80] E. La Croix, 'Vergelijkende studie van de opvattingen omtrent oorzaken, ziektemechanismen entherapieën van pest op basis van de Pesttraktaten van de Medische Faculteit te Parijs (1348–1349), van Joannes de Vesalia (na 1454), en van Thomas Montanus (1669), *Koninklijke Academie voor Geneeskunde van België*, LXI, no. 2 (1999), p. 361.

[81] See Carlo Cipolla, *Public Health and the Medical Profession in the Renaissance* (Cambridge, 1976), pp. 2–3, who asserts that before the seventeenth century, doctors 'chose *scientia* and left *ars* behind'. For a similar view of late-medieval and early modern physicians and science see Cantor, *In the Wake of the Plague*, pp. 17 and 196: 'Essentially it [pre-modern Europe] had only non-biomedical responses to devastation of breakdown in societal health—pray very hard, quarantine the sick, run away, or find a scapegoat to blame for the terror' (p. 196).

[82] Carmichael, 'The last past plague': 'This kind of medical commentary, characteristic of late-medieval plague treatises, was formulated with good Galenic universalism. It is difficult to deduce physicians' first-hand experience from the information included' (p. 158).

that all died almost without exception.[83] In recommending 'sanitary measures' for avoiding plague, a fourteenth-century doctor from Medenblick, 50 kilometres north of Amsterdam, began his tract by referring to his long and frequent experience with the plague, observing that 'the mixing with others' and visiting the sick often led to infection. As a preventative measure, he referred not to ancient texts but to contemporary experience in Italian city-states, advising that it was better to burn the commodities of plague victims than to sell them.[84]

An early fifteenth-century doctor from Bremen, like many of the authors of these tracts, saw the plague's contagion through observing patterns of mortality within households: if one case arose in a home, the others would likely catch the disease. He elaborated further: 'this infected household would then infect five others, and from them the plague would spread throughout an entire city or region'. He took this pattern of the plague's rapid spread (and not the plague boils) as its most significant 'sign'; only plague spread with such violent contagion. These findings he maintained 'we have seen from experience (*sicut nos vidimus ad experienciam*)'.[85] As testimony to such direct experience, most of these plague tracts were written in the midst of, or just after, a bout of plague, often beginning with the words: 'in tempore pestilencie'. Others confirmed their cures and theories with phrases such as that used by the famous doctor of the Milanese Visconti, Pietro da Tossignano, 'and this I have seen by experience'.[86]

John of Burgundy went further, boasting that his advice came from 'long experience'. He claimed to have 'liberated from death' plague victims in many places since the age of twenty-four. He legitimated his recipes and cures: 'not only would they have the approval of classical authors (*auctores*), they have been proven by long experience'. The plague had given John and his generation of practitioners a new seal of authority. His subsequent references to these 'auctores' were hardly obsequious. Along with Galen, he added to the list Hellenistic, Arabic and Jewish compilers, doctors and natural philosophers—Diastorius(?), Damascius (c. 462–c.550), Serapion (of Alexandria, fourth century) Geber (Jābir ibn Hayyān, eleventh century), Mesue (Māsā Ibn Sayyār, eleventh century) Copho (late eleventh century), Constantine [of Africa] (mid-eleventh century), Rhazes, Avicenna, and Algagel (al-Ghazālā, late eleventh century)—as authorities who had never witnessed a plague of the duration and magnitude of the plagues in his day. Because of their lack of experience, he concluded, 'the knowledge found from Hippocrates on had now become obsolete'. Just as these masters had to rely on experience for treating the diseases of their day,

---

[83] Campbell, *The Black Death*, p. 56.
[84] [19], pp. 420–1.
[85] [9bis], p. 85.
[86] [41], p. 395; also, see [48], p. 341: 'et sic etiam experientia demonstavit maxime'.

experience ought to become the key for healing once again (*quod experientia facit artem*). He then claimed that from this 'long experience modern practitioners everywhere (*magistri moderni ubicunque terrarum*)' are now more expert in curing pestilence and epidemic diseases than all the doctors of medicine and authors from Hippocrates onward.[87]

John was not alone in this positive vision of his generation's knowledge and his progressive view of the history of medicine made possible by the present plagues. By the third plague, Johannes Jacobi of Montpellier said much the same: since the plague had invaded us so frequently, we have much to say from experience, while 'the ancients could say little'.[88] By the next plague, in 1382, the papal doctor Raymundus Chalmelli de Vivario was even less respectful. The ancients did not understand the causes of plagues or know how to deal with them and 'plainly could not cure' them. Rather, they had 'left everything in confusion'.[89] In 1406 the physician of the King of Aragon added Hippocrates, Galen, Alexander, Serapion, Rhazes, Averrois, and Haly to the list of ancient authorities who were of no use with the current plague. Not even Avicenna provided effective cures or preventatives. In place of this 'scientia', he ended by trumpeting his own credentials, 40 years of plague diagnosis in Toulouse, Montpellier, and Sicily.[90] Although such confidence and sweeping indictments against the ancient authorities may have waned later in the fifteenth century, doctors such as Johannes Cleyn of Lübeck continued to believe that he and his generation of doctors 'because of their great experience' had surpassed the ancients.[91]

Far from being a thin veneer of central Italians, those further from the centres of the Renaissance may have been the most liberated from the doctrines of the 'auctores', and especially of the giants, Hippocrates and Galen. A fifteenth-century doctor from the diocese of Besançon asserted that in Bologna, where he had previously practised, the doctors had no remedies for plague, because they relied on Hippocrates and other ancients, who had no knowledge of the present plague. 'Without wasting words' he then described his many remedies, which he claimed had worked against plague.[92]

This new emboldened view of their science spelled a new confidence in their powers to heal. Guy de Chauliac's about-face, from the first plague to the next, from no cures to specific recipes, was hardly unique. Other doctors cured themselves (or so they believed) and wished to make their experiences and remedies available to fellow doctors, their 'own citizens

---

[87] [27 and 28], p. 68
[88] Cited in [26], p. 58.
[89] [257], pp. 38–9.
[90] [273], p. 104.
[91] Cited in [256], p. 21.
[92] [262], p. 54. Later in his plague tract, he claimed, as did Johannes Jacobi and others, that the ancients had nothing of use to say since this plague had not struck in their times (p. 55).

and to the world'.[93] At the end of the fourteenth century, a Dr Stephanus of Padua also turned to personal experience, describing his own and his wife's affliction with plague—four days 'of horrendous fevers and the detestable signs' with himself 'at the head of the bed and she at the foot', but, as he proclaimed, they had 'triumphed over the plague' with a regime of cures, which afterwards he used to cure 'many other citizens of Padua'. He now wrote these down to benefit his fellow citizens—to whom he dedicated his tract.[94]

With confidence, others pointed to specific clinical histories of patients to testify to the success of their remedies. At the time of the third (1372) or fourth plague (1382), John of Tornamira, a professor and practising physician at Montpellier, supported one of his procedures for bloodletting and another for surgery on a boil by referring to treatments of specifically named patients.[95] While others did not name their patients, they were no less confident about their procedures based on experience. In a tract from 1371–72, doctor Heinrich Rybinitz of Bratislava recommended rubbing plague boils with his specially concocted recipe for a 'tyriaca'. He maintained that this was a more cautious method of healing 'as I along with many others have seen and experienced'.[96] A late-fourteenth-century doctor in Venice claimed to have cured a hundred patients with his plague recipes.[97] The doctor of the Portuguese Cardinal Philip of Alenzolo claimed that none had died under his care during the last big plague (at the beginning of the fifteenth century); 'his methods' had cured 'an infinite number'.[98] At about the same time, a doctor from Danzig claimed that his concoction called 'lutum armenicum' mixed with weak wine had cured many plague victims.[99] At the end of the fifteenth century, a doctor from Cologne began his tract by saying that his 'little work' had already proven itself successful for the treatment of plague cases in Rome and other places throughout Italy. Unlike the doctor from Besançon, for him and others north of the Alps as evinced by their training and earlier practice in Italian towns, the Italian experience was the model: as the Cologne physician pointed out, 'through their industry and medical procedures many plague victims had been sagaciously liberated from the illness'.[100]

The doctors also assured themselves, their colleagues, and their patients

---

[93] 'Ex libro Dionysii Secundi Colle', p. 169.

[94] [54], p. 356.

[95] [24], p. 53.

[96] [9], p. 222.

[97] Varanini, 'La peste del 1347–50', p. 305. Unfortunately, Varanini neither names the doctor nor cites the source.

[98] [49], p. 342.

[99] [122], p. 174.

[100] [229], p. 152; although less praising of the Italians, the fifteenth-century doctor from Besançon began his tract by bragging that he had previously practised in Bologna; [262], pp. 53–4.

that certain preventative measures were effective in warding off plague. They described fires to be burnt from exotic woods, the use of scents in homes, and special diets and herbal recipes, the best directions for houses to face and the opening and closing of windows and doors depending on the seasons, the stars, and the winds. Others recommended simple sanitary measures—washing hands with warm water after coughing and defecating, covering mouths and noses with bread or sponges soaked in vinegar and rose water when near the infected, and simply avoiding public and especially enclosed places, such as churches, in times of plague. At least one modern commentator on these texts with a professional competence in pharmacology and herbal medicine has remarked that these fires, scents, and herbs would have served as effective disinfectants and would have had value—not against modern bubonic plague—but in protecting against a number of airborne diseases.[101] Further, the doctors' stress on cleanliness and elementary sanitation (seen in these texts as well as in post-plague sanitary manuals, which also soar in number)[102] may not have been without beneficial consequences, especially if the disease, as they maintained and our quantitative sources underline, was highly contagious. The proof of their methods, at least as far as they and their patients were concerned, was their own survival. No doubt, it had less to do with their recipes than their bodies' immune systems adapting to the new toxic germ, which, as our death data has shown, was rapidly becoming domesticated over its first hundred years of invasion.

*   *   *

This book has seen the about-face in mentality from the first to later plagues of the fourteenth and early fifteenth century as connected to the character of the disease. Unlike modern bubonic plague, for which human hosts have no natural or acquired immunity, our charts have shown the opposite for the plagues of the fourteenth and early fifteenth centuries. In most places, mortalities declined rapidly after the first bout of plague in 1347–51, and by the end of the century it had become largely a disease of children. The speedy adaptation of host and parasite appears to have been more rapid than many other infections diseases such as influenza or tuberculosis, whose microbes change radically to offset the human body's adaptation or smallpox in which the process of immunisation is complex.

Historians of medicine have yet to compare the relative rates by which various human societies have adapted to different diseases, at least before the nineteenth century. But smallpox in the New World and plague in the

---

[101] A. Trillat, 'Étude historique sur l'utilisation des feux et des fumées: Comme moyen de défense contre la peste,' *AIP*, XIX (1905): 734–52; and Panebianco, '"De preservatione a pestilencia"', p. 352.

[102] On these see, Castiglioni, 'Ugo Benzi da Siena'; 'Consiglio medico di maestr' Ugolino da Montecatini', 140–52.

Old might provide a beginning point. The mortalities from smallpox in Mexico City during the early modern period, instead of tracing a history of progressive immunisation, show a see-saw movement over time,[103] not the steady downward thrust of the plague over its first hundred years as seen from the quantification of death documents in Siena, Florence, Bologna, Orvieto, Besançon, and London. The steepness of the trend in these places rivals the progressive eradication of childhood diseases in England and Wales from the mid-nineteenth century to the 1920s. Of measles, scarlet fever, diphtheria, and whooping cough, only scarlet fever's decline in mortality dropped more rapidly than the Black Death's over its first century (see Fig. 9.1).[104]

Afterwards, this pattern may have changed, at least in the south of England, where historians such as John Hatcher and Barbara Harvey have utilised records of longevity (even if for monastic and not general lay communities). Another cycle of plague mortalities may have then begun, brought on either by a new strain of the disease or from a loss in human

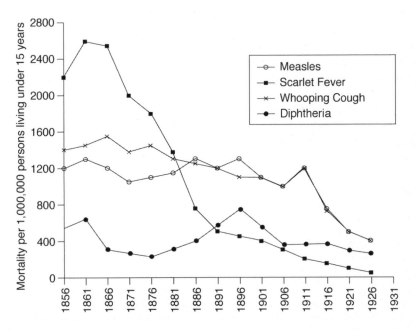

Figure 9.1 Death rates from infectious diseases: England and Wales, 1856–1926

---

103 Robert McCaa, 'Revisioning smallpox, inoculation and vaccination: a view from Mexico 1520–1950', talk at the Wellcome Unit, University of Glasgow, 13 June 2000.
104 For the mortality table of these childhood diseases, see Greenwood, *Epidemics and Crowd Diseases* (London, 1935), pp. 181ff.

immunity derived from the body's previous success.[105] Certainly with the seventeenth century places in Europe became in effect 'virgin-soil populations': Genoa and Naples (unscathed by the plague of 1629–30) lost as much as three-fifths of their populations in the plague of 1656–57, losses that may have even exceeded those of 1348.[106]

Historians have yet to study the long cycles of plague, either for understanding medical history or the plague's changing relation to the culture and psychology of Western Europe. But for the plague's first hundred years, I am ready to make several claims. The epidemiology of the late-medieval plagues was not like syphilis or other venereal diseases that (even in the twenty-first century) weaken and slowly kill their patients, and whose death counts mount progressively before beginning their decline. Nor was it like modern bubonic plague, which also recurs year after year with mounting and then erratic ups and downs in mortality before declining. As a result, in the full-bloom of colonial glory and industrial and scientific progress, the British medical corps in India faced the plague's mounting annual death tolls with fatalistic resignation, even though these plague mortalities never approached those scored in 1348 or thereafter in any region of India or the world.[107] By contrast, the mortality trends of the more devastating late-medieval plagues allowed doctors to congratulate themselves on what they and their patients perceived as successful medical intervention, the discovery of new remedies and measures for prevention. Medicine became the first field of secular endeavour in which late-medieval moderns claimed to have surpassed the ancients. Such an about-face in confidence began just after the second bout of plague in the 1360s.

To be sure, mendicant preachers and some humanists prompted their audiences to dwell on death; 'the art of dying well' (*Ars moriendi*) as a literary genre increased in importance over the Renaissance. Further, at least north of the Alps, obsession with death finds invigorated expression through *transi* tombs glorying in the decomposition of worm-wizened flesh and by the *danse macabre* in painting and poetry. Both in support and against the Renaissance affirmation of life and hope in the late fourteenth

---

[105] Hatcher, 'Mortality in the fifteenth century: some new evidence', *Economic History Review*, 2nd ser. XXXIX (1986): 19–38; Harvey, *Living and Dying in England*, ch. 4. For Florence, there seems to have been no such increase in plague mortalities in the second half of the fifteenth century. According to the mortalities charted by young girls registered in the city's dowry fund, the worst plague from 1430 to 1560 was that of 1430; Morrison *et al.*, 'Epidemics in Renaissance Florence', p. 530. But given what Ficino and others said about the devastation of the plague of 1480, one might want to question the adequacy of this source for judging the severity of plague in Florence. Again, more work needs to be done with the city's Libri dei morti.

[106] On Genoa and Naples see Cipolla, *I Pidocchi e il Granduca*, p. 79. Further, the plague of 1630 in Venice, when as many as 80,000 perished, assumed the characteristics of a disease striking a virgin soil population, not only in its extreme levels of mortality but also in the age structure of those who died. According to Ell, 'Immunity as a factor', p. 872, children were spared and able-bodied young men were its chief victims.

[107] Hirst, *The Conquest of Plague*, p. 451.

or fifteenth century, these are the voices and images intellectual and cultural historians continue to parade before us in introductory texts as well as specialised studies. For Alberto Tenenti these were the signs of a Renaissance love of life and a desperate clinging to it even past the grave,[108] while Huizinga, Philippe Ariès, Delumeau, and others have read it more straightforwardly as the morbid preoccupations of a depressed civilisation.[109] But no matter how it is read, at the same time, another voice resonated and, according to Arturo Castiglioni, was fast becoming part of popular culture by the beginning of the fifteenth century.[110] This was the voice of the doctors, and their message was the opposite. To answer the riddle of why some people died of plague, others became ill but recovered, and still others never caught it, the doctors turned from miasmic theories—all breathed the same air—to states of mind as the preconditions influencing susceptibility to plague. Instead of dwelling on death, they vigorously preached the opposite: along with melancholy, anger, struggle, sadness, trouble, torment, envy, fury, and confusion, the thought of death was to be shunned at all costs.[111] The mid-fifteenth-century doctor of Padua Michele Savonarola added to the list of dangerous sentiments: 'heavy thoughts (*gran pensieri*)' of which the thought of death was the worst.[112]

With the plague tracts, the earliest advice on these states of mind came with the second plague. The Florentine Tommaso del Garbo advised his patients to think only of delectable things and 'above all else' not about death in times of plague. Instead, they should tell amusing stories, fables, sing, and do loving deeds to make others feel happy. In addition, he advised his fellow Florentines to surround themselves with beautiful things—gold, silver, precious gems—and to robe themselves in expensive clothing, although he realised that not all might have access to such remedies.[113] Others added to the list of delectable pastimes for plague time: singing

---

[108] Tenenti, *Il senso della morte e l'amore della vita nel Rinascimento (Francia e Italia)* (Turin, 1957); more recently, see Paul Binski, *Medieval Death: Ritual and Representation* (London, 1996): 'The art of the macabre can only be understood as the final phase in the relationship between death and individualism', p. 131; and Aberth, *From the Brink of the Apocalypse*, pp. 229–57, especially his analysis of Archbishop Henry of Chichele's and other fifteenth-century English double decker *transi* tombs, which he reads as a proclamation of 'hope in the resurrection of the body at the Apocalypse, not just morbid meditation on the theme of corruption and decay' (p. 234). One must realise, however, that these *transi* tombs were extremely rare.
[109] In addition to Huizinga, see Ariès, *The Hour of Death* (New York, 1981), pp. 123–33; and Delumeau's trilogy on fear and guilt (see note 2).
[110] Castiglioni, 'Ugo Benzi da Siena', p. 75: 'La letteratura medica in lingua volgare comincia verso il principio del Quattrocento con libri di carattere quasi esclusivamente popolare.'
[111] For these tracts, see [29], pp. 80–2; [34], p. 339; [45], p. 322; [50], p. 346; [58], pp. 374–5; [110], p. 61; [117], p. 136; [122], p. 174; [24b], p. 33; [265], p. 87; [282], p. 128; [173], p. 9; Tommaso del Garbo, *Consiglio contro la pistolenza*, pp. 40–2.
[112] Savonarola, *I trattati in volgare della peste*, p. 15.
[113] Tommaso del Garbo, *Consiglio contro la pistolenza*, pp. 40–2. Tommaso's tract is undated and the earliest surviving manuscript is the mid-fifteenth century. But it is dedicated to his fellow citizens of Florence. At the time of the first plague, Tommaso was residing in Bologna,

melodies, inventing stories, reading history, playing delectable games, and these not in religious solitude but like Boccaccio's *brigata* in the company of small groups of good and trusted friends.[114] As the famous doctor from Padua Giovanni da Santa Sofia put it in his plague tract for the town council of Udine at the end of the fourteenth century, 'in place of anger, grief, and many worries, one should live and mix with friends in alacrity and good hope, casting all fears aside.'[115] Later, the northern German Dr Johann Widmans recommended: 'to resist the infection in the air, as much as one can, it is best to enjoy life to the fullest in the delectable close company of friends with a joyous and pleasant mind.'[116] The fifteenth-century doctor from Istria, Giovanni de Albertis, went further, telling his patients not only to stay happy and in good humour, but to stay away from sad people and avoid boring conversation. Ascetic activities such as fasting were also to be avoided; they simply made one weaker and thus more susceptible to plague. Instead, fine foods and good wine were to be enjoyed in plague time.[117]

The only activity scorned by the preachers that the doctors also warned against was sex. But unlike the arguments of moralising religious chroniclers such as Jean de Venette or John of Reading, the doctors' caution had no traces of moral censoring. Instead their concerns arose from fears of the plague's contagion, and their strictures appeared in the same chapters that warned against rigorous exercise, hot baths, and heavy work: all produced sweat and thus opened the pores to disease.[118] Doctors such as Cardo, personal physician to the late fourteenth-century Visconti, warned only against having 'too much sex' during plague, but 'salva pace christiana' in moderation it was not only all right, it was recommended.[119]

Such early Renaissance optimism seen in merchant chroniclers[120] and doctors' tracts does not support the French view of the Renaissance as a thin veneer of Tuscan intellectual culture overlying a mental world warped with anxiety-ridden wrecks. Indeed, because of Sudhoff's sampling, Prague or Bratislava, more than Florence, appears as the frontrunner of this new medical optimism at the beginning of the fifteenth century. Doctors'

---

where he taught at the medical school. The earliest date of his return to Florence is 1357, when he was made reader of physics at the University of Florence and shortly thereafter elected as a Prior and Gonfaloniere of Justice. He went to Milan in 1368 and died in 1370; see A. De Ferrari, 'Del Garbo, Tommaso' in *Dizionario Biografico degli Italiani*, vol. XXXVI (Rome, 1988), pp. 581–5, and Katharine Park, 'The readers at the Florentine *Studio* according to Communal Fiscal Records', *Rinascimento*, ns 20 (1980), pp. 253 and 258. Curiously, Park (*Doctors and Medicine in Early Reneissance Florence* (Princeton, 1985), p. 162) says Tommaso was teaching at Florence in 1348 but cites no evidence of it.

[114] Savonarola, *I trattati in volgare della peste*, p. 15.
[115] [50], p. 346.
[116] [173], p. 9.
[117] 'I libri italiani della pestilenza', p. 165.
[118] [46], pp. 329–30; [74], p. 108.
[119] [45], p. 322; also see *Practica Antonii Guainerii*, f. 108r.
[120] Morelli began his career as a dyer.

cautions against thoughts of death and recommendations for pleasurable worldly games, songs, and stories appear as far from Florence as Danzig and in country districts in the west of France.[121] In fact, the doctor with the most reservations about such entertainment, the only one with a tinge of sexual morality, was the Florentine Tommaso del Garbo, who recommended that his patients stay away from 'big drinkers, loose women, big eaters who greedily gorged themselves, and Jews' in plague time.

To be sure, with the first strike of plague chroniclers such as the ones of St. Denis and the Monastery of Neuberg reported that survivors reacted to the plague by indulging in merrymaking, as though dancing, singing, drumming, and the bagpipes might keep it at bay.[122] For others, such as Matteo Villani and Agnolo di Tura, the sins of those who escaped were worse: 'priests, nuns, lay men and women all indulged in sensual pleasures (*godevano*). Each thought himself rich since he had escaped and gained in the world. No one could restrain himself from doing anything.'[123] These authors of the first plague certainly did not advise such activities; instead, they pointed to them as at best in vain and at worst an incentive for God to renew the punishments. Furthermore, historians of literature now even question that Boccaccio intended his *Decameron* as reverse moral *exempla* for the enjoyment of a carefree, uncensored, sex-filled life in the face of the Black Death's doom.[124] Nonetheless, not a single one of the doctors' recommendations to strike out against the ascetic life and in its place sing delectable tunes, tell stories, indulge in other materialistic pleasures as antidotes to plague can be clearly dated to the first plague. Instead, they begin with the second one and cluster in the first half of the fifteenth century. Unlike the chroniclers' comments about pleasure-seeking in the first plague, the doctors' remarks elicited by these later plagues were prescriptions, not descriptions.

*   *   *

Practising doctors and their audiences of fellow citizens may have represented a cut beneath the intellectual horizons of humanist writers such as Petrarch. But can we step still lower down the cultural and intellectual ladder? In two previous books I have quantified thousands of last wills and testaments that reached into the worlds of peasants, artisans, and workers. From these, I found a remarkable change, not with the first plague of 1348, but with the second and successive plagues of the second half of the fourteenth century. From patterns of giving in which the rich and the poor alike

---

[121] [122], p. 174; [262], p. 54.

[122] For bagpipes, see the St Denis chronicle, Horrox, p. 58.

[123] *Cronaca Senese attribuita ad Agnolo di Tura*, p. 566

[124] Aldo S. Bernardo, 'The plague as key to meaning in Boccaccio's "Decameron"', in *The Black Death: The Impact of the Fourteenth-Century Plague. Papers of the Eleventh Annual Conference of the Center for Medieval and Early Renaissance Studies*, ed. by Daniel Williman (New York, 1982), pp. 39–64.

attempted to spread their remaining worldly goods over a vast landscape of pious beneficiaries—parishes, hospitals, confraternities and individual hermits, and the poor—testators of the last decades of the fourteenth century began to focus their bequests on a few causes and increasingly commissioned objects to recall their names and memories in both the terrestrial and celestial spheres. This change in mentality had an immediate impact on burial practice and the demand for funerary art ranging from monumental graves and frescoed vaults to ten-lire paintings placed above their last remains. This new zeal for 'fame and glory' supports the Burckhardtian view of the Renaissance, however, only in part. At least in Tuscany and Umbria it was a 'fame and glory' not of the 'individual' but of the family and, in particular, a male version of it—the lineage of male ancestors.

The present study of the disease adds another dimension to our understanding of this change: inherent in the disease itself were the makings of a new sense of progress and even triumph over the natural world. As we have argued, plague did not persist year after year, oppressing a community and its civilisation, but instead returned with a cyclical periodicity in which microbes adapted rapidly to their human hosts at least for the plague's first hundred years. Such optimism might even help to explain the decline and end of that genre in art, 'The Triumph of Death' which preceded the Black Death.[125]

But was the body's success and its implications for the psyche everywhere the same? Certainly, from the work of Michael Dols, the Middle East's late-medieval plague experience does not reveal any such optimism. Instead of the development of new territorial states with more efficient and larger bureaucracies accompanied by humanist mentalities, state power dissolved in Asia Minor; its mental world fits closely Thucydides's, McNeill's, and Delumeau's picture of post-plague despair. In Muslim society the plague treatises appear wholly different from those in the West. According to Dols, Middle Eastern plague tracts were guided by religious doctrine, limited intellectual discussion, and reflect a distinctive Middle Eastern attitude towards plague and death.[126]

Even across Western Europe were the plague's mental consequences everywhere the same? Indeed, for Douai and Tournai—the heartland of Huizinga's late fourteenth and fifteenth-century culture—the curve of adaptation to the plagues sketched by last wills and testaments differed from that in Tuscany, Umbria, and Bologna. For Douai the first big bout did not come until 1400; in Tournai the plague of 1383 relative to the then

---

[125] See for instance Joseph Polzer, 'Aristotle, Mohammed, and Nicholas V in Hell', *Art Bulletin* 46 (1964): 457–69, on the chronology of the Camposanto 'Triumph of Death' in Pisa.
[126] Dols, *The Black Death in the Middle East*, pp. 4, 266, 272, 281–302; 'The comparative communal responses'; and 'The Second Plague Pandemic', pp. 180–3.

surviving population may have been as devastating as its first plague in 1349.[127] For parts of Holland, little evidence points to 1348–50 as a devastating plague, but it certainly hit districts such as Noordholland in 1360. Further, plague deaths increased over previous strikes with the third plague of 1383, according to the number of lost inheritances of dead tenants ('*bersterften*'), and remained at about the same level for the fourth plague in 1400.[128] Further, for Paris, its mid-fifteenth-century diarist reported that the plague of 1418 'was worse than anything for three hundred years or so the old folks said' and 'no one who caught the disease escaped'. He estimated that 50,000 died in the capital, and his description of mass burial—30 or 40 in a pit laid in rows like sides of bacon—recalls Boccaccio's or Stefani's lament for 1348.[129] Although the Parisian Bourgeois later contradicted himself by claiming that the death rate for next major plague of 1432 was worse than anything since 1348 (1418 was not mentioned),[130] early and mid-fifteenth-century plagues appear to have been far worse in Paris, Burgundy, the north of France, and Picardy than in the Mediterranean. The plague of 1438–39 swept through northern Europe and is commented upon by numerous northern chroniclers but few in the Mediterranean south noticed it. In Bruges, a fifth of the city is said to have disappeared in 1438,[131] while in the south of Europe, in places such as Bologna, Florence, Siena, and Rome, where testaments, obituaries and other death documents survive in sufficient numbers, this plague along with others between 1400 and 1450 produce only slight ripples.[132] A new 'triumph over plague' may have appeared less convincing in places such as northern France and Burgundy than in Tuscany. Differences in the disease's mortalities may have conditioned different mental responses—cultural 'atrophy', pessimism, and totemistic dependence on charms and saints, as Huizinga has described for the north; 'fame and glory' as Burckhardt saw it for Renaissance Italy.

The surviving last wills and testaments, however, do not reinforce such a vision of Europe, radically split in its psychology following the plagues. As in Tuscany, testators from Tournai and Douai exhibited a new consciousness about earthly remembrance when it came to their last rites, and especially their burials, by the early fifteenth century. In these places, I have

---

[127] Although difficult to interpret, the tutelage records in Ghent suggest that its second plague in 1360–61 was more severe than the first in 1349. Also, the second plague was more devastating than the first in parts of Hainault.

[128] Boer, *Graaf en Grafiek*, pp. 64 and 339–40. On the other hand, the *necrologium* of Saint Lebuinus at Deventer shows a steep fall in mortalities after its first plague in 1350; see Blockmans, 'The social and economic effects', pp. 840–4, 856–7.

[129] *Journal d'un bourgeois de Paris*, p. 111.

[130] Ibid., p. 288.

[131] Blockmans, 'The social and economic effects', p. 857

[132] The most serious plague after 1400 may have been in 1438, but in marked contrast with French chroniclers only two Italian chroniclers in my database mention it, *Historia di Bologna*, p. 53 and *Diario Ferrarese*, p. 22.

argued Burckhardt's Renaissance 'individualism' appears more intact than it does in Renaissance Florence. Instead of recalling the male-line and a new worship of the ancestors, testators in these northern cities commemorated themselves, or at most themselves along with their spouses and occasionally the nuclear family, in their last prayers, masses, and sculpted figures to rest on their tombs and celebrate their earthly love and achievements.[133]

From the last three decades of the fourteenth and increasingly into the early fifteenth century husbands and wives in Douai and Tournai commissioned burial slabs, bas-reliefs, and free-standing sculpted figures of themselves lying next to one another to commemorate their loving, life-time partnerships and to preserve their memories in marble, bronze, or stone. As with Florence and other central Italian towns of the late fourteenth century, these northerners clearly wished to be remembered by their commissioned works of art. In some cases they even instructed that after their deaths their executors were to judge whether the post-mortem effigies bore a 'true likeness' to the testators themselves. Further, nothing like this artistic celebration for the remembrance of the individual amongst his or her nuclear family survives in the numerous testaments for Douai or Tournai before 1348 or, for that matter, in Tuscany and Umbria. Unlike the Florentines, when these northerners commissioned the sculpting of an ancestor or instructed post-mortem prayers, none went further back than a father or mother. Instead the lifespan of the testator was their frame of remembrance. Often husbands would commemorate more than one wife both with prayers as well as figures to lie above his grave even if such devotion might later complicate the paths of inheritance between rival groups of offspring.[134] No such multiple spousal devotion can be spotted in the wills of the lineage-conscious Florentines of the late-fourteenth or fifteenth centuries.[135]

*   *   *

---

[133] Cohn, 'The place of the dead in Flanders and Tuscany: towards a comparative history of the Black Death', in *The Place of the Dead: Death and Remembrance in Late Medieval and Early Modern Europe*, ed. by B. Gordon and P. Marshall (Cambridge, 2000), pp. 17–43; and idem, 'Two pictures of family ideology taken from the dead in post-plague Flanders and Tuscany', *The Household in Late Medieval Cities: Italy and Northwestern Europe Compared*, ed. by Myriam Carlier and Tim Soens (Leuven, 2001), pp. 165–78.

[134] Although Tournai's rich archival resources went up in smoke in May 1940, testaments which contained artistic commissions had been previously extracted and transcribed by A. de la Grange, 'Choix de testaments tournaisiens antérieurs au XVIe siècle,' *Annales de la société historique et archéologique de Tournai*, ns II (1897): 1–365. These include portions of testaments from the earliest examples in the thirteenth century (1267) to 1425. The earliest to demand figures of the testators themselves came in 1350, the year after the plague in Tournai. Also see L. Nys, *La pierre de Tournai: Son exploitation et son usage aux XIII, XIV, et XVième siècles* (Tournai, 1993) for exempla and fragments that survive. A widower in 1394 ordered six figures to reside on his tomb; de la Grange, 'Choix de testaments tournaisiens', p. 339.

[135] Cohn, 'The place of the dead'.

In conclusion, the epidemiology of the Black Death and its successive strikes through the first half of the fifteenth century portrays a disease that was strikingly different from the rat-based bubonic plague with its dependence on rat-fleas and resistance to human immunity. The speed of transmission, the numbers killed, the seasonality, the relation to grain, the sex and ages of the victims, and the pace of adaptation distinguish the one from the other, ruling out fleas and rats as the transmitters of plague and hence the major protagonists of post-Black Death Modern Europe. Even the late-medieval buboes—supposedly *Yersinia pestis'* 'unmistakable' sign—turn out not to have been so unmistakable. The cutaneous signs of the two hardly match in their positions on the body, number, or character. The Bombay plague report at the end of the nineteenth century showed that in 94 per cent of cases, the victims had only a single boil, that 57 per cent of them were in the groin and in not a single case of over 3000 clinical studies did the boils spread from the lymph nodes, bursting into tiny black, green, and red pustules across the body. By contrast, for the medieval plague two-thirds of the cases showed multiple boils; the neck, not the groin was the boils's pride of place, and one chronicler after another from Wales to Novgorod, Sicily to Uzbekistan described the invasion of small pustules preceding, accompanying, or following the formation of boils.

In place of *Yersinia pestis* I offer no alternatives. In fact, no disease that I know of from scanning the thousand pages of the most recent editions of *Manson's Tropical Diseases* easily fits the Black Death. Perhaps, veterinarians or zoologists with their larger databases can be called on for help. But need the disease now exist in happy symbiosis or somewhere lurking to assault humankind with the next environmental crisis? As with mammals and other forms of life, microbes are born, evolve, and become extinct.[136] Many historians have more willingly accepted that other diseases could have disappeared, such as late fifteenth-century 'sweating', which killed as swiftly and horribly as the Black Death (but not nearly as in great numbers) in northern France and southern England.[137] The virulence of streptococcal

---

[136] One disease that fits the late-medieval descriptions better than modern bubonic plague is Melioidosis, a water-borne disease that can appear in sheep, horses, pigs, cats, and dogs. Like bubonic plague, the mortality can be extremely high; the incubation period is shorter than plague, as little as three days as opposed to ten to fourteen days. It is spread by rats but does not depend on a prior epizootic of them. It is spread through the pulmonary and intestinal tracts; pneumonia usually accompanies cutaneous signs of pustules, rashes, and swellings. Sputum is profuse and often bloodstained. Its signs, however, like the later medieval disease, vary. Death occurs after a few days. It does not depend on an insect vector but arises from stagnant water and infected soil. Little can be done to control its spread. Few cases occur among women, and, most importantly, the natural immunity among humans is high. I know nothing of its climatic limits or cycles. See *Manson's Tropical Diseases*, 19th ed., pp. 603–5; and Thin *et al.*, *Quarterly Journal of Medicine*, 39 (1970), pp. 115–25. Others have recently speculated on the basis of sixteenth- and seventeenth-century parish records that the disease was a filovirus similar to Ebola; see Richard Trueman, 'Mistaken identity', *Guardian: Science* (21 June 2001), p. S3.
[137] Some historians have identified the disease as flu (Aberth, *On the Brink of the Apocalypse*,

infections and measles has lessened so as no longer to be the killers they once were, and smallpox has gone, albeit as a consequence of medical intervention. Why not the plague?

Recently, a team of paleomicrobiologists at Marseilles has claimed to have ended 'the controversy: Medieval Black Death was plague.'[138] Their triumph rests on testing for the DNA of *Yersinia pestis* from the pulp in teeth recovered from two fourteenth-century graves at Montpellier. However, before ending the controversy, perhaps we should await for corroboration from other graves. After years of such testing in other places in Britain, France, and Denmark from well-preserved plague hospital graves of the late Middle Ages as well as the seventeenth century, no such positive results have turned up.[139] As Alan Cooper and Hendrik Polnar have pointed out, the extraction of DNA from ancient bones is fraught with technical difficulties.[140]

If the results from Montpellier should be confirmed, new questions will be raised not only for the plague but more generally for the evolution of bacteria or viruses and human responses to them. As we know from even the short timespan of the twentieth century, pathogens can mutate and in some cases, such as tuberculosis, the signs and symptoms change beyond recognition between their first strikes on virgin-soil populations and later ones. For this reason scientists such as Macfarlane Burnet have cautioned historians to pay more attention to epidemiological patterns of diseases than to their surface manifestations.

Indeed, some historians have suggested that the differences between the Black Death and the late nineteenth-century bubonic plague can be explained by the agent's mutation.[141] In fact, however, over its first hundred years and probably into the eighteenth century the Black Death appears remarkably consistent in many of its traits—not only the epidemiological

---

p. 129), others, as Hantavirus pulmonary syndrome, but these diseases have failed to match contemporaries' descriptions; see E. Bridson, 'The English "sweate" (Sudor Anglicus) and Hantavirus pulmonary syndrome', *British Journal of Biomedical Science* 58 (2000): 1–6.

[138] Didier Raoult, Gérard Aboudharam, Eric Crubézy, Georges Larrouy, Bertrand Ludes, and Michel Drancourt, 'Molecular identification by "suicide PCR" of *Yersinia pestis* as the agent of Medieval Black Death', *Proceedings of the National Academy of Sciences*, 97 (7 November 2000): 12800–3.

[139] Their first results, 'Detection of 400-year-old *Yersinia pestis* DNA in human dental pulp: An approach to the diagnosis of ancient septicemia', ibid. 95 (October 1998): 12637–40, supposedly finding DNA traces of *Yersinia pestis* in the dental pulp from sixteenth- to eighteenth-century graves in Provence came under heavy criticisms with rumours of *Yersinia pestis* contamination in their laboratory, which the authors in their publication of 2000 suggest may have been the case. By contrast Alan Cooper of the departments of Zoology and Biological Anthropology at the University of Oxford has been working at Black Death and early modern plague sites in London, Copenhagen and two places in France with no such findings of *Yersinia pestis*.

[140] Such headline pronouncements fail to show the 'criteria of authenticity' as they have set out Cooper and Polnar, 'Ancient DNA: do it right or not at all', *Science* 289 (18 August 2000), p. 1139.

[141] Horrox, pp. 7–8.

ones such as its seasonality in the Mediterranean, but also in its signs and symptoms. From its first strike in the Byzantine Empire or Messina in 1347 to successive ones described in the fourteenth and fifteenth centuries, buboes formed in the lymph nodes, primarily the neck, and spread along with pustules over the body; some sufferers had the buboes only; some spat blood; some, the pustules; and some took on all three forms. Although the disease tended to kill fewer and became largely a childhood disease with successive strikes over its first hundred years, the germ appears to have remained ferocious, killing its victims in about three days on average. If the identity of the late-medieval and modern is to be explained by mutation alone, why not name any modern-day pathogen as the Black Death's mutant agent? Indeed, other bacteria and viruses would require fewer mutations than *Yersinia pestis*.[142]

If the bacillus of the Black Death had been *Yersinia pestis*, the disease would have had to change much more fundamentally than just in its clinical manifestations and in ways not yet encountered in microbiology. First, the trend with rat diseases that invade human populations has been on the lines of typhus. Once it was a disease of rats; it then evolved so that humans were capable of transmitting it without the rat intermediary, not the other way around as would have been necessary had the medieval and modern diseases been caused by the same agent.[143] With the pressures of natural selection, pathogens seek out more efficient means to propagate their populations and to survive, and not ones that are less effective. Second, Christopher Wills has recently argued that with progressive biological diversity, human defence against microbiotic attack has strengthened and that the ever-increasing bombardment from new diseases and mutations of older ones is the source of this strengthening.[144] Even if his view is overly optimistic, why would human populations that once possessed natural immunity to a bacillus with the ability to adapt to it with remarkable speed in the fourteenth to eighteenth centuries have then lost all traces of that ability by the end of the nineteenth century? That is, humans would have lost not only their immunity to the bacillus (which can vanish with a population's long-term absence from a virus's or bacterium's invasion) but all their former ability to acquire immunity. Could a major change in the human genome in the late eighteenth or nineteenth centuries have affected not just one people in one eco-niche but humankind globally, all at about the same time? We know of no instance of such speedy genetic change within so few generations that suddenly removed or conferred protection against a virulent disease over such a wide expanse of the globe.

Another possibility for uncovering the Black Death's pathogen might be to explore the genotypes of the present-day descendants of the Black

---

[142] See note 134.
[143] *Manson's Tropical Diseases*, 19th ed., pp. 213–18; Zinsser, *Rats, Lice, and History*, pp. 263–9.
[144] Wills, *Plagues*, chs 11–12.

Death. One such study conducted by 39 scientists has made such an attempt, receiving headline attention in the United States and Britain.[145] Sometime in the relatively recent past (that is, 275 to 1875 years ago) Western Europeans acquired the AIDS-resistant allele, CCR5-Δ32, which has resulted today in Europeans having greater immunity to AIDS than other peoples across the world. The authors then speculate that that moment 275 to 1875 years ago was the Black Death of 1348. Their assumption is that only Western Europeans must have experienced the Black Death, a historical fallacy made worse by the fact that they assume that the Black Death was *Yersinia pestis*. It is as though those in India, China, and elsewhere in the subtropics never experienced this rat-based plague in their medieval pasts or later. Nor does any other pathogen render their argument for 1348 any more plausible. The disease spread across the then known world with horrific mortalities in China, India, northern Africa and the Middle East. In fact, the researchers show that resistance to AIDS rises as one moves northward in Europe with the lowest rates of resistance in the Mediterranean, the highest in Scandinavia.[146] As we have seen, neither chroniclers nor statistics confirm any such trends with the Black Death's mortalities. The most horrific casualties may have occurred in the Mediterranean, both in Europe and the Middle East, while the Black Death's mortalities were lower in Holland and may never have struck Finland.[147]

* * *

No matter what the germ may have been, diseases are not just germs; rather, they are relationships between microbes and hosts in which both sides have

---

[145] I saw articles in the *New York Times* and the *Guardian*, which presented conclusions that were far more brazen than those actually presented by the researchers. It also seems to be accepted by biologists currently working on the early modern plagues, see Trueman, 'Mistaken identity'.

[146] Clairborne Stephens *et al.*, 'Dating the origin of the CCR5-Δ32 AIDS-resistance allele by the coalescence of haplotypes', *American Journal of Gentics* 62 (1998): 1507–15. Curiously, the Chinese are at the bottom of the list and the Swedes at the top (p. 1508).

[147] J.M.W. Bean, 'The Black Death: The Crisis and its social and economic consequences', in *The Black Death*, ed. by Williman, pp. 26–7, suggests that the Black Death's mortality was higher in England, northern France, and Provence than in inland Tuscany, but his argument is based on no statistics; rather since the plagues of Tuscany were summer ones, he argues they must have been bubonic and thus less lethal than elsewhere. For Holland and the Low Countries more generally, see Blockmans, 'The social and economic effects of plague in the Low Countries'. Also Poland, whose Black Death heirs rank near the top on the list of rates of HIV immunity (fourth) was only grazed by plague in 1347–51. For evidence of high mortalities in the Middle East, see Dols, *The Black Death*, and Abraham Udovitch, 'Egypt: crisis in a Muslim land', in *The Black Death: A Turning-Point?*, ed. by William Bowsky (New York, 1971), pp. 122–5. A better candidate for the genetic shift would be the famines and their accompanying diseases of 1315–19, especially ergotism, which were specific to transalpine Europe with only minor ripples in the Mediterranean. Of course over the timespan from circa AD125 to 1725 many other candidates might arise, almost any of which would make better sense than the Black Death and especially bubonic plague, given the geography of the CCR5-Δ32 genotype.

a history and usually a capacity for adaptation and change.[148] With human hosts the adaptation can take various forms—endogenous ones orchestrated by the body's immune system and exogenous ones initiated from individual medical treatment or from political and social reforms and public health controls. Regardless of human action, the character of the relationship is as vital for understanding culture and psychology as it is for demography and economics. The psychological effect of childhood diseases will differ from diseases that cut down principally able-bodied adults or mostly the old, not only in the speed by which populations can reproduce themselves but also in how they might educate and value their offspring or even reckon the afterlife. Against William McNeill's single-stranded relation between disease and culture, I would claim that diseases in which the adaptation between microbes and humans is rapid with steadily declining rates of morbidity and mortality will have different psychological and cultural consequences, no matter how high the mortalities, than diseases that return year after year hammering their hosts with rising or random levels of morbidity and mortality.

Such a proposition needs to be tested by studying comparatively the histories of other infectious diseases and other cultures. For now I contend that the unquestioned orthodoxy that the late-medieval plagues had to have been modern bubonic plague is not only wrong, it has retarded our knowledge of both the disease and its social and cultural consequences.

Instead of pinning down the disease with a modern equivalent, this book ends with a practice borrowed from late-medieval doctors, who sometimes closed their plague tracts with doubts and 'Quaestiones'. Perhaps there has been some progress; the mid-fifteenth century doctor Saladino da Ascoli posed 39 questions; I will ask only twelve. Why did the late-medieval plagues recur with striking consistency during the hottest and driest months of the year in the Mediterranean but north of the Alps later in the cooler and wetter autumn? Why did plagues after the first strike tend to kill men more than women? Why did subsequent plagues assume a class dimension: did it result from differences in exposure or did the rich possess a better biological defence? Why should the plague assume the pneumonic form with one family member and the bubonic with another in the same season as seen in Ser Iacopo of Lucca's patient diary? Why did the disease skip over some places, even as central to European trade routes as Milan or Douai, in 1348–50? Why did the plague spread, as though the sun had cast a shadow on one field while shining on others nearby? What were the long waves of the plague's history through the eighteenth century? Why did the disease not spread back to southern Europe with the throngs of pilgrims

---

[148] On this notion of disease and biological diversity, see Wills, *Plagues*, chs 11–12; on the historical development of the laboratory 'construction' of diseases as the same as their agents, see Cunningham, 'Transforming plague'.

who processed to Rome in the Jubilee of 1350? How stable was the bacillus? Did the signs, symptoms and epidemiological patterns change fundamentally over the long term? Why were the cultural consequences so different in the Middle East from the West? Were the cultural and psychological reactions similar throughout Western Europe: can we keep both Burckhardt and Huizinga?

This book has sought to liberate the Black Death from the late nineteenth-century prison of that era's bubonic plague and, in so doing, to give grounding for a new history of disease and culture in the West. By looking at the Black Death afresh I have sought to solve a fundamental enigma of the early Renaissance: why did a new culture of 'fame and glory' spring forth from the West's most monumental mortality? Why were those most intimately associated with death—plague doctors—the first to give expression to a new Renaissance psychology, one grounded in hope and hubris?

Appendix I
Miraculous plague cures

Date	Place	Position	Number	Age	Sex	Symptoms
1. 1373.xi.23	S. Angelo in Vado Central Italy	I	2		F	Fe
2. 1374.ix.11	" "	Tibia	1		M	Fe
3. 1374.iv.26	" "	R. axilla	1		F	Contagion
4. 1374.xii.10	" "	Pectinis	3	4	M	Fe, 3 days
5. 1374	" "	Sub sustel- lam dextra	1		M	Fe a few days
6. 1450	Viterbo	I	1	28	F	Pustules
7. 1452	"	Tibia	1		F	
8. 1435	"	Facia	Many	P	F	Disfigured
9. 1450s	"	Tibia	18		F	
10. 1451	"	Tibia	1		F	
11. 1450	"	G	Many		F	Can't swallow
12. 1453	"	Tibia	Many		F	
13. 1449?	"	Mamilla	1		F	Pustules
14. 1444	C.Vitorchino		1		M	Pustules
15. 1449.vii	Viterbo	Many	P		F	Can't swallow
16. 1448.vii	"	I, Brachio	3	P	F	Lenticulae
17. 1449	"	Tibia	1	P	M	
18. 1449.vii	"		Many	P	F	Lenticulae
19. 1451	"	I			F	
20. 1451	"	G	1	16	M	
21. 1451.x.28	"			24	F	3 days
22. 1450.iv.23	"				F	Pustules, a few days
23. 1450	"			6	M	Pustules
24. 1450	"				F	7 Nuns contagion
25. 1450	"	I		28	M	
26. 1454		Mamilla	1		F	Contagion
27. 1451	Rome	G	1	Juvenis		
28. 1363	Signa		1	13	M	Fe

Table continued

Date	Place	Position	Number	Age	Sex	Symptoms
29. 1363	Signa	Mamilla	1	P	F	Paucos dies
30. 1348	Signa	Pectore	1		M	
31. 1366	Signa		Many		M	3 days
32. 1383.viii	11 "		1		M	5 weeks, Fe
33. 1360s?	Signa	—	1		F	
34. 1348	Signa				M	3 days
35. 1439	Pisurae B. Felice	G	1		M	

Miracles without the plague dates specified

Date	Place	Position	Number	Age	Sex	Symptoms
36.	Rome Francesca Romanae, 1440				F	F
37.	Rome "				M	P
38.	Rome "				F	P
39.	Niclolai de Rupe Anacho early 14th century	Shin	3	Adol	M	
40.	S. Francesco di Paola (1416–1471)				M	
41.	"		3		M	
42.	"		2		M	
43.	S. Vincent, 1419	I	2		M	
44.	"	G	2		M	
45.	"	I	1		M	
46.	B. Wernherii	Shin	18	18	M	Pustules
47.	"	Collo	2		M	
48.	B. Aegidio 1184–1265 Portugal	Cervium et fauces	Plural		F	3rd day
49.	"	Collo	Many		F	2nd day
50.	"	Collo	Many		F	
51.	Isidore Agricolae 1130		Many			Pustles, Fe
52.	"	Axilla	1		F	
53.	Peter the Confessor 13th century	G	1		F	
54.	S. Stanislao of Krakow	G	Plural		M	Apostemate can't eat or drink
55.	" "	G	1			
56.	Magdelena [Albrica] 1430–65	G	2		F	Dolore

P: puer/puella; F: female; M: male; Fe: fever, I: inguine; G: in gutare, in throat.

Appendix II
Chronicles, annales, calendars

ITALY

1. Mons. Gasparo Negri, 'Memorie storiche della città e diocesi di Parenzo' *Atti e memorie della società istriana di archeologia e storia patria*, III (1887), 111–78.
2. Raphayni de Caresinis cancellarii Venetiarum, *Chronica [1343–1388]* ed. Ester Pastorello in *Rerum Italicarum Scriptores* [hereafter *RIS*] XII/2 (Bologna, 1922).
3. *Venetiarum Historia vulgo Petro Iutiniano Iustiani filio Adiudicata*, ed. Roberto Cessi and Fanny Bennato, in Deputazione di Storia Patria per le Venezie (Venice, 1964).
4. Lorenzo de Monacis, *Chronicon de rebus venetis et carmen de Carolo II Rege Hungariae et alia* (Venice, 1758).
5. Marino Sanuto, *Vitæ Ducum Venetorum italice scriptæ ab origine urbis, sive an. CCCXXI suque MCCCCXCIII in RIS*, ed. Ludovico Muratori [hereafter Muratori], XXII (Milan, 1733); *Le Vite dei Dogi di Marin Sanudo*, ed. Giovanni Monticolo, *RIS*, XXII/4 (Città di Castello, 1900).
6. B. Riccoboni, *Cronaca del Corpus Domini*, pp. 257–94, in B. Giovanni Dominici OP, *Lettere spirituali*, ed. M.-T. Casella and G. Pozzi, Spicilegium Friburgense, 13 (Friburg, 1969).
7. Inscription on the facade of the Scuola grande di S. Giovanni Evangelista: reproduced in *Venezia e la peste*, pp. 81–2.
8. *Notae Veronenses, 1328–1409* in *Antiche Cronache Veronesi*, I, ed. by Carlo Cipolla, Monumenti storici publicati dalla R. Deputazione Veneta di Storia Patria, ser. III: Cronache e diarii (Venice, 1890).
9. *Cronichetta in Volgare, 1259–1354*, ibid., pp. 480–1.
10. *Exerpta quaedam nondum edita, 899–1381*, ibid., pp. 483–96.
11. *La Cronaca di Cristoforo da Soldo [1437–1468]*, ed. by Giuseppe Brizzolara, RIS, XXI/2, (Bologna, 1938–42).

12. *Chronicon Parvum Ripaltae seu Chronica pedemontana minora*, ed. Ferdinando Gabotto, *RIS*, XVII/3 (Città di Castello, 1911).

13. *Chronicon Bergomense guelpho-ghibellinum ab anno MCCCLXXVIII usque ad annum MCCCCVII*, ed. by Carlo Capasso, *RIS*, XVI/2 (Bologna, 1926–40).

14. *Continuatio Chieriensis et pedemontana posterior*, ibid.

15. *Breve Chronicon Montisregalis, 1390–1403*, ibid.

16. *Dalla Cronaca di Giampaolo Miolo, 985–1415*, ibid.

17. Galeazzo e Bartolomeo Gatari, *Cronaca Carrarese confrontata con la redazione di Andrea Gatari [1318–1407]*, ed. Antonio Medin and Guido Tolomei, vol. 1, *RIS*, XVII/1 (Città di Castello, 1931).

18. Cortusii Patavini duo, sive Gulielmi et Albrigeti Contusiorum, *Historia de Novitatibus Paduae, et Lombardiae ab anno MCCLVI usque ad MCCCLXIV*, in Muratori, XII (Milan, 1728); *Guillelmi de Cortusiis, Chronica de Novitatibus Padue et Lombardie*, ed. Beniamino Pagnin, *RIS*, XII/5 (Bologna, 1941, complete only to 1339).

19. *Gravina: Additamenta recentioris scriptis ad hanc Historiam*, in Muratori, XII (1728).

20. *Storia della città di Parma continuata da Angelo Pezzana*, I: *1346–1400* (Parma, 1837).

21. *Petri Azarii, Liber gestorum in Lombardia*, ed. Francesco Cognasso, *RIS*, XVI/4 (Bologna, 1925–39).

22. *Annales Mediolanenses Anonymi auctoris* (MCCXXX usque MCCCCII), in Muratori, XVI (1730).

23. *Gualvanei Flammae Manipulus Florum sive Historia Mediolanensis . . . usque MCCCXXXVI ab alio continuatore . . . usque MCCCLXXI*, in Muratori, XI (1727).

24. Gabriele de' Mussis, *Historia de Morbo*, pp. 15–26, in Haeser, *Geschichte der epidemischen Krankheiten*, II, pp. 157–62.

25. *Chronicon Placentinum ab anno CCXXII usque ad annum MCCCCII auctore Johanne de Mussis Cive Placentino*, in Muratori, XVI (1730).

26. *Breve Chronicon Monasterii mantuani sancti Andree ord. Bened. di Antonio Nerli (800–1431)*, ed. Orsini Begani, *RIS*, XXIV/13 (Città di Castello, 1910).

27. *'Aliprandina' o 'Cronica de Mantua' per Bonamente Aliprandi*, ibid.

28. Iohannis de Bazano, *Chronicon Mutinense [1188–1363]*, ed. Tommaso Casini, *RIS*, 15/4 (Bologna, 1917–19).

29. *Chronicon Estense cum additamentis usque ad annum 1478*, ed. Giulio Bretoni and Emilio Paolo Vicini, *RIS*, XV/3 (Città di Castello and Bologna, 1908–37).

30. *Annales Estenses Jacobi de Delayto cancellarii D. Nicolai Estensis . . . ab anno MCCCXCIII usque ad MCCCCIX*, in Muratori, XVIII (1731).

31. *Polyhistoria fratris Bartholomæi Ferrariensis ordinis Prædicatorum ab*

MCCLXXXVII usque ad MCCCLXVII, called *Libro del Polistore*, in Muratori, XXIV (1738).

32–33. *Corpus Chronicorum Bononiensium*, ed. Albano Sorbelli, *RIS*, XVIII/1 2 vols (Città di Castello, 1910–38): *Chronica A* and *Chronica B*.

34. *Matthaei de Griffonibus, Memoriale Historicum de rebus Bononiensium [AA. 4448 a.C.–1472 d.C.]*, ed. Lodovico Frati and Sorbelli, *RIS*, XVIII/2 (Albano Castello, 1902).

35. *Historia Miscella Bononiensis ab anno MCIV usque MCCXCIV auctore præsertim Fratre Bartolomæo della Pugliola Ordinis Minorum. Continuatio usque MCCCCLXXI*, in Muratori, XVIII (1731).

36. *Historia di Bologna del R.P.M. Cherubino Ghirardacci*, ed. Albano Sorbelli, RIS, XXXIII/1 (Città di Castello, 1915).

37. *Chronicon Regiense* (1272–1388), in Muratori, XVIII (1731).

38. *Cronaca di Ser Guerriero da Gubbio dall'anno MCCCL all'anno MCCCCLXXII*, ed. G. Mazzatinti, *RIS*, XXI/4 (Città di Castello, 1902).

39. Georgii et Iohannis Stellai, *Annales Genuenses*, ed. Giovanna Petti Balbi, *RIS*, XVII/2.

40. *Cronice de Ianue edite anno a verbi nat. MCCCCV*, ibid.

41. *Chronicle of the Villa di Santa Maria Maddalena*, in *Cronichette antiche di varj scrittori* (Livorno, 1733).

42. Simone della Tosa, *Raccolta di Cronichette*, ibid.

43. *Cronichetta d'incerto*, ibid.

44. Giovanni di Pagolo Morelli, *Ricordi* in *Mercanti Scrittori: Ricordi nella Firenze tra Medioevo e Rinascimento*, ed. Vittore Branca (Milan, 1986).

45. Bonaccorsi Pitti, *Ricordi*, ibid.

46. Giovanni Villani, *Nuova cronica*, ed. Giuseppe Porta, 3 vols (Parma, 1990–91).

47. Matteo Villani, *Cronica con la continuazione di Filippo Villani*, ed. Giuseppe Porta, 2 vols (Parma, 1995).

48. *Cronica di Filippo Villani*, ibid.

49. Marchionne di Coppo Stefani, *Cronica fiorentina*, ed. Niccolò Rodolico, *RIS*, XXX/1 (Città di Castello, 1903).

50. *Cronica volgare di Anonimo Fiorentino dall'anno 1385 al 1409 già attribuita a Piero di Giovanni Minerbetti*, ed. Elena Bellondi, *RIS* XXVII/2 (Città di Castello, 1915–18).

51. *Annales Florentini 1288–1431*, in *Fontes rerum Germanicarum*, ed. Johannes Friederich Böhmer, vol. IV (Stuttgart, 1868).

52. *'Necrologio' di S. Maria Novella*, ed. Stefano Orlandi, 2 vols (Florence, 1955).

53. Leonardo Bruni, *Historiarum Florentini populi, Libri XII [Dalle origini all'anno 1404]*, ed. Emilio Santini, *RIS*, XIX/3 (Città di Castello, 1914).

54. 'Frammenti d'una cronica dei Cerchi', *Archivio Storico Italiano [ASI]*, LXXVI (1918), 97–109.

55. Boccaccio, *Decameron*, ed. Vittore Branca (Milan, 1976).

56. *Diario d'anonimo fiorentino dall'anno 1358 al 1389*, ed. Alessandro Gherardi, Documenti di storia italiana, VI: *Cronache dei secoli XIII e XIV* (Florence, 1876).

57. *Annales Pistorienses sive Commentarii Rerum Gestarum in Thuscia . . . ab anno MCCC usque ad anno MCCCXLVIII auctore Anonymo Sychrono*, in Muratori, XI (1727).

58. *Specimen Historiæ Sozomeni Presbyteri Pistoriensis ab an. MCCLXII usque ad MCCCX*, in Muratori, XVI (1730).

59. *Sozomeni Pistoiensis Presbyteri Chronicon Universale [1411–1455]*, ed. Guido Zaccagnini, *RIS*, XVI/1 (Città di Castello, 1908).

60. *Cronache di Ser Luca Dominici*, ed. Giovan Carlo Gigliotti, I: *Cronaca della venuta dei Bianchi e della Moria 1399–1400* (Pistoia, 1933).

61. *Cronica dei Fatti d'Arezzo di Ser Bartolomeo di ser Gorello*, ed. Arturo Bini and Giovanni Grazzini, *RIS*, XV/1 (Bologna, 1917).

62. *Annales urbis Arretinæ ab an. MCXCII usque MCCCXLIII actore anonymo*, in Muratori, XXIV (1738).

63. *Chronica antiqua Conventus Sanctae Catharinae de Pisis*, ASI, VI/3 (1848).

64. *Ricordi de me Sere Perizolo da Pisa notaro Imperiale, raccolti en Livorno 1492*, ASI, VI/2 (1845).

65. *Cronaca di Pisa di Ranieri Sardo*, ed. Ottavio Banti, Fonti per la Storia d'Italia 99 (Rome, 1963).

66. *Cronaca senese attribuita ad Agnolo di Tura del Grasso detta La Cronaca Maggiore [1300–1351]* in *Cronache senesi*, ed. Alessandro Lisini and Fabio Iacometti, *RIS*, XV/6 (Bologna, 1931–7).

67. *Cronaca senese di Donato di Neri e di suo figlio Neri [1352–1381]*, ibid.

68. *Cronaca senese conosciuta sotto il nome di Paolo di Tommaso Montauri [1381–1431]*, ibid.

69. *Cronaca senese di Tommaso Fecini [1431–1479]*, ibid.

70. *Annales seneses 1107–1479*, in *Monumenta Germaniae Historica* [MGH], XIX, ed. G.H. Pertz (Hanover, 1866).

71. *I Necrologi di Siena di San Domenico in Camporegio (Epoca Cateriniana)*, ed. M.-H. Laurent, Fontes Vitae S. Catherinae Senensis Historici, XX (Siena, 1937).

72. *Johannis Ser Cambii, Chronicon de rebus gestis Lucensium ab MCCCC usque MCCCCIX*, in Muratori, XVIII (1731).

73. Giovanni Sercambi, *Novelle*, ed. Giovanni Sinicropi, Scrittori d'Italia 250 (Bari, 1972).

74. *Cronica latina, anonimo (Ser Angelo Cerboni)*, in *Due cronache quattrocentesche*, ed. Angelo Ascani (Città di Castello, 1966).

75. *Cronaca dei Laurenzi*, ibid.

76. *Marcha di Marco Battagli da Rimini [1212–1354]*, ed. Aldo Francesco Massèra, *RIS*, XVI/3 (Città di Castello, 1913).

77. *Continuatio cronice dominorum de Malatestis di Tobia Borghi Veronese (1353–1448)*, ibid.

78. *Croniche de la città de Anchona*, ed. Pietro Frassica, *Studia Historica et Philologica*, VIII, (Florence, 1979).

79. *Brevi annali della Città di Perugia dal 1194 al 1352 da uno della famiglia Oddi*, in *Cronache e storie inedite della città di Perugia dal MCL al MDLXIII*, ed. Francesco Bonaini, Ariodante Fabretti and Filippo-Luigi Polidori, *ASI*, XVI (1850).

80. *Cronica della città di Perugia dal 1309 al 1491 nota col nome di Diario del Graziani*, ibid.

81. *La Cronica di S. Domenico di Perugia*, ed. Andrea Maiarelli (Spoleto, 1995).

82. *Annales Forolivienses ab origine urbis usque ad annum MCCC-CLXXIII*, ed. Giuseppe Mazzatinti, *RIS*, XXII/2 (Città di Castello, 1903–9).

84. *Chronica breviora aliaque monumenta faventina a Bernardino Azzurrinio collecta*, ed. Antonio Messeri, *RIS*, XXVIII/3 (Città di Castello, 1905–21).

85. *Cronache Malatestiane dei secoli XIV e XV (1295–1385 e 1416–1452)*, ed. Aldo Francesco Massèra, *RIS*, XV/2 (Bologna, 1922–24).

86. *Ephemerides Urbevetanae dal Cod. Vaticano Urbinate 1745 (Discorso Historico)*, ed. Luigi Fumi, *RIS* XV/5 (Città di Castello, 1902–20).

87. *Cronaca di Luca di Domenico Manenti (1174–1413)*, ibid.

88. *Estratto dalle 'Historie' di Cipriano Manenti (1325–1376)*, ibid.

89. *Ricordi di Ser Matteo di Cataluccio da Orvieto (1422–58)*, ibid.

90. *Annales Caesenates auctore anonymo ab anno MCLXII usque ad anno MCCCLXII*, in Muratori, XIV (1729).

91. *Annales Veteres Mutinensium ab Anno MCXXXI usque ad MCCCVI cum Additamentis Auctore Anonymo*, in Muratori, XI (1727).

92. *Additamenta varia*, ibid.

93. *Chronicon sublacense (593–1369)*, ed. by Raffaello Morghen, *RIS*, XXIV/6 (Bologna, 1927).

94. *Fragmenta Chronici Forojuliensis auctore Juliano canonico Cividatensi cum additamentis ab MCCLII usque MCCCLXIV*, in Muratori, XXIV (1738).

95. *Cronica inedita di Giovanni da Parma Canonico di Trento*, in Angelo Pezzana, *Storia della città di Parma*, I (Parma, 1937), Appendice, pp. 50–79.

96. Michele da Piazza, *Cronica*, ed. Antonino Giuffrida (Palermo, 1980).

97. *Cronaca di Partenope*, ed. Antonio Altamura, Studi e testi di letteratura italiana, II (Naples, 1974).

98. Dominici de Gravina notarii, *Chronicon de rebus in Apulia gestis (1333–1350)*, ed. Albano Sorbelli, *RIS*, XII/3 (Città di Castello, 1903).

99. *Notae Casinenses*, in MGH, XIX, ed. Pertz (Hanover, 1866).

100. 'Fragmenta Historica, ex eodem vetusissimo Necrologio deprompta', in de Rubeis, *Monumenta Ecclesiae Aquilejensis* (Argentinae, 1740).

101. *Istoria della città di Viterbo di Feliciano Bussi* (Rome, 1742).

102. *Cronache di Viterbo e di altre città scritte da Niccola della Tuccia dall'anno 1417 al 1468*, in *Cronache e statuti della città di Viterbo*, ed. Ignazio Ciampi (Florence, 1872).

103. *Le croniche di Viterbo scritte da Frate Francesco d'Andrea*, ed. P. Egidi, in *Archivio della Società romana di storia patria*, XXIV (1901), pp. 197–252, and 299–71.

104. Antonio Ferlini, *Pestilenze nei secoli a Faenza e nelle valli del Lamone e del Senio* (Faenza, 1990) [citations from Antonio Ubertelli, 'Delle cose di Faventia. Dall'anno 1310 all'anno 1474', ms in Biblioteca Comunale di Faenza].

105. Jean Mactei Caccia OP, *Chronique du couvent des prêcheurs d'Orvieto*, ed. A.M. Viel and P.M. Girardin (Rome and Viterbo, 1907).

106. *Il Diario Romano di Antonio di Pietro dello Schiavo*, ed. Francesco Isoldi, *RIS*, XXIV/5 (Città di Castello, 1917).

107. *Cronache Siciliane inedite della fine del Medioevo*, ed. Francesco Giunta, *Documenti per servire alla storia di Sicilia*, ser. IV, 14 (1955).

108. *Cronaca Aquilana di Buccio di Ranallo*, ed. Vincenzo de Bartholomaeis, Fonti per la Storia d'Italia (Rome, 1907).

109. *Le Cronache di Todi (secoli XIII–XVI)*, ed. G. Italiani *et al.* (Florence, 1979).

110. *Chronica di Milano dal 948 al 1487*, ed. Giulio Porro Lambertenghi, in Miscellanea di Storia Italiano, ser. I, VIII (Turin, 1869).

111. *Alberti de Bezanis Abbatis S. Laurentii Cremonensis Cronica*, ed. Oswaldus Holder-Egger, MGH per usum Scholarum [SS], 9 (Hanover, 1908).

112. Anonimo Romano, *Cronica*, ed. by Giuseppe Porta (Milan, 1979).

113. *Diario della città di Roma di Stefano Infessura Scribasenatio*, ed. Oreste Tommasini (Rome, 1890).

114. I. Carini, 'Cronichetta inedita del monastero di Sant'Andrea ad Clivum Scauri', in *Il Muratori: Raccolta di documenti storici*, II (1893): 1–58.

115. I 'Fragmenta Romanae Historiae', Studio preparario alla nuova edizione di essi, *Archivio della Società romana di storia patria [ASRSP]*, XLIII (1920), 113–56.

116. Giovanni Cavallini de' Cerroni, *Polistoria*, in *ASRSP*, XLIV (1921): 37–59.

117. Fr. Johannis Ferrariensis, *Ex annalium libris Marchionum Estensium Excerpta [00–1454]*, ed. Luigi Simeoni, *RIS*, XX/2 (Bologna, 1920).

118. Conforto da Costoza, *Frammenti di storia vicentina (1371–1387)*, ed. Carlo Steiner, *RIS*, XIII/1 (Città del Castello, 1915).

119. *Chronicon Fratris Hieronymi de Forlivio (1397–1433)*, ed. Adamo Pasini, *RIS*, XIX/5 (Bologna, 1931).

120. *Juliani Canonici Civitatensis Chronica (1252–1364)*, ed. Giovanni Tambara, *RIS*, XXIV/14 (Città di Castello, 1906).

121. *Diario Ferrarese dall'anno 1409 sino al 1502 di autori incerti*, ed. Giuseppe Pardi, *RIS*, XXIV/7 (Bologna, 1928–33).

122. *Cronicon Siculum incerti authoris de rebus Siculis (340–1396) in forma diary*, ed. Giuseppe de Blasiis in *Società di Storia Patria: Monumenti Storici*, ser. I: *Cronache* (Naples, 1887).

123. *Cronache della Città di Fermo, 1445–1557*, in Documenti di storia italiana, IV.

124. *Cronache anteriori al secolo XVII concernenti la storia di Cuneo*, ed. Domenico Promis, in *Miscellanea di Storia italiana* 12 (Turin, 1871).

125. *Chronica Parmensia a sec. XI ad exitum sec. XIV*, in *Monumenta Historica ad provincias Parmensium et Placentinam*, 10 (Parma, 1858).

126. *Chronica abreviata de factis civitatis Parmae cum aliquibus adjunctis 1030–1443*, ibid.

127. *Chronica abreviata Fr. Johannis de Cornazano OP*, ibid.

128. *Necrologio del Liber Confratrum di S. Matteo di Salerno*, ed. C.A. Garufi, *Fonti per la storia d'Italia* (Rome, 1927).

FRANCE

129. *Richardi Scoti Chronicon*, in *Chronique de Richard Lescot religieux de Saint-Denis (1328–1344) suivie de la continuation de cette chronique (1344–1364)*, Société de l'histoire de France, ed. Jean Lemoine (Paris, 1896).

130. *La Chronique Latine inédité de Jean Chartier (1422–1450)*, ed. Charles Samaran, Bibliothèque du XVe siècle (Paris, 1928).

131. Guillaume Gruel, *Chronique d'Arthur de Richemont, Connétable de France, Duc de Bretagne (1393–1458)*, ed. Achille le Vavasseur (Paris, 1890).

132. *Chronique du Mont-Saint-Michel (1343–1468)*, ed. Siméon Luce, 2 vols (Paris, 1879).

133. *Chronique normande du XIVe siècle*, ed. Auguste and Emile Molinier (Paris, 1887).

134. *Chronique normande de Pierre Cochon, notaire apostolique à Rouen*, ed. Charles de Robillard de Beaurepaire (Rouen, 1870).

135. *Chronique Rouennaise 1371–1434*, ibid., pp. 316–56.

136. *Journal d'un bourgeois de Paris 1405–1449*, ed. Alexandre Tuetey (Paris, 1881).

137. *Chronicon Abrincense 837–1359*, in Recueil historique de Gaules [RHG], XXIII (1876).

138. *Chronique des comtes d'Eu depuis 1130 jusqu'en 1390*, ibid.

139. *Les Grandes Chroniques de France*, ed. Jules Viard, 9: *Charles IV Le Bel, Philippe VI de Valois* (Paris, 1937).

140. *Les Grandes Chroniques de France: Chroniques des Règnes de Jean II et de Charles V*, ed. R. Delachenal, I: *1350–1364* (Paris, 1910).

141. Gilles le Bouvier dit le Héraut Berry, *Les chroniques du roi Charles VII*, ed. Henri Courteault and Léonce Celier, Société de l'histoire de France (Paris, 1979).

142. *La Chronique d'Enguerran de Monstrelet, 1400–1444*, ed. L. Douët-D'Arcq, vol. 5 (Paris, 1861).

143. *Chronique latine de Guillaume de Nangis de 1113 à 1300 avec les continuations de cette chronique de 1300 à 1368*, ed. H. Géraud, II (Paris, 1843).

144. *Cronique des quatre premiers Valois (1327–1393)*, ed. M. Siméon Luce (Paris, 1862).

145. *Histoire écclésiastique et civile de Bretagne*, ed. P.-H. Morice (Paris, 1750–6).

146. *Petite chronique françoise de l'an 1270 à l'an 1356*, ed. M. Douet d'Arcq in *Mélanges de littérature et d'histoire recueillis et publiés par la société des bibliophiles français*, 2e pte (Paris, 1867): 1–30.

147. *Les Cronicques de Normendie (1223–1453)*, ed. A. Hellot (Rouen, 1881).

148. E. Littré, 'Opuscule relatif à la peste de 1348 composé par un contemporain', *Bibliothèque d'École des chartes* II (1841): 201–43.

149. 'La Messe pour la peste', ibid., LXI (1900): 334–38.

150. *Chronique d'Antonio Morosini*, ed. Germain Lefèvre–Pontalis, 4 vols (Paris, 1898–1901).

151. *Chronique du religieux de Saint–Denys, contenant le règne de Charles VI, 1380 à 1422*, ed. M.L. Bellaguet, 6 vols, Collection des documents inédits (Paris, 1839–52).

152. *La chronique du bon duc Loys de Bourbon*, ed. A.-M. Chazaud (Paris, 1876).

153. *Journal de Clément de Fauquembergue, Greffier du Parlement de Paris 1417–1435*, ed. Alexandre Tuetey, 3 vols (Paris, 1903–15) .

154. *Journal de Nicolas de Baye, Greffier du Parlement de Paris, 1400–1417*, ed. A. Tuetey, 2 vols (Paris 1885–8).

155. *Chroniques de Perceval de Cagny*, ed. H. Moranvillé (Paris, 1902).

156. *Chroniques de J. Froissart*, ed. Siméon Luce, IV: *1346–1356* (Paris, 1873).

157. *Chronique de Bertrand du Guesclin par Cuvelier*, ed. E. Charrière, 2 vols (Paris, 1839).

158. *Chronographia Regnum Francorum*, ed. H. Moranvillé, 3 vols (Paris, 1893–7).

159. *Chronique de Jean le Bel*, ed. Jules Viard et Eugène Déprez, 2 vols (Paris, 1904–5).

160. *Chronique de Jean le Fèvre, Seigneur de Saint-Remy*, ed. François Morand, 2 vols (Paris, 1876–81).

161. *Le livre de Podio ou Chroniques d'Etienne Médicis, bourgeois du Puy*, ed. Augustin Chassaing, 2 vols (Le Puy-en-Velay, 1869).

162. *Annales S. Victoris Massilienses 1000–1542*, ed. Pertz, in MGH, XXIII (Hanover, 1874).

163. Stephanus Baluzious, *Vitae Paparum Avenionensium*, I, ed. G. Mollat (Paris, 1914).

164. *La chronique Avignonaise de Guillaume de Garet, d'Etienne de Governe et de Barthélèmy Novarin (1392–1519)*, ed. P. Pansier, in *Annales d'Avignon et du Comtat Vebaissin*, II (1913) 39–112.

165. *Annales Avignonaises de 1370 à 1392 d'après le Livre des Mandats de la Gabelle*, ed. P. Pansier, ibid., III (1914): 5–72.

166. *Chronicon parvum Avinionense de Schismate et beilo (1397–1416)*, ed. F. Ch. Carreri, ibid., IV (1916).

167. Guillaume Leseur, *Histoire de Gaston IV, Comte de Foix*, ed. Henri Courteault, 2 vols (Paris, 1893–6).

168. Thomas Basin, *Historie de Charles VII*, ed. and tr. Charles Samaran, 3 vols (Paris, 1933–44).

169. *Chronique de Mathieu d'Escouchy*, ed. G. du Fresne de Beaucourt, 3 vols (Paris, 1863–4).

170. Roger Berger, *Le Nécrologe de la confrérie des jongleurs et des bourgeois d'Arras (1194–1361)* (Arras, 1963–70), 2 vols.

FLANDERS AND THE LOW COUNTRIES

171. [Sanctus] Andries Welkenhuysen, 'La peste en Avignon (1348) décrite par un témoin oculaire, Louis Sanctus de Beringen (édition critique, traduction, éléments de commentaire)', in *Pascua Mediaevalia: Studies voor Prof. J.M. De Smet*, ed. R. Lievensm E. van Mingroot and W. Verbeke (Leuven, 1983), pp. 452–92 (text, on pp. 465–9); and *Breve Chronicon Clerici Anonymi*, pp. 5–30, in *Recueil des Chroniques de Flandre publié sous la direction de la Commission Royale d'histoire*, ed. J.-J. de Smet, t. III (Brussels, 1856).

172. *Laetste Deel der Kronyk van Jan van Dixude 1420 à 1440*, ibid.

173. *Chronique des Pays–Bas, de France, d'Angleterre et de Tournai*, ibid.

174–5. *Chronique et annales de Gilles le Muisit (1272–1352)*, ed. Henri Lemaître (Paris, 1906).

176. *Chronique de l'Abbaye de Floreffe, de l'Ordre des Prémontrés dans l'ancien comté de Namur*, in *Momuments pour servir à l'histoire des Provinces Namur, de Hainaut et de Luxembourg*, ed. Le Baron de Reiffenberg, VIII (Bruxelles, 1848).

177. *Annales de L'Abbaye de Saint–Ghislain*, ed. Dom Pierre Baudry, ibid.

178. *Chroniques des Ducs de Brabant, par Edmond de Dynter*, ed. P.F.X. de Ram, II (Brussels, 1854).

179. *Res Gestae ab anno M.CCC.LXXXIII ad Annum M.CCCC.V. auctore anonymo*, in *Chroniques relatives à l'histoire de la Belgique sous la* *domination des Ducs de Bourgogne*, ed. Kervyn de Lettenhove (Brussels, 1876).

180. *E Scriptis Petri monachi Bethleemitici chronica excerpta*, in ibid.

181. Ferreoli Locarii Pavlinatis, *Chronicon Belgicum ab anno CCLVIII ad anno usque MDC III* (Atrebati, 1516)

182. *Istore et croniques de Flandres d'après les textes de divers manuscrits*, ed. Kervyn de Lettenhove, II (Brussels, 1880).

GERMANY, SWITZERLAND, AND AUSTRIA

183. *Chronicon Hildesheimense*, MGH, SS 7 (1846).

184. *Chronicon de ducibus Bavariae, 1311–1372*, in *Fontes rerum Germanicarum*, 4 vols (Stuttgart, 1843–68), I, pp. 137–47.

185. *Annales Windebergenses, 1218–1392*, ed. Johannes Friederich Böhmer, ibid., III, 524–5.

186. *Annales Seldentalenses, 1108–1347, 1455*, ibid., III, 526–9.

187. *Heinricus de Diessenhofen und andere Geschichtsquelen Deutschlands im späteren Mittelalter*, ed. Alfons Huber, in ibid., IV.

188. *Cronica de Berno 1191–1405*, in ibid.

189. *Henricus Dapifer de Diessenhoven, 1316–1361*, in ibid., pp. 16–126.

190. *Excerpta ex expositione Hugonis de Rutlingen in Chronicam Metricam, 1218–1348*, in ibid.

191. *Matthiae Nuewenburgensis Cronica 1273–1350*, in ibid.

192. *Contiuationes Cronice Matthie Nuewenburgenisis, 1350–1355*, in ibid.

193. *Narratio de rebus gestis Archiepiscoporum Moguntinorum, 1138–1410*, in ibid.

194. *Chronici Moguntini miscelli fragmenta collecta, 1329–1501*, in ibid.

195. *Notae Historicae Blidenstadenses, 1346–1391*, ibid.

196. *Annales Francofurtani, 1306–1358*, ibid.

197. Iohannes Latomus, *Acta aliquot vetustiora in civitate Francofurtensi . . .* , ibid.

198. *Acta aliquot Francofurtana collecta a Caspare Camentz, 1338–1582*, ibid.

199. *Chronikalien der Rathsbücher, 1356–1548*, in *Basler Chroniken*, ed. August Bernoulli, IV (Leipzig, 1890).

200. *Hans Brüglingers Chronik, 1444–46*, ibid.

201. *Die Chronik Erhards von Appenwiler, 1439–71*, ibid.

202. *Anonyme Zusätze und Fortsetzungen zu Königshofen, nach der Abschrift Erhards von Appenwiler, 1120–1454*, ibid.

203. *Die grösseren Basler Annalen, 238–1416*, in *Basler Chroniken*, V (Leipzig, 1895).

204. *Die Kleineren Basler Annalen, 1308–1415*, ibid.

205. *Die Röteler Chronik, 1376–1428*, ibid.

206. *Die Chronik Henmann Offenburgs, 1413–1445*, ibid.

207. *Die Chroniken Heinrichs von Beinheim, 1365–1452*, ibid.

208. *Anonyme Chronik von 1445*, ibid.

209. *Die Chroniken der niedersächsischen Städte: Bremen*, ed. Hermann Meinert, MGH, (Bremen, 1968).

210. *Die Chroniken der niedersächsischen Städte: Magdenburg* (Leipzig, 1869).

211. *Chronicon Moguntinum 1347–1406 und Fortsetzung bis 1478*, in *Die Chroniken der niedersächsischen Städte: Mainz*, ed. J. Hegel (Leipzig, 1882).

212. *Liber de Rebus Memorabilioribus sive Chronikon Henrici de Hervordia*, ed. Augustus Potthast (Göttingen, 1859).

213. *Magnum Chronicon . . . Belgicae*, in *Rerum Germanicarum Veteres*, ed. Ioannis Pistorii (Regensburg, 1726).

214. *Chronicon Episcoporum Minensium*, ibid.

215. *Fritsche (Friedrich Closener's) Chronik*, in *Die Chroniken der oberrheinischen Städte: Strassburg* (Leipzig, 1870).

216. *Chronik des Jacob Twinger von Koninigshofen*, ibid.

217. *Chronika der Stadt Bern*, in Conrad Justinger, *Die Berner-Chronik des Conrad Justinger*, ed. G. Studer (Bern, 1871).

218. *Cronica de Berno*, ibid.

219. *Anonyme Stadtchronik*, ibid.

220. *Anonymus Friburgensis*, ibid.

221. *Detmar-Chronik von 1105–1386*, in *Die Chroniken der deutschen Städte vom 14. bis 16. Jahrhundert, 19: Lübeck*, ed. C. Koppmann (Leipzig, 1884).

222. *Detmar-Chronik von 1101–1395 mit der Fortsezung von 1395–1400*, ibid.

223. *Die Chroniken der Stadt Eger*, ed. Heinrich Gradl (Prague, 1884).

224. *S. Petri Erphesfurtensis auctarium et continuatio Chronici Ekkehardi*, in *Monumenta Erphesfurtensia saec. XII. XIII. XIV*, ed. Oswaldus Holder-Egger (Hanover, 1899).

225. *Cronicae S. Petri Erford, cont. III*, ibid.

226. *Continuatio II*, ibid.

227. *Chronici Saxonici continuatio (Thuringica) Erfordensis*, ibid.

228. *Die Chroniken der Stadt Konstanz*, ed. Ph. Ruppert (Konstanz, 1891).

229. *Die Limburger Chronik*, ed. Otto S. Brandt (Jena, 1922)

230. *Chronica de ducibus Bavariae, 1301–72*, ed. Leidinger, MGH, SS, 19 (1918).

231. *Chronica Universalis Mettensis, 1274–1509*, MGH, SS 24 (Hanover, 1879).

232. *Chronica Villariensis Monasterii, 1146–1485*, ed. G. Waitz, MGH, SS 25 (Hanover, 1880).

233. *Continuatio tertia auctore francone, 1346–1459,* ibid.
234. *Continuatio Mellicensis, 1124–1564,* in MGH, IX, ed. Pertz (Hanover, 1851).
235. *Continuatio Lambacensis, 1212–1348,* ibid.
236. *Continuatio Novimontensis, 1329–1396,* ibid.
237. *Codex Novimontibus,* ibid.
238. *Annales Zwetlenses,* ibid.
239. *Continuatio Zwetlensis, IV: 1348–1390,* ibid.
240. *Kalendarium Zwetlense,* ibid.
241. *Continuatio Claustroneoburgensis, V,* ibid.
242. *Continuati Claustroneoburgensis, VII,* ibid.
243. *Annales Matseenses, 1327–1394,* ibid.
244. *Continuatio Monachorum Sancti Petri,* in MGH, ed. Pertz, X (Hanover, 1852).
245. *Annales Neresheimenses, 1049–1406,* ibid.
246. Iohanne Schweickhofer Abbate Neresheimensi, *Continuatio II 1411–1545,* ibid.
247. *Chronicon Elwacense, 1–1477,* ibid.
248. *Annales Zwifaltenses, 1–1503,* ibid.
249. *Chronica Episcoporum Merseburgensium, Continuationes 1138–1514,* ibid.
250. *Continuatio tertio, 1341–57,* ibid.
251. *Gesta abbatum Trudonensium, Continuationis tertiae pars secunda, 180–1366,* ibid.
252. *Annales S. Vitoni Viridunensis, 96–1481,* ibid.
253. *Notae S. Victoris Xantensis, 1081–1411,* in MGH, XIII, ed. Waitz (Hanover, 1881).
254. *Annales S. Stepani Frisingenses, 711–1380,* in MGH, XIV, ed. Waitz (Hanover, 1883).
255. *Gesta archiepiscoporum Magdeburgensium, Continuatio I, 1143–1367,* ibid.
256. *Annales Floreffenses, 471–1482,* ed. Ludovico Bethmann, in MGH, XVI, ed. Pertz (1859).
257. *Annales Sancti Iacobi: Continuationis annorum, 1164–1393,* ibid.
258. *Annales Colonienses: Annales Agrippinenses, 1092–1384,* ibid.
259. *Annales Wormatienses,* in MGH, XVII, ed. Pertz (Hanover, 1861).
260. *Annales hospitalis Argentinenses, 1279–1389,* ibid.
261. *Annales Marbacenses, 631–1375,* ibid.
262. *Annales Engelbergenses, 1147–1489,* ibid.
263. *Notae Altahenses, 765–1585,* ibid.
264. *Notae . . . Baumburgenses, 1058–1383,* ibid.
265. *Annales Osterhovenses, 1365–1433,* ibid.
266. *Notae Weltenburgenses, 1046–1358,* ibid.

267. *Notae S. Emmerammi, 1052–1468*, ibid.

268. *Notae S. Petri Babenbergenses, 1024–1472*, ibid.

269. *Versus memoriales Babenbergenses, 1278–1349*, ibid.

270. *Annales Bohemiae*, ibid.

271. *Notae Petri Passerini, 1343–64*, in MGH, XIX, ed. Pertz (Hanover, 1866).

272. *Annales Prussiae, 1029–1450*, ibid.

273. *Annales Dunemundenses, 1211–1348*, ibid.

274. *Annales Colbazenses*, ibid.

275. *Notae Colbazensae, 1307–1349*, ibid.

276. *Continuatio II Arnoldo Borchout, 1342–1404*, in MGH, XX, ed. Pertz (Hanover, 1868).

277. *Chronicon Holtzatiae, 800–1428*, in MGH, XXI, ed. Pertz (Hanover, 1869).

278. *Notae S. Amati Duacenses, 1206–1358*, in MGH, XXIV, ed. Waitz (Hanover, 1879).

279. *Annales Wernheri, 1156–1455*, ibid.

280. *Notae Boemicae, 1278–1356*, ibid.

281. *Annales Frisacenses, 1217–1300*, ibid.

282. *Ex chronico pontificum . . . Ratisponensi*, ibid.

283. *Frisingensium: Continuatio, 1231–1495*, ibid.

284. *Chronica universalis Mettensis: Continuatio, 1153–1509*, ibid.

285. *Notae S. Blasii Brunsvicensis,, 1294–1482*, ibid.

286. *Notae Gaudavenses, 1348* in MGH, XXV, ed. Waitz (Hanover, 1880).

287. *Gesta episcoporum Eichstetensium, 1279–1445*, ibid.

288. *Cont. hist. Pataviensis, 1254–1451*, ibid.

289. *Ex annalibus S. Ebrulfi Uticensibus, 755–1370*, in MGH, XXVI, ed. Waitz (Hanover, 1882).

290. *Die Kölner Weltchronik 1273/88–1376*, ed. Rolf Sprandel, MGH, ns *Scriptores rerum Germanicarum*, XV (Munich, 1991).

291. Thomass Ebendorfer, *Chronica Austriae*, ed. Alphons Lhotsky, MGH, ns t. XIII (Berlin, 1967).

292. *Die Weltchronik des Mönchs Albert, 1273/77–1454/56*, ed. Rolf Sprandel, MGH, ns XVII (Munich, 1994).

293. *Die Chronik Johanns von Winterthur*, ed. Friedrich Baethgen MGH, ns III (Berlin, 1924).

294. *Cronica Heinrici Svrdi de Selbach*, ed. Harry Bresslau, in MGH, ns (Berlin, 1922).

295. *Chronik der Stadt Zürich*, ed. Johannes Dierauer, *Quellen zur Schweizer Geschichte*, 18 (Basel, 1900).

296. Heinrich Brennwalds, *Schweizerchronik*, ed. Rudolf Luginbühl, *Quellen*, neue folge, I (Basel, 1908).

297. *Die Chronik des Mathias von Neuenburg*, ed. Adolf Hofmeister MGH, ns IV (Berlin, 1924).

298. *Gesta Bertholdi Episcopi Argentinensis (Mathiae de Nuwenburg),* MGH, ns IV/2 (Berlin, 1936).

299. *Chronik des Burkard Zink, 1368–1468,* in *Die Chroniken der deutschen Städte vom 14. bis 16.,* ed. C. Hegel (Leipzig, 1866).

EASTERN EUROPE AND POINTS BEYOND

300. *Chronicon Viennense, 1367–1405,* ed. K. Höfler, in *Fontes Rerum Austriacarum,* I ser II (Vienna, 1856).

301. *Chronicon Bohemie, 824–1419,* ibid.

302. *Chronicon Bohemie, 1348–1411,* ibid.

303. *Chronicon Universitatis Pragensis, 1348–1413,* ibid.

304. *Chronicon Palatinum, 1346–1438,* ibid.

305. *Chronicon Treboniense, 1419–1439,* ibid.

306. *Chronicon capituli Metropolitani Pragensis,* ibid.

307. *Chronicon veteris Collegiati Pragensis, 1419–1441,* ibid.

308. *Chronicae Boemiae,* in *Fontes Rerum Austriacarum,* ed. Höfler, I ser VI (Vienna, 1865).

309. *Chronicon presbyteri Pragensis,* ibid.

310. *Annales magistratus Wratislaviensis, 1149–1491,* in MGH, XIX, ed. Pertz (Hanover, 1866).

311. *Annales Wratislavienses Maiores, 1230–1371,* ibid.

312. *Annales Polonorum III, 899–1415,* ibid.

313. *Continatio annalium Poponorum, 1344–1415,* ibid.

314. *Annales S. Crucis Polonici, 966–1410,* ibid.

315. *Ephemerides Wladislavienses, 1294–1366,* ibid.

316. *Notae Ephemerides Wladislavienses, 1345–53,* ibid.

317. *Miechowski, 947–1434* ed. A. Bielowski, in *Monumenta Poloniae historica* [series I], 2 (Lvov, 1872).

318. Joannis de Czarnkow, *Chronicon Polonorum,* ibid.

319. *Annales dicti Sandivogli, 965–1360,* ibid.

320. *Chronica principum Polonie,* ibid., ser I, 3 (Lvov, 1878).

321. *Chronica Olivensis auctore Stanislao, abbate Olivensi,* ibid., ser. I, VI (Lvov, 1893).

322. *Annales Olivenses [1356–1545],* ibid.

323. *Annales seu Cronicae incliti Regni Poloniae opera venerabilis domini Joannis Dlugossii canonici Cracoviensis,* ed. I. Dabrowski, 10 vols (Warsaw, 1964–85).

324. *Monumenta Ragusina: Libri Reformationum,* II (1347–52, 1356–60), ed. Fr. Racki, in *Monumenta spectantia Historiam Slavorum Meridionalium,* 13 (Zagreb, 1882).

325. *Annales Ragsuni Anonymi item Nicolai de Ragina,* ed. Speratus Nodilo (Zagreb, 1883).

326. *Ecclesia Spalatensis* in *Illyrici sacri,* III (Venice, 1765).

327. *Chroniques d'Amadi et de Strambaldi*, ed. M. René de Mas Latre, in *Collection de documents inédits* (Paris, 1891).

328. *Chronicon Posoniense*, ed. M. Florianus, in *Historiae Hungaricae Fontes Domestici*, IV (Budapest,1885).

329. *Cronica regni Hungarie*, ibid.

330. *Ducum ac regum Hungariae Genelogica Triplex*, ibid.

331. *Petri Ransani epitome rerum Hungaricarum*, ibid.

332. *The Chronicle of Novgorod, 1061–1471*, tr. Robert Michell and Nevill Forbes, Camden Society, 3rd series, XXV (London, 1914).

333. *Les Chroniques de Zar'a Yâ equob et de Ba'eda Mâryâm, rois d'éthiopie de 1434 à 1478*, ed. Jules Perruchon (Paris, 1893).

334. Joannes Cantacuzenes, *Historiarum*, liber IV, in Haeser, pp. 161–2.

335. Nicephorus, *Historia Byzantina*, ibid., pp. 162–3.

336. Abu-Giaphar Ebn Ali Ben Khātema, *Historia pestis 1347–49*, ibid., p. 177.

337. Ibn-Khaldûn, Abd al-Rahmān ibn Muhammad, *Muqaddmah: An Introduction to History*, tr. Franz Rosenthal (London, 1958), 3 vols

338. *Arabic Annals of Abu L-Mahasin Ibn Taghrā Birdī*, tr. by William Popper, in *History of Egypt 1382–1469 AD* University of California Publications in Semitic Philology, 13, 14, 17–9, 22–4 (Berkeley, 1954–63), 8 vols.

339. Maqrīzī, *Al-sulūk li-ma 'rifat duwal al-mulāk* (hereafter *Sulūk*), tr. Gaston Wiet, 'La grande peste noire en Syrie et en Egypte', *Etudes d'orientalisme dédiées à la mémoire de Lévi-Provençal*, I (Paris, 1962) pp. 367–80.

340. 'Relation d'Ibn Katīr', ibid., pp. 381–4.

341. 'Ibn al-Wardā's *Risālat al-nabā 'an al-wabā* (a major source for the history of the Black Death in the Middle East)', tr. Michael Dols, in *Near Eastern Numismatics, Iconography, Epigraphy and History: Studies in Honor of George C. Miles*, ed. Dickran K. Kouymjian (Beirut, 1974), pp. 269–87.

342. Ibn Sasrā, Muhammad ibn Muhammad, *A Chronicle of Damascus, 1389–1397* (Berkeley, Ca., 1963), 2 vols

IBERIA

343. *Epidemiología Española: o Historia cronológica de las pestes, contagios, epidemias y epizootias . . .* (Madrid, 1802).

344. *Chronique Catalane de Pierre IV d'Aragon III de Catalogne dit le cérémonieux ou Del Punyalet*, ed. Amédée Pagès (Toulouse, 1942)

345. Pedro Lopez de Ayala, *Cronicas de los Reyes de Castilla*, 2 vols, in Colección de *las cronicas y memorias de los reyes de Castilla* (Madrid, 1779–80).

346. *Crónica del Racional de la Ciutat de Barcelona (1334–1417)*, in Recull *des Documents i estudis*, I, ii (Barcelona, 1921).

347. *Cronicón de Valladolid*, ed. Pedro Sainz de Barbanda, in Colección de Documentos inéditos para la historia de España, XIII (Madrid, 1848).
348. Dom Nuno Alvarez Pereira, *Chronica do condestabre de Portugel*, Subsidios para o estudo da Historia da Litteratura Portuguesa, XIV (Coimbra, 1911).
349. *Crónicos dos sete primeiros reis de Portugal*, ed. Carlos da Silva *Tarouca Fontes Narrativas da Historia Portuguesa*, vol. 1 (Lisbon, 1952).

BRITISH ISLES: ENGLAND

350. *Chronicon Galfridi le Baker de Swynebroke*, ed. Edward Maude Thompson (Oxford, 1889).
351. *Chronicle of Dieulacres Abbey, 1381–1403*, in *Bulletin of the John Rylands Library*, 14 (1930): 164–81.
352. *The Anonimalle Chronicle 1333 to 1381*, ed. V.H. Galbraith, Historical Series, XLV (Manchester, 1927).
353. *The Westminster Chronicle 1381–1394*, ed. L.C. Hector and Barbara Harvey (Oxford, 1982).
354. *The St Albans Chronicle 1406–1420*, ed. V.H. Galbraith (Oxford, 1937).
355. *Eulogium . . . Chronicon ab Orbe condito usque ad annum Domini M.CCC.LXVI. a Monacho quodam Malmesburiensi Exaratum*, ed. Frank Scott Haydon, in Rerum Britannicarum Medii Aevi Scriptores, 9/3 (London, 1863).
356. *Polychronicon Ranulphi Higden Monachi Cestrensis*, ed. Joseph R. Lumby, ibid., 41/8 (London, 1882), pp. 344–8.
357. *Thomae Walsingham, quondam monachi S. Albani, Historia Anglicana*, ed. Henry T. Riley, I: *1272–1381*, ed. Henry T. Riley, ibid. 28/1 (London, 1863).
358. Johannis de Trkelowe et Henrici de Blaneforde, monachorum S. Albani et quorundam anonymorum, *Chronica et annales, regantibus Henrico tertio, Edwardo secundo, Ricardo secundo et Henrico quarto, 1259–1406*, ibid. 28/3 (London, 1866).
359. *Gesta Abbatum Monasterii Sancti Albani*, a Thoma Walsingham, ibid., 28/4 (London, 1869).
360. *Annales Monasterii S. Albani a Johanne Amundesham (AD 1422–1431)*, ibid., 28/5 (London, 1870).
361. *Chronicon Rerum Gestarum in Monasterio Sancti Albani (A.D. 1422–1431)*, ibid., pp. 3–71.
362. *Chronica Monasterii S. Albani: Ydodigma Neustriae a Thomas Walsingham*, ibid. 28/4 (London, 1876).
363. *Chronicon Abbatiae de Evesham ad annum 1418*, ed. by W.D. Macray, ibid., 29 (London, 1863).

364. *Annales Monastici: Annales Monasterii de Bermundeseia (AD 1042–1432)*, ed. Henry Richards Luard, ibid., 36/3 (London, 1866).
365. John de Waurin and anon., *A Collection of the Chroniclers and Ancient Histories of Great Britain, now called England*, ibid., 40 (London, 1864–91).
366. *Chronica Monasterii de Melsa, a fondatione usque ad annum 1396, auctore Thoma de Burton, Abbate*, ed. Edward A. Bond, ibid., 43/3 (London, 1868).
367. *Chronicon Angliae ab anno Domini 1328 usque ad annum 1388, Auctore monacho quodam Sancti Albani*, ed. E.M. Thompson, ibid., 64 (London, 1874).
368. Adae Murimuth, *Continuatio Chronicarum*, ed. E.M. Thompson, ibid., 93 (London, 1889), pp. 3–219.
369. *Robertus de Avesbury de Gestis Mirabilibus Regis Edwardi Tertii*, ed. Thompson, ibid., pp. 279–471.
370. *John Capgrave's Abbreuiacion of Cronicles*, ed. Peter J. Lucas, Early English Texts Society, no. 285 (Oxford, 1983).
371. *The Brut or The Chronicles of England*, ed. by Friedrich W.D. Brie, ibid., no. 136 (London, 1906).
372. *Knighton's Chronicle 1337–1396*, ed. and tr. G.H. Martin (Oxford, 1995).
373. The 'Bristole Calendar for the year 1348' in Koenraad Bleukx, 'Was the Black Death (1348–49) a real plague epidemic?', p. 90.
374–5. *Chronica Johannis de Reading et Anonymi Cantuariensis*, ed. James Tait, University of Manchester Publications, no. LXXXVIII (Manchester, 1914).
376. *Historia Roffensis*, ed. and tr. R. Horrox, *The Black Death* (Manchester, 1994).
377. Antonia Gransden, ed., 'A fourteenth-century chronicle from the Grey Friars at Lynn', *English Historical Review*, LXXII (1957): 270–8.
378. *Pars Secunda: Continuatio Chronicae de Vitis Archiepicoporum Eboracensium per Thomam Stubbs, Dominicanum, ut fertur, Conscripta*, ed. J. Raine, in *Historians of the Church of York*, II (1879–94).
379. *Chronicon Abbatiae de Parco Ludae: The Chronicle of Louth Park Abbey*, ed. E. Venables (Horncastle, 1891).
380. *Chronicon Adae de Usk, AD 1377–1421*, ed. Edward Maunde Thompson, 2nd edn (London, 1904).
381. 'Chronicle of William Gregory, Skinner', ed. James Gairdner, Camden Society, ns XVII (London, 1876).
382. *A Christ Church Chronicle*, in *Archaeologia Cantiana*, 29 (1911): 56–84.
383. *The Kirkstall Chronicle, 1355–1400*, ed. M.V. Clarke and N. Denholm-Young in *Bulletin of the John Ryland Library*, 15 (1931): 100–37.

384. *An English Chronicle of the Reigns of Richard II, Henry IV, Henry V, and Henry VI written before the year 1471*, ed. by John S. Davies, Camden Society (1856).

385. From the continuation of the *Eulogium*: Cotton Ms. Galba e.VII, ibid.

386. *The Great Chronicle of London*, ed. by A.H. Thomas-Thornley (London, 1938).

387. *William Thorne's Chronicle of Saint Augustine's Abbey Canterbury*, ed. A. Hamilton Thompson, tr. A.H. Davis (Oxford, 1934).

388. Sir Thomas Gray of Heton, *Scalacronica: A Chronicle of England and Scotland from AD MLXVI to AD MCCCLXII* (Edinburgh, 1836).

389. *Chronicon Angliæ Petriburgense*, ed. J.A. Giles (London, 1845).

390. *Chronicles of London*, ed. Charles Kingsford (Oxford, 1905).

391. *Ms. of the Marquis of Bath (Longleat)*, pp. 99–101, in *Six Town Chronicles of England*, ed. Ralph Flenley (Oxford, 1911).

392. *Ms. Rawlison B. 355*, pp. 101–13, in ibid.

393. *A Short English Chronicle, from Lambeth MS. 306*, pp. 1–80, in *Three Fifteenth-Century Chroniclers*, ed. by James Gairdner, Camden Society, ns. XXVIII (Westminster, 1880).

394. William Langland, *Piers the Ploughman*, tr. J.F. Goodridge (Harmondsworth, 1959).

WALES, SCOTLAND, AND IRELAND

395. Llywelyn Fychan, 'Pestilence', in *Galar y Beirdd: Marwnadau Plant/ Poets' Grief: Medieval Welsh Elegies for* Children, ed. Dafydd Johnston (Cardiff, 1993).

396. *Brenhinedd y Saessin; or The Kings of the Saxons*, ed. Thomas Jones (Cardiff, 1971).

397. *The Original Chronicle of Andrew of Wyntoun*, ed. F.J. Amours, 6 vols (Edinburgh, 1903–14).

398. *Johannis de Fordun Chronica gentis Scotorum*, ed. William F. Skene, *The Historians of Scotland*, I (Edinburgh, 1871).

399. Walter Bower, *Scotichronicon*, ed. Der Watt, 9 vols (Aberdeen, 1987–98).

400. *The Dethe of the Kynge of Scotis*, tr. John Shirley, in *Death and Dissent: Two Fifteenth-century Chronicles*, ed. Lister M. Matheson (Woodbridge, 1999).

401. *Annalium Hiberniae Chronicon*, ed. R. Butler, *Irish Archaeological Society* (1849): 1–39.

402. *Annales Breves Hibberniae auctore Thaddaeo Dowling, Cancellario Lechlinensi*, ibid., pt. 2: 1–45.

403. *Annals of the Kingdom of Ireland by the Four Masters*, 2nd ed., ed. John O'Donovan, 4 vols (Dublin, 1856).

404. *The Annals of Clonmacnoise from the Creation to AD 1408*, ed. Rev. Denis Murphy (Dublin, 1896).

405. *Annála Connacht: The Annals of Connacht (A.D. 1224–1544)*, ed. by Martin Freeman (Dublin, 1944).

406. *Annala Ulah: Annals of Uster: A Chronicle of Irish Affairs AD 431 to AD 1540*, ed. William M. Hennessy, 4 vols (Dublin, 1887–1901).

407. *The Annals of Loch Cé: A Chronicle of Irish Affairs from AD 1014 to AD 1590*, ed. William M. Hennessy, 2 vols (London, 1871).

Appendix III
Plague tracts cited from
Sudhoff Archiv für Geschichte der Medizin

Numbers in brackets correspond to those Sudhoff assigned to the tracts; where he added and edited later versions of earlier texts I have added 'bis' to the number.

Band IV (1910)

[2] = 'Das Prager "Missum imperatori"' (1371), pp. 194–9.
[9] = 'Tractatus de praeservationibus . . . hinricum rybbinis de wartislavia', pp. 205–22.
[5] = 'Regimem Praeservativum et curativum (from Prague before 1400)', pp. 391–5.
[19] = 'Regulae technicae contra pestilentiam', pp. 419–22.
[20] = 'Ein kleiner lateinischer Pesttrakat', pp. 422–4.

Band V (1911)

[22] = 'Pestregeln des Magisters Bartholomäus von Brügge' (early fourteenth century), pp. 39–41.
[23] = 'Causa epidemiae et praeservatio eiusdem' (between 1348 and 1350), pp. 41–6.
[24] = Johanns de Tornamira 'Praeservatio et cura apostematum antrosum pestilentialium' (around 1360), pp. 46–53.
[26] = Die Identität des Regimen contra pestilentiam des Kanutus

Episcopus Arusiensis (1461–2) . . . mit der Pestschrift des Johannes Jacobi, pp. 56–8.

[27 and 28] = 'Die Pestschriften des Johann von Burgund und Johann von Bordeaux', pp. 58–75

[30] = Gentile da Foligno, 'Tractatus de pestilencia', pp. 83–7.

Band V (1912)

[31 and 32] = 'Zwei weitere Pestkonsilien des Gentile da Foligno an das Arztekollegium zu Genua', pp. 332–5.

[34] = 'Ein fünftes Pestkonsilium unter dem Namen des Gentile', pp. 337–40.

[35] = 'Pestkonsilium des Mag. Johannes della Penna aus Neapel (1348)', pp. 341–8.

[38] = 'Ein Consilium illatum contra Pestilentiam des Nicolo de Burgo, 1382', pp. 354–65.

[39] = 'Leve Consilium de pestilentia a Francischino de Collignano Florentiae 1382', pp. 365–84.

[41] = 'Der Pesttraktat des Pietro di Tussignano (1398)', pp. 390–5.

[42] = 'Die Pestschrift des Ugolino (di Caccino) da Montecatini', pp. 395–6.

Band VI (1913)

[43] = 'Fragmentarische Pestprophylaxe eines unbekannten italienischen Arztes (end of the fourteenth century)', pp. 313–16.

[44] = Pestkonsilium eines Meister Albertus (1348), pp. 316–17.

[45] = 'Ein "Regimen in pestilentia" eines fürstlichen Leibarztes Cardo zu Mailand (1378)', pp. 317–28

[46] = 'Pesttraktat des Doctor Francinus de Bononia', pp. 328–33.

[47] = 'Kurze lateinische Pestregeln eines Paduaner Anonymus (second half of the fourteenth century)', pp. 333–8.

[48] = 'Prophylaxe und Kur pestilentialischer Fieber nach Nicolaus Florentinus (Niccolò Falcucci, end of the fourteenth century)', pp. 338–41.

[49] = 'Eine Pestbeulenkur unter dem Namen des Kardinals Philipp von Alenzolo', pp. 342–4.

[50] = 'Ein Pestkonsilium des Giovanni Santa Sofia an den Rat der Stadt Udine', pp. 344–9

[52] = 'Ein italienischer Traktat "De pistelencia"', pp. 353–5.

[54] = 'Ein Paduaner Pestkonsilium von Dr Stephanus de Doctoribus', pp. 355–61.

[55] = 'Ein Pestregimen für Herzog Albrecht von Österreich von Meister Nicolaus von Udine, verfasst zu Wien 1390', pp. 361–9.

[56] = Doctor Johannes Aygeis von Korneuburg 'Regimen Pestilentiae' (early fifteenth century), pp. 369–73.

[57] = 'Doctor Jakob de Stockstals Pestregimen für Kloster Meik (around 1416)', pp. 373–4.

[58] = Dr Pankratius Creuzers of Traismauer, 'Pestregimen für Kloster Melk' (1444), pp. 374–5.

Band VII (1913)

[2bis] = 'Leipziger Universitätsbibliothek "Missum Imperatori"', pp. 58–60.

[2bis/23] = 'Missum est Imperatoris de pestilencia' (Prague, 1406), pp. 60–1.

[63] = 'Regimen tempore pestilenciali (Prague, 1416)', pp. 73–5.

[5bis] = 'Das kurze "Regimen praeservativum et curativum"', pp. 75–81.

[9bis] = 'Causae, signa et remedia contra pestilentiam edita per Magistrum Henricum (de Bremis oder de Ribbenicz)', pp. 81–9.

[61] = 'Die Pestschrift des Mag. Gallus (Mistr Havel) in Prag', pp. 68–72.

[64] = 'Sigmund Albich über die Pest' (1411 or 1412), pp. 89–99.

Band VIII (1914)

[74] = 'Canones seu Regulae in praeservatione a pestilentia (second half of the fifteenth century)', pp. 179–80.

[75] = 'Ein diagnostisch-prophylakitisches lateinisches Regimen (second half of the fifteenth century), pp. 181–2.

[78] = Dr Hans Würckers in Ulm 'Regiment sich zu behüten von der giftigen unreinen bösen Pestilenz' (before 1450), pp. 185–202.

[81] = 'Eine kleine Sammlung von deutschen Pestratschlägen in einer Marburger Handschrift (beginning of the fourteenth century)', pp. 214–15.

Band VIII (1915)

[83] = 'Ein kurzes Pestkonsilium eines Arztes aus Wetzlar für Abt Heinrich der Benediktinerabtei Amorbach' (Südtirol, before 1450), pp. 241–4.

[89] = 'Ein Regimen contra febrem pestilenciae simplicem' (end of the fourteenth century)', pp. 262–9.

Band IX (1916)

[95] = 'Ein Pestkapitel des Breslauer Arztes Thomas, Bischof von Sarepta', pp. 56–63.

[97] = 'Die Schrift des Magister Johannes, Archidiakon zu Glogau', pp. 65–78.

[98] = 'Collectorium minus' (Prague Medical Faculty, around 1406), pp. 117–37.

[103 and 104] = 'Ein Regimen praeservatium et curativum bonum' (Bratislava, early fifteenth century), pp. 159–66.

Band XI (1919)

[106] = 'Eine "Quaestio medica" über die Pest als Gottesstrafe und ihre natürlichen Ursachen aus den südlichen deutschen Grenzlanden', pp. 44–51.

[107] = 'Quaestiones über die Entstehung der Pestepidemie des schwarzen Todes und über Pestverhütung vom Jahre 1349', pp. 51–5

[108] = 'Pest-Quaestiones, aufgezeichnet in Lübeck (1411)', pp. 55–6.

[109] = Dr Johann Vinck (Fink) 1440–1505, 'Fragestellungen zur Pestätiologie, aufgezeichnet in einer Berliner Handschrift', pp. 56–9.

[110] = 'Ein Regimen praeservativum a pestilencia ex purificacione aeris', pp. 59–68.

[113] = 'Lateinische Pestvermeidungsregeln (Regimen bonum) aus einer Elbinger Handschrift', pp. 71–3.

[114 and 115] = 'Ein ausführlicher lateinischer Pesttraktat im Jahre 1405 der Stadt Erfurt gewidmet', pp. 74–92.

[116] = 'Der Pesttraktat Meisters Peter von Kottbus', pp. 121–32.

[117] = 'Ein lateinischer Pesttraktat aus Niederdeutschland in einer Leipzinger Handschrift', pp. 130–43.

[119] = 'Collectum de peste eines Lübecker Arztes aus dem Jahre 1411', pp. 141–63.

[122] = 'Ein Compendium epidemiae, aufbewahrt in Danzig' (beginning of the fifteenth century), pp. 165–76.

Band XIV (1922)

[123] = Mag. Gwillelmi de Monte Caprarum, 'De pestilencia aus Helmstädt (second half of the fifteenth century)', pp. 1–4.

[125] = 'Das kurze lateinische Regimen praeservativum et curativum (after 1450)', pp. 8–10.

Band XIV (1923)

[138] = 'Dr Johan Lochners Regimen praeservativum a pestilentia', pp. 84–9.

[140] = 'Mag. Hermann Schedels aus Nürnberg für seinem Diensthernn Bischof Johann von Aich zu Eichstädt, 1453', pp. 90–8.

[150] = 'De obitu ducis Johannis et pestis Epidemie', pp. 138–9.

[151] = 'Ein Pestratschlag Dr Hartmann Schedels für den Abt und die Ordensbrüder in Kloster Heilsbronn (1494)', pp. 140–2.

[152] = Dr Johanns Rosenbusch, 'Viele deutsche epidemiologische Fragen ohne Antwort (1450)', pp. 142–3.

[153] = 'Quaestiones zur Pestatiologie und prophylaktische Anweisungen (end of the fifteenth century)', pp. 143–5.

[161] = 'Ein Tractatus de febribus pestilencialibus (Bohemia, around 1400)', pp. 158–62.

Band XVI (1924)

[173] = Ein früheres handsschriftliches Pestregimen Johanns Widmans, pp. 5–10.

[175 and 176] = 'Pestanweisung dreier Strassburger Ärzte (second half of the fifteenth century), pp. 12–20.

[177] = 'Ein Compendium de Epidemia eines Mag. Johannes de Saxonia (in Strassburg)', pp. 20–9.

[182] = Thomas a Cempis, 'Consilium in peste von 1481', pp. 36–46.

[183] = Dr Johannes Hartmann, 'Praevisivum Regimen contra pestem', pp. 46–53.

[184] = Mag. Heidenricum, 'Regimen preservatiuum contra pestilenciam presentem', pp. 54–6.

[190 and 191] = 'Ein deutsches und ein lateinisches Pest-Regimen aus Bern', pp. 59–67.

[192] = 'Secreta Magistri Mathee phisici Gebenen' (end of the fifteenth century, Geneva), pp. 67–9.

Band XVI (1925)

[193] = 'Ein Pesttraktat eines Magister Berchtoldus' (1447 for Francesco Sforza), pp. 77–95.

[194] = 'Ein rein astrologischer kurzer liber de pestilencia Leipzig', pp. 95–102

[198] = 'Ein anonymer Tractatalus optimus de pestilentia', pp. 104–12.

[202] = Gabriel Prezatus, 'Flagellum Dei', p. 114.

[213] = 'Notizen zur Pestkur von Antonius de Salomonibus, Canonicus bei S. Petronio Bologna, 1464', pp. 124–5.

[215] = 'Opusculum fratris Bartholomaei de Ferraria' (written around 1400), pp. 126–31.

[220] = 'Jacobi Soldi opus insigne de peste 1440', pp. 136–7.

[42bis] = 'Zur Pestschrift des Ugolino (di Caccino) da Montecatini', p. 140.

[223] = 'Ein italienischer Pesttraktat von Mariano di Ser Jacopo di Siena, medico', pp. 140–8.

[229] = 'Ein 'Kölner Pestinkunabel kurz vor 1500', pp. 152–3.

[230] = 'Tractatus de epidemia anni 1424 (cuiusdam Papiensis scriptus anno 1431)', pp. 153–6.

[232] = Dr Magister Heidricus, 'Pest in Rom', pp. 157–61.

[233] = 'Ein Kassineser Pesttraktat', pp. 161–2.

[234] = 'Ein weiterer Tractatus de peste des Magister Johannes de Penna' (beginning of the fifteenth century), pp. 162–7.

[238] = 'Ein consilium . . . Jacobus de Manderano (Monterone) 1448', pp. 169–72.

[239] = 'Ein anonymer Pesttraktat zu Palermo', p. 173.

Band XVII (1925)

[256] = Johannes Jacobi, 'Tractatus de peste ad honorem sancte et individue Trinitatis', pp. 16–32.

[24bis] = 'Zu Johanns von Tornamira Pesttraktat', pp. 32–5.

[257] = 'Das Pestwerkchen des Raymundus Chalin de Vivario', pp. 35–9.

[258] = 'Aliqua breuia dubia cira materiam de Epidemia in Montepessulano' (by follower of Bernard Gordon, beginning of the fifteenth century), pp. 40–3.

[259] = 'Eine akademische Rede über Pest aus Montpellier' (around 1400), pp. 43–6;

[260] = 'Ein therapeutischer Pesttraktat von Mag. Michael Boeti' (from Milan, ca 1400–20), pp. 46–51.

[262] = 'Der Tractatus pestilentialis eines Theobaldus Loneti aus Aurigny in der Diözese Besançon', pp. 53–65.

[265] = 'Brevis tractatus contra pestem eines Magistrus Primus de Gorllicio' (Paris, first half of the fifteenth century), pp. 77–92.

[267 and 268] = Thomas Le Forestier of Avranches (Normandy), 'Regimen pauperum contra pestilentiam', pp. 92–7.

[273] = 'Die Pestschrift des "Blasius Brascinensis (Barcelonensis)" ', pp. 103–19.

[278] = 'Epistola de Maestre Jacme d' Agramont (24 April 1348)', pp. 120–1.

[279] = 'De Epidemia tractatus Costoffori, medici regis Anglie' (Oxford, end of the fourteenth century), pp. 121–4.

[282] = Johannes of Speyer, 'Ein Regimen preservativum de peste' (end of the fifteenth century), pp. 126–32.

[285] = 'Pestregel aus England' (end of the fifteenth century), pp. 136–8.

BIBLIOGRAPHY

Archives:

For the archival sources that comprise the formation of the six-city testament database, see Cohn, *The Cult of Remembrance*, pp. 381–3, or *Women in the Streets*, pp. 217–19.

Arezzo:

Archivio di Fraternità dei Laici: Libri di morti

Bologna:

Archivio di Stato, Bologna: Ufficio dei Memoriali, Liber memorialium contractuum et ultimarum voluntatum

Florence:

Archivio di Stato, Firenze:
Grascia: I libri dei morti
Provvisioni Registri
Diplomatico: Ospedale di Santa Maria Nuova

Rome:

Archivio Capitolino: Sezione I.
Archivio di Stato:
IMAGO parchment database
Collegio dei Notari
Biblioteca Apostolica Vaticana: Sant'Angelo in Pescheria, I.
Biblioteca Vittorio Emanuele: Codice, V.E. no. 528

Siena:

Archivio di Stato, Siena: Santa Maria della Scala, Spoglio

Douai:

Archives Municipales de Douai [AMD], FF series
Notaires

Rodez:

Archives départementales de l'Aveyron: Archives Notariales de l'Aveyron, série 3E.

St. Étienne

Archives départementales de Loire: série B

Printed sources:

Aberth, John. *From the Brink of the Apocalypse: Confronting Famine, War, Plague, and Death in the Later Middle Ages*. New York, 2000.

Acta Sanctorum, Analecta bollandiana, 67 vols. Paris, 1863–1983.

'Additional observations on the septicaemia in human plague', *Journal of Hygiene* [hereafter *JH*], 8 (1908): 221–35.

'On the seasonal prevalence of plague in India', *JH*, 8 (1908): 266–301.

Albertis, Giovanni de. *Il Libro della Pestilenza di Giovanni de Albertis da Capodistria (AD MCCCCL)*, ed. Arturo Castiglioni, in *Archeografo Triestino*, ser. III, 39 (1924): 163–229.

Albini, Giuliana. *Guerra, Fame, Peste: Crisi di mortalità e sistema sanitario nella Lombardia tardomedioevale*. Bologna, 1982.

Alexander, John. *Bubonic Plague in Early Modern Russia: Public Health and Urban Disaster*. Baltimore, 1980.

Allerston, Patricia. 'The market in second-hand clothes and furnishings in Venice, c. 1500–c. 1650', Ph.D thesis, European University Institute (1996).

Amayden, Teodoro. *La Storia delle famiglie romane*, 2 vols. Rome, 1910–14.

Amelang, James S. *The Flight of Icarus: Artisan Autobiography in Early Modern Europe*. Stanford, 1998.

Andel, M.A. van. 'Plague regulations in the Netherlands', *Janus*, 21 (1916): 410–44.

Archives Historiques du Rougergue, VII: Documents sur la ville de Millau, ed. Jules Artières. Millau, 1930.

L'Archivio della fraternità dei Laici di Arezzo: Inventari, ed. Augusto Antoniella. Florence, 1985–9, 2 vols

Ariès, Philippe. *Centuries of Childhood: A Social History of Family Life*, tr. Robert Baldick. New York, 1962 (originally published Paris, 1960).

Arnold, David. *Colonizing the Body: State Medicine and Epidemic Disease in Nineteenth-Century India*. Berkeley, 1993.

——— , ed. *Warm Climates and Western Medicine: The Emergence of Tropical Medicine, 1500–1900*. Amsterdam, 1996, pp. 1–19.

——— . *Science, Technology and Medicine in Colonial India. The New Cambridge History of India*, III, 5. Cambridge, 2000.

Arrizabalaga, Jon. 'Facing the Black Death: perceptions and reactions of university medical practitioners,' *Practical Medicine from Salerno to the Black Death*, ed. Luis García-Ballester, Roger French, Jon Arrizabalaga and of Andrew Cunningham. Cambridge, 1994, pp. 237–88.

——— , John Henderson and Roger French. *The Great Pox: The French Disease in Renaissance Europe*. New Haven, 1997.

'A study of the bionomics of the common rat fleas', *JH: Plague Supplement III* (1914): 447–654.

Aubry, Martine. 'Mortalités lilloises 1328–69', *Revue du Nord*, 65 (1983): 337–60.

Bacot, A.W. and C.J. Martin, 'Observations on the mechanism of the transmission of plague by fleas', *JH: Plague Supplement III* (1914): 432–9.

Bacot, George Petrie, and Captain Ronald E. Todd. 'The fleas found on rats and other rodents, living in association with man, and trapped in the towns, villages and Nile boats of upper Egypt', *JH*, 14 (1914): 498–504.

Bannerman, W.B. 'The spread of plague in India', *JH*, 6 (1906): 179–211.

Bannerman and R.J. Kápadiâ. Chapter XXVII, *JH: Plague Supplement II*, (1908), pp. 209–20.

Barkai, Ron. 'Jewish treatises on the Black Death (1350–1500): a preliminary study', in *Medicine from the Black Death to the French Disease*. ed. by French, Arrizabalaga, Cunningham and García–Ballester. Aldershot, 1998, pp. 6–25.

Barrett, O. 'Alexandre Yersin and recollections of Vietnam', *Hospital Practice*, 24 (1989).

Bartsocas, Christos S. 'Two fourteenth-century Greek descriptions of the "Black Death"', *Journal of the History of Medicine and Applied Sciences*, 21 (1966): 394–400.

Baschet, Jérôme. 'Image et événement: l'art sans la peste (c. 1348–c. 1400)?', in *La Peste Nera: Dati di una realtà ed elementi di una interpretazione. Atti del XXX Convegno storico internazionale, Todi, 10–13 ottobre 1993*. Spoleto, 1994, pp. 25–48.

Basset, Steven, ed. *Death in Towns: Urban Response to the Dying and the Dead*, 100–1600. Leicester, 1992.

Bean, J.M.W. 'The Black Death: The Crisis and its social and economic consequences', in *The Black Death: The Impact of the Fourteenth-Century Plague. Papers of the Eleventh Annual Conference of the Center for Medieval and Early Renaissance Studies*, ed. Daniel Williman. New York, 1982, pp. 23–38.

Benedict, Carol. *Bubonic Plague in Nineteenth-Century China*. Stanford, 1996.

Benedictow, Ole Jørgen. *Plague in the Late Medieval Nordic Countries: Epidemiological Studies*. Oslo, 1992.

Berlinguer, Giovanni. *Le mie pulci*. Rome, 1988.

Bernard, Noël *et al. Yersin et la peste*. Lausanne, 1944.

Bernardo, Aldo S. 'The plague as key to meaning in Boccaccio's "Decameron" ', in *The Black Death*, ed. Williman, pp. 39–64.

Bertram, Martin. 'Bologneser Testamente. Erster Teil: Die urkundliche Uberlieferung,' *Quellen und Forschungen aus italienschen Archiven und Bibliotheken*, 70 (1990): 151–233.

Bibliotheca Sanctorum, ed. Mons. Filippo Caraffa, Istituto Giovanni XXIII, 13 vols. Rome, 1961–69.

Billet, A. 'La Peste dans le département de Constantine en 1907: recherches particulières sur les rats, leurs ectoparasites et leurs rapports avec l'épidémie', *Annales de l'Institut Pasteur* [hereafter *AIP*], 22 (1908): 658–81.

Binski, Paul. *Medieval Death: Ritual and Representation*. London, 1996.

Biraben, Jean–Noël. *Les hommes et la peste en France et dans les pays européens et méditerranéens*, 2 vols. Paris, 1975–6.

——— . 'Les temps de l'Apocalypse', in Jean Delumeau and Yves Lequin, *Les malheurs des temps: Histoire des fléaux et des calamités en France*. Paris, 1987, pp. 177–92.

Bleukx, Koenraad. 'Was the Black Death (1348–49) a real plague epidemic? England as a case-study', in *Serta Devota in Memoriam Guillelmi Lourdaux*, ed. Werner Verbeke. Leuven, 1995, II, pp. 65–113.

Blockmans, W.P. 'The social and economic effects of plague in the Low Countries 1349–1500', *Revue belge de philologie et d'histoire*, 58 (1980): 833–63.

Blue, Rupert. 'Anti-plague measures in San Francisco, California, USA', *JH*, (1909): 1–8.

Boer, Dick de. *Graaf en grafiek: sociale en economische ontwikkelingen in het middeleeuwse 'Noordholland' tussen 1345 en 1415*. Leiden, 1978.

Bornstein, Daniel E. *The Bianchi of 1399: Popular Devotion in Late Medieval Italy*. Ithaca, 1993.

Bottero, Aldo. 'La Peste in Milano nel 1399–1400 e l'opera di Gian Galeazzo Visconti', *Atti e Memorie dell'Accademia di Storia dell'Arte Sanitaria. La Rassegna di Clinica, Terapia e Scienze Affini*, XLI, fasc. VI (1942): 17–28.

Boudet, Marcellin and Roger Grand. *Étude historique sur les épidémies de peste en Haute-Auvergne (XIVe–XVIIIe siècles)*. Paris, 1902.

Bowsky, William. 'The impact of the Black Death upon Sienese government and society', *Speculum*, 39 (1964): 1–34.

Bradley, Leslie. 'Some medical aspects of plague', in *The Plague Reconsidered: A New Look at its Origins and Effects in 16th- and 17th-Century England*. Cambridge, 1977, pp. 13–5.

Bridson, E. 'The English "sweate" (Sudor Anglicus) and Hantavirus pulmonary syndrome', *British Journal of Biomedical Science*, 58 (2000): 1–6.

Brooks, Ralph St. John. 'The influence of saturation deficiency and of temperature on the course of epidemic plague', *JH: Plague Supplement V* (1917): 881–99.

Brownlee, John. 'Certain aspects of the theory of epidemiology in special relation to plague', *Proceedings of the Royal Society of Medicine*, XI (1918): 85–127.

Burgess, A.S. 'Virulence, immunity and bacteriological variation in relation to plague,' *JH*, 30 (1930): 165–79.

Burnet, Sir Marfarlane. *Natural History of Infectious Disease*, 3rd edn, Cambridge, 1962. 4th edn by David. O. White. Cambridge, 1972.

Butler, Thomas. 'A clinical study of bubonic plague: observation of the 1970 Vietnam epidemic with emphasis on coagulation studies, skin histology and electrocardiograms', *American Journal of Medicine*, 53 (1972): 268–76.

———— . *Plague and Other Yersinia Infections*. New York, 1983.

Bynum, Caroline Walker. 'Disease and death in the Middle Ages', *Culture, Medicine and Pyschiatry*, 9 (1985): 97–102.

Calendar of Lincoln Wills, vol. I., ed. C.W. Foster, British Record Society, XXVIII. London, 1902.

Calendar of Wills: Court of Husting, London, AD 1258–AD 1688: The Archives of the Corporation of the City of London at the Guildhall, ed. Reginald R. Sharpe, 2 vols. London, 1889.

Campbell, Ann. *The Black Death and Men of Learning*. New York, 1931.

Campbell, Bruce. 'Population-pressure, inheritance and the land market in a fourteenth-century peasant community', in *Land, Kinship and Life-Cycle*, ed. Richard M. Smith. Cambridge, 1984, pp. 87–135.

Campbell, James. *Gazetteer of the Bombay Presidency. Bombay, 1877–1901*, 35 vols and 24 supplements.

Canard, Jean. *Les pestes en Beaujolais, Forez, Jarez, Lyonnais du XIVe au XVIIIe siècle*. 1979.

Cantor, Norman F. *In the Wake of the Plague: The Black Death and the World it Made*. New York, 2001.

Cappelli, Adriano. *Cronologia, Cronografia e Calendario perpetuo*. 7th edn. Milan, 1998.

Carmichael, Ann G. 'Contagion theory and contagion practice in fifteenth-century Milan', *Renaissance Quarterly*, XLIV (1991): 213–56.

———— . 'Bubonic plague: The Black Death', in *Plague, Pox and Pestilence*, ed. Kenneth F. Kiple. London, 1997, pp. 60–7.

———— . 'Tarantism: the toxic dance', in *Plague, Pox and Pestilence*, pp. 166–9.

———— . 'The last past plague: the uses of memory in Renaissance epidemics', *Journal of the History of Medicine and Allied Sciences*, 53 (1998): 132–160.

——— . *Plague and the Poor in Renaissance Florence*. Cambridge, 1986.

Carpentier, Elizabeth. 'Famines et épidémies dans l'histoire du XIVe siècle', *Annales: E.S.C.*, 17 (1962): 1062–92.

——— . *Une ville devant la peste: Orvieto et la peste noire de 1348*. Paris, 1962.

Castiglioni, Arturo. 'I libri italiani della pestilenza', in *Il Volto di Ippocrate: Istorie di Medici e Medicine d'altri tempi*, ed. Castiglioni. Milan, 1925, pp. 147–69.

——— . 'Ugo Benzi da Siena ed il "Trattato utilissimo circa la conservazione della sanitate" ', *Rivista di Storia Critica delle Scienze Mediche e Naturali*, XII (1921): 75–105.

Catanach, I. J. 'The "globalization" of diseases: India and the plague', *Journal of World History*, 12 (2001): 131–53.

——— . 'Plague and the tensions of empire: India 1896–1918', in *Imperial Medicine and Indigenous Societies*, ed. D. Arnold. Manchester, 1988, pp. 149–71.

Chiappelli, A., ed., 'Ordinamenti Sanitari del Comune di Pistoia contro la pestilenzia del 1348', *Archivio Storico Italiano* [hereafter *ASI*], ser. 4, XX (1887): 8–22.

Ciappelli, Giovanni. 'A Trecento bishop as seen by Quattrocento Florentines: Sant'Andrea Corsini, his "Life," and the Battle of Anghiari', in *Portraits of Medieval and Renaissance Life*, ed. S.K. Cohn and Steven Epstein. Ann Arbor, 1996, pp. 283–98.

Chalmers, A.K. *Corporation of Glasgow, Report on Certain Cases of Plague occurring in Glasgow in 1900 by the Medical Officer of Health*. *Glasgow*. Glasgow, 1901.

Chandavarkar, Rajnarayan. 'Plague panic and epidemic politics in India, 1896–1914', in *Epidemics and Ideas*, ed. T. Ranger and P. Slack. Cambridge, 1992, pp. 203–40.

'Characteristic appearances in plague-infected rats recognisable by naked-eye examination', *JH*, 7 (1907): 324–58.

Chase, Melissa P. 'Fevers, poisons, and apostemes: authority and experience in Montpellier plague treatises', in *Science and Technology in Medieval Society*, ed. Pamela O. Long. New York, 1985, pp. 153–69.

Chauliac, Guy de. *Chiurgia*, Tract. II, cap. 5, text found in Heinrich Haeser, *Geschichte der epidemischen Krankheiten* in *Lehrbuch der Geschichte der Medizin und der epidemischen Krankheiten*, II. Jena, 1865 [hereafter, Haeser], pp. 175–6.

——— . *La Grande Chirugie de Guy de Chauliac*, ed. E. Nicaise. Paris, 1890.

Chick, Harriette and C.J. Martin, 'The fleas common on rats in different parts of the world and the readiness with which they bite man,' *JH*, 11 (1911): 122–36.

Chojnacki, Stanley. 'Patrician women in Early Renaissance Venice', *Studies in the Renaissance*, 21 (1974): 176–203.

Cipolla, Carlo. *Cristofano and the Plague: A Study in the History of Public Health in the Age of Galileo*. London, 1973.

———. *Environment in the Pre-Industrial Age*, tr. Elizabeth Porter. New Haven, 1992.

———. *Faith, Reason and the Plague: A Tuscan Story of the Seventeenth Century*, tr. M. Kittel. Brighton, 1979.

———. *Fighting the Plague in Seventeenth-Century Italy*. Madison, 1981.

———. 'I Libri dei morti', in *Le fonti della demografia storica in Italia*. Rome, 1972, II, pp. 851–66.

———. *Miasmas and Disease: Public Health and the Environment in the Pre-Industrial Age*, tr. Elizabeth Porter. New Haven, 1992.

———. *I pidocchi e il Granduca: Crisi economica e problemi sanitari nella Firenze del '600*. Bologna, 1979.

———. *Public Health and the Medical Profession in the Renaissance*. Cambridge, 1976.

Cohn, Samuel K. *Creating the Florentine State: Peasants and Rebellion, 1348–1434*. Cambridge, 1999.

———. *The Cult of Remembrance and the Black Death: Six Renaissance Cities in Central Italy*. Baltimore, 1992 and 1996.

———. *Death and Property in Siena: Strategies for the Afterlife*. Baltimore, 1988.

———. 'Introduction' to David Herlihy, *The Black Death and the Transformation of the West*.

———. *The Laboring Classes in Renaissance Florence*. New York, 1980.

———. 'Labour legislation after the Black Death' (forthcoming).

———. The place of the dead in Flanders and Tuscany: towards a comparative history of the Black Death', in *The Place of the Dead: Death and Remembrance in Late Medieval and Early Modern Europe*, ed. B. Gordon and P. Marshall. Cambridge, 2000, pp. 17–43.

———. 'Two pictures of family ideology taken from the dead in postplague Flanders and Tuscany', *The Household in Late Medieval Cities: Italy and Northwestern Europe Compared*, ed. Myriam Carlier and Peter Soens. Leuven, 2001, pp. 165–78.

———. *Women in the Streets: Essays on Sex and Power in Renaissance Italy*. Baltimore, 1996.

Colussi, J. 'Population de Millau 1280–1363. Étude démographique' typescript, 91 pp. Toulouse, 1955, found in the Archives départementales de l'Aveyron: AA 157–21.

Condon, J.K. *The Bombay Plague . . . September 1896 to June 1899*. Bombay, 1900.

Conrad, L.I. 'Arabic plague chronologies and treatises: social and historical factors in the formation of a literary genre', *Studia Islamica*, LIV (1981): 51–93.

――――. Tā'ān and Wabā': conceptions of plague and pestilence in early Islam', *Journal of the Economic and Social History of the Orient*, XXV (1982): 268–307.

Contagion: Perspectives from Pre-Modern Societies, ed. by Lawrence Conrad and Dominik Wujastyk. Aldershot, 2000.

Cooper, Alan and Hendrik N. Polnar. 'Ancient DNA: do it right or not at all', *Science* 289 (18 August 2000): 1139.

Corradi, Alfonso. *Annali delle epidemie occorse in Italia dalle prime memorie fino al 1850*, 5 vols. Bologna, 1865–92.

Coulton, George. G. *The Black Death*. London, 1928.

――――. *Five Centuries of Religion*. 4 vols. Cambridge, 1923–50.

[Couvin, Simone], 'Opuscule relatif à la peste de 1348 composé par un contemporain', ed. by E. Littre, *Bibliothèque d'École des Chartes*, II (1841): 201–43.

Coville, Alfred. 'Écrits contemporains sur la peste de 1348 à 1350', in *Histoire littéraire de la France*, XXXVII. Paris, 1938, pp. 325–90.

Cragg, Major F.W. 'The geographical distribution of the Indian rat fleas as a factor in the epidemiology of plague: preliminary observations', *Indian Journal of Medical Research*, 9 (1921): 374–98.

Craven, Robert B. 'Chapter 159: Plague', in *Infectious Disease: A Treatise of Infectious Processes*, ed. P. Hoeprich, M. Jordan, and A. Ronald, 5th edn. Philadelphia, 1994, pp. 1302–11.

Crawfurd, Raymond. *Plague and Pestilence in Literature and Art*. Oxford, 1914.

Creighton, Charles. *History of Epidemics in Britain*, 2nd edn, ed. D.E.C. Eversely, E.A. Underwood and L. Ovenall, 2 vols, I: *AD 664–1666*. Cambridge, 1894; London, 1965.

Crosby, Alfred. *Ecological Imperialism: The Biological Expansion of Europe, 900–1900*. Cambridge, 1986.

――――. 'Influenza: in the grip of the grippe', in Kiple, ed., *Plague, Pox and Pestilence*, pp. 148–53.

Cunningham, Andrew. 'Transforming plague: the laboratory and the identity of infectious disease', in *The Laboratory Revolution in Medicine*, ed. Andrew Cunningham and Perry Williams. Cambridge, 1992, pp. 209–44.

Daniell, Christopher. *Death and Burial in Medieval England 1066–1550*. London, 1997.

Davis, David E. 'The scarcity of rats and the Black Death: an ecological history', *Journal of Interdisciplinary History*, XVI (1986): 455–70.

de Ferrari, A. 'Garbo, Tommaso del' in *Dizionario Biografico degli Italiani*, vol. XXXVI. Rome, 1988, pp. 581–5.

del Garbo, Tommaso. *Consiglio contro la pistolenza*, ed. Pietro Ferrato. Bologna, 1866.

Del Panta, Lorenzo. 'Cronologia e diffusione delle crisi di mortalità in Toscana', *Ricerche Storiche*, 7 (1977): 293–343.

Del Panta, Lorenzo and Livi-Bacci, Massimo. 'Chronology, intensity and diffusion of mortality in Italy. 1660–1850', in *The great mortalities: methodological studies of demographic crises in the past*, ed. Hubert Charbonneau and André Larose. Liège, 1979, pp. 69–79.

Delumeau, Jean. *Le péché et la peur: la culpabilisation en Occident (XIIIe–XVIIIe siècles)* Paris, 1983.

——— . *La peur en Occident (XIVe–XVIIIe siècle): Une cité assiégée*. Paris, 1978.

——— . *Rassurer et protéger: le sentiment de sécurité dans l'Occident d'autrefois*. Paris, 1989.

——— and Yves Lequin. *Les malheurs des temps: Histoire des fléaux et des calamités en France*. Paris, 1987.

Derbes, Vincent. 'De Mussis and the great plague of 1348: a forgotten episode of bacteriological warfare,' *Journal of the American Medical Association*, 196 (1966): 59–62.

Deregnaucourt, Jean-Pierre. 'Autour de la mort à Douai: Attitudes pratiques et croyances, 1250–1500', 2 vols. Thèse, Université Charles de Gaulle. Lille, 1993.

Desowitz, Robert. *Tropical Diseases from 50,000 BC to 2500 AD*. London, 1998.

Dhérent, G. 'Histoire sociale de la bourgeoisie de Douai', Thèse d'Ecole des Chartes (1981).

'The diagnosis of natural rat plague', *JH*, 7 (1907): 324–58.

'Digest of recent observations on the epidemiology of plague', *JH*, 7 (1907): 694–723.

Dols, Michael W. *The Black Death in the Middle East*. Princeton, 1977.

——— . 'The comparative communal responses to the Black Death in Muslim and Christian societies', *Viator* 5 (1974): 269–87.

——— . 'The Second Plague Pandemic and its recurrence in the Middle East: 1347–1894', *Journal of the Economic and Social History of the Orient*, XXII (1979): 162–89.

Dominici, Giovanni. *Regola del Governo di cure familiare*, ed. Donato Salvi. Florence, 1860.

Dubois, Henri. 'La dépression: XVIe et XVe siècles', in *Histoire de la population française*, ed. Jacques Dupâquier. Paris, 1988, I, pp. 313–66.

Ell, S.R. 'Immunity as a factor in the epidemiology of medieval plague', *Reviews of Infectious Diseases*, 6 (1984): 866–79.

——— . 'Interhuman transmission of medieval plague,' *Bulletin of the History of Medicine*, 54 (1980): 497–510.

Elliot, Sir H. M. and John Dowson. *The History of India as Told by its own Historians: The Muhammadan Period*, 8 vols. London, 1867–77.

Emery, Richard W. 'The Black Death of 1348 in Perpignan,' *Speculum*, 42 (1967): 611–23.

'Epidemiological observations in Madras Presidency', *JH: Plague Supplement IV* (1915): 683–751.

'Epidemiological observations in the United Provinces of Agra and Oudh, *JH: Plague Supplement V* (1917): 793–880.

'Epidemiological observations made by the Commission in Bombay City', *JH*, 7 (1907): 724–98.

'Ex libro vetusto Dionysii Secundi Colle', in Haeser, pp. 169–70.

Farrar, Steve. 'Bug that bears the mask of death', *Times Higher Educational Supplement*, no. 1431 (14 April 2000): 20–21.

Fawcett, Hugh A. 'Preliminary rat-flea survey and some notes on its relation to local plagues Hong Kong', *JH*, 30 (1930): 482–9.

Ferlini, Antonio. *Pestilenze nei secoli a Faenza e nelle valli del Lamone e del Senio* Faenza, 1990.

Ficino, Marsilio. *Consilio contro la pestilenzia*, ed. Enrico Musacchio. Bologna, 1983.

Fiétier, Roland. *La cité de Besançon de la fin du XII ème au milieu du XIVième siècle: Étude d'une société urbaine*, 2 vols. Paris, 1978.

Flynn, M. W. 'Plague in Europe and the Mediterranean countries', *Journal of European Economic History*, 8 (1979): 131–47.

Foa, Anna. *The Jews of Europe after the Black Death*, tr. Andrea Grover. Berkeley, 2000.

Fournial, Étienne. *Les villes et l'économie d'échange en Forez aux XIIIe et XIVe siècle*. Paris, 1967.

French, Roger. 'Gentile da Foligno and the *via medicorum*', in *The Light of Nature*, ed. J.D. North and J.J. Roche. Dordecht, 1985, pp. 21–34.

Gatacre, Brigadier-General W.F. *Report on the Bubonic Plague in Bombay, 1896–1897*, 2 vols. Bombay, 1897.

Gauthier, J.C. and A. Raybaud 'Des variétés de pulicidés trouvés sur les rats à Marseille', *Comptes rendus hebdomadaires des séances et mémoires de la société de biologie*, 67 (1909): 196–9.

'General considerations regarding the spread of infection, infectivity of houses, etc. in Bombay City and Island', *JH*, 7 (1907): 874–94.

Gimlette, J.D. 'Plague in Further India,' *JH*, 9 (1909): 60–9.

Ginzburg, Carlo. *Ecstasies: Deciphering the Witches' Sabbath*, tr. Raymond Rosenthal. London, 1991.

Goodes, A. 'Coventry at the time of the Black Death and afterwards', in *The Black Death in Coventry*, ed. M. Hulton. Coventry, 1998.

Gottfried, Robert S. *The Black Death: Natural and Human Disaster in Medieval Europe*. London, 1983.

———. Review of Twigg, *The Black Death* in *Speculum*, 61 (1986): 217–19.

Gras, P. 'Le registre paroissial de Givry (1334–1357) et la peste noire en Bourgogne', *Bibliothèque de l'École des chartes*, C (1939): 295–308.

Greenwood, Major. *Epidemics and Crowd Diseases*. London, 1935.

———. 'Statistical investigation of Plague in Punjab. Third report', *JH: Plague Supplement I* (1912): 62–156.

Guilbert, Sylvette. 'A Châlons-sur-Marne au XVe siècle: un conseil municipal face aux épidémies,' *Annales: E.S.C.*, 23, (1968): 1283–300.

Guerchberg, Séraphine. 'The controversy over the alleged sowers of the Black Death in the contemporary treatises on plague', in *Change in Medieval Society: Europe North of the Alps 1050–1500*, ed. Sylvia Thrupp. London, 1965, pp. 208–24.

Gwynn, Aubrey. 'The Sermon-Diary of Richard FitzRalph, Archbishop of Armagh', in *Proceedings of the Royal Irish Academy*, 44 (1937–8), Section C: 2–66.

———. 'The Black Death in Ireland', *Studies: An Irish Quarterly Review of Letters, Philosophy and Science*, 24 (1935): 25–42.

Gyug, Richard. *The Diocese of Barcelona during the Black Death: Register Notule Comunium (1348–49)*. Toronto, 1994.

———. 'The effects and extent of the Black Death of 1348: new evidence for clerical mortality in Barcelona', *Medieval Studies*, XLV (1983): 385–98.

Haeser, Heinrich. *Geschichte der epidemischen Krankheiten in Lehrbuch der Geschichte der Medizin und der emischen Krankheiten*, II. Jena, 1865.

Hamburger Testamente 1351 bis 1400, ed. Hans-Dieter Loose. Hamburg, 1970.

Hanawalt, Barbara A. *Growing Up in Medieval London: The Experience of Childhood in History*. New York, 1993.

Hankin, E.H. 'On the epidemiology of plague', *JH*, 5 (1905): 48–83.

———. 'La propagation de la peste', *AIP* 12 (1898): 705–62.

Harding, Vanessa. 'Burial choice and burial location in later medieval London', in *Death in Towns: Urban Response to the Dying and the Dead, 100–1600*, ed. Steven Basset. Leicester, 1992, pp. 119–35.

Hardy, Anne. *The Epidemic Streets: Infectious Disease and the Rise of Preventive Medicine, 1856–1900*. Oxford, 1993.

Harvey, Barbara. 'Introduction: the "crisis" of the early fourteenth century', in *Before the Black Death: Studies in the "Crisis" of the Early Fourteenth Century*, ed. Bruce Campbell. Manchester, 1991, pp. 1–24.

———. *Living and Dying in England, 1100–1540: The Monastic Experience*. Oxford, 1993.

Haas, Louis. *Renaissance Man and his Children: Childbirth and Early Childhood in Florence, 1300–1600*. London, 1998.

Hatcher, John. 'Mortality in the fifteenth century: some new evidence', *Economic History Review*, 2 ser., XXXIX (1986): 19–38.

———. *Plague, Population and the English Economy 1348–1530*. London, 1977.

Hawthorn, Geoffrey. *Plausible Worlds: Possibility and Understanding in History and the Social Sciences*. Cambridge, 1991.

Hayez, Jérôme. 'Quelques témoignages sur les épidémies à Avignon, deuxième moitié XIV siècle' (unpublished).

Hecker, I.F.C. *The Black Death in the Fourteenth Century*, tr. B.G. Babington. London, 1833 (originally published 1832) orig., 1832.

——— . 'The Dancing Mania', in *The Epidemics of the Middle Ages*, tr. Babington. London, 1844, pp. 79–174.

Helleiner, Karl F. 'Population of Europe from the Black Death to the Eve of the Vital Revolution', in *The Cambridge Economic History of Europe*, IV, ed. E.E. Rich and C.H. Wilson. Cambridge, 1966, pp. 1–95.

Henderson, John. 'The Black Death in Florence: medical and communal responses', in Basset, ed., *Death in Towns*, pp. 136–50.

——— . 'Epidemics in Renaissance Florence: medical theory and government response', in *Maladies et Société (XIIe–XVIIIe siècles): Actes du colloque de Bielefeld*, ed. Neithard Bulst and Robert Delort. Paris, 1989, pp. 165–86.

——— . 'The parish and the poor in Florence at the time of the Black Death: the case of S. Frediano', *Continuity and Change*, 3 (1988): 247–72.

Henderson, Mary. 'La Confraternità e la catastrofe: La Confraternità francescana di Orvieto e la peste nera', in *Bollettino dell'Istituto Storico Artistico Orvietano*, xlviii–xlix (1992–3). Orvieto, 1999, pp. 89–127.

Herlihy, David. *The Black Death and the Transformation of the West*, ed. by S.K. Cohn. Cambridge, Ma., 1997.

——— . *Medieval and Renaissance Pistoia: The Social History of an Italian Town, 1200–1430*. New Haven, 1967.

——— . 'Medieval children', in *Women, Family and Society in Medieval Europe: Historical Essays, 1978–1991*. Providence, R.I., 1994, pp. 215–43.

——— . *Pisa in the Early Renaissance: A Study of Urban Growth*. New Haven, 1958.

——— and Christiane Klapisch-Zuber. *Les Toscans et leurs familles: Une étude du Catasto de 1427*. Paris, 1978.

Hicks, E.P. 'The relation of rat-fleas to Plague in Shanghai', *JH*, 26 (1927): 163–9.

Hinnebusch, B. Joseph. 'Bubonic plague: a molecular genetic case history of the emergence of an infectious disease', *Journal of Molecular Medicine*, 75 (1997): 645–52.

Hirsch, August. *Handbook of Geographical and Historical Pathology*, 3 vols, tr. Charles Creighton. London, 1883–6.

Hirst, L. Fabian. *The Conquest of Plague: A Study of the Evolution of Epidemiology*. Oxford, 1953.

Hocquet, Adolphe. 'Table des Testaments', *Annales de la société historique et archéologique de Tournai*, ns, 6 (1901): 284–99; 7 (1902): 81–161; and 10 (1906): 1–197.

Hoeniger, Robert. *Der Schwarze Tod in Deutschland: Ein Beitrag zur Geschichte des vierzehnten Jahrhunderts.* Berlin, 1882.

Hopkins, G.H.C., 'Cotton and plague in Uganda', *JH*, 38 (1938): 233–47.

Hollingsworth, Mary F. and T.H. Hollingsworth, 'Plague mortality rates by age and sex in the parish of St Botolph's without Bishopsgate, London, 1603', *Population Studies*, 25 (1971): 131–46.

Horrox, Rosemary, ed. and tr. *The Black Death*, Manchester Medieval Sources series, Manchester, 1994.

Hossack, C. District Medical Officer, Calcutta, 'Influenza and plague', *British Journal of Medicine* (1900), II: 1244–7.

Howard-Jones, N. 'Kitasato, Yersin and the plague bacillus', *Clio Medica*, 10 (1975): 23–7.

Hulton, Mary. 'Introduction' to *The Black Death in Coventry*, ed. Hulton, Coventry, 1998.

Hunecke, Volker. 'Findelkinder und Findelhäuser in der Renaissance', *Quellen und Forschungen aus italienschen Archiven und Bibliotheken*, 72 (1992): 123–53.

Iacopo di Coluccino. *Il Memoriale di Iacopo di Coluccino Bonavia Medico Lucchese (1373–1416)*, ed. Pia Pittino Calamari, in *Studi di Filologia Italiana*, XXIV. Florence, 1966.

Ila, Balint. 'Contribution à l'histoire de la peste en Hongrie au XVIIIe siècle', in *The Great Mortalities: Methodological Studies of Demographic Crises in the Past*, ed. Hubert Charbonneau and André Larose. Liège, 1979, pp. 133–8.

'Interim report by the Advisory Committee' *JH*, 10 (1910): 566–8.

Inventaire général des chartes . . . appartenant aux hospices et au bureau de bienfaisance de la ville de Douai, ed. Félix Brassart. Douai, 1839.

Inventaire du trésor de St-Nizier de Lyon 1365–1373: Listes des sépultures de la paroisse 1346–1348, ed. Georges Guigue. Lyon, 1899.

Jacob, Robert. *Les époux, le seigneur et la cité: Coutumes et pratiques matrimoniales des bourgeois et paysans de France du Nord au moyen âge.* Brussels, 1990.

Johnston, Dafydd. *Galar Y Beirdd: Marwnadau Plant/Poets' Grief: Medieval Welsh Elegies for Children.* Cardiff, 1993.

Jordan, Karl. 'Suctoria,' in *Insects of Medical Importance*, ed. by John Smart, K. Jordan and R.J. Whittick, 3rd edn. London, 1956, pp. 211–46.

Jordan, William C. *The Great Famine: Northern Europe in the Early Fourteenth Century*, Princeton, 1996.

Jouet, Roger. 'Autour de la Peste Noire en Basse-Normandie au XIVe siècle', *Annales de Normandie*, 22 (1972): 265–76.

Kunhardt, J.C., Captain and Captain J. Taylor, 'Epidemiological observations in Madras Presidency', *JH: Plague Supplement IV* (1915): 683–751

Karlen, Arno. *Plague's Progress: A Social History of Man and Disease*. London, 1995.

Karlsson, Gunnar. 'Plague without rats: the case of fifteenth-century Iceland,' *Journal of Medieval History*, 22/23 (1996): 263–84.

Kedar, Benjamin. *Merchants in Crisis: Genoese and Venetian Men of Affairs and the Fourteenth-Century Depression*. New Haven, 1976.

Keene, Derek. 'Tanners' widows, 1300–1350', in *Medieval London Widows 1300–1500*, ed. Caroline M. Barron and Anne F. Sutton. London, 1994, pp. 1–27.

Kiple, Kenneth F. *Plague, Pox and Pestilence*. London, 1997.

Klebs, A.C. and E. Droz, *Remèdes contre la peste: facsimilés*. Paris, 1925.

Klein, Ira. 'Plague, policy and popular unrest in British India', *Modern Asian Studies*, 22 (1988): 723–55.

———. 'Urban development and death: Bombay City, 1870–1914', *Modern Asian Studies*, 20 (1986): 725–54.

Konrad von Megenberg. 'Tractatus de mortalitate in Alamannina', in Sabina Krüger, 'Krise der Zeit als Ursache der Pest?: Der Traktat De mortalitate in Alamannia des Konrad von Megenberg', in *Festschrift für Hermann Heimpel zum 70. Geburtstag am 19. September 1971*. Göttingen, 1972, II, pp. 839–83.

Kovalevsky, Maxim. 'Die wirtschaflichen Folgen des schwarzen Todes in Italien', *Zeitschrift für Sozial- und Wirtschaftsgechichte*, III (1895): 406–23.

Kriegel, Maurice. *Les Juifs à la fin du Moyen Age dans l'Europe méditerranéenne*. Paris, 1979.

Kupferschmidt, H. 'Development of research on plague following the discovery of the bacillus by Alexander Yersin', *Revue Médicale de la Suisse Romande*, 114 (1994): 415–23.

La Croix, E. 'Vergelijkende studie van de opvattingen omtrent oorzaken, ziektemechanismen entherapieën van pest op basis van de Pesttraktaten van de Medische Faculteit te Parijs (1348–1349), van Joannes de Vesalia (na 1454), en van Thomas Montanus (1669)', *Koninklijke Academie voor Geneeskunde van België*, LXI, no. 2 (1999): 325–61.

La Grange, A. de. 'Choix de testaments tournaisiens antérieurs au XVIe siècle', *Annales de la société historique et archéologique de Tournai*, ns II (1897): 1–365.

Lamb, H.H. *Climate, History and the Modern World*, 2nd edn. London, 1995.

———. *Climate, Present, Past, and Future*, 2 vols. London, 1977.

Landucci, Luca. *Diario fiorentino dal 1450 al 1516 continuato da un anonimo fino al 1542*, ed. Iodoco del Badia. Florence, 1883.

La Roncière, Charles-M. de. *Prix et salaires à Florence au XIVe siècle (1280–1380)*. Rome, 1982.

Lastri, Marco. *Recerche sull'antica e moderna popolazione della città di Firenze*. Florence, 1775.

Leela, B. 'Plague in Karnataka: 1896–1900', *Indica*, 35 (1998): 133–46.

———. 'Plague in Karnataka. Part 2: Mysore (1896–1900)', *Indica*, 36 (1999): 39–49.

Le Roy Ladurie, Emmanuel. 'A concept: the unification of the globe by disease (fourteenth to seventeenth centuries)', in *The Mind and Method of the Historian*, tr. Siân and Ben Reynolds. Brighton, 1981, 28–83. [Original *Revue Suisse d'Histoire* (1973): 627–96.]

Levett, Ada Elizabeth. *Studies in Manorial History*, ed. H.M. Cam, M. Coate and L.S. Sutherland. Oxford, 1938.

'Il "Libro dei Morti" di Santa Maria Novella (1290–1436)', ed. C.C. Calzolai, *Memorie Dominicane*, ns XI (1980): 15–218.

Lomas, Richard. 'The Black Death in County Durham', *Journal of Medieval History*, XV (1989): 127–40.

Lorcin, Marie-Thérèse. 'Clauses religieuses dans les testaments du plat pays lyonnais aux XIVe et XVe siècles', *Moyen Age*, 78 (1972): 287–323.

———. *Vivre et mourir en Lyonnais à la fin du Moyen Age*. Paris, 1981.

Lucenet, Monique. *Les grandes pestes en France*. Paris, 1985.

Lüneburger Testamente des Mittelalters 1323 bis 1500, ed. Uta Reinhardt. Hanover, 1996.

MacKay, Angus 'Popular movements and pogroms in fifteenth-century Castile', *Past & Present*, 55 (1972): 33–67.

Manson, Patrick. *Tropical Diseases: A Manual of the Diseases of Warm Climates*. London, 1898.

———. *Tropical Diseases*, 3rd edn. London, 1903.

Manson's Tropical Diseases, ed. Philip H. Manson-Bahr, 7th edn, London, 1921; 10th edn London, 1935.

Manson's Tropical Diseases, ed. P.E.C. Manson-Bahr and D.R. Bell, 19th edn. London, 1987.

Manson's Tropical Diseases, ed. Gordon Cook, 20th edn. London, 1996.

Maréchal, Griet. 'De Zwarte Dood te Brugge (1349–1351)', *Bierkorf-Westvlaams Archief*, 80 (1980): 377–92.

Marshall, Jr, J.D., R.J. Joy. N.V. Ai, D.V. Quy, J.L. Stockard and F.L. Gibson. 'Plague in Vietnam, 1965–1966', *American Journal of Epidemiology*, 86 (1967): 603–16.

McCaa, Robert 'Revisioning smallpox, inoculation and vaccination: a view from Mexico 1520–1950', talk at the Wellcome Unit, University of Glasgow, 13 June 2000.

McNeill, William. *Plagues and Peoples*. New York, 1976.

Meiss, Millard. *Painting in Florence and Siena after the Black Death*. Princeton, 1951.

Meyer, Jacob. *Commentarii sive Annales rerum Flandricarum*. Antwerp, 1561.

Michaud, Francine. 'La peste, la peur et l'espoir: Le pélerinage jubilaire de romeux marseillais en 1350', *Le Moyen Age*, 3–4 (1998): 399–434.

Michon, L.A. *Documents inédits sur la Grande Peste de 1348, Thèse de l'École de Médicine*. Paris, 1860.

Mollaret, H.H and J. Brossollet, *Alexandre Yersin ou le vainqueur de la peste*. Paris, 1985.

———. *Pourquoi la peste? Le rat, la puce et le bubon*. Paris, 1994.

Mollat, Michel. 'Note sur la mortalité à Paris au temps de la Peste Noire d'après les comptes de l'oeuvre de Saint-Germain-l'Auxerrois', *Le Moyen Age*, LXIX (1963): 505–27.

Monumenta Ragusina: Libri Reformationum, II, ed. Fr. Racki. Zagreb, 1882.

Moraglia, Giampaolo. 'Introduzione' to Ficino, *Consiglio contro la pestilenza*, pp. 1–50.

Morris, Christopher. 'The Plague in Britain', *Historical Journal*, 14 (1971): 205–15.

'Necrologio' di S. Maria Novella, 2 vols, ed. Stefano Orlandi. Florence, 1955.

Morrison, Alan, Julius Kirshner and Anthony Molho. 'Epidemics in Renaissance Florence', *American Journal of Public Health*, 75 (1985): 528–35.

Mueller, Reinhold C. 'Aspetti sociali ed economici della peste a Venezia nel Medioevo', *Venezia e la peste, 1348–1797*. Venice, 1979–80, pp. 71–92.

Naphy, Willaim. 'Learning to live with plague: the development of Genevan plague regulations, c. 1400–c.1530', seminars in the Wellcome Unit, University of Glasgow, 15 February 2000.

Naso, Irma. 'Individuazione diagnostica della "pesta nera". Cultura medica e aspetti clinici', in *La Peste Nera*, pp. 349–81.

Neustatter, Otto. 'Mice in plague pictures', *Journal of the Walters Art Gallery*, IV (1941): 105–14.

Neveux, Hugues. 'La mortalité des pauvres à Cambrai (1377–1473)', *Annales de démographie historique* (1968): 73–97.

Nirenberg, David. *Communities of Violence: Persecution of Minorities in the Middle Ages*. Princeton, 1996.

Nohl, Johannes. *The Black Death: A Chronicle of the Plague Compiled from Contemporary Sources*, tr. C.H. Clarke. London, 1926, reissued 1961.

Norris, J. 'East or West? The geographic origin of the Black Death', *Bulletin of the History of Medicine*, 51 (1977): 1–24.

Nuttall, G.F.H. 'Zur Aufklärung der Rolle, welche die Insekten bei der Verbreitung der Pest spielen', *Centralblatt für Bakteriologie, Parasitenkunde und Infektionskrankheiten*, XXII (1897): 87–97.

Nutton, Vivian. 'The seeds of disease: an explanation of contagion and infection from the Greeks to the Renaissance', *Medical History*, 27 (1983): 1–34.

Nys, L. *La pierre de Tournai: Son exploitation et son usage aux XIII, XIV, et XVième siècles*. Tournai, 1993.

'Observations made in four villages in the neighbourhood of Bombay', *JH*, 7 (1907): 799–873.

'Observations on plague in Eastern Bengal and Assam', *JH: Plague Supplement II* (1912): 157–92.

'Observations on the bionomics of fleas with special reference to *Pulex cheopis*', *JH*, 8 (1908): 236–59.

'On the existence of chronic plague in rats in localities where plague is endemic', *JH*, 6 (1906): 530–6.

'On the infectivity of floors grossly contaminated with cultures of *B. pestis*', *JH* (1906): 509–23.

Ogata, M. 'Ueber die Pestepidemie in Formosa', *Centralblatt für Bakteriologie, Parasitenkunde und Infektionskrankheiten*, XXI (1897); 769–77.

Orme, Nicholas. *From Childhood to Chivalry: The Education of the English Kings and Aristocracy 1066–1530*. London, 1984.

Otten, L. 'The problem of the seasonal prevalence of plague', *JH*, 32 (1932): 396–405.

Page, F.M. *The Estates of Crowland Abbey*. Cambridge, 1934.

Panebianco, Domenico. ' "De preservatione a pestilencia" di Cardone de Spanzotis de Mediolano, del 1360', *Archivio Storico Lombardo*, CII (1977): 347–54.

Panella, Emilio OP. 'Cronica fratrum dei conventi domenicani umbro-toscani (secoli XIII–XV)', *Archivum Fratrum Praedicatorum*, LXVIII (1998): 223–94.

Parenti, Giuseppe. 'Fonti per lo studio della demografia Fiorentina: I libri dei morti', *Genus*, 5–6 (1943–9): 281–301.

Park, Katharine. *Doctors and Medicine in Early Renaissance Florence*. Princeton, 1985.

———. 'The readers at the Florentine Studio according to Communal Fiscal Records', *Rinascimento*, ns 20 (1980): 249–310.

Peste Nera, La: Dati di una realtà ed elementi di una interpretazione. *Atti del XXX Convegno storico internazionale, Todi, 10–13 ottobre 1993*. Spoleto, 1994.

Petrarca, Francesco. *Le Familiari*, edizione critica, ed. Vittorio Rossi, II. Florence, 1934.

Philip, W.M. and L.F. Hirst. 'A Report of the outbreak of the plague in Colombo, 1914–1916', *JH*, 15 (1915–17): 527–64.

Piccolomini, Aeneas Silvius (Pope Pius II). *I Commentarii*, ed. Luigi Totaro, 2 vols. Milan, 1984.

'Plague in Parel Village', *JH*, 7 (1907): 843–65.

Plague Reconsidered: A New Look at its Origins and Effects in the 16th- and 17th-Century England, Local Population Studies Supplement. Cambridge, 1977.

Platelle, H. 'Chirographes de Tournai retrouvés dans un fonds de la Bibliothèque de Valenciennes', *Revue du Nord*, XLIV no. 174 (1962): 191–200.

Pollitzer, Robert. *Plague*. Geneva, 1954.

—— and Karl F. Meyer 'The ecology of plague', in *Studies in Disease Ecology*, ed. Jacques M. May. New York, 1961.

Polzer, Joseph. 'Aristotle, Mohammed, and Nicholas V in Hell', *Art Bulletin*, 46 (1964): 457–69.

Poos, Lawrence R. 'Population and resources in two fourteenth-century Essex communities: Great Waltham and High Easter, 1327–1389' Ph.D Fitzwilliam College 1983.

Practica Antonii Guainerii papiensis doctoris clarissimi et omnia opera. Florence, 1517.

Prosperi, Adriano. *Dalla Peste Nera alla guerra dei Trent'anni*. Turin, 2000.

Rabie, Hassanein. 'Some technical aspects of agriculture in medieval Egypt', in Udovitch, A., ed., *The Islamic Middle East, 700–1900: Studies in Economic and Social History*. Princeton, 1981, pp. 59–90.

Raoult, Didier, Gérard Aboudharam, Eric Crubézy, Georges Larrouy, Bertrand Ludes, and Michel Drancourt. 'Detection of 400-year-old *Yersinia pestis* DNA in human dental pulp: an approach to the diagnosis of ancient septicemia', *Proceedings of the National Academy of Sciences*, 95 (October 1998): 12637–40.

—— . 'Molecular identification by "suicide PCR" of *Yersinia pestis* as the agent of Medieval Black Death', ibid., 97 (7 November, 2000): 12800–3.

Renouard, Yves. 'Conséquences et intérêts démographiques de la Peste Noire de 1348', *Population*, 3 (1948): 459–66.

Rapp, Francis. *L'église et la vie religieuse en Occident à la fin du Moyen Age*. Paris, 1971.

Regesten der Lübecker Bürgertestamente des Mittelalters, ed. A. von Brandt, 2 vols. Lübeck, 1964.

Roberts, J. Isgaer. 'The carriage of Plague', *JH*, 34 (1934), 504–6.

—— . 'Plague conditions in an urban area of Kenya', *JH*, 36 (1936): 467–84.

—— . 'Plague conditions in a rural area of Kenya', *JH*, 36 (1936): 485–503.

—— . 'The relation of the cotton crop to plague and its role as a vehicle for rats and fleas in East Africa', *JH*, 34 (1934): 388–403.

Robo, E. 'The Black Death in the Hundred of Farnham', *English Historical Review*, XLIV (1944): 560–72.

Rocke, Michael. *Forbidden Friendships: Homosexuality and Male Culture in Renaissance Florence*. Oxford, 1996.

Ronen, Avraham. 'Gozzoli's St Sebastian altarpiece in San Gimignano', *Mitteilungen des Kunsthistorischen Institutes in Florenz*, XXXII (1988): 77–124.

Rosenberg, Charles S. 'Cholera in nineteenth-century Europe: a tool for social and economic analysis', *Comparative Studies in Society and History*, 8 (1965–6): 452–63.

Rothschild, Honourable N.C. 'Note on the species of fleas found upon rats, *Mus rattus* and *Mus decumanus*, in different parts of the world', *JH*, 6 (1906): 483–5.

Rubio, Agustín. *Peste Negra, Crisis y comportaminetos sociales en la España del Siglo XIV: La cuidad de Valencia (1348–1401)*. Granada, 1979.

Sarton, George. *Introduction to the History of Science*, III: *Science and Learning in the Fourteenth Century*. Baltimore, 1948.

Savonarola, Michele. *I trattati in volgare della peste e dell'acqua ardente*, ed. Liugi Beloni. Milan, 1953.

Schofield, Roger. 'An anatomy of an epidemic: Colyton, November 1645 to November 1646', in *The Plague Reconsidered*, pp. 95–126.

Sheel, Alok. 'Bubonic plague in south Bihar: Gaya and Shahabad districts, 1900–1924', *Indian Economic and Social History Review*, 35 (1998): 421–2.

Shrewsbury, J.F.D. *A History of Bubonic Plague in the British Isles*. Cambridge, 1970.

Siraisi, Nancy G. *Medieval and Early Renaissance Medicine: An Introduction to Knowledge and Practice*. Chicago, 1990.

———. *Taddeo Alderotti and his Pupils: Two Generations of Italian Medical Learning*. Princeton, 1981.

Sköld, Peter. 'The history of smallpox and its prevention in Sweden', paper at the 19th International Congress of Historical Sciences. Oslo, August, 2000.

Simili, Alessandro. 'Saladino Ferro da Ascoli', in *Atti e Memorie dell'Accademia di Storia dell'Arte Sanitaria*, 29 (1963): 26–46.

Simond, Paul–Louis. 'La propagation de la peste', *AIP*, XII (1898): 625–87.

Simpson, W.J. *A Treatise on Plague dealing with the Historical, Epidemiological, Clinical, Therapeutic and Preventive Aspects of the Disease*. Cambridge, 1905.

———. *Report on the Causes and Continuance of Plague in Hong Kong*. Hong Kong, 1903.

Singer, Dorothea Waley. 'Some plague tractes (fourteenth and fifteenth centuries),' *Proceedings of the Royal Society of Medicine*, IX, pt. 2 (1916): 159–214.

Sivéry, Gérard. 'Le Hainaut et la Peste Noire', *Memoires et publications de la Société des sciences, arts et des lettres du Hainaut*, 79 (1965): 431–47.

Slack, Paul. 'The Black Death past and present, 2: Some historical problems', *Transactions of the Royal Society of Tropical Medicine and Hygiene*, 83 (1989): 461–3.

———. *The Impact of Plague in Tudor and Stuart England*. London, 1985.

————. 'The local incidence of epidemic disease: the case of Bristol 1540–1650', in L. Bradley, *The Plague Reconsidered*, pp. 49–62.

Smith, Michael and Nguyen Duy Thanh. 'Plague' in *Manson's Tropical Diseases*, 20th edn.

Statutum Bladi Reipublicae Florentinae (1348), ed. Gino Masi. Milan, 1934.

Stein, Henri. 'Comment on luttait autrefois contre les épidémies', *Annuaire-Bulletin de la Société de l'Histoire de France*, LV (1918): 125–50.

Stella, Alessandro. *La révolte des Ciompi: Les hommes, les lieux, le travail.* Paris, 1993.

Stephens, Clairborne *et al.* 'Dating the origin of the CCR5-Δ32 AIDS-resistance allele by the coalescence of haplotypes', *American Journal of Genetics*, 62 (1998): 1507–15.

Steveni, William B. 'The ravages of the Black Death in the fourteenth century and its reappearance in the twentieth century', *Fortnightly Review*, 95 (1914): 154–64.

Sticker, Georg. *Abhandlungen aus der Seuchengeschichte und Seuchenlehre*, I. Gissen, 1908.

Stradario storico e amministrativo della Città e del Comune di Firenze. Florence, 1929.

Sudhoff, Karl. 'Pestschriften aus den ersten 150 Jahren nach der Epidemie des "schwarzen Todes" 1348', *Archiv für Geschichte der Medizin*, vols IV–XVII (1910–25). For individual Pestschriften, see Appendix III.

————. 'Nachträge und Verbesserungen', ibid., XVII (1925): 286–91.

Tenenti, Alberto. *Il senso della morte e l'amore della vita nel Rinascimento (Francia e Italia).* Turin, 1957.

Testa, Antonia Pasi. 'Alle origini dell'Ufficio di Sanità nel Ducato di Milano e Principato di Pavia', *Archivio Storico Lombardo*, CII (1977): 376–86.

Testamentary Records in the Archdeaconry Court of London, I., ed. by Marc Fitch, British Record Society, 89. London, 1979.

Testamente der Stadt Braunschweig, ed. Dietrich Mack, 5 vols. Göttingen, 1988–93.

Thompson, J. Ashburton. 'On the epidemiology of plague', *JH*, 6 (1906): 537–69.

————. 'A Contribution to the aetiology of plague', *JH*, 1 (1901): 153–67.

Thomson, John A.F. *The Transformation of Medieval England, 1370–1529.* London, 1983.

Thorndike, Lynn. 'A pest tractate before the black death', *Archiv für Geschichte der Medizin*, XXIII (1930): 346–56.

————. 'Some Vatican manuscripts of pest tractates', *Archiv für Geschichte der Medizin*, XXII (1929): 199–200.

Tiraboschi, Carlo. 'État actuel de la question du véhicule de la peste', *Archives de Parasitologie*, XI (1907): 545–620.

————. 'Les rats, les souris et leurs parasites cutanés dans leurs rapports avec la propagation de la peste bubonique', *Archives de Parasitologie*, VIII (1904): 163–352.

Titow, J.Z. *English Rural Society 1200–1350*. London, 1969.

Tour-Landry, Geoffroy de la. *The Book of the Knight of the Tower*. London, 1971.

Trexler, Richard. 'In search of father: the experience of abandonment in the recollection of Giovanni di Pagalo Morelli', *History of Childhood Quarterly*, 3 (1973): 225–52.

Trillat, A. 'Étude historique sur l'utilisation des feux et des fumées: Comme moyen de défense contre la peste', *AIP*, XIX (1905): 734–52.

Trueman, Richard. 'Mistaken identity', *Guardian: Science* (21 June 2001), p. S3.

Twigg, Graham. *The Black Death: A Biological Reappraisal*. London, 1984.

Udovitch, Abraham. 'Egypt: Crisis in a Muslim land', in *The Black Death: A Turning-Point?* ed. William Bowsky. New York, 1971, pp. 122–5.

Ugolino da Montacatini. 'Consiglio medico di maestr' ad Averardo de' Medici', ed. F. Baldasseroni and G. Degli Azzi, *ASI*, 5th ser., 38 (1906): 140–52

Varanini, Gian Maria. 'La peste del 1347–50 e i governi dell'Italia centro-settentrionale: un bilancio', in *La Peste Nera*, pp. 285–317.

Verger, J. 'Nouveaux fléaux, nouveaux recours', in Delumeau and Lequin, *Les malheurs des temps*, pp. 209–34.

Verlinden, Charles. 'La grande peste de 1348 en Espagne: contribution à l'étude de ses conséquences économiques et sociales', *Revue belge de philologie et d'histoire*, 17 (1938): 103–46.

Walz, P. Angelus OP. *Compendium Historiae ordinis praedicatorum*. Rome, 1948.

Washington Post Historical Weather Data (website).

White, G.B. 'Fleas', in *Manson's Tropical Diseases*, 19th edn, pp. 1482–6.

White, Norman F. 'Twenty years of plague in India with special reference to the outbreak of 1917–18', *Indian Journal of Medical Research*, VI (1918): 190–236.

Williams, Gwyn A. *From Commune to Capital*. London, 1963.

Williman, Daniel, ed. *The Black Death*: The Impact of the *Fourteenth-Century Plague*. Papers of *the Eleventh Annual Conference of the Center for Medieval and Early Renaissance Studies*. New York, 1982.

Wills, Christopher. *Plagues: Their Origin, History and Future*. London, 1997.

Winslow, Charles-Edward Amory. *The Conquest of Epidemic Disease*. Princeton, 1943.

——— . *Man and Epidemics*. Princeton, 1952.

Worboys, Michael. 'Germs, malaria and the invention of Mansonian tropical medicine: From "diseases in the Tropics" to "Tropical Diseases" ', in Arnold, ed., *Warm Climates and Western Medicine*, pp. 181–207.

Wu, Lien-Teh. *A Treatise on Pneumonic Plague*. Geneva, 1926.

———. 'First Report of the North Manchurian Plague Prevention Service', *JH*, 13 (1913–14): 237–90.

———. 'Historical aspects', in Lien-Teh Wu, J.W.H. Chun, R. Pollitzer, C.Y. Wu, *Plague: A Manual for Medical and Public Health Workers*. Shanghai Station, 1936, pp. 1–12.

———. *Plague Fighter: The Autobiography of a Modern Chinese Physician*. Cambridge, 1959.

———. 'Plague in the orient with special reference to the Manchurian outbreaks,' *JH*, 21 (1922–23): 62–76.

Yersin, Alexandre. 'La peste bubonique à Hong-Kong', *AIP*, 8 (1894): 662–7.

Yersin, A. Calmette, A. and Borrel, A., 'La peste bubonique', *AIP*, IX (1895): 589–92.

Zerner, Monique. 'Une crise de mortalité au XVe siècle à travers les testaments et les rôles d'imposition', *Annales: E.S.C.*, 34 (1979): 566–89.

Ziegler, Philip. *The Black Death*. Harmondsworth, 1970.

Zinsser, Hans. *Rats, Lice, and History*. London, 1935.

Zitelli, Andreina and Richard J. Palmer, 'Le teorie mediche sulla peste e il contesto veneziano', in *Venezia e la peste 1348–1797*. Venice, 1979, pp. 21–8.

INDEX